THE LETTERS OF
Samuel Pepys
AND HIS
FAMILY CIRCLE

Oxford University Press, Amen House, London E.C. 4

GLASGOW NEW YORK TORONTO MELBOURNE WELLINGTON
BOMBAY CALCUTTA MADRAS KARACHI CAPE TOWN IBADAN

Geoffrey Cumberlege, Publisher to the University

SAMUEL PEPYS

From the painting attributed to J. Closterman in the National Portrait Gallery

THE LETTERS OF
Samuel Pepys
AND HIS
FAMILY CIRCLE

EDITED BY

HELEN TRUESDELL HEATH

OXFORD
AT THE CLARENDON PRESS

FIRST PUBLISHED 1955
REPRINTED 1956

PRINTED IN GREAT BRITAIN

In gratitude and affection
the author dedicates this volume
to her son
CLIFFORD AMBROSE TRUESDELL III
and to her grandson
CLIFFORD AMBROSE TRUESDELL IV

PREFACE

THE editor wishes to acknowledge the kindness of the librarians of the Bodleian Library, the British Museum, the National Maritime Library at Greenwich, and the Pepysian Library at Cambridge in granting permission to reprint manuscripts from their collections. Especial gratitude is due to Mr. Arthur Houghton of Corning, New York, for his pains and courtesy in making his manuscript available to a stranger and in granting permission to reprint it.

To Miss Helen Darbishire, Professor D. Nichol Smith, Mr. Denholm-Young, Dr. Raymond Klibansky, Mr. Rice-Oxley, and Dr. Paul Spencer Wood goes deep-felt gratitude for their encouragement, patience, suggestions, and optimism in dark and difficult days. To many, many fellow-students, colleagues, and pupils go thanks for reading the manuscript in various stages and for help in typing and re-typing.

Particularly the editor must thank Mr. R. H. New for using his eyes on the revisions when she dared not use hers, and to Mrs. Rose Leys for expert work on the index when she could least spare the time from her own work.

Finally, there is a debt to the members of the staff of the Clarendon Press, from the compositors to the Delegates, all of whom have had to exercise forbearance and patience with an editor separated from them by an ocean and a continent, as well as by many years' difference in experience. In especial, the warmest of thanks go to Miss Withycombe, formerly of the Press, for verifying manuscript readings when the editor was seven thousand miles away, and to the Secretary's staff, under whose patient supervision all the strands were woven together to make this book.

H. T. H.

CONTENTS

INTRODUCTION   vii

LIST OF LETTERS   XXXV

THE LETTERS   I

A CALENDAR OF OMITTED PAPERS   231

APPENDIX I. S.P.'S 'PEDDEGREE'   244

    II. FAMILY TREE   245

PREVIOUS EDITIONS OF THE LETTERS   246

INDEX   247

PLATES

Samuel Pepys. From the painting attributed to J. Closterman
in the National Portrait Gallery   *Frontispiece*

Letter from Samuel Pepys to his Brother, John, dated March
26, 1670. Bodleian Library, MS. Rawl. 182
     Between pages 16 *and* 17

INTRODUCTION

'AND so I betake myself to that course, which is almost as much as to see myself go into my grave: for which, and the discomforts that will accompany my being blind, the good God prepare me!' So wrote Pepys as he closed the last page of his intimate diary. It is not surprising, then, to find Howarth, one of the recent editors of Pepys correspondence, remarking on the difficulty of realizing that life, even the busy life of Pepys, went on after that tragic day in its customary pace. Certainly the emphasis which has been placed of late almost exclusively upon the public life and service of the diarist has left the casual reader to wonder whether the man himself remained the same. The intense consciousness of home and family relationships and the intense personal savour of experience, of course, are not well expressed in the second diary or in the letters to public men. This problem, then, of Pepys's continuing family relationships is the unifying principle of the present collection.

The text has been assembled from letters passing between Pepys and his closest relatives, letters concerning those relatives exchanged between Pepys and persons outside the circle of kin, and other non-epistolary memoranda related to the subject-matter involved. Of the 188 documents here reprinted, 162 are for the first time reproduced in full, although short passages from some of them have been used in various biographical works.

Besides Samuel Pepys, the correspondents include the diarist's father, his two brothers, Thomas and John, his sister Paulina, his sister's husband, his wife's brother and her sister-in-law, and three nephews. Letters to Samuel's cousin, the Earl of Sandwich, are omitted, as also those to other cousins, in order to limit the collection to the concerns of the immediate family circle. The letters between the ageing Pepys and John Jackson, his sister's son, the nephew who inherited his estate, are so far from intimate in tone as to shed little light on the Pepys of the diary, and have been so fully reprinted by Tanner as to make their inclusion here superfluous. Included, however, are thirty-seven letters to and from persons outside the circle of relationship, but involved temporarily in the family concerns, letters throwing additional light on problems discussed in the family papers.

The significance of the present volume lies in its subject-matter, which is closer to the diary than any previous collection of letters. Whereas it is the Pepys of the diary who has endeared himself to readers, the Pepys revealed by previous collections of letters has been the secretary of the Admiralty or the aged, infirm, retired savant of Clapham. The present collection, however, returns us to the man of family pride, personal ambition, and meticulous responsibility whom diary readers watched at the outset of his career. It sets him again among the members of his family who have aroused the interest and curiosity of those readers.

THE TEXT

The text of all material is presented directly from the manuscript. The letters which I have transcribed are to be found chiefly in volumes 170 to 195 of the Rawlinson Collection in the Bodleian Library at Oxford, in the Admiralty volumes in the Pepysian Library at Magdalene College, Cambridge, and in one volume of the Cockerell Papers in the National Maritime Museum at Greenwich. Letter 188 is transcribed from the Cockerell papers in the possession of Mr. Arthur Houghton of New York.

In respect to the state of the text, the letters fall into three groups, as I have indicated at the first of each letter: originals, copies kept by the writer, and first drafts. By originals I mean the letters actually sent through the post, often preserved with cover, address, and seal. Most of the letters received by Pepys lie in this category. Some of the letters written by Pepys are also holographic originals, as the Rawlinson Collection contains unsorted remains of the private papers of Samuel's father and brother. Many of the original letters sent by Pepys, however, were not in his hand, but were written by secretaries, as he made use of amanuenses even before he gave up the diary, and increased the use of them with time. Some of these secretarial manuscripts have been revised in the hand of Pepys himself.

Copies kept by the writers are often the only surviving versions of the letters. Risks of the post or of a personal carrier made it wise to keep such duplicates or even to dispatch more than one copy to the recipient, as readers of the Pepys–Jackson letters in the Tanner edition, for example, will recall. Earlier, when Pepys was charged with treason in 1679 and his brother-in-law St. Michel was in France gathering evidence to clear him, Pepys caused a secretary to copy each letter, before sending, into a folio volume which he called his letter-book. He urged St. Michel to do the same. It happens that Pepys's letter-book, now in the Rawlinson Collection, is the only known surviving copy of this part of the correspondence. St. Michel's letter-book has not so far been found, nor have the originals from either correspondent come to light. Other letter-books are in the Pepysian Library and the National Maritime Museum.

The reader need not, however, suspect the authenticity of these copies or letter-books. Insecurity of the post gave the makers and preservers every reason to make sure of complete accuracy. In particular, absent-mindedness made it advisable for Pepys to have correct records, as even family letters were full of business dealings, money matters, or legal problems. These copies had to be genuine replicas. Even when the letter-book shows emendations in the hand of Pepys, we may be confident that the corresponding changes have been made in the letter posted.

The third class of texts, the rough copy or first draft, from which a fair copy was to be made to send through the post, has not been segregated, as far as I am aware, by other editors. Although these first drafts could be called, in one sense, 'originals', even though not sent through the post, they have been used in this collection only when the posted letter or the letter-book is not known to have survived, and in every case they are noted as drafts.

These first drafts Pepys sometimes dictated to a secretary, with emendations as the work proceeded, occasionally with a complete change of construction in mid-sentence. Sometimes a draft would be scratched by Pepys on the foot or back of a letter he had just received, usually in longhand but twice in shorthand.[1] Again, a letter begun with flourishes as an original would be so marred by changes during composition that it became merely a draft to be copied fairly. These emendations, which might well serve as lessons in epistolary care, are indicated in footnotes.

In presenting all three classes of text differentiated above, this edition remains faithful to whatever manuscript is available, repudiating the practice of reducing to modern usage all letters in the hand of a secretary. The comparatively ephemeral nature of handwritten manuscript binds a modern editor to preserve a faithful copy of what the page holds at the time of transcription. Besides, the scarcity of emendations occurring in those letter-books which bear evidence of Pepys's copyreading would indicate that the various secretaries held normally to the master's habits and preferences.

Most seventeenth-century writers used abbreviations habitually. The present edition extends conventional abbreviations, including the ampersand, the tilde over *m* and *n* to indicate doubling, and that over *con* to indicate *tion*. It expands *ye* into *the*, *yt* into *that*, *wt* into *what*, *wch* into *which*, and *yor* into *your*. The abbreviations *vizt* and *&c*, however, are retained as personal habits of Pepys and not conventions. The apostrophe is retained in past tenses such as *answer'd*, as Pepys evidently regarded this custom not as abbreviation but as a

---

[1] Letters 143 and 145.

form of spelling. Words clearly misspelled are reproduced exactly as the manuscript gives them.

Of each letter the provenance is given in a footnote with volume and folio reference, as well as page reference to the printed volume if the letter has been included by previous editors. The arrangement is chronological according to the modern calendar. The original date on each letter has been preserved and placed in the heading, even when written at the end in the manuscript, with the present editor's emendations or additions indicated by square brackets.

HISTORY OF THE TEXT

As far as this editor can determine, this collection represents the first attempt to segregate one complete section of Pepys correspondence. With the first edition of the diary in 1825, Lord Braybrooke published a random selection of letters. With subsequent fuller reprints of the diary, more letters were added, the text of each containing so many omissions and recastings as to be unreliable. In 1841 John Smith, the transcriber of the diary for Lord Braybrooke, published a two-volume edition of Pepys's Tangier diary and some other papers, entitled *Life, Journals, and Correspondence of Samuel Pepys.* Here again the selection of letters was random, and, where the originals survive, comparison shows that Smith emended ruthlessly.

Both early editors overlooked the intrinsic value of the family letters, giving preference instead to matters of historical importance. The latest and fullest[1] edition of the diary, 1893–7, omitted letters entirely. Tanner's three volumes of the letters, published 1926–9, are based wholly upon a particular collection, the four manuscript volumes known as the Pepys Cockerell letters, of which one is now at Greenwich and the other three are in the hands of Mr. Arthur A. Houghton of Corning, New York. Dr. Tanner does not reprint all the Pepys Cockerell letters in his three volume edition, nor does he classify them according to subject or correspondent. He does not indicate how much of any given letter he omits or changes.

Finally, there is Howarth's selection, in 1932, the *Letters and the Second Diary of Samuel Pepys,* a remarkably meticulous transcription and with careful notation of manuscript sources. As the 350 letters cover the full range of Pepys's many interests and many correspondents, however, only the dates furnish continuity. No one correspondence is represented with completeness. Almost half of the selections are drawn from Pepys's old age and retirement, when responsibility for the family was no longer his prime concern.

[1] *Wheatley.*

Introduction

THE LETTERS, THE DIARY, AND
RESTORATION ENGLAND

The family letters, exclusive and highly specialized as this collection is, must be read against a background of Pepys's England, the England of Charles II, of James II, and of William and Mary.

Confirmed Pepysians will recall that the diary commences with the return of the Stuart family from exile in Holland. The young Pepys, as secretary to his cousin Sandwich, is a member of the welcoming party which escorts home the new monarch, Charles II, and his brother the Duke of York, later to become James II.

The first letter of the present collection, dated 1663, indicates that the writer, already burdened by heavy responsibilities in the Navy office prior to the Second Dutch War, is being vexed by a lawsuit with the Trices concerning the Brampton inheritance. This estate, as readers of the diary will recall, has been left to the diarist's father at the death of Uncle Robert Pepys in 1661, thereby creating disputes at law with Uncle Thomas, a closer heir, and the Trices, sons of Uncle Robert's wife. Family difficulties are increased the next year by the death of Samuel's brother Tom.

Between the letters of 1665 and those of 1670, a period from which, apparently, no family letters have survived, although many must have been written, the diary reminds us of the victories of Lowestoft and of Sole Bay, of the diarist's increase in wealth through trading in captured prize goods, and of the plague and fire which disfigure London. Strangely no surviving letter mentions the death of Pepys's mother in 1666. After the war has been ended by the Peace of Breda, and the old Chancellor Clarendon has been dismissed and exiled, Pepys closes the diary for fear of losing his eyesight, and takes Elizabeth on a continental tour. On their return, Elizabeth dies, leaving Pepys a widower all his days.

After 1670, the year in which the letters recommence, Pepys is called upon to defend not only the Navy Office, but the Treasury as well from accusations of waste and inefficiency, brought by Buckingham and others in high places who hope to discredit thereby the Duke of York. The Third Dutch War commences, and Sandwich, 'my Lord' of the diary, dies in the second battle of Sole Bay. From this point family matters are so frequently mixed with business and history that segregation can be decided only arbitrarily.

When the Duke of York has to retire from public service under the Test Act, his office as Lord High Admiral is entrusted not to one man but to a commission, for which Pepys is named secretary. Throughout this period of reorganization Samuel works closely with

John Pepys and Thomas Hayter, who hold jointly his old office of Clerk of the Acts. When peace is signed with the Dutch in 1674, Samuel moves both office and residence to Derby House, and at the same time takes a seat in Parliament as member for Castle Rising. But the old enemies of his patron, the Duke of York, are not done with Pepys. They accuse him of popery. In this connexion St. Michel, his brother-in-law, writes the long and much-quoted letter of family history in vindication of Samuel's protestantism.[1] Shortly afterward Samuel loses his brother John, becomes Master of Trinity House and Master of the Cloth Workers Company, labours to refit the fleet for hostilities against the Algerines and the French, and founds modern naval administration by his three great reforms governing manning of ships, selection of chaplains, and training of lieutenants. At this period the exiled York gives his daughter Mary in marriage to the Hollander, William, Prince of Orange, who is to sit with her on the English throne in a little over ten years' time.

From October 1678 to June 1680 Pepys is under accusation of treason, and is lodged for a time in prison. For clarity the confused events of this period are set forth in a separate chapter. But no sooner is Pepys released from the false charges than fresh worries surround him. Paulina's husband dies in September 1680 and Pepys's father in October, leaving two estates to put in order. Paulina comes to London, Samuel himself falls ill with ague, and Paulina's two orphan boys are to be clothed and sent to school. At this juncture St. Michel's wife Ester brings down Samuel's wrath by overdrawing her allowance with him while her husband is off on his new appointment at Tangier. For a year the St. Michel household and the two estates at Brampton and Ellington are constant worries.

From this point the number of family letters decreases. In 1683, the year in which Pepys comes out of retirement to become Secretary of the Admiralty under the restored Duke of York and is sent to Tangier to evaluate property at the time the mole is demolished, the notorious Colonel Scott, the instrument of Pepys's imprisonment and subsequent anxiety, confesses his former perjury. Pepys becomes M.P. for Harwich, president of the Royal Society, and for the second time Master of Trinity House. He walks as one of the barons of the Cinque Ports in the coronation of James II.

The family letters of 1688 do not record the flight of the king. On the evening of 19 December 1688 Pepys receives a note from William Hewer, 'a letter of great tendernesse at a time of difficulty' as he endorses it. 'You may rest assured that I am wholly yours', writes the staunch friend who was the boy Will of Seething Lane in

[1] Letter 21.

the days of the diary, 'and that you shall never want the utmost of my constant, faithfull, and personal service . . .; And . . . as all I have pro-seeded from you soe all I have and am, is and shalbe at your service. I have noe reason to complaine as yet of any hardshipp, but to morrow shall know the utmost and then I shall waite on you.'[1] The family letters of 1689 do not chronicle Pepys's retirement from office, nor his being imprisoned once more briefly on a fantastic charge of plots with the French. With the letters to St. Michel in this year the family records stop, leaving Pepys still thirteen years to live in retirement in York Buildings and later at Clapham with the faithful Hewer, who has been almost a son to him.

Pepys's parents and brothers are dead; Paulina and her husband are dead; a gulf of silence and bitterness separates Pepys and St. Michel. The old gentleman's days of bustle and activity are over. His patron James II lives in exile; William and Mary of Orange rule England. Such letters as Pepys now writes go quietly to his nephew John or to elderly friends such as the Houblons and the other diarist, John Evelyn.

THE TRIAL

The accusation and imprisonment of Pepys, which form the background for many of the letters, were part of a larger political plot against James, the Duke of York. Shaftesbury, Buckingham, and a number of other anti-papists in high places had at no time, it appears, entirely abandoned their attempts to discredit the king's brother, but in 1678 their plans took a decidedly practical and personal turn.

The action involving Pepys began in October with the disappearance of Sir Edmund Berry Godfrey, a well-known and upright Protestant magistrate. Days later, his body, run through with a sword, was found in a ditch. Clues were scanty and conflicting. The perpetrators, it is now thought, had originally planned to implicate Pepys in the murder, in order to discredit his patron, the Duke of York. But Pepys's being out of town at Newmarket, on unexpected summons from the king, removed him from immediate connexion with events. Thus, in order to involve him indirectly, the conspirators caused the arrest of his clerk, Samuel Atkins, on evidence which later proved so palpably false that the young man was acquitted.

During the imprisonment of Atkins, however, as Pepys accumulated evidence to clear the boy's character and prove an alibi, the design of the whole became apparent. One of the accusers of Atkins

---

1 Howarth, R. G., *Letters and the Second Diary of Samuel Pepys* (London, Dent, 1932), p. 198.

was that ubiquitous renegade, Colonel John Scott, whose career has been set forth in detail by Arthur Bryant.[1] An adventurer whose excursions into real estate promotion, gun manufacture, map-making and selling, and matrimony involved him in escapades on both sides of the Channel and both sides of the Atlantic, he did not scruple to invent evidence against Atkins at this time nor against Pepys himself later.

Atkins was cleared and liberated in February 1678/9. By May the opposition had fabricated so much testimony that they were emboldened to arraign and imprison Pepys and his friend the shipbuilder, Sir Anthony Deane, upon charges of piracy, popery, and treachery. Briefly, an attempt was first made to link Pepys with the joint enterprise of Deane and Balthasar St. Michel, who had borrowed the King's sloop *Hunter* during the Dutch wars and chartered it as a privateer. The unreliable captain of the sloop, who had not confined his actions to enemy ships, but had preyed upon English vessels as well, had seriously embarrassed his employers. Second, every effort was made to show that Pepys had secretly turned to the Catholic Church, had hidden crucifixes in his home, had consorted with Catholics. Third, the notorious Scott was intended to be the instrument of proving that Pepys had sold copies of English coastline maps to French officials through the agency of Deane, who had once made a trip to France to deliver certain English-built ships.

To all who knew the almost fanatical patriotism and protestantism of the serious little man, such charges against Pepys must have appeared patently untenable. But the urgency was to obtain definite evidence for defence admissible in an English court. The letters from the Tower and subsequently from York Buildings, where Pepys, allowed out on bail, repaired as guest of his friend and clerk, Will Hewer, trace the quest of this evidence.

St. Michel, just appointed Naval Storekeeper at Tangier, received the king's permission to delay his embarkation in order to secure French witnesses for Pepys. He went to Paris under the care and direction of the Secretary of the British Embassy, John Brisbane, and of Henry Savile, the Ambassador. Through Pepys's Huguenot friends in London, Mr. Houblon and Mr. Trenchepain, St. Michel was able to make contact with the families of a M. Pellissary and of a certain Captain de la Piogerie, both of whom had been named by Scott as recipients of English coastal maps sold by Pepys and delivered by Antony Deane. During the weeks in Paris St. Michel also developed a certain intimacy with such underworld characters as Foster, Joyne, Sherwin, and Fielding, all cronies of Scott, but most

[1] Arthur Bryant, *Samuel Pepys: The Years of Peril* (n.e. London, 1948), passim.

of them willing to become character witnesses against their former friend in the forthcoming trial of Pepys.

Previously, of course, Pepys had resigned his naval secretaryship, which was given to Thomas Hayter. During the period of his accusation he was without public employment, although the king still called for his advice upon occasion. It is interesting to note that Pepys and Deane were among the first to test the recently enacted Habeas Corpus Act, a statute which put into writing a long-accepted principle of English common-law. But as the Act had been supported by the enemies of the Crown to safeguard their own rights and not those of the king's friends, the plea for a speedy trial was in this case rejected. Through the months the postponement and delay were repeated, as the great men back of the plot found it impossible to secure genuine evidence to support their charges. Scurrilous pamphlets appeared against Pepys and against his host, Will Hewer. Even though King Charles had already sent his brother York into exile in Holland, the campaign continued.

Finally in 1680 Pepys's erstwhile butler, John James, who had been dismissed because of an amour with the housekeeper, lay on his death-bed. In this emergency he confessed in writing that he had vengefully perjured himself in accusing Pepys of popery, and named the Naval Administrator William Harbord as instigator of the plot against Pepys.

Quite suddenly the opponents retreated, the charges were dropped, and on 28 June Pepys and Deane were set free without a trial. This absence of public vindication went so hard with Pepys that he compiled all the testimony that he had gathered, not of his own doings only but of all the details concerning his accusers and vilifiers, into two great folio volumes, calling them his Volumes of Mornamont, a name taken from a fictitious title assumed by Colonel Scott in one of his scoundrelly undertakings. These volumes, which Pepys for some time hoped to publish in order to humble his accusers, are now a part of the Pepysian Collection at Cambridge University, the only official monuments to a trial which never took place.

THE PEPYS OF THE LETTERS

Biographers and editors have spent time and paper in speculation over what manner of man Pepys became after abandoning his diary in his thirty-sixth year. Likewise, readers of the published letters of the post-diary days, noting the sedate and scholarly poise of the man, have lamented the apparent absence of the diarist's curiosity, liveliness, and whimsicality. The thoughtful student is thus reminded that the Pepys of the diary was a many-sided man, and that the personal nuances revealed in the diary may have found only partial expression in the writer's various personal relationships. He is forced to recognize also that biographers have not dealt adequately with such other problems as the emotional immaturity of both Samuel and Elizabeth at the time of their marriage, nor Samuel's youthful inability to resolve the dichotomy of his nature, nor the background of family poverty, bickering, and mismanagement which furnished neither Samuel nor Elizabeth the pattern for a wholly satisfying partnership.

Although the present small and special collection furnishes only one clue to the complex problem outlined above, it is not too much to expect that a full publication of all Pepys's letters, if it is ever made in one edition, will provide important materials for the study of the man in all aspects.

The present collection, limited in scope as it is, assists the reader to trace the development of a young Pepys whose concept of family loyalty was at first external, traditional, even sentimental, into a mature man whose genuine sense of family invests both himself and his beneficiaries with dignity.

The first of the letters antedates the close of the diary by six years, revealing in 1663 a Clerk of the Acts of the Navy Office, aged thirty, who prospers, takes dancing lessons, and beautifies his house in the Navy yard, meanwhile urging his parents to survey their income and expenditures with an eye to better use of the sums at their disposal. Nine documents here reprinted overlap the period of the diary and corroborate part of it. After a silence from 1666 to 1670 the letters resume, with the diary closed, Elizabeth dead, and Samuel committed to responsibility for his wife's family as well as his own. The letters continue till 1689, the year of the writer's retirement to private life in York Buildings on the Thames.

What sort of man revealed himself through these letters? Although he may have felt as impatient with his relatives as the diary would indicate, he wrote urbanely to them as he gave money and advice, helped the younger men to employment, and settled the estates and debts of his two brothers. He rose in office from Clerk of the Acts to Secretary of the Office of Lord High Admiral without changing the tone of his writing to his family.

The same ability to separate intellectual and emotional reactions can be traced during Pepys's unjust accusation and imprisonment for popery and high treason. The present publication of his letters written during this period makes it possible to trace the clear thinking of the man from day to day and to admire his freedom from acrimony as he concentrated his faculties upon the legal problem of clearing his name instead of upon the danger to his life.

Released from prison, Pepys took up family troubles again with the same patience as of old, to untangle the involved estates of his sister's husband and of his own father, to provide for his sister and her two orphaned sons, to bring order into the finances of his wife's brother. In 1684, when the English withdrew from Tangier, Pepys was sent to that port to liquidate claims of property holders. In 1687 and 1688, while he was reorganizing the navy in an anxious attempt to protect his king and country from invasion, he was still offering advice to the same feckless brother-in-law, St. Michel. After the flight of James II, so staunch a friend of the exiled monarch as Pepys could not expect to remain in office, and with his retirement this series of family papers ends. The reason for excluding later letters to his nephew has been given on page vii of this introduction.

Surveying the present collection as a whole, we find the style of the writing an index to the writer. There is little of Pepys's private life or of his lightest moods in letters to the family, for the relatives are, for the most part, not of his lively disposition. They are engaged chiefly in seeking money or advice or practical help from him. In view of the cringing servility of their thanks, it is to Pepys's credit that he does not become unctuously benevolent, but remains cordial and matter-of-fact.

On the other hand, Pepys is far from brusque or impatient with this often shiftless crew. When he feels compelled to point out the defects of character or conduct which have led to misfortune, he addresses his kin with the same tact and diplomacy which he would employ to a fellow-committeeman, albeit in simpler terms. This patience, which in regard to his father was tinged with amusement in the pages of the diary, takes on in the letters a deference which is the more surprising as the son was clearly the superior in practical matters as well as in education. Also, the ability to analyse a situation into its several aspects, which was a part of Pepys's genius for administration, pervades his intercourse with his family. When he does a favour for a relative, he refers to it frankly as a favour, with no hypocritical pretence that it is no trouble, and he always makes clear exactly upon what grounds he performs it. Similarly, when he acknowledges an obligation, he is equally frank. He is constant in his praise of St. Michel for his industry in gathering evidence which is to clear Pepys of the treason charge, without sentimental iteration of his own gratitude. When he has to caution St. Michel about the size of his expense account, he also takes care to commend his zeal. There is mental health in this clear-headedness.

Introduction

The sense of family in Pepys is always tempered by personal honour. He will recommend for appointment or promotion only those of his relatives whom he could recommend conscientiously without the relationship. From St. Michel's complaints, indeed, we infer that Pepys sometimes strains a point to see superior merit in persons not related, rather than be guilty of nepotism. He will refuse to intervene for even the most deserving when he finds them in the wrong on so much as a single count, choosing instead to analyse their conduct dispassionately and candidly. When accused, even wrongfully, he will refuse to aid his own just cause by anything equivocal or even by anything honest that could be twisted to false-seeming by his bitterest enemy, cautioning himself to 'be most slow to believe what we most wish should be true'.[1] And this is neither the Puritan nor the wily strategist. This is the familiar Pepys of the diary, who liked to have all fine and neat about him in his home; his integrity demanded the same criteria for his personal acts.

One more quality, less elevated than scrupulous honour, but perhaps more intimately appreciated by the family, is Pepys's moderation. He refuses to become abusive or impatient, even under provocation. This merit shines not only through his letters to those who exceed their allowances, lose important papers, or involve themselves in unseemly controversies, but as well through the letters written to him in which these simple souls lay before him their misdeeds, their confusions, their bewilderment. However busy he is, they feel free to spread their woes loquaciously over much paper. They are confident in the humanity of the man they address.

THE CORRESPONDENTS

Chief among the writers and receivers of letters in this collection stands Samuel Pepys himself, who has been the subject of the previous chapter. Next to him one would like to place his wife Elizabeth, but search has revealed so far not one scrap of writing in her hand, nor any letter from her husband to her. The blind spot that enables some readers of the diary to join heartily in Pepys's outbreaks of impatience with his wife without sharing his equally frequent moods of tenderness has allowed some readers to infer that Elizabeth was probably not one to appreciate or treasure her husband's letters. To refute this fallacious inference one needs only the diary of 9 January 1662 in which Pepys in a fit of temper destroys all his wife's store of sentimental treasures and notes, even to his own earliest love-letter, which she has been cherishing. It is apparent from the diary that Elizabeth often sent her husband notes to his office. That this inveterate

[1] Letter 91.

preserver of documents should have destroyed them forthwith is unlikely in view of the Rawlinson Collection, which preserves even begging letters from total strangers, neatly folded and labelled with memoranda such as 'Gave her nothing'. We wonder if Pepys ever answered his wife's notes. Sometimes, we know, he ran home to reply in person. To other persons it was his custom to send a brief note of explanation when he was detained. If he showed a like courtesy to Elizabeth, the evidence has disappeared.

John Pepys, Senior

Nearest in relationship to Pepys among those whose letters survive is the diarist's father, John Pepys. The old gentleman is sixty-two years of age when he receives the first letter in this collection. In 1661 he has inherited the estate of his elder brother Robert, with its debts and responsibilities, and has moved down to the country-house at Brampton in Huntingdonshire. To his son Thomas he leaves the London tailor shop, the inventory of which is reprinted in this collection. After coming up to London briefly for Samuel's help in April of 1663, the old gentleman has returned to Brampton. He then receives the letter that begins the series: Samuel, after a study of the tangled records, has drawn up a programme of economy for his parents and a schedule of benevolence for himself that is to found securely the Brampton estate, later passed on to the Pepys descendants. Mention of this estate is to recur throughout Samuel's letters to all members of the circle.

Pepys's mother does not appear directly or indirectly in the letters. The diary furnishes us with meagre details concerning the character and death of Margaret Kight Pepys, sister of William Kight, the butcher. Apparently of lower social standing than her husband, she figures in the diary solely by her improvidence and quarrelsomeness. We do not know even the date of her birth, as it is not given in the Brampton register which records her death on 25 March 1667.

The birth-date of Samuel's father is to be inferred from the baptismal record in Impington, 14 January 1601. Although of a fen-land family, John Pepys lived for thirty-six years, 1613 to 1649, in St. Bride's Churchyard, London, as tailor's apprentice and masterman. He married Margaret Kight in Newington, Surrey, 15 October 1626, and buried in infancy seven of his eleven children, as the St. Bride's register shows. After the death of his wife, as appears from both diary and letters, he lived with his married daughter, Paulina Jackson, made comfortable by letters and gifts from his sons in London. He died 4 October 1680.

Throughout his lifetime the father is treated with respect and thoughtfulness by all his children, apparently, although his letters reveal no outstandingly lovable traits in himself. The cramped, awkward penmanship reveals a writer not too literate, nor too much at ease with the pen. He reveals no spiritual gifts in any letter to his children. 'Pray good Child let thare be something done in it' strikes the keynote of all his messages. His prayer that his one prosperous son may survive him lest he suffer from his own ineptness makes him an unheroic figure. The letters do not reveal him a success in either city or country, or even a figure of esteem among the relatives. True, his brother Robert leaves him an estate, but so hedged about with restrictions and with other bequests that we can see the testator's underlying intention that the property shall revert ultimately to Samuel. There is internal evidence that more letters were exchanged between the diarist and his father than have been preserved; the surviving letters are consistent in revealing a father never quite equal to the occasion, always demanding or receiving some type of aid.

Thomas Pepys

Next come the two brothers, Thomas and John, who with Samuel and Paulina make up the four survivors of the original eleven. Neither brother has been pictured favourably by biographers, nor does the diary give stature to either. Thomas, born 18 June 1634, took over the London tailor shop in 1661, on terms never made clear beyond the hint in the diary that he would miscarry for want of brains and care. Documents included in the present volume record the conflicting assertions and recriminations of the persons involved. Perhaps most of the contenders were mistaken in what they thought they knew, although it seems possible that some were perjuring themselves. Samuel, in any event, was left to compose the quarrel and satisfy the law.

That Thomas was not a financial success is no mark against his character. The inaccuracy of his book-keeping, even though regrettable, was not outstanding in an age when even the royal accounts were often confused, and when Samuel Pepys made a name for himself by an honesty and an accuracy in public accounting that were held unprecedented. The pitiful fragment listed as Letter 3 in this collection is the only writing we have in Tom's own hand. Clearly the man was not quite equal to life; he died on 15 March 1664. It is from the diary that we know of the family's surprise to learn that Tom, who had resisted the paternal attempts to marry him, had fathered twin bastards, one of whom survived him to become a family problem. So far it has been impossible to follow the subsequent fate of this child, which, after adoption by one Cave, was apparently forgotten by the Pepys family.

John Pepys, Junior

To John Pepys, the other brother, no biographer has given praise; and yet the letters in this collection should go some way at least towards establishing his character. Born 26 November 1641, John is twenty-eight when we first come upon him in this collection, the brother John with whom the diary has shown indignation over his poor scholarship at Cambridge and his spiteful letters about Samuel. These spiteful letters unfortunately are not preserved in the untidy collection of papers relative to John in the Rawlinson Collection. In 1670 John is being summoned to London, where Samuel finds employment for him as a clerk in Trinity House and sets him upon the road to prosperity. Samuel has evidently forgotten his resolution to carry his grudge against John through life.[1] A letter from Samuel to Sir Richard Browne at this period declares that mere family relationship could not tempt him to recommend John were not the young man's sobriety, diligence, and education so far above those of the last incumbent that it is a service to the corporation to name him. This praise is the likelier to be accurate, as Samuel is at this time involved in clearing the Navy Office of charges of corruption and inefficiency. Two years later, when Samuel is made an Elder Brother of Trinity House, the centre of merchant marine activity, the two Pepyses work together to keep all official transactions clear and businesslike.

The death of Sandwich at Sole Bay in 1672 and the voluntary exile of James Stuart in 1673 after the passage of the Test Act leave Samuel without his two great patrons, although he is still expected to guide and protect all his kin. Although biographers have accepted John customarily as one of the family parasites, the letters in this collection reveal him as a faithful collaborator with Samuel at this tense period in dispatching weekly news to the querulous father in Brampton, in packing up and sending off gifts of food and money, even in undertaking a thousand-pound bond. In Letter 23 we find John busying himself in good works for St. Michel, Samuel's brother-in-law. Letter 40 from the father is an indication of how much the family depends upon John, while Letters 43 and 44 show Samuel's dependence upon his brother for honesty and efficiency in naval duties. Among John's papers is a memorandum,[2] evidently a duplicate of one given to John Jackson, Paulina's husband, with notes and advice on all the perplexities of the Jackson household. Although

---

[1] *Diary*, 21 March 1663/4.   [2] Letter 45.

corrections in Samuel's hand indicate that the two brothers are collaborating in this assistance, the presence of the paper in John's files shows that Samuel is delegating to his younger brother essential family responsibility.

And then in 1677 young John Pepys dies at the age of thirty-six and is buried in St. Olave's Churchyard, London, leaving a confused estate for Samuel to administer, and one more burden of debt and worry, which Samuel assumes at once. It is customary for biographers to comment at this point upon John's shortcomings. Data have never been complete enough, however, to justify the assertion of some editors that Samuel actually had to pay 300 pounds to Trinity House to make up a deficit for his brother. The fact is that records were so involved that it could not be seen at once whether John was debtor or creditor. His salary had been unpaid for three years, during which time he had expended from his own purse large sums on behalf of the corporation, sums for which he had expected to be reimbursed. That Samuel at once insisted upon depositing 300 pounds with Trinity House is clear, but there is no record available to show whether he ultimately paid more after going over the accounts, or whether this sum or even a larger one was repaid to Samuel as John's heir.[1]

Paulina Pepys Jackson

If the readers of the diary carry away an unflattering portrait of Samuel's sister Paulina, often called Pall, these letters will not greatly heighten her reputation. We know from the record of her baptism in St. Bride's that she was born in London, 18 October 1640. We know from the diary that Samuel worried over her because she was unattractive, unpleasant to live with, and unsought in matrimony, and that he stirred himself to find a husband for her. The biographer Whitear has compiled a list of eight candidates under consideration, including Pepys's faithful clerk William Hewer, who remained a bachelor until his death, possibly because he had earlier assured his master and mistress that he had no thought to change his condition. In the present collection Paulina first appears as the recipient of Letter 3, the enigmatical fragment from her brother Tom. When she is next seen, she has been married for three years to John Jackson, whom the diary describes as uneducated, untalented, and plain, but handsome enough for Pall. The diarist adds, 'Though I shall, I see, have no pleasure nor content in him.'[2]

Although Paulina's report to her brother John, dated 5 March

---

[1] See Master and Wardens of Trinity House to S. P., Bodleian Library, Rawlinson MS. A. 191: 83–4, reprinted as Number 63 in this collection; also Rawl. A. 182: 263–89.   [2] *Diary*, 7 Feb. 1667–8.

1672, shows small literary merit or warmth of affection, it deals capably with family matters. By 1675, in her letter to her father who is visiting in London, she is more affectionate, and in addition, definitely conscious of responsibility, already aware perhaps of her husband's inadequacy in practical dealings. In the light of subsequent events, it is pathetic to read her assertion that Samuel is to have no fear of not seeing his money again, as she will sell all she possesses if driven by necessity rather than disoblige him. This boast she never makes good.

Samuel's frankly unflattering estimate of John Jackson in a letter to Dr. Turner doubtless explains why all business is transacted through Paulina. Jackson's one appearance in this collection, a querulous wail when his wife is ill, is followed by Paulina's memorandum to her brothers, a list of the errands in London with which she has charged her husband, but which she evidently has no confidence in his remembering.

Paulina's hour of greatest dignity, perhaps, is reflected in Samuel's laying upon her the family responsibilities while he is in prison. He writes as to one who can be trusted to stand fast in time of doubt and danger, explaining to her the false accusation of his clerk Atkins and the implied threat to himself, assuring her of his innocence, and trusting her to understand his inability to write frequently. Although none of her bulletins has yet come to light, it is to be hoped that Paulina sent the weekly reports on family matters which her brother requested, in order that family anxieties need not be added to those arising from the dangers which threatened his life.

Not long after Samuel's release, however, John Jackson is dead, leaving less than enough resources to satisfy his creditors, some of whom are reported clamorous. Papers included in this collection show Paulina's dignified attempts to handle the problem and to provide for her sons. Within a month the old father too is dead, and Samuel must administer the estate, relying to a certain extent upon Paulina's moral support. But Paulina is no mainstay. She falls ill and must be brought to London; her sons are left in the school of a kinsman, one John Matthews, and Samuel must assume responsibility for their education, their clothing, and their choice of career. The house at Brampton now being vacant, Samuel sends down the St. Michels, who are still there when Paulina recovers in 1682 and resumes direction of her estates. This is our last glimpse of Paulina; from the inscription in Brampton Church, we know only that she died 17 November 1689, leaving two sons.

Introduction

Balthasar St. Michel

In Balthasar St. Michel, 'my wife's brother Balty' of the diary, we come upon the most colourful of all the correspondents in the family group. Pepys secured for the young man the post of muster-master at sea on Harmon's flagship in 1666, and that of deputy treasurer of the fleet in 1667. Thus commences the long career of St. Michel in the service of his nation. The first letter[1] from St. Michel himself is a description of the arrival of a Dutch boat at Deal, where he has just been made muster-master. It is to be noted that life in Balty's eyes is never matter-of-fact. Every wind is a hurricane, every mishap a near-catastrophe, every hardship a hell. Readers must lament the letters from him which have been lost and the diary which he never wrote.

The letters here reprinted outline the rise of St. Michel under the advice and patronage of Pepys, and the fall of his fortunes when he no longer has a protector. Samuel's first letter to his protégé advises the young man prophetically not to rely upon the continuance of present prosperity or of Samuel's influence, but to put by savings against the future. This advice is never heeded, for Balty is always in need of money, and Pepys becomes, as the biographers phrase it, a father to St. Michel. Perhaps the most noteworthy and most informative letter from St. Michel is Letter 21, in which is vividly sketched the family background from which he and his sister, Pepys's wife, have emerged. Here is depicted as delightfully erratic a family as anyone could wish to choose a wife from.

Two letters of 1675, those of 13 and 29 August, require comment at this point, not because they are supremely important biographically, but because together they clarify an incident hitherto obscured by the publication of only one. Together, they reveal one of the less admirable aspects of Balty's impetuous nature. What seems at first a simple request to Pepys to save a seaman from imprisonment for debt, a request answered by Pepys's hint that His Majesty need not yet rob the gaols in order to man his ships, turns out to be a flagrant and wilful misrepresentation on Balty's part. He has, in fact, misused his office and influence to interpose in a suit at law between two of his acquaintances, to handicap the one and favour the other.

Unstable as Balty often appears in personal relationships, he is clearly an efficient public servant, both as muster-master at Deal and later as Deputy Commissioner of the Sick and Wounded during the Dutch war. As neither Pepys nor John Evelyn, St. Michel's superior officer, is an indulgent critic when matters go wrong, the absence of

[1] Letter 11.

xxiv

censure alone would be a tribute, even without the frequent commendations by Pepys.

One other incident requires clarification, an unfortunate venture into which St. Michel was lured by his ambition for money. With the shipbuilder Sir Anthony Deane and others, St. Michel formed a partnership to borrow the sloop *Hunter* from the king and fit her out as a privateer to prey upon Dutch shipping during the war. One of the captains of the ship, apparently Thomas Swaine, presumed to license the ship in a French port to prey upon English shipping as well. Finally, as noted in the section on Pepys's trial, one of the other captains, Moon or Mohun, attempted either profit or revenge by accusing Deane and his partners of treason. Even Samuel, who was wholly unrelated to the venture, shared the unpleasant publicity with the partners, who had been deceived and swindled by their employee.[1]

St. Michel's greatest service to his benefactor was performed in connexion with the previously mentioned imprisonment of the diarist. As both Pepys and Sir Anthony Deane were in the Tower, it was St. Michel who went to Paris to unearth information about the scoundrel Scott, their accuser. Although the subject-matter is amply clear from Pepys's letters, the only part of the correspondence preserved, St. Michel's missing reports would doubtless be the more exciting version. It is evident, despite complaints of hardship and homesickness, that Balty relishes the investigation, which he protracts unmistakably. The amazing sums of money which he draws indicate that he is not living too abstemiously, as he pursues a sort of double life between the wealthy merchants of Pepys's acquaintance, on the one hand, and the rogues and vagabonds who consort with the nefarious Colonel Scott on the other. Protesting that he is so overworked as to need an assistant, he is nonetheless visibly disappointed at being taken at his word, when a prosaic Mr. Denise of London comes to share the credit and perhaps moderate the glamour.

St. Michel's taste for the grandiose is reflected in his reluctance to return quietly to England when the investigation is complete; he prefers to continue in France until he can escort the French witnesses at the time of the trial, or, as an alternative, to bring them all over to England at once to live in the interim at Pepys's expense. And finally, he must have exasperated even Pepys by his suggestion that a special warrant from the king would be needed to land French Catholics upon English soil.

When the case is dismissed and the witnesses have returned to France, St. Michel is again free to serve the navy and depart for

[1] See abstract of accusation in *Mornamont Papers*, i. 5–7, Pepysian Library, Cambridge University, England.

Introduction

Tangier. His melodramatic account of unspeakable hardships on the road from London to the Downs would be merely laughable if he had not undertaken to prove that the misfortunes clearly brought on by his own poor planning were traceable to Pepys's precepts of economy. A florid account of cruel hardships in Tangier is rendered less realistic by insistence that the absence of a letter from Pepys is the most insupportable of all his griefs. Although, four months later, his miseries, caused in his estimation by the enemies of Pepys, have passed the expression of the tongue, his pen continues adequate to record them.

While St. Michel, arrived home without leave in order to complain of his grievances, is being remanded to duty by the Navy Office and is again embarking for Tangier, a remarkable epistolary duel is taking place between Pepys and St. Michel's hopelessly inefficient wife Ester. She is unable to live within her allowance, although Pepys has installed her in his house at Brampton rent free, and yet is unable to report where the money has gone. Social historians will find these letters valuable in their wealth of detail on daily living, and students of human nature will appreciate the ageless picture of domestic infelicity and mismanagement, presented with a realism in direct contrast to St. Michel's trite and rhetorical descriptions of marital bliss. After Balty's reference to his sweet little family, his five small babes crying after him, and his dearest love for his wife, it is sobering to come upon Ester's confession of 'being a stranger as well to my husbands estate as Actions, alwayes in a worse condition then the meanest servant he kept . . . but when I chuse for my ease it shall not be an husband, with home I never had any.'[1]

But the problems of this family are not susceptible of permanent solution. When St. Michel is promoted to Resident Commissioner of the Navy at Deptford and Woolwich, Pepys tries gently to leave the family to its own resources, but Ester dies shortly thereafter in childbirth, leaving her husband with seven children and many problems. For a time the correspondence is largely formal, and then a serious personal break occurs. No biographer has found an explanation beyond mere conjecture of the nature of the quarrel which leads St. Michel to complain in May 1689 that he is damned unheard and that Pepys's housekeeper, Mary Skinner we presume, is a 'female Beast', maliciously inventive.[2]

From this time, or before, St. Michel is evidently not welcome as a guest. It is clear, however, from papers reprinted in this collection[3] that Pepys is seeking to have his brother-in-law's old age provided for officially. The Rawlinson Collection contains St. Michel's petition

[1] Letter 142. [2] Letter 181.
[3] Letters 182, 183.

xxvi

for re-employment, as the new régime after 1688 did not retain old servants loyal to James II. On 20 March 1692 he appeals to Pepys in a letter characteristically florid[1] asking for old clothes and wigs and expressing gratitude for some recent unspecified generosity. It is not known whether Pepys relieved St. Michel's distress with money as well as old clothes. Even such welcome pensioning would be grim solace for the man who had once enjoyed grandiose dreams of himself as the cherisher and protector of Samuel's old age. Years later, we find St. Michel still in want, still forgotten by the world. In April 1703 Samuel Pepys, near his mortal end, interrupts his own last illness to petition Sir George Rooke, Commander-in-Chief of the Fleet, to secure for St. Michel the relief 'universally enjoyed by other persons under his circumstances of age and length of service'.[2] St. Michel, he says, has been unaccountably for 'many years together wholly overlookt in the Navy, and with his numerous family exposed to and continued in a known state of want' and has without compensation served the seamen of England for all these years as an Elder Brother of Trinity House. The result of the appeal is unrecorded in these papers. We know that the widowed St. Michel had married again on 29 January 1688/9, one Margaret Darling, of whom only her name is known, and that he was alive to attend, with his daughter Mary, or perhaps Elizabeth, Pepys's funeral in 1703.

This daughter of St. Michel has been the subject of so much dispute that, although she is not one of the correspondents, it is worth summarizing in this place all that has been said and known of her. The confusion arises from William Hewer's mention of Mary St. Michel[3] as a recipient of a mourning ring at the funeral of Samuel Pepys, and from the young Samuel St. Michel's message in Letter 186 to a sister Elizabeth. Having seen an early document signed by Pepys and witnessed by Elizabeth St. Michel, Mr. Edwin Chappell inclines to believe that Mr. Hewer's memory of the name is faulty[4] and that Mary and Betty are the same person. We see from Letters 96 and 101 of the present collection a bit of evidence not heretofore mentioned by Pepysian scholars, that there was a Betty among St. Michel's children in 1679. But Mr. Hewer was ordinarily the most meticulous of men, especially in records and accounts. It is surely possible that among the seven children there may well have been at least three daughters: Elizabeth, named for her aunt, Pepys's wife, acting perhaps as head of her father's household after the mother's death, and married and removed elsewhere by 1703; Mary, a spinster living

[1] Letter 188.
[2] Tanner, J. R., *Private Correspondence . . . of Samuel Pepys* (London, 1926), ii. 307–8.
[3] Tanner, *Private Corr.* ii. 314. [4] *Notes and Queries*, 13 May 1933, p. 327.

xxvii

with her father at the time of the funeral in question; and Hannah, either too young or too ill to go to the funeral in 1703, or living elsewhere, but surviving in 1762, when an entry in the Contingent Accounts, which Mr. Chappell has called to the attention of the present editor, records ten guineas 'Paid to Hannah St. Michel, by order, for her Relief, in regard to her being Daughter to Balthasar St. Michel, who was formerly a Captain and a Commissioner of the Navy, and that she had a brother killed in the service of the Crown.'[1]

Samuel St. Michel

The family circle is now complete except for the nephews. Of the nieces, Pepys takes no notice. This present collection reprints the earliest known letter from a nephew. Only an uncle, perhaps, would enjoy the mincing tone of Letter 67 from St. Michel's son, the only son to whom reference is ever made by either Pepys or St. Michel, a boy usually referred to as 'little Samuell' or 'your littel disiple', but here signing himself, for no discernible reason, 'Chevalieu St. Michel'. Perhaps Chevalieu was a pet name of Pepys's for the lad, or perhaps the reference is to the gentlemanly polish which the boy is supposed to be acquiring, for the occasion is St. Michel's trip of investigation to France in 1679, when the small son is taken along to perfect his French and his dancing. Although we do not know whether St. Michel carried out his project of bringing home a French tutor, we do know from the mother's letter that the boy was subsequently under the care of a tutor who lived with the family. Nothing definite is to be learned of the lad himself. From the mother's letters in 1681, it is to be inferred that he had weak eyes and that his Uncle Samuel had complained of his bad manners or his indolence or both. It would be unreasonable to expect too much of a lad from such a chaotic home, but no direct evidence is available to explain why the uncle did not promote more zealously the career of his namesake. From the boy's letter to his father in 1689, forwarded to Pepys in an attempt to heal the family breach, it appears that young Samuel came in time to follow the sea. This supposition is corroborated by the reference quoted above in regard to the charitable grant to his sister Hannah.

Samuel Jackson

On the Jackson nephews we have vastly more data. After the death of their father in 1680 their care fell directly upon their uncle Samuel. Letters to Mr. Matthews show the uncle to be eager that young Samuel Jackson, who showed some 'genius' for penmanship or mathematics or both, should be put to a suitable vocation, by which

[1] Charles Fearne's Contingent Accounts. *Public Record Office*, Ad. xvii, 7.

Introduction

Pepys meant, of course, the sea. But as young Samuel did not justify his early promise, changes in the uncle's will recorded progressive disappointment with the boy, who ultimately found himself disinherited by reason of an ill-advised marriage. The boy's only representation in the present collection, or in any collection, is one seafaring letter[1] describing the death of Sir John Narborough with a certain maritime gusto that smacks of folk-poetry, if one ignores the garnish of servile compliment.

It appears that on the death of the mother, Paulina, young Samuel Jackson came ashore and set himself to the care of the estates, residing with his old schoolmaster and kinsman Matthews. Born in 1669, he would then be twenty years of age. Letters between Pepys and Matthews, which the present editor has not seen, but which are quoted in Sotheby's Catalogue of the Pepys Cockerell Sale of 1931, show that Pepys had cause to be uneasy about his nephew. By 1 April 1693 his nephew had unlawfully made away with some sixty-nine pounds of revenue from the estate, ten pounds of which he repaid, whereupon his uncle forgave the rest of the debt. By 1695 he was engaged in a lawsuit which had been pending since the days of his mother's stewardship, the outcome of which was the loss of the Ellington part of the estate and such a large bill for arrears and costs that the uncle had to pledge the Huntingdon estate for four years to raise the sum. The uncle is silent upon the subject from 1696 to 1701, when he writes to Matthews: 'I do not remember my having wrott one word even to my Nephew Sam: Jackson . . . since I last wrote to you; but contented myself with the Belief of his being still under the same Directions of yours which to my great Content I then left him. And a very unwelcome surprise it is, to understand from you now that 'tis otherwise; as suspecting his being guilty of something worse on this Occasion, than (for his sake) you have thought fitt to tell me. Which however I shall at present forbear any further Enquiry after.'[2]

The undesirable activities of the young man were evidently connected with marriage to a young woman whose name is unrecorded. This marriage must have occurred between 2 August 1701, the date of Pepys's will which makes young Samuel the chief heir, and 12 May 1703, the date of the codicil which substitutes the younger brother John as heir and leaves Samuel an annuity of only forty pounds, as he 'has thought fit to dispose of himself in marriage against my positive advice and Injunctions and to his own irreparable prejudice and dishonour'.[3]

---

[1] Letter 173.   [2] *Sotheby Catalogue of the Relics of Samuel Pepys*, 1931, pp. 23–24.
[3] Wheatley, H. B., *Pepysiana* (London, 1899), appendix i, pp. 251–70.

Introduction

Perhaps the marriage took place shortly after 21 April 1702 when the uncle writes to Matthews of his 'weak nephew', his 'hopeless kinsman', whose 'folly, Undutifulness, and Obstinacy' have incensed him to exclaim: 'As to whom, I protest to you, Sir, I am so full of Solomon's thoughts, that Bray a—— in a Mortar and you know what follows, that when I reflect upon the Perverseness as well as Stupidity legible in what he writes, I think it were best both for you and me, to rid our hands of him.'[1]

John Jackson

John the studious fulfilled all hopes. He graduated from Cambridge so sensible and capable as to be almost indispensable to his uncle, but so promising that it would have been unwise not to allow him foreign travel. Samuel Pepys had gained so much from three brief trips abroad, the first a ceremonial excursion to accompany the return of Charles II, the next a pleasure trip to the Continent with his wife in 1669, and the last an official trip to Tangier and Spain in 1683,[2] that he felt particularly keenly the value of travel for young men. Accordingly, in 1699 and 1700, John Jackson made the grand tour of the Continent, the uncle furnishing both means and advice, the nephew reporting decorously the sights he saw, the persons he met, the money he spent, the purchases he made, the music he heard. Undoubtedly the uncle enjoyed the boy's letters more than most modern readers, who find the series in the Tanner volumes pretentious and dull.

In the present collection this nephew is represented by Letter 170, carefully folded away and labelled 'My Nephew John Jackson's first Letter to me after his going to reside in Magdalen College in Cambridge'. John it was who comforted his uncle's old age and provided living justification of his uncle's taste and philosophy of education. A dispute among biographers has undoubtedly made too much of a letter which this nephew wrote to William Hewer as the uncle lay dying.[3] He has never known, he says, what disposition his uncle has made of the property, nor has he been curious, having already received greater benefits than a lifetime could repay in gratitude. This statement has been labelled untruthful and hypocritical. Of course, he must have known that his uncle was worried over young Samuel's misdoings at Brampton and must have inferred that the displeasure was approaching a crisis which might involve disinheritance. But he also realized that his uncle was far too ill to wrestle with the necessity

---

[1] *Sotheby Catalogue of the Relics of Samuel Pepys*, 1931, pp. 23–24.
[2] Cf. Tangier Diary.
[3] Tanner, *Private Corr*. ii. 309–10.

of making his will proof against the foolishness of the young. Thus, when the young man writes Hewer that a dutiful regard for his uncle will remain indelible, that he will labour by all laudable means to improve and never impair whatever bequest is made him, and that in whatever matters are left undetermined he will always act suitably to his uncle's inclinations and to the honour of his illustrious name, the poor young man is probably trying indirectly to assure a very sick old uncle that he need not trouble himself painfully over details in revising the will, because his nephew will try honourably to avoid the mistakes of young Samuel. Neither decency nor grief will allow him to speak on this point to his uncle directly, he says, but his letter to the uncle's secretary undoubtedly means to assure the invalid that he will not marry unworthily or jeopardize the property foolishly or scatter the proceeds upon beneficiaries of whom his uncle would not approve. Biographers surely need infer no mercenary motives behind the comfort which the young man's presence brought during the final hours. So well had the nephew come to understand his uncle that he was able to base his reassurance upon exactly those points of greatest concern to Samuel Pepys.

Later, at an unknown date, John Jackson, having inherited the bulk of his uncle's estate, married Anne Edgeley, a niece of William Hewer, the former clerk and lifelong friend of Pepys, a capable man who had risen with his benefactor to a position of public service and much wealth, and who gave his niece a marriage portion of 3,300 pounds and in 1715 a dying bequest of 1,000 pounds.[1] John Jackson died in 1724, aged fifty-one. Among his seven children, his daughter Frances, who inherited both the Pepys and the Hewer fortunes, founded the present Pepys Cockerell family.

PEPYS IN HIS PERSONAL LETTERS

When the whole body of Pepys's letters goes to press one day in a definitive edition, readers will still look upon the family letters as the heart of the collection, because Pepys the man felt his sense of family and family continuity as a solid core or centre in the midst of all his activities. Indeed, in all of Pepys's relationships a clear awareness of the other person as an individual distinct from all others is evident. Even officials to whom he writes, as well as his intimate friends, are clearly sensed as persons. The self-awareness from which such objectivity springs is in turn based upon a sense of his place in his own family.

In assessing the value of the Pepys letters in the long series of personal documents stretching from the Paston letters in 1434 to the

[1] Whitear, *More Pepysiana* (London, 1929), p. 140.

very present, one must consider many writers with whom a comparison would be illuminating. Any reader who has worked with the vast mass of correspondence left by Horace Walpole, for example, will be tempted to compare the two men who were eager watchers of the pageant of their respective centuries. Both wrote to a variety of correspondents, Pepys, however, as a man of the people counting more of earth's simple souls among his friends than did Walpole. Pepys was also the more deeply involved in the subject-matter of his letters, being actor rather than spectator. On the other hand, Pepys's letters to women were the more tepid, being less consciously gallant than Walpole's, and lacking entirely the emotional tension which unifies the Walpole letters from the friendship of Madame du Deffand to that of Mary Berry. Pepys's letters to men, however, carry a robust warmth and vigour seldom attained by Walpole's.

The considerations above are almost superficial, however, when we compare the Pepys letters and the fifteenth-century Paston correspondence, both animated always by a practical motive. In both there is always an errand to be done, money to be obtained, a question to be asked, a sorrow to be assuaged, a misunderstanding to clarify. Neither Pepys nor the Pastons had leisure, it seems, to spin an entertaining letter out of nothing or out of boredom.

Dorothy Osborne, Pepys's contemporary, is nearer to the eighteenth century than Pepys in her leisurely conversational tone and her ability to found a letter upon a mental state rather than an external need. But Pepys also wrote as if speaking, even though necessity dictated the contents of the letter. Never until old age, apparently, had he complete leisure of the sort that produces the letter merely as a work of art. Even in retirement he was in a constant bustle to reorganize his library, recatalogue his prints, search out some new book, write a history of the navy; these activities he interrupted by letters only for some specific purpose. Even though his library contained a section devoted to personal letters, including those of Cicero and James Howell, he did not write in the consciousness of posterity. Like the Pastons, he was too robustly involved in living to send a letter except for a purpose.

Among the qualities of the Pepys letters, a student using the original manuscript will note first a care for the exact word. The first drafts show meticulous revisions, not for a more felicitous phrase merely, but often for a more tactful wording, an approach more neatly calculated to induce the desired response from the recipient. In the final copies alterations of a single word for exactness of meaning indicate both a similar care and a scrupulous verbal accuracy which corresponds to the writer's delicacy in personal relationships.

Introduction

The very sedateness and meticulousness of the style have caused disparaging comment. Among early critics this adverse opinion may have arisen partly from the somewhat unrepresentative examples of letters chosen for publication, and partly from editorial revision and tampering with the text. Those limitations do not apply, however, to the latest editor, R. G. Howarth, some of whose strictures are not completely borne out by the letters which he reprints. Pepys's correspondence as a whole surely cannot be said to 'suffer' from 'a restraint and a sense of personal dignity'.[1] Pepys, it is true, is very much a man of the seventeenth century, but the customary civilities of his day do not constrain him in his letters as a whole, and certainly not in his correspondence with his family. One who will read several hundred letters by various writers of that century will probably be struck by the uncommon grace with which the small ceremonies of address blend themselves with the diction of Pepys. So genuine is the man that even the customary forms are infused with a robustness and a masculinity lacking in less vigorous writers of the age.

Ceremony there is, let there be no doubt about that, even during times of stress and suspense, but always incidental to the main purpose. However urgent the letter, none sets forth without its small courtesies, for the decencies of deportment have become habitual to the pen as well as the bearing of the erstwhile tailor's son. The touch of friendliness and courtesy is not protracted or elaborate, often indeed is surprisingly brief and direct, as in a letter to St. Michel during the heat of preparation for the trial: 'Very sorry I am for the Indisposition you have been under in your health, and no less gratified with the advice you give me of your recovery, which I wish perfect to you, and remain. . . .'[2]

No problem of elevated diction arises in letters to the simple persons who were Pepys's family. The letters of this collection refute Mr. Howarth's too sweeping remark, 'Pepys rarely writes simply and candidly.'[3] That is exactly how he did write to his kin. Missing here are sallies of pleasantry or the deftness and airiness of phrase found in letters to the Houblons or to Lady Mordaunt and her sister Mrs. Stewart, for no one in the family could share his moods of persiflage. There is, however, simplicity, a bareness that is almost beautiful, from the first letter, in which he cautions his father against extravagance and domestic wrangling, to the last letter, in which he conveys frankly without whining that he is too old and too ill to continue his supervision or benevolence to the improvident clan of St. Michel. There is also throughout the collection a refreshing candour,

[1] Howarth, xiv.
[3] Howarth, xiv.

Letter 72.

xxxiii

accompanied by tact. The style of the letters parallels so closely the character of the man that it is hard to separate the two.

To Pepys a letter is always a personal encounter. A reader may look in vain for indication that the writer expects to be read by posterity or even to be read by a critical reader, for Pepys assumes a letter to be not a thing in itself but a bridge for personal contact. Far from aping the manners of polished conversation, Pepys sometimes neglects syntax, his pen running ahead of his mind as fast as the tongue of an excited speaker. This is not careless thinking; it is the enthusiasm of direct communication, in which gesture sometimes supplements grammar.

The immediacy of contact between writer and recipient, coupled with subject-matter ranging from the price of a ball of whiting to the efficiency of His Majesty's navy, anticipates the nineteenth century, in which the writing of a letter came to be what the lifting of a telephone receiver is to the twentieth. But no letter writer even among the greatest Victorians exceeds the span of Pepys, who knew the small world of fens or of tailor shops as intimately as he knew Greenwich docks or Whitehall; who could be as tactful with an improvident Ester St. Michel as with a Sir Hans Sloane or a Mr. Evelyn; who could help a Godfrey Kneller to renown in art as simply as he trained a Balthazar St. Michel for a useful career in the nation's service. No one else in any day of the English personal letter has gathered for us a more vivid, more Hogarthian gallery of rogues, fools, incompetents, blockheads, wits, fops, scholars, preachers, honest countrymen, merchants, artists, courtiers. To each correspondent Pepys offered a sincere part of himself. The reader of the diary who seeks a genuine portrait of Mr. Pepys will find it, not in the National Portrait Gallery or in the halls of Cambridge, but in the diverse files of his letters.

LIST OF LETTERS

1663

*1. S.P. to John Pepys Senior — 16 May
*2. The Rents of the Brampton Estate — Undated

1664

*3. Fragment: Thomas Pepys to Paulina Pepys — 16 January
*4. S.P. to Cozen Scott — 20 April
*5. Dr. Thomas Pepys to John Pepys Senior — Undated
*6. S.P. to Mr. Pearson — 3 July
*7. John Pepys Senior to S.P. — 10 July
*8. The Inventory of the Tailor Shop — Undated

1666

*9. John Pepys Senior to Mr. Smith — 8 April

1670

10. S.P. to John Pepys Junior — 26 March
*11. B. St. Michel to S.P. — 11 June

1672

*12. Paulina Jackson to John Pepys Junior — 5 March
13. Memorandum for Will of John Pepys Senior — 7 April
14. S.P. to B. St. Michel — 22 June
15. B. St. Michel to S.P. — 14 August
*16. B. St. Michel to S.P. — 11 September

1673

*17. Promissory Note from John Pepys Senior to S.P. — 2 July

1674

*18. S.P. to B. St. Michel — 19 January
*19. S.P. to B. St. Michel — 23 January
*20. Samuel Francklin to John Pepys Senior — 28 January
21. B. St. Michel to S.P. — 8 February
*22. John Pepys Junior to John Pepys Senior — 12 March

* Not heretofore reproduced.

*23. B. St. Michel to John Pepys Junior   26 July
*24. S.P. to John Pepys Junior   30 September
*25. S.P. to B. St. Michel   28 December

1675

*26. S.P. to B. St. Michel   11 January
*27. S.P. to B. St. Michel   18 February
*28. S.P. to B. St. Michel   24 June
*29. S.P. to B. St. Michel   6 July
30. S.P. to B. St. Michel   13 August
*31. S.P. to B. St. Michel   29 August
*32. Paulina Jackson to John Pepys Senior   8 September

1676

*33. S.P. to B. St. Michel   27 January
*34. John Pepys Senior to John Pepys Junior   3 February
*35. S.P. to B. St. Michel   4 February
*36. S.P. to B. St. Michel   28 February
*37. John Pepys Junior to S.P.   4 April
*38. Dr. Thomas Pepys to John Pepys Senior   9 May
*39. S.P. to B. St. Michel   10 July
*40. John Pepys Senior to John Pepys Junior   23 August
*41. John Jackson to John Pepys Junior   23 August
*42. Paulina Jackson to John Pepys Junior   3 October
*43. S.P. to John Pepys Junior   11 October
*44. S.P. to John Pepys Junior   25 October
*45. Memorandum My Brother Jackson   6 November
*46. Notes on Ellington by John Pepys Junior   Undated
*47. S.P. to B. St. Michel   24 November
*48. S.P. to B. St. Michel   1 December
*49. S.P. to B. St. Michel   13 December
*50. S.P. to B. St. Michel   20 December

1677

*51. S.P. to B. St. Michel   22 January
*52. S.P. to B. St. Michel   23 January
*53. S.P. to B. St. Michel   31 January
*54. S.P. to John Pepys Senior   20 June

* Not heretofore reproduced.

55. S.P. to John Pepys Senior — 1 September
56. Sir John Bernard to S.P. — 4 September
57. S.P. to John Pepys Senior — 15 September
58. S.P. to Sir John Bernard — 15 September

1678

*59. S.P. to B. St. Michel — 14 January
60. S.P. to B. St. Michel — 17 January
*61. S.P. to B. St. Michel — 22 January
62. S.P. to B. St. Michel — 26 January
*63. Account of John Pepys with Trinity House — 3 March
*64. S.P. to B. St. Michel — 26 September
65. S.P. to Paulina Jackson — 5 December

1679

*66. S.P. to B. St. Michel — 19 June
*67. Samuel St. Michel to S.P. — 22 June
*68. S.P. to B. St. Michel — 26 June
*69. S.P. to B. St. Michel — 3 July
*70. S.P. to B. St. Michel — 7 July
*71. S.P. to B. St. Michel — 14 July
*72. S.P. to B. St. Michel — 17 July
*73. S.P. to B. St. Michel — 21 July
*74. S.P. to B. St. Michel — 24 July
*75. S.P. to B. St. Michel — 26 July
*76. S.P. to B. St. Michel — 7 August
*77. S.P. to B. St. Michel — 11 August
*78. S.P. to B. St. Michel — 18 August
*79. S.P. to B. St. Michel — 25 August
*80. S.P. to B. St. Michel — 28 August
*81. S.P. to J. Pepys Senior — 30 August
*82. S.P. to B. St. Michel — 1 September
*83. S.P. to B. St. Michel — 4 September
*84. S.P. to B. St. Michel — 11 September
*85. S.P. to B. St. Michel — 18 September
*86. S.P. to B. St. Michel — 25 September
*87. S.P. to B. St. Michel — 29 September
*88. S.P. to B. St. Michel — 29 September

* Not heretofore reproduced.

*89.	S.P. to B. St. Michel	2 October
*90.	S.P. to B. St. Michel	6 October
*91.	S.P. to B. St. Michel	9 October
*92.	S.P. to B. St. Michel	13 October
*93.	S.P. to B. St. Michel	16 October
*94.	S.P. to B. St. Michel	23 October
*95.	S.P. to B. St. Michel	30 October
*96.	S.P. to B. St. Michel	3 November
*97.	S.P. to B. St. Michel	6 November
*98.	S.P. to B. St. Michel	10 November
*99.	S.P. to Mr. Hayter	11 November
*100.	S.P. to B. St. Michel	13 November
*101.	S.P. to B. St. Michel	17 November
*102.	S.P. to B. St. Michel	24 November
*103.	S.P. to B. St. Michel	27 November
*104.	S.P. to B. St. Michel	1 December
*105.	S.P. to B. St. Michel	8 December
*106.	S.P. to B. St. Michel	15 December
*107.	S.P. to B. St. Michel	18 December

1680

*108.	S.P. to B. St. Michel	1 January
*109.	S.P. to B. St. Michel	5 January
*110.	S.P. to B. St. Michel	8 January
*111.	S.P. to B. St. Michel	12 January
*112.	S.P. to B. St. Michel	19 January
*113.	S.P. to B. St. Michel	26 January
*114.	S.P. to Mr. Brisbane	20 February
*115.	S.P. to B. St. Michel	4 March
*116.	S.P. to B. St. Michel	8 March
117.	S.P. to J. Pepys Senior	27 March
*118.	S.P. to Lord Brouncker	11 May
119.	Dr. John Turner to S.P.	20 May
*120.	Dr. John Turner to S.P.	10 June
*121.	Dr. John Turner to S.P.	21 June
*122.	S.P. to Dr. John Turner	4 August
123.	Dr. John Turner to S.P.	26 August
124.	S.P. to Dr. John Turner	3 September

* Not heretofore reproduced.

*125. Dr. John Turner to S.P.   7 September
*126. Dr. John Turner to S.P.   14 September
*127. B. St. Michel to S.P.   24 September
*128. B. St. Michel to S.P.   29 September
*129. B. St. Michel to S.P.   2 October
*130. S.P. to Paulina Jackson   14 October
*131. S.P. to Sir Nicholas Pedley   26 October
*132. S.P. to William Hewer   4 November
*133. Fragment: S.P. to Paulina Jackson   – December
*134. B. St. Michel to S.P.   13 December

1681

*135. S.P. to Commissioners of the Navy   24 March
*136. S.P. to Mr. Matthews   26 March
*137. S.P. to Roger Pepys   26 March
*138. B. St. Michel to S.P.   21 April
*139. S.P. to Mr. Loke   23 April
*140. Mr. Hunter to S.P.   14 July
*141. S.P. to Bursar of Peterhouse   29 June
*142. Ester St. Michel to S.P.   28 August
*143. S.P. to Ester St. Michel   24 September
*144. Ester St. Michel to S.P.   24 September
*145. S.P. to Ester St. Michel   1 October
*146. Ester St. Michel to S.P.   5 October
*147. Mr. Matthews to S.P.   20 October
*148. Mr. Matthews to S.P.   6 November
*149. S.P. to Mr. Matthews   12 November
*150. Mr. Matthews to S.P.   21 November
*151. Mr. Matthews to Paulina Jackson   21 November
*152. Ester St. Michel to S.P.   29 November

1682

*153. S.P. to B. St. Michel   7 January
*154. S.P. to Mr. Matthews   7 January
*155. S.P. to Mr. Matthews   12 January
*156. B. St. Michel to S.P.   5 March
*157. B. St. Michel to S.P.   9 March
*158. B. St. Michel to S.P.   12 March
 159. Ester St. Michel to S.P.   5 April

* Not heretofore reproduced.

*160. Dr. John Turner to S.P.   13 April
*161. S.P. to Paulina Jackson   29 April
*162. Ester St. Michel to S.P.   1 August

1683
*163. B. St. Michel to S.P.   27 June

1686
164. S.P. to B. St. Michel   11 December

1687
*165. B. St. Michel to S.P.   24 January
*166. S.P. to B. St. Michel   27 January
167. Mr. Tilghman to S.P.   9 February
168. Mr. Tilghman to S.P.   10 February
*169. B. St. Michel to S.P.   14 February
170. John Jackson to S.P.   24 February

1688
*171. B. St. Michel to S.P.   23 May
*172. S.P. to B. St. Michel   7 June
173. Samuel Jackson to S.P.   20 July
*174. S.P. to B. St. Michel   14 September
*175. B. St. Michel to S.P.   18 September
*176. S.P. to B. St. Michel   19 September
*177. B. St. Michel to S.P.   21 November
*178. B. St. Michel to S.P.   23 November
*179. B. St. Michel to S.P.   25 November

1689
*180. B. St. Michel to S.P.   25 January
*181. B. St. Michel to S.P.   28 May
*182. S.P. to Sir Richard Haddock   21 April
*183. S.P. to Sir John Lowther   9 May
*184. His Majesty to the Commissioners   11 July
*185. B. St. Michel to S.P.   22 July
186. Samuel St. Michel to S.P.   2 August
187. B. St. Michel to S.P.   6 August

1692
188. B. St. Michel to S.P.   20 March

* Not heretofore reproduced.

1. S.P. TO JOHN PEPYS SENIOR[1]

May 16, 1663

Sir.

believing that the wearysomenesse of your late journy is by this time throughly over, and being unwilling to delay the stateing to you in writing the present posture of our affaires for a guide to you in your future expences (which for the time to come I hope you will understand it to bee necessary by all ways possible to lessen) I have thought fitt to take this time of doeing it, and in the first place must reminde you, that after our many great disbursements upon Repayres, funeral charges, paying of debts and legacys, and a deare housekeeping there remaynes yet behinde, Six hundred and fifteene pounds unpayd in debts and Legacys; Towards which wee have comeing to us[2] by your hands and myne according to the perticulers mentioned in a paper annexed[3]—376 Ł 09s 00d, which as fast as it comes in is to bee employed towards the payment of the aforesayd Debt. And there will remayne to bee provided for, the sum of 238 Ł 11s 00d more then wee have any mony comeing to us to make good, but what shall arise out of the rents of the estate.

Now the Rents of the estate, which remaynes unsold at this day amount to 75 Ł, 09s, 00d per annum all taxes and charges deducted, as by the enclosed accompt you will perticularly see. Out of which 75 Ł 09s 00d wee being to pay 25 Ł to my uncle Thomas and Aunt Perkins,[4] there will rest but 50 Ł and 9s per annum towards your maintenance and the payment of the above-sayd debt of 238 Ł 11s 00, which debt however seeing it must bee payd soone or late and that wee may the sooner bee ridd of all trouble and clamours, wee did at your being here conclude it necessary to sell Sturtlow, which by Will Stankes's[5] reckoning may yeeld 480 Ł out of which my Brother Thomas may bee supplyed with 200 Ł for his share (which will bee a very plentifull provision for him) and pay the debt of 238 Ł 11s 00,

---

[1] Rawl. A. 191 : 224–5. Original, with red wax seal. Holograph. Endorsed : 'May 16, 1663. The Present Generall State of Our affaires at Bramton, given my Father for his future direction therein. S.P.' Cf. *Diary*, 6–9 July 1661; 1–8 May 1663. Also Whitear, *More Pepysiana*, pp. 145–8.

[2] *either*, canc.

[3] The Rawlinson MS. does not contain this listing of funds owing to the estate; but the 'enclosed accompt' of the rents referred to below is reprinted as the second item in the present volume.

[4] The father's elder brother Robert had left the major portion of his estate to the diarist's father, slighting an intermediate brother, Thomas, to whom and to whose married sister he left only annuities. For the poverty of the latter, see *Diary*, 17 Sept. 1663.

[5] The bailiff of the Brampton estate. *Diary*, 19 July 1661.

besides a remaynder of 41 £ 09s 00d, which it is too probable wee shall have occasions enough of laying out in charges of Courts, repayres, and following the law against Tom Trice,[1] with other charges I cannot now thinke of.

But that which follows next to bee considered is how you and my mother shall bee maintayned out of what remaynes when Sturtlow[2] is sold which will bee but 29 £ per annum. This I confesse is a very sad consideration, That after soe much expectation, trouble and removing your selfe from a better condition you should finde noe better provision made for you then a house to live in and 29 £ a yeare. But Sir as it helpes us nothing to afflict ourselfe for what wee cannot prevent, soe doth it concerne us more to study how to improve the best wee can that little which is left. And that I may not appeare wanting to the best of my ability to encourage and assist you herein, I am contented to make up the losse of Sturtlow to you out of my owne purse, soe that you may have entire 50 £ a yeare to live upon, till by the death of my uncle Thomas, or the falling of the Wardrob's plase[3] it may bee raysed to you some other way. You cannot but thinke that for mee to part with twenty pounds a yeare out of my purse in steade of haveing 30 £ a yeare and the rent of Sturtlow as the Will[4] gives mee is an unwellcome burthen; but Sir I have two designes[5] (besides my duty in generall to bee assisting to you) which if I bee not disappointed in I shall thinke my parting with that Summe very well bestowed.

1. I would by this oblige my mother and you to the study of thrift and quietnesse, that I may heare noe more of those differences, which to my great griefe I have of late understood doe often arise betweene you. From whence they come I know not, nor am willing to enquire, But this I know, that it did not use to bee soe, nor I trust in god will bee here after, there being nothing that I can hope or doe wish for you more, then that the abatement of your plenty may bee made up in the encrease of your peace.

2. I hope hereby not only my selfe to bee at a certainty, what it is

---

[1] Tom Trice was Uncle Robert's foster-son, by a marriage in 1630 with Ann Trice, a widow with seven children. The will excludes her specifically by reason of alleged fraud in the marriage settlement. A caveat against the estate was being entered in her name by her two sons, Tom and Jasper Trice. Cf. Whitear, *More Pepysiana*, pp. 46–49.

[2] The sale of Sturtlow is mentioned in the *Diary*: 11 Feb. 1661/2; 1 May 1663; 15 Sept. 1663.

[3] Master of the Wardrobe was one of the posts given by Charles II to Samuel's cousin, the Earl of Sandwich. Samuel secured the promise that the post of Yeoman Tailor in this establishment might revert to his father when it should next fall vacant. *Diary*, 3 June 1661; 6 June 1664.

[4] By the will Samuel was entitled to these benefits as soon as the debts and legacies should be paid.

[5] *encouragements*, canc.

that I must provide to spare out of my owne expences for you, but you alsoe when you shall see thoroughly what it is and noe more that you can expect either from the estate, or mee, will not (as you have hitherto) spend at a guesse but will bee able at every months or Quarters end to tell, whether you doe excede or come[1] within your allowance.

And I must needs further say, that considering you live rent free, and I hope free from any future charge for my Brother John or any of your Children but Pall, that 50 Ł a yeare will bee thought a good competence. Especially if all ways of thrift bee studyed, as I hope you will all of you thinke it necessary from hence forward to doe. And by the way lett mee tell you, that if I understand any thing of thrift, it cannot bee any good husbandry to such a family as yours to keepe either hoggs, poultry, sheepe, cowes, (or horses more then one) there being meate of all sorts, milke, butter, cheese eggs fowle and every thing elce to bee had cheaper and I am sure with more quiet at the market, if not at your doore, then for you to keepe them besides the danger of theyr dying or being stolne. This I desire you and my mother to consider of, and if you judge it as I doe to bee good husbandry, then not to scruple the parting with them upon any other pretences, but sell them off; by which, being now on even ground and the rents from Lady day last comeing to you, you will bee the better[2] able to spare the other monys mentioned in the enclosed paper for the payment of Debts and Legacys, without which we shall never bee able to cleare our selfes thereof.

But if after all this you shall finde, that 50 Ł per annum will not doe; I beleive you cannot but know that for that mony you and my mother may bee boarded well either in City or Country and (Pall being placed abroad in some good service) spend your days without further cares or charge.[3]

All this I doe earnestly recommend to your selfe and my mother to consider of, it being the greatest wish I have in the world, that by my advice and purse (soe farr as I can without wrong to her whom I am obliged to make provision for) I may bee able to assist you in makeing such provision for you as may enable you to passe the remaynder of your time with a sufficiency of estate and ease. Soe craving your blessings I remayne

Your ever obedient Sonn
SAMUEL PEPYS

I have sent you alsoe herein a Copy of the Severall lands wee have in Brampton, how they are lett and to whom, that you may see what

[1] *Short*, canc.   [2] *a little*, canc.
[3] Cf. *Diary*, 23 Aug. 1661; 1 and 4 Apr. 1663; 15 Sept. 1663.

3

the rents of the whole come to, and what the taxes and other charges thereupon doe amount to.

For my father.

2. THE RENTS OF THE BRAMPTON ESTATE[1]

A perticuler accompt of the Rents of our lands at Brampton; how they are disposed of, and what taxes and charges lye upon them.

		£	s	d
	1. To Tom Head 38 acres and a halfe by lease for 15 yeares from Lady day. 1662. at the yearely rent of ..	14.	00	00
	2. To Gransden a close of Pasture at	02	00	00
	3. To Newberry a close for 3 yeares at	02	00	00
	4. To William Ratford 3 acres of pasture for three yeares at the yearely rent of	01.	16.	00
These are letten	5. To John Stankes an acre of pasture at	00	12.	00
	6. To John Stankes an acre & halfe of Meadow	01.	05.	00
	7. To Richard Hall an acre of Meadow.	00.	16.	00
	8. To William Newberry an acre of Meadow	00	15	00
	9. To John Chaford and Richard Ireland 6 acres & a halfe in Long fishers meadow at	04.	06.	00
	10. To Medborough 2 acres & halfe of Meadow	02.	00	00
	11. Three acres & halfe of Peggs hedge close	01.	15.	00
These are unlett	12. Eight acres in Good Cow and Brants willows close	04.	00.	00
	13. Bayliffes close 2 acres	01.	00.	00
	14. Fishers meadow 6 acres	03.	00.	00
	15. Tobys house	00.	15.	00
	Totall ..	40.	00.	00

[1] Rawl. A. 191 : 226. Original.

Out of which 40 £ a yeare is to bee taken

	£	s	d
1. For Taxes at 6s a month ..	2	08.	00
2. For Lords rents for a yeare ..	2.	00	00
3. For the Minister & Clerke &c.	0.	13.	00
4. For the parish dutys of 10 acres which must bee kept in our hands to preserve a horse's commoning	0.	10.	00

05. 11. 00

Soe the cleare yearly value of Brampton lands after all charges deducted is .. ..

£	s	d
34.	09.	00

An account of our Yearely Rents.

	£	s	d
1. Offord letts per annum for	23.	00.	00
Out of which abate for Taxes and Lords rent ..	03.	00	00
There remaynes cleare per annum	20.	00	00
2. Bugden letts per annum for	24.	00	00
Out of which abate for Lords rent, 26s and 8d and for Taxes 33s.	03.	00	00
There remaynes cleare per annum	21.	00	00
3. Brampton letts per annum according to the perticulers annexed for	40.	00	00
Out of which abate for Taxes &c.	05.	11.	00
There remaynes cleare per annum	34.	09.	00

Soe the Cleare yearely value of all three places comes to 75. 09. 00

Out of which wee being to pay yearely to my uncle Thomas 20 £ & to my aunt Perkins 5 £ There will remayne cleare after the payment of those annuitys .. ..

£	s	d
50.	00.	00

Our present condition therefore is, Wee have Fifty pounds Rents yearely comeing in, & a debt of Two hundred thirty eight pounds eleven shillings to pay out of it.

3. FRAGMENT: THOMAS PEPYS TO PAULINA PEPYS[1]

London January 16th 1663/[4]
would doe well to make goeing [or][2] comming for Brampton and
...[2] thus may Shaddow Banberye.[3] Pray gitt my Father to resinge
over the goods, for Likely that may be one point of theirs and doe it
now, for if my Father continue a well wisher to my frind,[4] when it
pleas god I am well,[5] I am now resolved to make a bolt or a shot of it,
and that Suddenly. Pray Let my Father know that I shall not doe any
thing in it that shal [be][2] with out his knowledg I shall pay you your
quarterage[6] assoon as it comes to my hands. Doctor Brough, your
frind is not in town but I exspeckt him to Lye at my house next week
for Dean Honiwood has invited him to Lye their. If he comes to
town I shall be sure to remember[7] you: Pray Let my Father know
alderman Pepys gives this Answer. After his commendations to all
He is willing the boy[8] should come to him. But not to Rub horse
heeles and he is willing he should doe anithing that may be fitt for
him to doe. Theirfore he will allow four pounds a year, furnish him
suffitiently with close at presant but what Ever the boy wants hereafter my Father must be at the charg. I desire my Father will send
answer one Munday to be here for the Alderman will call one purpose for an answer, some thing I have forgott to write to you, but
now you are with my Father I hope you will remember me in every
thing. Not Else at presant but all frinds Loves to you all with my most
Humble duty to father and mother true Love to your good self
(sister Pal) I take Leve as Ever to be

Your truly Loving Brother
till Death
THOMAS PEPYS

... John Pep. ... neer Hunt[ington] with care and speed. Huntington
Sheire.[9]

---

[1] Rawl. A. 182 : 342. Fragment. Original. This fragment is evidently the 'other paper'
referred to in Letter 7. Facts are lacking to clarify many of the vague hints herein.
[2] Torn.
[3] Mistress Hobell, one of the young ladies under consideration as a bride for Tom,
resided in Banbury. Apparently Tom, dissatisfied with the progress of his father and
Samuel, was undertaking further negotiations secretly through Paulina and John.
Cf. *Diary* 23 Aug., 30 Sept. 1662; 20 Mar. 1664.
[4] *Friend* was a not unusual term for fiancée or suitor.
[5] Cf. *Diary*, 20 and 27 Jan. 1664.
[6] This is the only intimation that we have that Paulina was on an allowance from
her brother Tom. But from Letter 5, by Dr. Thomas Pepys, it would appear that Tom
made an allowance also to his brother John.   [7] *writ*, canc.
[8] The editor is unable to identify this boy or to account for Tom's concern. This cannot be Tom's bastard, for she was a girl who went under the name of Elizabeth Taylor;
her existence was not discovered by the family until after Tom's death. *Diary*, 6 Apr.,
4 May, 4 June, 25 Aug. 1664.   [9] Address on the back. Torn.

4. S.P. TO COZEN SCOTT[1]

[Aprill. 20. 1664.]

Good Cozen[2]

I wrott the last night to my father touching the businesse you wrott to mee about and am sorry to finde you soe soone[3] discon-[ten]ted at that which I am sure was proposed to you by him[4] and accepted of by you as a friendshipp done to your selfe; for you very well know Dr. Pepys would have been glad to have administred, and that my father (who lives soe farr off) would never have done it, had not your undertakeing to act as his atturney encouraged him there-unto. Wherefore lett mee desire[5] you to consider the prejudice which may arise to your selfe as well as[6] him by an over hasty receding from what you have obliged your selfe to. For my part I am sure I shall bee a deepe sufferer who ever lookes after the businesse. However I will soe far concerne my selfe in the matter as to endeavour (by calling upon you shortly)[7] to instruct you the best I can in the accounts which are left with you. In the meane time you neede not wonder that noe mony is left with you, since[8] to my knowledge my father hath pay'd the summes following,

To my Cosen Stradwiche for biskett	4.	11.	00
To Mr Sexton for wine	2.	2.	06
Church dutys	2.	8.	00
Coffin	1.	9.	00
Doctor	1.	0.	00
Wages to the mayd & for mony my Brother[9] had of her	5.	5.	00
Takeing out letters of Administration and other charges	2.	17.	6
Rent to his Landlord	5.	13.	9
	25.	06.	09

besides other layings out which I know not of.

The Inventory you say comes to but 15 £ odd mony, and the best part of his wearing cloths you have in your Custody, Soe that for

---

[1] Rawl. A. 182 : 312. Holograph. Rough draft. Endorsed: 'Aprill 20. 1664. My answer to my Cozen Scott about his declining to act as atturney to my father in his Administratorship to my Brother Tom. S.P.'   [2] *Cozen Scott*: canc.
[3] *I am sorry you should soe soone bee*, canc.   [4] *my father*, canc.
[5] *advise*, canc.   [6] *to*, canc.
[7] MS. altered from: concerne myselfe to let my father know what you write, and shall endeavour to finde a time (by calling upon you shortly) that to my power I may give you the best helpe I can in understanding the accounts. But to take a dup— ....
[8] *when*, canc.   [9] *hee*, canc.

7

ought appeares hee hath layd out more then hee hath yet received[1]
and that only for Funerall expences, Rent and Servants wages which
had beene but a greater trouble to you to have looked after. You are
very well secured your owne Mony, and can bee accountable for noe
more then you receive, and therefore neede not disquiet your selfe
at any Creditors demands more then to give them the hearing, and
satisfaction when you shall bee enabled.[2] I will see you very shortly
and hope this will cleare your present doubts. I remain your [and]
J V['s] very affectionate Cozen

S Pepys

5. DR. THOMAS PEPYS TO JOHN PEPYS SENIOR[3]

1664[3]

May 21. Cozen
Upon my coming to London, I heard of your manner of g[oing][4]
out of towne, as alsoe of your doeing in towne when you had made
as much moneye as you could how you went away as if you had bin
affraid of an attachment to have bin made upon the hundreds pounds
you have wrongfull in past made and taken to your use, and you have
left my Cozen Scot to receave your troubsome debts, without particulars direck[4] but he is wise, and will not bringe him selfe into
trouble. I have seen your false inventorie, and know of the indirect
severall wayes of priseing and prisein[g] without bringe in a particular inventorie to every roome, and wheras the goods in the house
found; you pratended they ware but lent to your sonne, my broth[er]
Roger and others can testifie they ware given him, and soe will your
letters, and you told my[5] at brampton in your garden for and in consideration of what you had done for Thomas, your sonne In givening
him all thos goods, you expected he should allow his brother John
an allowance and you demanded 20 £ per annum. I told you how
unreasonable it was for him that had nothing but what he earnt hardly
to doe, soe you proceeded noe further, yet I know he did doe for him
and yourselfe more then 20 £ which you never put it into his debt,
and other will testifie as much that your sonne departed hath said
soe; for the old plate that he chaunged, I can witnesse in the old baylie

---

[1] *of my Brothers estate*, canc.
[2] *I am heartily sorry to heare my poore Cosen continues soe ill and remayne*, canc.
[3] Rawl. A. 182: 340–1. Two sentences quoted in Bryant, i. 226. Dr. Thomas Pepys
was one of the executors of the will.
[4] Interpolations in square brackets in this letter indicate cuts or tears in the paper,
or blots.   [5] Probably *me*.

upon discourse how you gave it him, and you put into the inventorie
ij shillings and 6 pence for I pounde, and soe you doe with Cistorn
Andiron and other goods, as for the pewter you carry that away, or
give it wher you please to defraud the creditors, and wronge your own
Cride[t] which once was good, but it stincks now by your base action
be you assured if you give not a new and true inventorie, without con-
cealing or cloaking any thing noe not the new cloacke which made
of the reliquies of the high Sheriffe of your counties livery, expect a
summons at the Civill law, as well as at the Common. I will spend as
much againe as my debtes if you promise me noe payment, nor make
a new inventorie with[out] cosening or jugling and then if bounds be
first paid my bill will be paid to without relying upon your courtisie,
if I had nott dealt with your sonne more kindly living then you have
living or dead, or thos of his nearest relation, by lending him Supplies
of moneys from time to time, which you nor his brother never did,
except one ten pounds which was his owne befor, you let him have
it, but you left him 20 in debts to pay for it, then you might blame
me for my plaine but true writing but your telling me you gave noe
body leave to trust him either with goods or moneys and therfor they
that had done soe must get it as they could makes me be that sharpe
with you, seeing your embezeling your sonnes proper goods to a
contrary use, his proper linnen you could tell me he had non, noe not
soe much as 3 bands for his owne use, what Should he have done with
his halfe Shirts his brother hath now, to repeat noe more send me an
answer what you will doe as to my selfe, or I must send you a processe,
for I will not be satisfied with thes doings I writ this because I have
spooke as much to some of your frind but you shall hear it first from
my selfe; If you had not medled, or had bin but a stranger I should
have let you alon[e] as a K[nave], without troubling my selfe for soe
inconsidrable debt neither shall I be persuaded easely to be deceaved
by any I beleeve if you and I accord noe better, you will repent of
your Administratorship, See that you breake not your oath nor forfitt
your bound; I will put you upon the tryall. I wish you may prove
honest at last and not discredit the deceased, which of all men I
thought his nearest relations would not have done, wow[1] should
rather Covered faults, then defame him, whome you both have done.
farewell. My love to you all.

Your well wishing friend
T H O M A S   P E P Y S

To his loving Kinsman Mr John Pepys at his house in Brampton
near Huntington thes Huntingtonshire

---

[1] MS. *how*, emended to *wow*, for *who*.

6. S.P. TO MR. PEARSON: CASE OF J. P. ADMINISTRATOR[1]

T.P. dyes intestate. J. P. his father administers, Receives 32 Ł. Pays in funerall Charges, Rent, Servants wages &c 28 Ł is accountable for the rest.

Makes a letter of Atturny to B. S. who in a bond of 300 Ł obliges himselfe to performe the trust reposed in him by the letter of atturney in receiving the Deceased's estate and giving J. P. an account of his receipts and Disbursments

B.S. would fling up his letter of atturney, and JP his letters of administration.

Q. how either of them can doe it?

Q. whether B S can have any plea to reject his Attornyship, because J. P. did for the present receive and pay the 2 summs while in towne and hath about 4 Ł in his hands; or whether the Letter of Atturny did exclude himselfe out of all power of acting but by his atturny. The Bond is dated Apr. 2. 1664. Upon April 13, following JP did at his goeing out of towne collect and cause to bee delivered to BS a perticuler of all T P's debts and Credits and the bookes etc denoting them, which B S did receive of JP's messenger without any scruple.

Q. whither the mistake of leaving out 24s for Shirts in the Inventory and 40s for som Cloath which JP made use of may not be rectifyed. And for an old Sute and bands JP gave them to T P's servant, according to Covenant.

Q. whither if Dr TP wont, JP may not[2] procure another to receive the power of Administrator from him?

Q. what I can doe for my 87 Ł?

7. JOHN PEPYS SENIOR TO S.P.[3]

July 10th. 1664

dear Soon

you will find by the inclosed[4] that the foule mouthed docter is resolved to be troublesom it was with the consent of his brother mr Roger for

---

[1] Rawl. A. 182: 316. Evidently a copy. Addressed: Mr. Pearson's house in Stanhop streete. Endorsed in S.P.'s hand: July. 3. 1664. State of J.P.'s administration to his son T.P.   [2] *make*, canc.

[3] Rawl. A. 182: 329. Original. Holograph. One sentence quoted in Bryant, i. 227. Written in a seventeenth-century hand of individual peculiarities, with exaggerated ascenders and descenders, *i*'s dotted cursively, open vowels, and capitals and lower-case letters hard to distinguish. Punctuation is so erratic that the editor cannot always be sure where the sentence ends.

This letter carries a marginal note in S.P.'s hand: '3 ½ shirts 24 s.'

[4] Possibly Letter 5 or a similar letter. That the diarist shared his father's opinion of

thay ware both with mr fillips[1] that brought me this letter. thay gote a promise from him to be for them befor thay told him aganst home it was. and sent the note to him after ward and docter tomess note that he had under your brother hand for Ł 10 but noe seal to it. he did acknowleg to me and your brother John that it was but Ł 8 pound that was due to him and thare was 19s and 6d was in your brothers book which was due to him of that Ł 8.) i was with mr fillips this morning & he shoed me the note for the 10 pound. and I see noe seal to it /, & i told him thare shuld be noe need of troubling a baly to serve the leet./[2] therefore pray good child let thare be som theng done in it. nether can i know how an new inventery can be mad the goods is so disparsed. if you have aded the mony which is 24s for the 3 shirtes and 40s for the clothe. and a letter case. I can but tak my oth—as i have done all redy— that i have mad a true inventery of all things that was his I hope you have receved my last letter with the [receipt] inclosed under toms hand[3] for an acknowlegment that the goods were mine with the other paper[4] which was writ not a quarter of a year before he died whare in he wished i wold mak and asinement of my goods over to him. now in answer to your last I have spoken to will Stancks and he will sift out Steven wilson and foxe[5] what was due when your uncle died he is afeared that foxe hath payd your uncle. I wished w. Stancks to let him know if he pleeds [,] that he had noe write to it tell he was admited to it. and for ashtone[6] Stanckes cannot tell what it shuld be for that thare shuld be mony due from him for the close. thar was an acker that belonged to an other man that your uncle never agreed for but thinking he might have it at any time yelded to pay 8s a year tell he had concluded for it. and soe your uncle set trees and dichet and set a queck set as far as that acker went [.] he that ode [owned] it being dead it is Latin [letten] to an nother and he hath taken it to his one use. it was the land that the hay cock stood one. Stanckes gote the gate removed when i was at london last. so prices mony is not to be payd tell mickellmus or the next cort that we give

---

Dr. Thomas Pepys is apparent from such epithets as *simple, puppy,* and *doating coxcomb* in *Diary,* 1 July 1663; 14 Mar. 1663/4; 22 Aug. 1664.

[1] 'Mr Phillips the lawyer' at Brampton. *Diary,* 12 Feb. 1661/2. It was this man's nephew, John Jackson, who later married Paulina, the diarist's sister. Whitear, *More Pepysiana,* p. 22.

[2] *wrote,* canc. Leet: manorial court.

[3] The receipt is the latter part of Entry 8 in this edition. Evidently, this is the inventory which the father caused to be made when turning over the tailor shop to Tom. But the systematic inventory made upon Tom's death, as referred to in *Diary*: 16 Mar. 1663/4, may have been lost, to judge by the accusations of forgery.

[4] This paper may be the fragment printed as Entry 3, p. 6.

[5] Evidently Fox and perhaps Steven Wilson also had purchased land previously from Uncle Robert; neither appears in the *Diary.*

[6] Ashton does not appear as either person or place in the *Diary.*

up our write to him in the land. for the Ł 39 pound which is yet due to us from piget[1] i doe not know what securi[ty][2] we are like to have from him for it more then we have all redy. we must indever to mak sale of soe much as is left for soe much as is left unpayd. i doe not yet understand hoe it is that is to give sattisfackshon for the none payment of [rent][3] from the time that it shuld be payd. as for barten bisnes thare is 7 rodes of that land your uncle had of old barten[4] which is worth a matter of 15 or 16 Ł to be sold. thes and soe much more as mad it up 14 or 16 Ł a yeare was geven to old barten and his wife and to the are male of them to after thare desest. this was geven 4 years befor the oner died. when he died he gave all the rest of his estate to old barten. if we cannot find any writing that bartan was ingaged to your uncle for to cleare this. if we cold find any thing then we cold tak a corse with the old man. if we cannot if the old man die it comes to the young man and we cannot hinder him. Mr Narborow hath a good bart of this land and hath sold it to price[5] and price hath the bennefet of it this year. it is thought he refueses to paye mr narborow tell he hath cleared this thing. i desird he wold act for us as wel as himself and according to the valluashan of ours we wold contribute toward the charges. you will doe very well to write to him and at your uncle whiles you may know how to have your letter convade. not receveing a letter by york[6] makes me fear thare is som hinderance of my daughters[7] coming next week. if thare be i shall be very sory for it for i shold be very glad to see her hear as sone as can be. dear Child I am very much troubled what my lords potiecarries[8] fear is of you—that you have an ulser

[1] The diarist and his father were involved in a dispute with the Trices over a mortgage held by Uncle Robert on the land of one Piggott. *Diary*, 11, 12, 13, 14 Oct. 1662; 27 Oct. 1663; 27, 28 Sept. 1664.

[2] Edge of paper.

[3] MS. Blot over word.

[4] John Barton, married to Elizabeth Kight, sister of Samuel's mother (Margaret Kight Pepys), was an alderman and burgess of Huntingdon and apparently an intimate of Sandwich. But when Bryant (i. 14) mentions him as a local fellmonger, he must be confusing the elder man with his nephew and namesake. (Whitear, *More Pepysiana*, pp. 13–14.) From the Diary it is apparent that 'Barton's business' refers to the sale of a house which Uncle Robert had bought of Barton, but to which Barton's title had been dubious, as appeared when one Prior offered to buy the place from John Pepys Senior. *Diary*: 31 Oct. 1661; 13 Oct., 20 Dec. 1662; 15 Oct. 1664.

[5] Neither Narborow nor Price figures in the Diary; one wonders whether this Price may not be the Prior of the Diary, since the shorthand symbols for the two names would be similar. Or the father may be absent-mindedly miswriting the name, for certainly Prior was engaged in buying Barton's property. *Diary*, 24 Sept. 1664: 'This night Prior of Brampton came and paid me Ł 40, and I find this poor painful man is the only thriving and purchasing man in the town almost.'

[6] York the carrier. See Letter 22.

[7] Elizabeth, Samuel's wife, visited Brampton in July. *Diary*, 11 July 1664.

[8] [apothecary]. Dr. Alexander Burnett, Honorary Fellow of the College of Physicians. See *Diary*, 1 July 1664, for this diagnosis and the prescription therefore, and *passim* for other references to Dr. Burnett.

groeing in your kidnes. for godsak let me beg of you that you will
have mr holards[1] advice and som able docter of his acquantance with
as much speed as you can. and to beg a blesing from the lord that your
life may be preserved for what a sad condishan shuld your poor old
father and mother be in if the lord shuld tak you before us. i shall be
very glad if any lines com to will stanck to day for our bisnes requires
his spedie asistance. thiss with mine and your mothers very kindely be
presented to you both with your sisters service i rest hoe shall ever be

Your very loving father
J OHN P EPYS

8. THE INVENTORY OF THE TAILOR SHOP[2]

An Inve[n]tarye of all the goods that is Left.

Shopp chamber

2 flock[3] bedds, 4 boulsters, on pair of blankets, on rugg, 2 Liste[4]
coverlids, on sea chest, on trunk.

Cutting Board upper chamber & mayds beed

on cutting board, 2 nest of Drawers, shelfs, on Looking glass. a
bi—.[5] on Joynt Stoole. 2 boxses & other Lumber. 2 Bedsteds with
curtaines & vallence on stripte the other Darnix.[6] On grate chest.
a press. on trundle bedd. on bedd. 2 feether Beds on flock bed on bolster
on quilt 2 pillows a pair of blankets 2 coverlids on Looking glass,
other on coverlid 2 blankets & 2 pillows, on close stoole & 2 muskets.
mayds bed. 2 flock bolsters on flock beed on Blanket on coverlid. a
grate green rugg.

2 chamber

A larg standing Bedsteed, purple curtaines & vallence a counter
pain of the same, 7 back stooles on elbow cheir kivered with the same
on Feather bedd & bolster, on pillow, on pair of blankets. A pair of
brass Andirons & Snuffers, a pair of Iron Doggs tongs & shovvel with
brasses a pair of Bellows. A lowe wainskote table with a drawer a
rownd folding table, on rose carpet & 2 stripte carpetts a cheest of

[1] Dr. Thomas Hollier or Holyard of the *Diary, passim.*
[2] Rawl. A. 182: 311. In the hand of Thomas Pepys.
[3] Flock bed, stuffed with coarse wool.
[4] *List*: border. (French: *liste*.) Johnson's Dictionary.
[5] Edge of paper torn.
[6] Darnix, Darnick, Dornick: a fabric for hangings, originally Flemish. *O.E.D.*

Drawers a Lookinglass a Trundle bedd the room hung with Stript hanging, with maps. On Feather bedd bolster & coverled a pair of virginals & a Frame In the closset to this chamber 4 Stooles on hye rose work & 3 loe with glassen & Earthen Potts & a bruch

i chamber

on Larg hye bedsted redd serg curtaines & vallence & cups[1] with silk fringe, the room hung with stripe hangings & curtins of the sam A large ovell Table 2 Joynt stooles a turne up table & a corte cubberd,[2] A larg Turkey carpett, 6 cheirs & an elboe cheir of the same the bedd is off. kivvered all with redd covers a Loe Joint-stole. a pair of brass Andirons a pair of Doggs with brass knobs a pair of bellows with a Lookinglas & a larg mapp on feather beed on bolster on pillow 2 blankets on rugg. a pair of tongs & fier shovell with brasses a pair of brass snuffers
Studdy to this chamber
A round folding table a large elboe chair a loe Joynt Stoole a lookinglas window curtins & shelfs

Parler

6 Leather chairs on Joint Stoole a foulding table a rose work carpet 2 cuchings of the same 2 branches on Lookinglass a cronacle & the histery of England Scotland & Ierland a pair of snuffers

Kiching & yard

6 grate diches 3 pye plates on bed pan on close stoole pan 6 small diches 9 porringers a brass pessle & morter on brass candlestick 4 pewter candlesticks 2 pewter saltsellers on trencher salte 7 sallet dishes & on dussen of plates. on thrundle[3] pott on wine thurnill pint[4] on pint on half pint pott all pewter 2 rosters of tin & a brass branch on table 2 chairs & on Stoole i pair of Large grates a long Iron before i fier shovvell i pair of tongs i fire fork 2 slises 2 sliding racks on plane on 2 racks for the Spit i pair of bellows i Jack & wayts 2 drippin pans on pudding pann 3 spits 2 Smothing Irons i bason i spice box The yard 6 disshes 4 sausers i cullender on copper on brasskillet 2 copper skillets on bras pott on kittle 2 scummers on basting Ladle i Leaden seston[5] i salt box 4 chamber potts pewter a choppin knife

---

[1] Possibly *caps.*
[2] Court cupboard: a movable cabinet used to display plate. *O.E.D.*
[3] i.e. trundle.
[4] Turnel: shallow oval tub. *O.E.D.*
[5] i.e. cistern.

In the Seller

on stand Woching Tubs a cole hole a boarded seller with Lock
& key & other nessessaryes as 3 powdring tubs
Their is a Silver Tankard & spoone

August. 25. 1661.[1]

I hereby acknowledge the Goods in the above-written inventory to
belong to my father Mr. John Pepys, and by him at my request lent
to mee for my present accomodation.
Which sayd goods I doe hereby promise and engage to preserve with
all care, and to see the same returned safe to my sayd father or his
executors or assignes upon his or theyr demand. Wittnesse my hand
this 25. of August. 1661.

THOMAS PEPYS

Witnesses hereunto
Samuel Pepys.
Wm. Hewer.

A note of the linning that I left at London[2]
4 paire of fine sheets & 7 paire of ordinary sheets 2 dozen of strong[3]
diaper napkins, a table cloth, & cupbo [ard] cloth, 1 dozen of ordinary
napkins. 4 towels diaper, 2 paire of pillowbeares.[4]

9. JOHN PEPYS SENIOR TO MR. SMITH[5]

Brampton Aprill 8th 1666

Sir.
    in answer to yours of the 26th of March I asure you I have no
more doubt of the Justness of your Debt then of any of those which
my Son had contracted, and for which Bonds and Bills under his
hand appear at this day, as (among others) neere an hundred pounds
to his Brother[6] which he had supplyed him with.
    That I received mony for the lease of my house and what goods
I Judged convenient to leave behind mee I acknowledge, but that
my Son had no right in either needs noe other testimony then an
angagement I have under his owne hand to bee accountable to mee
for them, I leaveing them at my Comeing from London for his
present accomodation only.

---

[1] This receipt is in the hand of Samuel Pepys. The signature is Thomas's. Endorsed
in S.P.'s hand: 'TP's bond to redd on demand.'
[2] A note on the back of the sheet, evidently dictated to S.P. by his father.
[3] *course*, canc.   [4] i.e. pillow-cases.
[5] Rawl. A. 182: 334. First draft, probably composed by S.P.   [6] Samuel.

15

It is true I finde hee had made bold with some of the things and changed them, the difference between the vallue whereof (which is very inconsiderable) I owne my selfe accountable for, and have disposed thereof duly as administrator.

This I am ready to shew you or whome you shall desire, being resolved to doe every man right, and refuse no man satisfaction that apprehends I have done him wrong. I am

Your very Loveing Friend and Servant

JOHN PEPYS

To Mr Smith

10. S.P. TO JOHN PEPYS JUNIOR[1]

March 26. 1670

Brother.

something hath offered it selfe which may prove of advantage to you, that makes it necessary for mee to have you here on Tuesday night next. It is an employment into which some or other must bee elected on Wednesday morning. If my endeavours for you succede it will bee a good provision for you. If it doe not, it is very well worth a journy to attempt it.

I am sensible this may bee inconvenient to my Brother Jackson; but I hope some way or other may bee found to putt off the meeting on his businesse for a few days. For whither this succedes or not, you shall bee at liberty in a few days to returne for a little time. Therefore pray fayle not to bee here on Tuesday night next. I begg my fathers blessing and rest

Your loving Brother

S PEPYS

For my Loving Brother Mr John Pepys at Ellington neere Huntington. Leave this with the Post-maister at Huntington, to be speedily sent as directed. S.P.

---

[1] Rawl. A 182 : 475. Original. Holograph. Printed: Bryant, ii. 50–51. Having taken his B.A. degree at Cambridge in 1662/3 and his M.A. in 1666, John was evidently helping Paulina's husband while awaiting an appointment in the church.

The opportunity referred to was the clerkship of Trinity House, to which John was duly elected. For the duties and privileges of Trinity House as set forth by Samuel, see Rawl. A. 178 : 214. For the letters of recommendation which Samuel wrote to the Duke of York, Lord Sandwich, Lord Craven, and Sir Richard Browne: Rawl. A. 180 : 175, 293; A. 182 : 410, 413, 457; H.M.C. Rept. 8 (Trinity House 254); Howarth, pp. 38–39.

11. B. ST. MICHEL TO S.P.[1]

Honoured Sir   Deale the 11th June 1670

This comes humbly to acquinte you that yesterday Sailed out of the Dounes the faulcon and Speedwell (bound for the River Thames), and that i have a parfect muster-booke from the Purser of the falcon now, whoe brought it me a Shore acording to Promise and I am a preparing them to be Sent to your Office within this 2 days which i hope wilbe time Enough for the Shipps be-fore thay be paid off,

Yesterday there came into the Downes a Duch plesure boat with a penant above her anchent which when i Saw (walking upon the beach with Mr Coulmer) i said to Mr Coulmer, let you and I goe on board her, and See what Shee doth heere, Soe wee went and founde on board 2 or 3 brave gallants amongst whome (as hee Said) the Duch Imbassadors brother whose plesure boat this was; hee kindely Entertained us with a botell of wine, and tould us hee came for plesir to See all along the Coast, Saing hee had bine at Dover, and that after hee had bine ashore at Deale, hee woold goe to Sandwich, from thence to, and through all the Creekes and view Sherenesse, and Chatham and then to London; and woold if hee could (hee Said) saile his boat for 100£ with any of the Kings plesure boats I haveing nothing more of Newes to present you with, (with all our most humble Dutys: Respects, and Serveces to you) I remaine

Your Most faithfull and Obedient
Servant

B st Michel

for his Majesties Service. To the Honourable Samuell Pepys Esquire at the Navy Office in Seathing lane. these. London.

12. PAULINA JACKSON TO JOHN PEPYS[2]

Good brother   March the 5: 1671[/2]

Wee all retorn our harty thanks to you for your very good Ioysters, which my father will repaye you, what you have desbursd for them and the lettell boyes hate,[3] which as yet wee have not received.

[1] Rawl. A. 195 : 237. Original, with cover and seal. Holograph. In 1666 Pepys had secured his brother-in-law a post as muster-master on the *Henry*. In 1670 he was promoted to be muster-master at Deal.

[2] Rawl. A. 182 : 410. Original. Holograph. The country household had by now moved from Brampton to Ellington. Paulina had married John Jackson on 27 Feb. 1667/8, and S.P.'s mother had died in March of the same year, leaving the father to reside with Paulina.

[3] Paulina's son, Samuel, S.P.'s namesake, born 1669, would be about two years old at this date. Chappell, *Eight Generations*, p. 66.

as for the mony you shall not fale of the greatest part of it the next week—thoe it pots us to some inconvenince. for with in thes month wee have lade out above a hundered pound in barly for molting[1] but you shal not be long with out the rest with all due thanks to you for your love to us / I bles god my father is in good health and your boye[2] thrifes bravely all our respects love and service presented to you— I remane

Your most afectshonat Sister
P AULLINA J ACKSON

For Mr John Pepys in the Navy Office in Sething Lane London

13. MEMORANDUM FOR THE WILL OF JOHN PEPYS SENIOR[3]

Aprill: 7th: 1672

Memorandum, that I John Pepys of Ellington in the county of Huntington Gentleman doe declare my mind in the disposall of my worldly goods, as followeth.

First. I desire that my Lands and goods left mee by my Brother Robert Pepys deceased, bee delivered up to my Eldest Son Samuell Pepys of London Esquire according as is expressed in the last will of my Brother Robert aforesaid.

Secondly, As for what goods I have brought from London, or procured since, and what monyes I shall leave behind mee or due to mee I desire may bee disposed off, as followeth.

Imprimis, I give to the stock of the poore of the parish of Brampton (in which Church I desire to bee enterred) five pounds.

Item, I give to the poore of Ellington fourty shillings.

Item, I desire that my two Grandsons Samuell and John Jackson have ten pounds apiece.

Item, I desire that my daughter Paulina Jackson may have my Largest Silver Tankerd.

Item, I desire, that my Son John Pepys may have my gold-seale-ring.

Lastly I desire, that the remainder of what I shall leave bee equally distributed between my Sons Samuel and John Pepys, and my daugh-

---

[1] i.e. malting.

[2] Whether this reference is to the same child who was to receive the hat is uncertain. The John Jackson who was to be the namesake of his father, his grandfather, and his uncle and later the heir of his uncle Samuel was not yet born. Two other infants, however, came to birth and death between these two survivors, at least one of whom is known to have been named John. Chappell, *Eight Generations*, p. 66.

[3] Rawl. A. 182 : 413. Not in the hand of the testator. Endorsed: My Fathers Will. Filed among papers of John Pepys Junior. Printed: Braybrooke, *Mem.* ii. 300; Braybrooke, 3rd ed., v. 446; *Diary*, I. xvi–xvii.

ter Paulina Jackson; All which I leave to the care of my Eldest Son
Samuel Pepys to see performed, if he shall think fitt.
In witnes hereunto I sett my hand.[1]

14. S.P. TO B. ST. MICHEL[2]

22 June 1672

Brother Balty
   I came last night home from the Fleete, where I have spent about
5 days. I thanke God I am well, saveing some little disorder an uneasy lodgeing for so many nights hath given me.
   At my comeing backe I finde a very kinde Letter from your selfe
for which I am your Debtor, and alsoe for your last, wherein you
take notice of some of the worlds late discourses, and your hopes
nevertheless concerneing me, the success whereof what ever it may
be; I cannot but advise you to make this use of it, that even dilligence
and integrity its selfe is not always defence enough against censure,
nor can be while Envy remaines in the world, and that therefore you
are by all honest improvements of your time to provide against a
Day where possibly I in my place may not be able to helpe you, nor
you in yours be able to helpe your selfe.
   I tell you this out of a very serious reflection upon what you may
very possibly finde my condition to prove; and to shew you the more
that I am not without apprehensions of that sort, I have laboured now
within a day or two to get that from the Duke for you, which I have
respited for so many yeares to looke after, least it should fall out of my
power to procure it, I meane his Royal Highness's Commission to
you for your present Employment. Wherein I doe both desire and
charge you to behalfe your selfe soe, that your owne merit (if possible)
may continue you in that, which the endeavour of your freinds have
by Gods blessing brought you into. I say not this with soe much a
seemeing Melancholly, as if I would have you lay aside your expectations of good success, but to caution you against the worst effects of
bad. A doctrine which I the rather press upon you from the trouble
that it in some degree gives me, that I noe sooner learnt it my selfe.

---

[1] No signature.
[2] Pepys MS. 672–3, National Maritime Museum, Greenwich. Secretarial copy in
letter-book. Printed : Tanner, *Further Correspondence*, pp. 271–2. The two letters from St.
Michel referred to have not been found. S.P.'s prospects for becoming secretary to the
Duke of York, who was then lord high admiral, are the hopes mentioned. Matthew Wren,
the incumbent, had been wounded at Sole Bay; S.P., however, was not promoted to the
vacancy. St. Michel's present employment was muster-master at Deal.

Soe with my blessing to my God Sonn and Love and Service to all.
I remaine,
            Your very affectionate Brother and Servant
                             S P

15. B. ST. MICHEL TO S.P.[1]

Deale the 14th August 1672

Honoured Sir

You dayly and howerly soe comble[2] me with (not only Expresions
but allsoe) deeds of your worthyness, and Goodness, as well to my
selfe, as the rest of your most devoted humble Creaturs heare, that I
am (as well as my poore drooping mother,[3] whoose continuall illness
since the death of my father, gives me but litell hopes shee will survive him longe (only but to be sumthing longer a living wittness of
your deareness to her poore Childe, your Late deare Consort, My
beloved sister) by that your Noble, worthy, and kinde Expresions
and promices to be still her benefactor, for which shee hath only
(saith shee) the capasity lefte her, to Bless god for your prosperity,
and to Continue still her prayers to the allmyty god, to power[4] upon
you, and yours Multitude of heavenly Blessings; theese Sir are her
owne Expresions, and I am sure from the very Botome of her harte
and sowle) I am then sir as I said Confuted in my selfe how I may
Ever strive to deserve, the least of those your manyfould, gratious,
good, kinde, Fatherly, and Deare (not only Expresions) but Efects
which I for Ever shall owne.

    well sir since I fear it will never lye in my power to serve you as
I ought (without devoteing My life and fortunes at your feete be
pleased to acept, and Comande both upon all Occasions. which you
will finde, with soe Much Zeale still; for you, and your Cause, that
never Man living, will Ever be Named more Gratefull (as I am In

---

[1] Rawl. A. 174 : 235. Original. Holograph. Printed: *Mem.* ii. 25–26; 1848; 1854;
Howarth, pp. 40–41. Endorsed: 'My Brother St Mitchells acknowleging letter to mee
upon mine to him upon the death of his Father.' As long as S.P.'s wife lived, she dispensed
the benefactions to the parents, who lived so meanly that she and S.P. often felt dis-
graced. After Elizabeth's death S.P. evidently took the responsibility for their welfare
upon himself. St. Michel is thirty-two years of age at this time, and has been married
almost ten years.

[2] i.e. crown or shower.

[3] We know little of the mother of Elizabeth Pepys and St. Michel, other than that
she was daughter to Sir Francis Kingsmill, and that she was the widow of an Irish squire
when she married Alexander le Marchant de St. Michel. See Letter 21.

[4] i.e. to pour.

duty bounde) to your Favours and More Zealous for your Consernes, and interest; then him whoe is proud to be sir
Your Most Faithfull and Obedient humble servant
B St MICHEL

Litell Samuell (whoe Speakes now very pretely) desiers to have his most humble duty presented to his Most Honoured Uncle, and God-father, which please to accept from your Most humble litell disiple.

This day the dragon is come into the Downes which to moroe god willing I intend to Muster. pray present my most kinde and Humble service to my Cosen John Pepys.
B St M

To the Honourable Samuell Pepys Esquire at the Navy Office in seathing Lane. these. London.

16. B. ST. MICHEL TO S.P.[1]

Deale the 11th September 1672

Honoured Sir

I have perused and Studied upon your most Dear and more then fatherly kinde advices, for which you may Sir beleeve, and know, how much I finde in my very harte and sowle that I am obliged to your goodness for which I cann returne nothing but my most humble thankes with Offers of my perpetuall Obedience, not only in relation to this perticular of Sick and woonded, but allsoe those others favours past, (but never my Memory) wherein you have shewed your selfe for goodness and kindeness (not only to my selfe; but allsoe to the rest of your Humble Creaturs my relations) farr Exceeding (for Honour and Dear Kindeness) all the Expresions (in acknowledgement there-of) I am able to Utter. Now Sir in answer to your kinde lignes and advice of the 7th instant, you may please to know that I have and shall, take soe much care to keepe my selfe from Hazarding much of my owne, either by Credit or Specie that I hope never to give you Cause to accuse me of Unadvisedness; therefore I humbly begg you will please to goe on, with my former desier in the getting Mr Peirce[2] the Chyrurgn Generall (to whoome be pleased to present my most

---

[1] Rawl. A. 187 : 357. Original. Holograph. England was engaged in the Third Dutch War. By September the fleet was returning to harbour for the winter and paying the men. Samuel's letter of advice, evidently cautioning St. Michel against advancing money of his own to finance the care of the wounded in the then low state of the king's finances, has not been found. See Letter 19.

[2] James Pearse, a surgeon met frequently in the *Diary*, was at this time surgeon-general to the navy. Tanner, J. R., ed., *A Descriptive Catalogue of the Naval MSS.*, &c. (Printed for the Navy Records Society, 1903), i. 137.

Humble Service) his favour and kindeness to me and this towne for
the sending Sick and woonded men Heare, where thay are not and
have not bine only provided for (I am sure) better then any other
place, but allsoe from whence noe Complaint since my time hath
Ever bine made for theire ill Usage or want; besides wee haveing soe
few heere now, wilbe the better argument (had Mr Peirce noe
perticular kindeness for me though i doubt not but hee hath) for sick
men to be sent hither, where our cleanly nurses houses are redy now
to reseave them being now Emtey I haveing pretty well Cleared this
towne, and Consequently Eased his Majesty's Charges by returning
them as fast as posible I could when Cured to theire respective shipps
soe that wee have very few heere now, and as I said before the nurses
houses redy to reseave others when thay shall come, better I say then
to be thronged upp and indeed partely murthered (as at Gravesende)
occasioned by theire Multitude at one place, and want of good payment (may be) from my breatheren Deputy Comissioners,[1] the latter
of which i thanke god hath not bine heere, which makes that my
Nurses heere flock about me to receive them, when thay come on
Shoare. besides in my aprehention you may please to tell Mr Peirce,
twoold be much Easier for the poore sick men, and less Charge to
his Majesty, to sende from the Bouy of the Oare[2] some by sea to this
place and heare abouts, then a glutt of 700 at Gravesende from
whence thay must [be] hurryed (when sick to the very harte) in
Cartes and wagons (which I aprehende is but litell Ease to poore sick
men) when the towne is or was full to the adjasant Country Vilages,
but if Every place had theire proportion (when neere anough) it woold
hinder those Contagious diseases, which multitudes of sick in one
place may Occasion. this Sir I only mention to your perticular selfe
and noe other. Thus begging your pardon for this long truble, and
desiring you woold please to write to Mr Peirce Speedely to be soe
kinde to his humble servant as to sende us sume heither and I shall
be Much Obliged to him as well as Our Churgeon Mr Hannam
whoose profiet it is to have many haveing soe much a Cure. which
with Litell Samuell['s] humble returne of thankes for your Most
Kinde remembrance of your litell disiple and the most humble devotions of all the rest of yours heare I remaine
      Sir
        Your Most Faithful and obedient humble servant
           B St Michel

To the honourable Samuel Pepys Esquire at the Navy Office in
Seathing Lane These London

---

[1] St. Michel was one of fifteen deputy-commissioners for the care of sick and wounded
in various ports.   [2] Buoy of the Nore.

17. PROMISSORY NOTE FROM JOHN PEPYS
SENIOR TO S.P.[1]

[2 July 1673]

Know all Men by these prasents, that I John Pepys of Ellington in the County of Huntington Gentleman doe owe, and stand indebted unto Samuel Pepys of the City of London Esquire the sum of thirty pounds,[2] which I promise to pay him upon demand being in part of a debt of eighty seven pounds owing to him from Thomas Pepys late of the City of London Merchant Tayler deceased, to whom I was Administrator. Witnesse my hand and seale this second day of July in the twenty fift yeare of his Majesty's Reigne Annoy Domini 1673

JOHN PEPYS

18. S.P. TO B. ST. MICHEL[3]

Derby House January 19th [16]73[/4]

Brother Balty.

I have seen your letters to Mr Evelyn[4] and am Sorry for the Obstruction which the refractoriness of the two persons you name occasions to the Kings Service. I desire you to Lett me know whatt Obligations the King can bee thought to have upon those men, by which hee Should exact this Service from them more then from any other of the Towne, Whether there bee not moneys att this day due to them for former disbursements in this Servise, And whether their refuseall to proceed further in this Service, bee grounded upon any other reason then the want of the money they have allready disbursed, which is all att present from

Your affectionate Brother and Servant,

S.P.

This I do, that I may know what to informe his Majesty, and my Lords touching the true ground of your Complaints and what may be reasonable to advise should be done for the correcting of the misbehaviours of the persons you complaine of.

1 Rawl. A. 182 : 308. Original.
2 Rawl. A. 182 : 306. '1673. Received of Mr John Pepys in part of a debt of eighty seven pounds due from Mr. Thomas Pepys deceased the sum of thirty pounds . 30 £ S. Pepys.'
3 Admiralty Letters, iii. 44, Pepysian Library, Cambridge. Secretarial copy in letterbook. Marginal entry: About 2 persons that refuse the Quartering of Sick men.
4 John Evelyn, the diarist and a friend of Pepys, was at this time one of the Commissioners for the Care of the Sick and Wounded.

19. S.P. TO B. ST. MICHEL[1]

January 23d [1674]

Brother Balty.

I have received your letter of the 21th instant and am extreamly afflicted att the trouble you are putt to, though much more for that which is the ground of it, I meane, the Calamitous condition of the poore sick Seamen and the indigence of those by whom it is expected they Should bee enterteyned and all through the want of money. Butt what to say to it I protest I know not, for as it would at no time bee thought reasonable so neither att this time in particular would it bee thought excusable that those poore people who have already trusted Beyond their Strength, Should bee urged to goe on further in trusting, or that others who observe the Evill Effects of it to their neighbours Should bee pressed by any Violence to the Exposeing themselves to the like inconveniences, by giveing entertainment to the persons you would put upon them without better Security of their being reimbursed. A case in which (to tell you the truth) I thinke itt unbecomming me either with respect to prudence, or my place to become an adviser in, and therefore have written to Mr Evelyn[2] that hee may not expect more from mee then the laying before his Majesty and my Lords of the Admiralty the Contents of his late letters, which by the Grace of God I will not faile to doe with all the efficacy I can but without undertakeing or answering for the Same.

As to the present therefore in reference to your Selfe, I doe charge you by all the respect that you beare either your Selfe or me, that you endeavour above all things to preserve your Self from being transported (by any thing that Shall be offered to you of difficulty or abuse in this matter from others) to the doeing or saying any thing that Shall appeare like violence, makeing itt rather your choyce to Suffer reproach then offer any; And to gett Your Selfe discharged of your Employment Seasonably and decently and thereby eased of the feares of any further inconveniences that may arise to you or your family from it, Then continue to hold it upon termes dishonourable to the King, Unsatisfactory to the poore Seamen, Injurious to your poore neighbours, and unsafe to your selfe.

This (Brother) is the summe of what I shall say to you upon this subject and which upon the Foresight, I long agoe had of some Such like consequences as these, Led me (as you may well remember) to the adviseing you to the considering well what you were goeing about

---

[1] Adm. iii. 56. Secretarial copy in letter-book. Extract quoted in Bryant, ii. 108.

[2] See Adm. iii. 55, dated 23 Jan. 1674. S.P. urges Esquire Evelyn to explain to king and council that failure of the government to repay the people of Deal for their previous care of the wounded is the reason for their refusal to take any more into their houses.

when you first Sought for this Employment[.] Therefore in a word lett mee perswade you to make itt your business to bee as Serviceable to the King, and carefull of your Selfe as you can while you are in itt, and unless you can have any reasonable hopes given you from Mr Evelyn that Matters will goe better with you hereafter as to Payment,[1] labour with as much decency, prudence, and Speed as you can to gett out of it, and So god blesse you. I remaine
            Your very affectionate Brother and Servant
                                  SP
Mr St. Mitchell

20. SAMUEL FRANCKLIN TO JOHN PEPYS SENIOR[2]

                              Doctors Commons
                           28 January, 1673/4
Worthy Sir
There hath been all possible meanes that can be used for the getting of a copy of this Inventory, It doth appeare by the Registry of the prerogative that the Inventory was Exhibited, and putt into a bag as is usuall in like cases, and that bag hath been diligently searched, and it cannot be there found, If it were a thing in my power to serve you in, You might be well assured that I would serve you therein, but the matter being in the Custody of Others, I can not serve you as I would, However I shall Cause the Clerke of the Office to make a farther search herein, Sir, I am
                          Your very humble servant
                          SAM: FRANCKLIN
To John Pepys Esq these

21. B. ST. MICHEL TO S.P.[3]

                 Deale, the 8th February 1673/4
Honoured Sir
In answer to yours of last night which received this morning at 8 of the Clock: I wonder indeed that you, whoose life and Conversation, hath bine ever knowne to be a Ferme Protestant, shoold now

---

[1] Point is given to S.P.'s remark by the fact that in 1702 John Evelyn was still submitting to the Crown bills for arrears due to him.
[2] Rawl. A. 182 : 320. Original.
[3] Rawl. A. 185 : 440–1. Original. Holograph. Printed: Smith, i. 146–53, with revisions; Howarth, pp. 44–47. Endorsed by S.P.: 'Brother Balty's letter to mee giveing an account of the Fortune of his Family, perticulerly done for the cleareing the imputation layd on mee in Parliament of my turning his Sister from a Protestant to a Catholique, S P.'

be Caled in question of being a papist; but Sir Malice and Envey will still oppress the best of Men; wherefore Sir to the hazard of my life i will proove (if Occasion be) with my sworde in my hand (since it hath touched soe neare of the memory of my Dear sister) that your Competitor is a False lier in his throught, as to your haveing Eather an Alter in your House, or that my Dear sister Ever since shee had the Honour to be your wife, or to her Death had the least thoughts of Popery, this I know, by my not only often Conversation with her my selfe, but in my Presence on time, i remember, shee haveing some discourse with my Father, conserning your life and Conversation, as well as Fortunes; this was his speech with her, that amongst the Greatest of the Happinesses hee injoyed in his minde, was that shee had by matching with you, not only wedded wisdome; but allsoe one whoe by it, hee hoped in Christ, would quite bloute out, those Foolish, Phopish thoughts, shee might in her more tender yeares have had of Popery, theese (to the Best of my memory) ware his very words; to which her reply was (Kissing his Eyes, which shee loved dearly) dear Father said shee, though in my tender yeares I was, by my low Fortune in this world deluded to popery by the Fonde-didly thereof; I have now a man to my husbande soe wise, and one so religious in the Protestant religion (Joyned with my riper yeares which gives me more understanding) to Ever suffer my thought to bende that way any more.

But Sir, I have given you two much truble with one thinge; Now to what you desir as to the Knoledge how, and when, the Popish Fancis ware first put in my Poore Dear Sisters head; which (to the best of my memory) in Every Pointe I shall declare to you. First my Father, Sonn to the High-Shreeve of Boge (in Anjou in France) a Papist and all his Famely, in which religion, allsoe my Father was bread, and continued in, till hee was 21 yeares, at which time, (hee being then in the German service) turned Protestant, and without trubling you with the rest of his life there, till hee returned to France, I shall only say that hee did soe; where hee Found his Father Dead, haven given all hee had (heering of my Fathers being turned Hugenot as hee termed it) in mariage with his Daughter (my Fathers only sister) soe that my Father, being disinherited of all for his religion-sake, had nothing lefte but his sword and Freindes, to preferr him in the world (though an Uncle of my Fathers a Chanoine of Parris whoe loved [him] soe well, that hee promised to make him his Aire and Give him 200 000 livres Tournois which is about 20 000 £ sterling, if he woold but goe to mass againe, but all (to this deare man whoe lived and died a sai[n]tely life) nor any thing could shake his resolutions of Continuance in the true Protestant Cause; at last Fortune in this world seemed to smile one him againe, hee being (as you knew Sir) a Gentleman, Extreamely well-bread, got him the Frends (to geather with his Name and Quality being of a very Good house in France) to preferr him (when the Match was Concluded, between his Majesty Charles the First of Blessed memory, and the Daughter of France, to be of her retenue, in the Place of one of her Gentlemen Carvers, soe hee Came over with her Majesty, but longe had hee not Continued heere in her service, but the Cloudes of his Misfortunes (as to the Losse of his place) Frowned on him againe, being tooke notice of by some of the Friers that hee came not to Mass, was by it imediattly knowne to be what hee was Viz: a Very strong and Firme protestant, soe that the Queene dismissed him, his imployment, hee having in discourse and Controversy of religion struck a Frier: Well (as I said before and as your Honour knew) hee being a man not only Extreame Hansome, but allsoe of mightey winning Courtely Partes, went For Irelande where hee soone by it wone the Afection of my mother, Daughter, to Sir Francis Kingsmall[1] and then late widow to an Irish Esquire, soe my Father, After hee had Maried her, though much to the dislike of her Freinds (my Lord Moore, &c) with what moneys thay could then raise being 1500 £, intended for France againe (with his wife my mother, to indeavour by Law (to recover if Posible some parte of his Fathers Estate,) with his sister; but in his prosedure haveing turned the moneys hee had into Goods marchandable For France, at sea hee and Goods were all tooke by the Dunkirckers, and hee allsoe prisoner some munths, soe that hee and my Mother were again to begeen the World, but hee, being Bread to Nothing but the sworde; that was his recourse, and by it had in his time many Very Honourable Comisions both in France, Holland and Germany as well as England; hee For some time settled him selfe upon that litell hee hadd in Devonsheire at a Place Caled Bidiford, where, and thereabouts my sister and wee all ware borne. Sir my Small age at those times hinders my giving you soe Exact accompt as I could wish; how-that, at last my Father, Mother and Famely went For France againe, neather cann I tell on what accompt only at First I remember that hee Caried a Compagny of Foot under his Comande by order of Englande, to Assiste the French against the Spaniard in the taking of Dunkirck, and Arrass which was about the yeare 1648 or 9 neather any Further acompt cann I say wee went to parris about, but that my Father (at last) grew Full of wheemesis, and Propositions (of Perpetuall Motions &c) to Kings, Princes, and others, which

---

[1] See *Diary*, 10 April 1664. 'Lord's Day . . . . . . We spent the day in pleasant talke and company one with another, reading in Dr Fuller's book [*Worthies*] what he says of the family of the Cliffords and Kingsmills.'

Soaked his Pockett, and brought all our Famely soe low (by his not minding anything Elce spending all hee had or had Gott and Getting noe other imployment to bring in More) as nothing more, and my Mother (For Feare of her Childrens want) into Extreame trubles, at last shee was persuaded by some deluding Papists, namely Madame Trouson, a Rich Counselers wife, Mr Duplesis a Rich Advocat of the Parlement, with many others Pretended Devouts, that if my Mother with her Children would gett From her husbande my Father, that Damned trublesome Hugenot (as thay Cauled, him) thay woold provide For all of uss namely my Mother, sister and selfe by Allowing her a Considerable allowance Fitting a Gentlewooman of her Quality, Give a Rounde some of Moneys and Make My sister a Nunn, and my selfe Page to the Popes Nuncio (by which i might [have been] since I have thought on it Either a Cardinall, or a Bardache;) then at Parris resident; in order to theese persuasions, my Mother agrees, apointes the day and Howr, when Exactly Came 2 Coashes on of Madame Trouson Aforesaid, and the other of Mr Dupl[e]cy and Madam Trouson in hers caries Mother and sister a way as sweefte as litening For Feare of my Fathers interest and Furies, and putts them both into the Nouvelle Catholique of Weemen, and I in Mr Duplecys convaid to that of Garsons, at last my Deare sister being Extreame Hansome was deluded into the Nuneries of the Urselines (all this about her 12 or 13 yeare of age) where shee was received with Gladness, thinking to have her there sure Enough it being the stricktest Nunerys in all Parris, but shee was not there longe I meane not 12 days Eare my Father by some stratageme or other I know not well How, gott her out, and uss all, hee haveing bine allmost distracted about it (Poore Deare man) but in Fine hee gott uss all For England againe, where after some time wee had the Honour to be related to you by my Dear sisters match, which was of Extreame Content to my Father, that his deare child had an other Ferme Protestant Protector, and Guide. Truly Sir I beleeve (that could I remember or that of my mother whoe by Her Absence From my house at this present, For health sake I can have noe accompt of) that never man For Religion in thees later ages hath sufered what my Father hath. and now sir I doe declare From my very soule, and am Extreamely well satisfied that you kept my Dear sister in the true protestant Religion till her death. I am your Honour's most obedient humble Servant.

B[althasar] Michel

22. JOHN PEPYS JUNIOR TO JOHN PEPYS SENIOR[1]

March: 12: 1673[/4].

Honored Sir

I have received yours of the 20th Instant. I assure You I sent the Canary by York last weeke, and my Boy went with the Porter and see it delivered at the Inn; I hope the Carrier will not abuse You, for it was choice wine.

I shall remember some Clarett next weeke, I proferd 20s for a Joale of Sturgeon, but when the kegg was opened, it was not sweet; If any good can bee gott for mony my Sister shall have some next weeke, or if shee will have some at a Venture, I will send her the best can bee gott.

As for the mony, pray draw a bill on mee for two hundred and fifty pounds, I will pay it here at sight, but pray bee sure that it be transmitted to You by good hands.

If I can, I will send you an account of what I have disbursed for You and Bray[2] by Saturday's post, but pray doe not pay any mony to him, till I have sent You the bonds, which hee is to signe to secure mee, and my Cosen Pepys,[3] wee have enterd into a thousand pound bond to secure my Ant Wight[4] from any other Relations, Debts, &c.

Pray, Remember, that I have taken a bond[5] of Bray in your Name, that hee shall secure one third part of what hee shall receive for the Use of his wifes 2 Children, and it is reason hee should bee held to it.

The Articles of Peace[6] are too bigg to send in a Letter:

I shall remember a Dogg for my Brother.

My Brother some time since desired mee to returne his thanks for my Sister's kind token, and promised hee would write himselfe to her; but busines hath prevented him I thought I had given you an account of it.

---

[1] Rawl. A. 183 : 51. Original. Holograph. This letter is filed among S.P.'s papers for 1680, after the death of his father, endorsed: 'My Brother John Pepys to my Father.' John Pepys the younger became with Thomas Hayter Joint Clerk of the Acts in 1673, still retaining his post and salary as clerk to Trinity House, and thus becoming able to assist his father financially. See Rawl. A. 180 : 189, copy of warrant of appointment.

[2] Thomas Bray had married Elizabeth Perkin, daughter of Aunt Perkin, and niece of John Pepys Senior. These people and all other surviving relatives, including the Pepys family, became involved in the litigation when Uncle William Wight, half-brother on the mother's side to the elder John Pepys, died intestate in 1672. Ultimately, John Pepys Senior was awarded one-sixth of the £4,000 estate.

[3] One of the parties to the lawsuit was Thomas Pepys, son of Uncle Thomas Pepys.

[4] The widow of the deceased ultimately received one-half of the estate.

[5] See Rawl. A. 180 : 284: 'Copy of a bond given by John and Thomas Pepys respecting the distribution of the property of William Wight . . . fishmonger, their deceased brother by the mother's side, 24 Feb. 1673/4.'

[6] The Third Dutch War came to an end with a peace signed 9 Feb. 1674 at Westminster and proclaimed 28 Feb.

The remainder of monyes which shall bee in my hands after I have sent my account shall bee returned by your first order.

My humble duty to your selfe, kinde respects to Brother Sister &c I am

Sir

Your Obedient Son

J. PEPYS

For Mr John Pepys at Ellington neer Huntington These with care

23. B. ST. MICHEL TO JOHN PEPYS JUNIOR[1]

Deale the 26 July 1674

Honoured Sir

I returne you my most humble Thankes For your most kinde of the 24th instant and am not a litell reioyced to my very harte, that you are satisfied in my last (most Just and trew) Sir, your Generosity, and goodness will still shew it selfe to your humble servant, which is only unhapy in that it is not yett in his power to shew with what Zeale hee woold acknoledge your manyfould Favours, and allthough I value not the world as to theire slanders,[2] yett you have shewd your perticular goodness soe plainely to me that I shall never Forgett it;

I heere of noe bills assined For me as you are pleased to instance to be last weeke, save one of 150 £ imprest For which I returne the Board, and your Favour my most humble thankes For, and that being but one i humbly begg your Favour in promoting the Furtherance For the Assigning my others which are (since you Comande to know them) one of 111£: 5s: 7d one of 120 £: 2s: 10 both which are to Cleare the imprest of 200 £ For my French voyage &c (soe long Depending) and an other of 61 £: 2s: 10d Clearly Disbursed out of my owne pockett; besides my salareis at Laddy day last and mid somer past, and of which, i have last post perticularly write to my Lord Brouncker,[3] wherefore I humbly Begg your Favour in the seconding

---

[1] Rawl. A. 180 : 214. Original. Holograph. This letter is further evidence that John Pepys is helping to lighten the worries of his brother Samuel, especially as the St. Michels can scarcely be considered his responsibility.

[2] Despite the efficiency of the relatives for whom S.P. secured appointments, there were frequent rumours of family patronage.

[3] The Lord Brouncker of the *Diary* was comptroller of the Treasurer's Accounts. (Tanner, *Cat.* ii. 121.)

the same; as to the 20 £ Bill For my reward when it is assined I shall
by it reimbu[r]se your Favours which is all at present From Sir
Your Most Affectionat Kinsman and
humble servant
B St. Michel

To the Honourable John Pepys Esquire at the Navy Office in Mark
lane. London

24. S.P. TO JOHN PEPYS JUNIOR[1]

D[erby] H[ouse] 30th September [16]74
Brother
Beleaveing that it may not only be usefull in some sort but alsoe
of some Reputation to the Brotherhood of Trinity Howse that some
3 or 4 of the ancientest and ablest members thereof (I meane besides
those that are of the Navy Office) should be put into the Commission
of Oyer and Terminer for the Admiralty which will shortly be
Issued, Pray some time this day send me a perfect List of all the present Elder Bretheren with a marke on those whom you conceave
may be the fittest to be incerted the length of whose experience may
be best able to enlighten the Court in any matters relateing to the
Customs of the Sea, To which there wilbe some necessary references
to be made at the Sessions upon some points which I know wilbe
handled I am
Your affectionate Brother
S P
Mr John Pepys

25. S.P. TO B. ST. MICHEL[2]

28th December [16]74
Brother Balty—
This comes only to own my receipt of your Letter since your return
to Deale where I wish you health and not doubting your Continuance

---

[1] Adm. iii. 321. Secretarial copy in letter-book. Pepys was made an Elder Brother of
Trinity House in 1672. John was clerk to the same organization. The definite request
for advice in this letter is refutation of those biographers who have implied that John
was lacking in talents and industry.
[2] Adm. iii. 426. Secretarial copy in letter-book.

of your Care for the deserveing all kindness that is, or can be shown you by mee I remain

Your very affectionate Brother and Servant
SP.

Mr Mitchell—Deale

26. S.P. TO B. ST. MICHEL[1]

Derby-House January 11th 1674[/5]

Brother Balty,

I have been prevented by business in giving you my thanks so soon as I should have done for your great care and trouble in the business of putting the money for Tangier on Board the Dragon, and procuring me Sir Roger Strickland's Receiptes in due forme for the same: the Copies whereof you give me in your Letter of the 5th instant, but the Originals by Mr Gibson's kinsman are not yet come to my hand: But I suppose he may have deliver'd them to Will. Hewer, who is not at present in the way to informe me. What your Disbursements are on this, or have been on any other occasion for me, pray forget not to give him a Particular of, for all; besides I must remaine your Debtor and

Your truely affectionate Brother to serve you.
SP

Mr St Michel

27. S.P. TO B. ST. MICHEL[2]

Derby-H[ouse] 18th February 1674[/5]

Brother Balty,

This comes only to tell you that I have received yours of the 18th instant being very glad of your safe returne and your leaving the Child well at Calais. As to the Maister of the Vessel that carried you, I am very well satisfied with the occasion of his so long stay, and shall see that no inconvenience attend it to him. So I remaine,

Your very loving Brother
SP

Mr St Michel

---

[1] Greenwich MS. 700. Secretarial copy in letter-book.
[2] Greenwich MS. 701. Secretarial copy in letter-book. The reason for St. Michel's trip is not clear. The child must be Samuel's godson, whose ability to speak French was apparently a matter of importance. This trip is evidently one of those foreign journeys so confusedly referred to by Mrs. St. Michel in a later argument. See Letter 142.

28. S.P. TO B. ST. MICHEL[1]

24 June [1675] past 12 at night

Brother Balty

It being midnight I shall not say more then to desire you to find some meanes of informing as soone as may be every Ship and Vessell of his Majesty's now in the Downes, that his Majesty purposes to Imbarke upon his Yachts for Portsmouth on Satturday morning next at Gravesend, Desireing them to putt themselves into a condition of Sayleing soe as to be ready to attend his Majesty thither at his passing through the Downes, for which they shall have his Majesty's particular Orders this Serveing only to prevent their Surprise and his Majesty's finding them unready, pray therefore see that this notice be as timelyly given them as you can. Which is all at present from

Your very affectionate Brother to Serve you
SP.

Mr Mitchell at Deale

29. S.P. TO B. ST. MICHEL[2]

Derby House 6th July 1675

Brother Balty

This comes only to thanke you for your Letter of the 29th June, which I mett with at my returne home from Portsmouth last night. You did very well in attending his Majesty and the Duke, and makeing them the little Present of the Lambe and Fish you mention, the King haveing neede enough of it (I beleive) before he gott on Shore at the Isle of Wight.

Pray take Care for the imediate conveying of the inclosed Letters to the Ships in the Downes, Which is all at present from

Your very affectionate Brother to Serve you
SP.

Mr St Mitchell at Deale

30. S.P. TO B. ST. MICHEL[3]

August 13th 1675

Brother Balty

I have received your Letter of the 9th instant, though, by my being out of Towne, not so soon as you might have expected, however

[1] Adm. iv. 155. Secretarial copy in letter-book.
[2] Adm. iv. 166. Secretarial copy in letter-book.
[3] Greenwich MS. 713–14. Secretarial copy in letter-book. Printed: Tanner, pp. 281–2.

soon enough in reference to the matter of it; there being nothing wherein My Lords of the Admiralty receive less satisfaction than in that of being apply'd to for Protection for Seamen, and others, under pretence of their Employment in the Navy, from being arrested, and consequently from being oblig'd to do right to their Creditors. A Priviledg which indeed his Majesty's Service dos give, but such a one as ought to be us'd with great gentleness, and principally (if not only) in time of war, or other great action,[1] and not in Peace, when plenty of men may be had to answer all His Majesty's occasions, without robbing of the Goales. Upon which account it is that My Lords have at noe time entred into any consideration of the particular Rights of Man and Man; but upon application made by any person for leave to arrest any Officer or Seaman in His Majesty's Service, their course is to give that Officer or Seaman 12 days to satisfy their Creditors, or shew their Lordships good reason why they should not deliver him up to the Law: Upon failure whereof, My Lords have never yet denied liberty to any Plaintiff, after leave thus asked to take his remedy at Law, which will certainly, if Mr Lodge insist upon it be granted him in this case of his; though probably My Lords will demand satisfaction from him for his arresting a Seaman in His Majesty's Pay without leave. But I must tell you in the first place, I do by no means approve of your concerning yourselfe in any thing of this kind, the Priviledge that a Seaman has being a matter that the King's Honor only and his Service ought to be concern'd in, and not any private Man's: Besides, I do not think it for your Credit, that it should be thought you cannot find men enough to mann a Boat, without obliging His Majesty's Service to a dependance upon such persons as are not Maisters of their owne Liberty. To which, when all is done let me add, that a man's being imployed in the King's Service at day-wages,—not constantly, and too, not under any certain Muster, will not be reputed such a relation to the King's Service, as will give him Protection from it; and that, I fear, is the case of the person you are concerned for. But whether it be or no, pray for the time to come keep your owne Credit to depend upon yourselfe, and not the good or ill deportment of other people. As for the present Case I have written to Mr Lodge as much as is fit for me to write, a Copy whereof I enclose to you; which when I have received his Answer to, I shall be able to say more to the business; but till then cannot. Which is all at present from

Your affectionate Brother to serve you
SP

Mr. St Michel at Deale

---

[1] *occasion*, canc.

31. S.P. TO B. ST. MICHEL[1]

29th August 1675

Brother Balty,

I have received yours of the 15th in answer to mine of the 13th instant touching the Business of Lodge and Bowles, by which and what I have met with since from other hands, I find much more dissatisfaction in the Matter, than I conceiv'd, from your first representation of it, though even that[2] gave mee enough: For instead of its being a case of the common sort, I mean, that of Debtor and Creditor, (according to which apprehension of it, the whole stile of my said answer of the 13th runs) I find it to be a business much less becoming you to be an Interposer in, as being grounded upon a private squabble between those two persons, wherein whatever you tell me in yours of the 15th of Lodge's ill usage of Bowles his misbehaviour towards him by ill Language, threats and personal assaults, besides an action first entred by him against Lodge which is still depending. One part of which your selfe confess, I mean, his ill language, which of it selfe is enough to make it very unfit for you to become his or any man's Advocate in: For 'tis not to Lodge alone, but to all the World that you administer matter for the lessening you in your authority (which seems the great thing that touches you) while you shall pervert that Authority of yours to uses it was never given you for. If Bowles had decently by Petition resorted to My Lords with his Complaint of being without their leave arrested, and thereby interrupted in the execution of his Duty to the King, or shall still, I don't doubt but (his relation to the King's Service first appearing) My Lords would in right to His Majesty, and not in complement to him call Mr Lodge to an account for the indignity done the King therein; and if a Petition so prepar'd had been handed to My Lords from you as the Petitioner's next Superiour Officer and no more, your concernment therein soe far might have been well enough admitted. But for you to imbark your selfe in the merits of the quarrel, mixing prejudices of your owne in the matter, and this in favour of One who whilst he pleads the King's Service for his not being arrestable, can find leisure from it to attend a Suite against the said Person by whom he would not be sued, is a piece of presumption, and can by no means excuse you; and the less by how much I may have any reason of thinking it grounded upon any relyance you may have of my supporting you in it, which you know how often I have advised you to avoid any

---

[1] Greenwich MS. 716–17. Secretarial copy in letter-book. It is unfortunate that the preceding letter has heretofore been reprinted without the accompaniment of this sequel.
[2] *you*, canc.

thoughts of, as being, besides the injustice of it, too conscious of frailties of my owne and the care due to my selfe under them, to take upon me the answering, and therefore much less the patronizing the faults or misbehaviours of others, especially where (as in your Case) the nearness of relation suffices to make me a partaker in the blame, though never so much a stranger to the guilt or matter of it, as you know to how much trouble to me it did in the late case of the Privateer.[1] In a word therefore I do conjure you whatever present reflection you think it may have upon you to let fall whatever concernments you shall have in this quarrel, and for the time to come reckon it the best means of preserving your Authority to restrain the use of it, to Causes honourable, and such as properly come within your Cognizance, and no other; assuring you, that as in general I shall never interest my selfe in your defence while you do otherwise, so I know not what you can expect of Friendship from me in the present Case, more than the perswading of Mr Lodge to withdraw his Action upon condition of Bowles[']s[2] doing the like with mutual promises of peace on both sides. All which I pray you to take in good part from me, as proceeding from the truth of the love I[3] bear you, and which shall never suffer you to be injur'd by any man, where any thing within my power can right you. So I remaine

Your truely affectionate Brother and Servant
SP

Mr Balthazar St Michel at Deale

32. PAULINA JACKSON TO JOHN PEPYS SENIOR[4]

[Ellington] September 8 1675

Honoured Sir

your boyes thinkes your next letter a long time acoming that thay may know when you will bee pleased to Set your time of coming. Sir yesterday Mr Jackson wated upon Sir John,[5] and found him most Extriordnary Ready to asist him in his busnes. and hee dose desire both your Self and my husband, if you have any ocashan for advice mak use of him it shall cost you nothing

   hee Read over our leas and informd him selfe what it hath bine let for

---

[1] The reference is to the sloop *Hunter*, in the incident outlined in the section of the Introduction on St. Michel. For Pepys's own account, see Mornamont Collection, Pepysian Library, Cambridge University, i. 5–7.

[2] Secretary erroneously wrote: 'Bowless;'.   [3] *truly*, canc.

[4] Rawl. A. 180 : 275. Original. Holograph.

[5] Sir John Bernard, of the Diary, was S.P.'s frequent advisor in questions of property.

and he doth protest the Coledg[1] hath mad the leas soe stricket that hee is confident, when takes[2] are to be payd thare is not twelfe pence to be gote out of it. he hath promised to meet these Jentellmen, when thay set thare time-and-place-and hee dose protest he will get them to give as much as posible he cane but he sese hee cannot prosed with them tell hee hath a Sight of the leas that was last mad by the Coledg to Mr Jackson—which my Brother Pepys hath. which I desire hee will be pleased to Send downe as Spedily as posible hee can for wee expect thare Sending a mesenger to Set the place of meeting every day.

and pray Sir let my Brother not at tall Distrust our Justnes in Repaying what wee Stand bound to him for, upon my life what ever nesisity I am dreven to I will sell all that ever I have before I will disobleag Shuch a Reall freand as hee is, or let him lose any part what I am in deated to him, but upon your Returne you shall ether have the leas or the mony in your Costitie[3]

if that had bine bought my boye you shuld not have stad long without your mony[4]

My most humble duty to your self Respects and Service to my Brothers Craveing your blesing I rest

Sir

Your Most obedint daughter
PAULINA JACKSON

33. S.P. TO B. ST. MICHEL[5]

27th January [16]75/6

Brother Balty—

I have received your Letter of the 24th instant and according to your desire doe inclosed send you a Letter to the Captain of the Greyhound to transport you over to Calais Wherein wishing you a good Voyage I am

Your very affectionate Brother to serve you
SP—

Mr Mitchell at Deale

---

[1] St. Peter's College, Cambridge, owned the land which Jackson leased at Ellington. See also Rawl. A. 194 : 253; 189 : 298, 300, 302.

   [2] i.e. taxes.   [3] i.e. custody.

   [4] The meaning of this sentence is unclear. Perhaps : If the lease had been brought down by Mr. Boye, you would have had your money sooner.

   [5] Adm. iv. 355. Secretarial copy in letter-book. For letters of S.P. to Captain Clements of the *Greyhound*, see Adm. iv. 357, 29 Jan., asking him to carry St. Michel to Calais; and Adm. iv. 361, 4 Feb., asking him to return St. Michel from Calais. See Letter 35.

34. JOHN PEPYS SENIOR TO JOHN PEPYS JUNIOR[1]

[Ellington] February 3th 1675/6

Dear Sonn I have Receved a bill from Mr Mason but hee Settes downe Severall thinges in it that Mr Jackson and I know wee lade downe mony our Selves for

tharefor I desire you will not paye him any mony upon our acount tell I Come to discos with him at his Retorne and if you have payd him any mony upon my acount pray send me word all due love and Respects

with my prayers to god to bles you I rest

Your most afeckshinat father
JOHN PEPYS

For the Wright Worshipfull John Pepys Esquire in the Navy office in Mark lane Present London

35. S.P. TO B. ST. MICHEL[2]

4 February [16]75[/6]

Brother Balty

I have received your Letter of the 2d instant, and in answer to it the Greyhound doth with this come to fetch you backe, with Orders to stay one day for you, Soe as I presume you will have opportunity to see the close of the Carnavall, to which I have nothing to add but my blessing to my Godsonne, and Service to my Sister, with wishes of a safe returne to you, remaining

Your very affectionate Brother to Serve you
SP.

Mr Michell at Calais

36. S.P. TO B. ST. MICHEL[3]

Derby-House ultimo February 1675/6

Brother Balty,

I have received your Letter of yesterday's date and am very well satisfied with the reason of your desire of coming up to Towne; So

---

[1] Rawl. A. 180 : 286. Original. Holograph. Filed among: Papers Publick and Private of Mr John Pepys (Junior).

[2] Adm. iv. 361. Secretarial copy in letter-book.

[3] Greenwich MS. 736. Secretarial copy in letter-book. Evidently John Evelyn, in his capacity as Commissioner for the Sick and Wounded, had called for the accounts of all his deputies. St. Michel made the trip to London, but was unable to secure an interview.

that as soon as you have the like from the Principall Officers of the Navy (which on this occasion and at this time I presume they will not deny you) you are at liberty to begin your Journey; hoping that you are on your part ready in every respect to discharge yourselfe as you ought to doe in all you have been concerned in, though I have reason very much to doubt it of some others, whose failure I understand to have been the occation of this General Summons. Soe I remaine

Your truely affectionate Brother and Servant
SP

Mr St Michel at Deal

37. JOHN PEPYS JUNIOR TO S.P.[1]

[Trinity House] 4. April [16]76

Sir:

If you have discoursed with Sir William Turner; concerning the mony in the Bankers hands, the Deputy Master of Trinity house[2] desires to have a Court held either on Thursday next, or some time the next weeke, according as you shall appoint.

If you please, I will wait on you to morrow morning for what you shall please to send into the Country.

I am
Your most humble Servant
JP

Sam Pepys

38. DR. THOMAS PEPYS TO JOHN PEPYS SENIOR[3]

Maij the 9th 1676

Good Cosen if it maie sute with your conveniencie praie bee pleased to favor me with the contents of this bill and you will at this time doe me a kyndnes and much oblidge your Loving Cosen

THOMAS PEPYS

For my Loving Cosen Mr John Pepys

[1] Rawl. A. 180 : 343. Rough draft. Holograph.
[2] Samuel Pepys became Master of Trinity House in 1676.
[3] Rawl. A. 180 : 243. Original. Holograph.

39. S.P. TO B. ST. MICHEL[1]

10th July 1676

Brother Balty,

Yours of the 7th came to me this afternoone after the little[2] I had wrote to you this morning touching my Godson, and very glad I am, and much content it gives me that you have managed your trust so, as to be able to give Mr Evelyn[3] the answer which you have sent him, as relying upon it, that it is a true one; and taking the liberty only of noting to you, that it had been enough in the close of your Letter to have undertaken against any man's giving a more just, instead of engaging that none should give so just an Account as your selfe: Which amounts to noe less than your arraigning them all of being unjust. This I observe to you only for future caution; and as to the present business shall add noe more than that I will speak to Mr Evelyn about it, as soon as I see him, and would have you, in case you have not an answer from him very suddenly, to remind him very civilly by another from yourselfe of your desire of knowing what part of the 10000 £ you are to reckon your selfe to have received, taking occation therewith to put him in mind of the Journey you lately took, and chargeable stay you made here upon no other score than the tendring to him and soliciting him to receive and examine your Accounts and Vouchers for all your Receipts and Payments from the beginning of this Action, but could not obtaine it. One thing more there is indeed which I would mention to you, namely, That noe longer since than on Saturday last My Lord Treasurer being ledd to take notice to His Majesty, in my hearing, of the business of the Sick and Wounded upon occation of some Petitions presented the King from some of the Districts for reliefe under their want of Payment, his Lordship was pleas'd among other grounds of dissatisfaction, which he thought fit to take notice of, in relation to the management of that matter, to observe to His Majesty that the general Debt of the Sick and Wounded, which before the last 10000 £ supply'd towards it, was computed but at 21000 £ has been represented to him (since and over and above the Payment of that 10000 £) to be encreased to 25000 £; and that since his Lordship's having supply'd them with 2000 £ more it is reported to him[4] to amount to 28000 £. The use which I would make of this is my desiring you to consider whether

---

[1] Greenwich MSS. 744–6. Secretarial copy in letter-book.

[2] Possible secretarial error for *letter*. This reference points to an important letter not yet found.

[3] John Evelyn, who had turned over his post as Commissioner for the Sick and Wounded to Dr. James Pearse in 1674, was attempting to balance his accounts. As late as 1702 he was still petitioning the Crown for arrears of payments on this score.

[4] *now*, canc.

this uncertain Calculation of the General Debt has arisen in any degree from any uncertaine reports thereof in what relates to your province, and to give me the satisfaction[1] of knowing whether it has so, or no. Which is all at present from

Your very affectionate Brother and Servant
SP

Mr St Michel at Deale

40. JOHN PEPYS SENIOR TO JOHN PEPYS JUNIOR[2]

July the 18 1676

Dear Sonne

tell I have Received my rent from my tennant at Storkloe which hath bine due ever sence lady day

l can not Set my time to Come to See you.

your brother and Sister is troubled that you are not more puncktuall in your advis. now thare is to Jentellmen a bought it and it is thought hath bid as much to the full as it Can posible be worth.

for it Can not be thought that any man will give 12 years birches[3] for a thing that thare is bot 14 years in all to Com in it tell it is renewed agane. but wee Stood for 400 £ and thay to Renew. and not one foote of our one land belonging to it.

thay are in a great Strate what to doe leste thay are to displeas you. and how to Stoope deates thay Cannot tell.

the Colledg[4] rent is 4 Score and 10 £ thes year. mr Crow Calls in his 60 £ or Requires new Security now mr Rolte is dead. wool and t[he] hay[5] thay know not what to doe with them. thare is noe rent for them. hee went with gelding to fotheringay fare to sell [.] not one body bad mony for him [. He was] fane to bring him back agane.

now the Coledg expect thar rent, and thay have not 20 pound toward it nor know not what to doe.

truly it is a greef to mee to see thare great trouble.

I give you heartie thanks for the bottell of Sperites you Sent. with that I received from the Carriers a boxe of sweetmeets wade 10 ll. directed to me but noe letter. if you know hoe sent it pray send word

---

[1] S.P. evidently felt the need for being answerable on short notice for the doings of all his relatives.
[2] Rawl. A. 180 : 293. Original. Holograph.
[3] i.e. purchase.
[4] Peterhouse, or St. Peter's College, Cambridge.
[5] Emendation of difficult passage suggested by Mr. Kenneth Sisam.

and I will give them thankes. my kind love with all due Service from brother and Sister beseching the lord to bles and keep you I rest

your most afectshinat father

JOHN PEPYS

For the Wright Worshipfull John Pepys Esquire in the Navy Office in Mark lane London

41. J. JACKSON TO JOHN PEPYS JUNIOR[1]

August 23 1676

Sir

Wee are very much troubled that wee have not had a letter from you nor my father above this weeke, my wife and bouth my little boyes are very ill I do desire that wee maye heere from you by the next bost

I have sent you and my father 1 fat pig 2 Geese, and I have ordered Edward Johnson to send a brase of hares which I suppooses hee will not faile thus with all our humble Searvice present to you and our duty to my fathe[r] I conclud

Your loving brother to Command

JOHN JACKSON

This To the Worshipfull John Pepys Squire at Trinitye house in Water lane neere the Custum house Present London

42. PAULINA JACKSON TO JOHN PEPYS JUNIOR[2]

[Ellington,] October the 3 1676

Honered Sir

I hope before this Comes to your hand, My Husband will be Com Safe to towne, to wate one you, to Crafe your asistance, in thes following Conseirnes.

in the first place to Relate what discorse hath bine about Bartones busnes

---

[1] Rawl. A. 180 : 347. Original. Holograph. Endorsed by J. P.: '23 August. Mr. Jackson abouto bee cancelled.' Possibly intended for: Mr. Jackson's lease about to be cancelled, thus furnishing a clue to the father's errand in London.

[2] Rawl. A. 180 : 323. Original. Holograph. Date blotted. Filed among: Papers Publick and Private of Mr John Pepys (Junior).

in the next place how unhansom Mr Merrett lettes Brampton hous[1]
fall out of Repares

and then, to have Counsell about old thomas Hensones acount and
whether, wee Can bring the towne to Make a More Exact tarer of
thare Estates

and how an Impropriater aught to be lade to taxes and leives and if
it be possible to Mak freands to bee Eased in the Melisha Sir I doe
most Humbly begg your asistance and Countinance in these Severall
acashan, for with out it I know not how to live in the parsonage[2] the
towne are Soe unworthy

I shall not trouble you with more att present but am
Sir

Your Sister and Servant to comemand
PAULINA JACKSON

hee must bee shure to doe what hee Cane to gett the grant for the
Sett in the Church.

43. S.P. TO JOHN PEPYS JUNIOR[3]

D[erby] H[ouse] 11 October 1676

Brother,

I have received your Letter this morning, and cannot see upon
what inducements my Brethren should be of opinion to put out these
words; (And without any encrease of Duty to be expected for the
same.) Since they are the only Words that doe our Corporation most
Honour and Right, and are imply'd in the other parts of the Paper,
where we say we do it at our own Cost for the publick benefit of
Navigation: Which would not be true, if we intended that Navigation should be taxed towards it; besides that we pretend what we have
done to be only the amendment of an old Light, for which a Duty is
already settled, and not the erecting of a new one that should give
any ground to the laying a new. But that which sways most of all with
me, is that we have under all our hands (which I am sorry should be
so soon forgott) declar'd in an Answer to Sir John Clayton's Petition,
that what we are doing at Lestoffe,[4] we do without any expectation of
profit; and which is yet more, the Act of Parliament that impowers
us to erect Lights, expresly excludes us from acting any thing therein

---

[1] Presumably the old home which still stands on the main road in Brampton and is
known as the Pepys House. On 23 Nov. 1680 (Rawl. A. 194 : 234) S.P. sent his secretary, Paul Lorraine, to supervise extensive repairs to this dwelling.

[2] The house in Ellington to which the Jacksons removed for a time was known as the
parsonage, probably from a former tenant, as Jackson was unconnected with the Church.

[3] Greenwich MS. 751–3. Secretarial copy in letter-book. Samuel as Master of Trinity
House writes to his brother as clerk of the organization.   [4] Lowestoft.

otherwise than at our owne Charge both in the building and maintaining of our Sea-marks: So that if we cannot justify our selves in our expectation of any profits from it, and have already declared that we would look for none; Why should we deny ourselves the credit and reputation justly due to us by omitting to publish it to the World, that what we doe is for publick good, at our private cost; it being alsoe the only advantage we have over Sir John Clayton in his present pretensions, and every private man that do's as he do's under pretence only of benefit to the Publick, but in reality at the Publick's Charge. Nor[1] am I of opinion that our publishing these words will at all hinder us from any future favour we may hope for from His Majesty; but rather further us therein more than if these Words were left out; they shewing both our conforming our selves to the Law, and willingness to serve the Publick as far as we are able; the want whereof in our Predecessors is that (I doubt) which first ledd the Crowne to the granting Patents to private Men for erecting of those Lights; which had our Corporation done at their owne Charge it is not to be thought but the consideration of its being done out of the Poor's Money[2] would some time or other have prevail'd with the Crowne to have relieved the Poor, by granting them some allowance for it, rather than doe what it has done at the importunity, and for the gratifying of private persons, and perhaps prevented many of those attempts, which have been made (and some with success) by such private persons, of obtaining Patents for the erecting useful Lights at the Publick's Charge, I mean, if our Corporation had timelily apply'd themselves to the providing of those Lights; which (through our failure) have been done by private men and found as useful as those which the Trinity-House has been the Founders of. Upon which considerations I am in my particular judgment fully of opinion, that it should be published to the World that we have not presum'd or design'd what we have now done with any purpose of an increase of charge to Navigation; but I submitt it to Sir Thomas Allyn and the rest of my Brethren, to whom I would have you instantly communicate these my thoughts and shall stay for their answer (which pray send me by noon) before I proceed to the offering our Papers to the Press.

Your Loving Brother
SP

Mr John Pepys

---

[1] *I*, canc.

[2] Trinity House had under its care a number of 'alms people'. On 30 Oct. John Pepys wrote his brother concerning the agenda for a meeting, enclosing revised rules for the care of the poor of Deptford. (Rawl. A 180: 320.) Also, Rawl. A. 178: 214 outlines the duties of Trinity House.

44. S.P. TO JOHN PEPYS JUNIOR[1]

Derby House 25th October 1676

Brother

That the Labour taken by my selfe and the rest of my Brethren yesterday at Deptford may not be lost, nor the use of it delayed, pray see that some Orders be drawen up pursuant to the Severall points then Concluded on, that soe I may call a Court for the confirming it, and putting them all in a way of execution and pray lett some thoughts be spent in the drawing of them up, that they may be effectuall, and forgett not to invite the Church Wardens and Overseers of Deptford to come to Us when our next meeting is, which shalbe in a morning.

I remaine

Your very affectionate Brother

S Pepys

For John Pepys Esquire at the Navy Office These

45. MEMORANDUM MY BROTHER JACKSON NOVEMBER 6TH 1676[2]

Bartons Land

My Brother will look over his papers for what concernes Bartons Land and then wee will goe to Councell, In the meane tyme I desire my Father to look over his papers and old Bonds and informe me whom the Land was bought off, and whether he has any security for the title; I desire also the Coppy of Mr Merritts Letter concerning this Land which I lately sent.

Old Henson

Nothing can be said in it till wee see his declaration put into the Court of Common pleas—In the meane tyme Mr Jackson must proceed upon his Suite in the Commisary Court except a prohibition come from the Court of Common pleas to stop it; and Mr Jackson will doe well to gett a determination of his Suite in the Commisaries Court—Lett him also be fully satisfied that neither of his Tithingmen or Servants had notice from Henson that he would lay out his owne

---

[1] Rawl. A. 180: 317. Original. Written by secretary, signed by S.P. The Brethren and the Court referred to are, of course, those of Trinity House.

[2] Rawl. A. 180: 202–3. Secretarial copy, with many corrections almost certainly in S.P.'s hand. Endorsed as in the title and filed among the papers of John Pepys junior. The phrasing of the text, which strongly resembles that of S.P., may have been dictated for John by S.P., as the 'My Brother' of paragraphs one and three must surely be Samuel.

Tith, and enquire whether any of his Tithingmen or Servants did acquaint Henson that he has laid out his Tith wrong.

The Militia

My Brother will speake with Sir Lionell Walden—if there be a Muster very suddenly let Mr Jackson hire for the present a couple of Musketts—and afterwards if he finds himselfe agreiv'd by being laid too much lett him state the Case to me, and I will advise him how to apply himselfe to the Lieftenancy for Releife.

Tax for the poore

Lett him compare an old Leavy with an new and if he finds himselfe wrong'd lett him state the Case and apply himselfe to a Justice of peace, and if he can have noe releife from the Justice then lett him gett a Sessions writt and have the Case brought before the Justices at the Sessions—Lett him also take perticuler Care to see the Ancient Deed for the Stock given to Church and poore that he may know how much is given to the Church and how much to the poore—If the Towne refuse to shew him that Deed the Justices at the Sessions can compell the Towne to produce it.

A pew in the Church

I desire my Father would not be troubled for such little things, and pray that in Case Owen and he cannot agree about it (which I beleive may be done with good words) Mr Jacksons Pew may be made Comodious for my Father, but if that cannot be done and my Father wilbee at the Charge (which wilbee about 20 s) I will move the Chancellor to the Bishop for an Order to add the pew in the Chancell to the other.

Mrs Trice

If shee has any lawfull claymes on Mr Jackson and the Throgmortans lett her take her course at Lawe, and lett it not be referr'd to the Lieftenancy.

Colledg Lease

I will tak care to gett Mr. Wright's Assistance in Brampton Howse I desire my Father either to send me Merritts Lease or at least a Coppy of that part of it which relates to Merritts keeping the howse in repair.

Mr Haughtons Bill

I will send it into the Country by the next post.
Memorandum at the palace of St Michaell Cornehill in London the parishoners laid out their stock which was given for the poore for the rebuilding of their Church, but afterwards were compeld to repay some of the monyes and dispose of it to the poore and a Suite of Lawe is now depending to make them pay the whole Summe.

46. NOTES ON ELLINGTON BY JOHN PEPYS JUNIOR[1]

Matthew Ensam had the Lease of Ellington parsonage for Lives— Loosing mony by it hee agreed for a Lease for 21 yeares—running out 18 yeares of his 21 his rent was doubled—As wee are informed—

A dispute was with Robert Ensam and others about this Estate— hee to secure it give the College theire owne proposal of fine[2] (and rent agreed for before)

Jackson succeeds R. Ensam—hearing some dispute would bee about the Title—he complyes with the Terms of Fine and the old rent proposed by the College.

The ground conveyance from Queen Elizabeth was to keep a free schoole, which was nor is performed.

Q. what a Clergyman may doe for to get it.

A yeares rent &c Clare is to be paid customarily for a Fine.

Jackson hath layd out 200 Ł on it

   is ruined

   hath lost 400 Ł by it

   besides 80 Ł of his owne per annum

rent is not proposed for the parsonage

Computes 7 yeares charge for payments rents Taxes &c

   Send mee the abstract of accounts for 7 yeares

8 yeares of Jacksons Lease is run out

Oath to bee taken that 30 Ł per annum omnibus annis can be got by it &c.

   Clare consider the Improvements on the House—Land—&c

40 Ł will be given

500 Ł run out already. Time given to pay it—

My Father keeps house there and helps them.

Owen—

Cosen Roger Pepys to consult with.

but 200 Ł bid for the parsonage and Crop

Correct the error of their Lands and Jacksons which by the Turnings given in by Jackson was false.

90 Ł paid at the last reconing

Q. if it can be brought to ——[3]

v. the customary boke for Letting of Lands by consent of the Lord

---

[1] Rawl. A. 180: 322. Notes are scratched rapidly in John Pepys's hand. No title or date or endorsement. Probably 1676.

[2] *Fine*: a sum of money paid by the tenant . . . in order that his rent may be small or nominal. *O.E.D.*

[3] MS. illegible.

47. S.P. TO B. ST. MICHEL[1]

Derby House 24th November [16]76

Brother Balty

This comes upon an occasion of some thing that I have been lately led to the Suspition of, touching the behaviour of Comanders of his Majesty's Shipps Imployed in the Downes, Namely that too much Liberty may be taken by them and possibly their under Officers and Companies of spending their time on shore, to the neglect of their duties on board, and generall dishonour to his Majesty, as well as lesening of the Service to the benefitt of his Subjects. Particulars I have none to instance in, but as I said before am not without some grounds of doubt concerning it, sufficient to lead me to the Comitting it to your private Care and Observation, as being agreable to the very Office you serve his Majesty in where you are, that noe such Disorders or neglects of Duty come to your knowledge, but you give me advice of it. Not that I have any purpose of Exposeing the good Office you shall doe his Majesty therein, soe as to make it liable to the occasioning you any prejudice, but to improve it silently to such use as may Serve for the provideing timely Cautions and Admonitions to our Comanders for the remedying of the Evills which must attend any such Liberties should they remaine unobserved. Which is all at present from,

Your very affectionate Brother to serve you
SP.

Mr Michell at Deale

48. S.P. TO B. ST. MICHEL[2]

1st December [16]76

Brother Balty.

I have received your letter of the 26th November in answear to mine of the 23 and 24th of the same, and was in very good Earnst when I told you that I meant it not in respect to any particular Comander when I gave you that advice but onely of a generall apprehension which I have of late had Some Seeming grounds to entertaine of the Liberty taken by Comanders in the Downes of resorting to and Lying on Shoare to the neglect of his Majesty's

---

[1] Adm. v. 255. Secretarial copy in letter-book. This letter and the others following, concerned with laxity in the Navy, will remind readers of passages in the Diary.
[2] Adm. v. 263. Secretarial copy in letter-book. No signature.

Service on float and am not les glad to find by you the little cause there is of any Suspitions of that kind, then I should be Sorry to understand the contrary and missed of being informed therein from your selfe. In which relying upon your care and faithfullnes to his Majestie I remaine,

Your very affectionate Brother to serve you

Mr Michell at Deale

49. S.P. TO B. ST. MICHEL[1]

13th December [16]76

Brother Balty.—

One particular hath lately come to my knowledge relateing to the matter I lately wrott to you about, concerning Captaine's spending time on shore at Deale, while they should be attending to his Majesty's Service on board; Namely That in my Enquiry after the reason why Captain Temple in the Dartmouth did not with his Fleet to Virginia gett out of the Downes the Same day when the Merchant Ships bound to the Streights did, (by which had the winds changed noe man knowes the Consequence it might have been to his Majesty) I understand that though Captain Temple excuses it by another reason, Namely that being himself under Saile the Merchant men could not gett all under saile before night, soe that he was forced to anchor againe, some Masters of the Merchant men have given it out by way of Complaint, that it arose from his not being to be gott timelily from the shore. The truth of which being very desirous to know, pray lett me comitt it to you to make some Enquiry in, and if you can learn any thing therein lett me understand it. The day upon which the Streight's Shipps sailed was the 2d instant when by very good Authority (Sir Richard Haddock I mean) I have understood they were gott clear of the Foreland by 2 of the Clock in the afternoone. Which is all at present from,

Your very affectionate Brother and Servant
SP.

Mr Michell at Deale

50. S.P. TO B. ST. MICHEL[2]

20th December 1676

Brother Balty

I have received your Letter of the 15th instant, in answer to mine about Captain Temple's not getting under saile with his Ships bound

---

[1] Adm. v. 281–2. Secretarial copy in letter-book.
[2] Adm. v. 290. Secretarial copy in letter-book.

with him to Virginia, soe soon as the others to the Streights did, in which account of yours I doe acquiesce relying upon the truth of your Report in it, and remaine,

Your very affectionate Brother and Servant
SP.

Mr Michell at Deale

51. S.P. TO B. ST. MICHEL[1]

Brother Balty.   Derby House 22th January 1676/7

I have received your Letter of the 19th of January and thank you for your Care of the Packetts therein mentioned.

As to the Character you give of Captain Carverth it is noe more then what I verily beleive you think just, and is soe, but pray tell me whether or noe you doe not think the great ground of his Complaint for want of Men to arise not soe much from the lowness of his Complement (which is the same which was allotted by the Officers of the Navy and accepted of by him for the carrying her to the furthermost part of the Baltick) but from the weakness of that Number by the Sickness that is among them, which he seemed to mention to me in a late Letter, and if that be the reason, it seems not to be the adding of more Men that he wants, but the changing of those he hath for better; however I doe acknowledge that the Number he hath is less then her Complement need to be but yet is more then his Majesty will need to have for the manning of the Spragg, in case he expects to return with her to his old Station at Guernsey and Jersey, which I presume his Majesty and my Lords will rather incline to have done, then employ a more chargeable Shipp there, then is necessary for that Service, and then hath hitherto been allow'd for it wherein at Captain Carverth's return pray advise with him, and lett me know his answer. Soe I remaine

Your very affectionate Brother to serve you
S P

Mr Michell at Deale.

52. S.P. TO B. ST. MICHEL[2]

Brother Balty   23th January [16]76/7

This comes only to take notice of, and to give you thankes for the great Care which I have understood (though not from your Selfe)

---

[1] Adm. v. 323. Secretarial copy in letter-book.
[2] Adm. v. 327. Secretarial copy in letter-book.

you tooke in the over takeing of the Adventure, and delivering his
Majesty's Orders to her Comander timely enough to bring her backe
to the Downes; Though I am sory it was accompanied with soe
much paine to you. But dilligence will some time or other bring it's
owne reward, and I would not have you dispare but it will doe soe to
you Soe I remaine

Your very affectionate Brother and Servant
S. P.

Mr Michell

53. S.P. TO B. ST. MICHEL[1]

Derby House 31th January [16]76[/7]

Brother Balty

In answear to yours of the 28th instant, touching the Francis's
number of men. I am as I have heretofore tould you as much Captain Carverts friend as he can expect, and if the King shall thinke fitt
to increase his charge for the Service of Jersey's and Guernsy's I shall
move that her Complement may be increased but if his Majestie
shall judge the charge of the Spragg as much as it is adviseable for him
to beare for that worke, or needfull for the doeing of it, Captain
Carverth will not appeare soe discreeet in repining to returne to that
Command, which though in a time of Action he may deserve, and
looke for a better, he thought very well worth his while to accept,
which is all at present from

Your very affectionate brother to Serve you
S P.

Mr Michell at Deale

54. S.P. TO JOHN PEPYS SENIOR[2]

Derby House. 20th June 1677.

Honoured Sir

I doe acknowledge my selfe to be greatly in arreare to you for the
Severall Letters I have received from your selfe and my Sister, which

---

[1] Adm. v. 328. Secretarial copy in letter-book.
[2] Greenwich MS. 35 (MS. 0209). Original. Dictated to secretary, revised by S.P.,
with holograph postscript. Endorsed: 'June the 20th 1677 Mr Samuell Pepys's Letter
to his Father Mr John Pepys—relating to the State of their Affaires at Brampton.'
Single MS. in cover. John Pepys Junior, Samuel's youngest and last surviving brother,
had died in the spring of 1677.

truly Sir doth not arise from any defect in my duty to you, or unkind-
nesse to her, but from the misfortune I lye under of not being able
to write with my owne Eyes,[1] without a great deale of paine and the
muchnesse of my businesse preventing my doeing it by other hands;
but Sir for the fuiture I will take Care that either from my selfe, or
from one of my Clerkes my Sister shall heare weekely[2] from me, and
have answer to any thing, that either from her selfe, or by your Command I shall have occasion of writeing to you.

And now to the great businesse which you propose touching
Brampton Estate, I will as I said doe any thing that is in my power
for the bringing about that which you desire on behalfe of my little
Nephews, nor did I faile to speake to Sir John Bernard twice about
it, when hee was in Towne, with whom upon perusall of your paper
of particulars I am fully Satisfied that the Payments Wee have made
doe arise very farr towards, if not exceede[3] the full value of the Estate
my Unckle left, But our misfortune is, that it hath not been in your
memory or mine to gett that Stated[4] and acknowledged under two
of the hands to whom by our agreement at first with my Unckle
Thomas[5] the stateing of the matter was referred. Not but that it is
true, I doe firmely beleive, that Wee may have remedy in Chancery
in it, but it is my opinion, that it wilbe much better to gett that done
while it pleaseth God that you and I shalbe liveing, then to leave it to
be hereafter disputed by the Children who wilbe lesse able to mannage
it for themselves then wee, and may be lesse able to beare the Charge
of it. And this I hold the more necessary alsoe from the consideration
of my Cozen Thomas declineing to come to any composition with
Us at least as Sir John Bernard tells me, who as I remember did
before his goeing to the Bath acquaint me that hee had offered him
100 Ł for his Satisfaction in it, soe as it doth appeare that he doth putt
waite upon the hopes hee has that[6] this little Estate will fall to him
and his family in case I die without Children, as in all probability

---

[1] Recent medical opinion holds that Pepys's eye trouble was not blindness, but astig-
matism and severe strain, which modern optometry would relieve with glasses, and which
perhaps Pepys himself could have relieved substantially with the 'tubes' mentioned in the
Diary, had he experimented with the lenses. (*Diary*, 31 July, 11, 12 Aug., 24 Oct. 1668.)
Power, 'An Address on Why Samuel Pepys Discontinued his Diary', *Occasional Papers
. . . of the Samuel Pepys Club*, 1; also, *Lancet*, 24 June 1911; also McLaurin, *Post Mortem*,
p. 162.

[2] This promise, of a type that Pepys would not have taken lightly, indicates that
many letters are still missing.

[3] *exceeded*, canc.   [4] *Ruled*, canc.

[5] The claim of Uncle Thomas and his heirs would be somewhat nebulous by reason
of the annuity they were already receiving from the estate. As the line of inheritance
determined by Uncle Robert ran exclusively through the male heirs, and as Samuel was
a childless widower, the death of John now left Paulina's sons as Samuel's heirs.

[6] *of*, canc.

I shall; and soe will have a just right to expect the Estate, unlesse Wee doe while Wee are alive bring to a plaine understanding and determination[1] the State of Our case in relation to this Estate, and thereby prevent both an Errour on our side in leaveing to the Children a provision that wilbe disputable, and on theirs, the misleadeing them to a Chargeable Suite at Law in expectation of recovering from the Children what perhapes had they known the truth of the Case, they would not have looked after. Wherefore truely Sir if you please, I doe thinke the best that Wee can doe in this matter is, as soone as Wee can, to have the Will looked over.[2] As alsoe the Agreement betweene my Unckle Thomas and Us, together with the true value not only of the yearely Revenue, but of the monies, and Stocke that my Unckle left Us, and alsoe of Our Payments both in Legasyes and annuall Pentions, and the maintenance my Unckle expresly allowed to you out of it for your life, and that being done, to have the opinion of some good Lawyers in it, and if then upon the same being made knowne to my Cozen Thomas Pepys, he shall not thinke fitt to submitt[3] to it to take such course for the haveing Our right Settled in our life times, that Wee may know what Wee have upon this Estate to leave the Children, and see the same done soe legally, as that they may have noe controver[s]y about it when Wee are gone, nor wee mislead to thinke of a Provision left them out of this Estate, when God knowes it may otherwise amount to nothing to them. And this Sir is what I have to offer you upon this Subject praying you to consider it, and if you find reason of differing[4] from me, in any thing that I have said, be pleased to tell it me, and I shall most readily submitt to that which you shall judge the best.

Very glad I am that my Sister hath disposed as shee tells me of her[5] troublesome pa[r]sonage, I pray God blesse her and hers in what she doth therein, and shall desire to know whether Brampton house wilbe free for you at the time of her leaveing of the house shee is now in, or whether else she purposeth to remove, that it may be to your content, and much it would be alsoe to my Satisfaction to know the truth of her condition and the condition of her Family, which shee in her Letter tells me I shall have when shee comes to remove.

I hope you have had some Wine lately, and desire that before your Stocke be out, you would give me notice of it, that I may provide more for you, and what ever else either your health or pleasure shall require from hence.

---

[1] *of*, canc.   [2] *out*, canc.
[3] *a proposition*, canc.   [4] *departing*, canc.
[5] Ellington. This letter, heretofore unpublished, helps to establish one of the disputed dates of Paulina's various moves.

As to my Brother Thomas's Debt I have heard nothing from the Man, nor that I remember any thing from my Brother John while hee was alive, but truely Sir if I could have a true accompt of all my Brother Thomas's just debts, and that I knew what the whole would amount to, and what (if any thing) there is yet to come in towards the Satisfying them, I should be inclined to beare with a little Charge to my selfe for the cleareing them.

As to what relates to my Brother Johns Accompt[1] I doe hope in a very little time, soe soone as Will Hewer shall come to Towne againe, which wilbe at the end of this Weeke, to be able to finish my lookeing over all his Papers, and see in what condition hee has left the World, and shall give you and my Sister a speedy and cleare Accompt of it. Which with the tenders of my most humble Duty to you and prayer to Almighty God to preserve you in health, with my true love to my Brother and Sister Jackson, and Blessing to the Children is all at present from

Your most Dutifull Sonne.
S PEPYS

Sir Lionell Walden did tell mee the other day, that hee has made my Brother Jackson an Assessor of the Tax in Ellington.

55. S.P. TO JOHN PEPYS SENIOR[2]

D[erby] H[ouse], 1 September, 1677

Honoured Sir

I hope e're this come to your hand you will have received mine of the 28th of the last, with one enclosed from Mr Hollyer, to which I much long for an answer, and hope to receive it by Monday's Post, that I may understand the present condition of your health, with the effects of his advice and what you shall please to direct me to supply you further with from hence, and particularly about some wine.

I did also in the same Letter give you an expectation of my full answer to you in the business of my Sister; but because I would leave no stone unturned that may conduce to your satisfaction and hers in that matter, I have determined upon taking some advice here more than my owne therein, that I may as much as it is possible secure myselfe against any imputation of doing any thing misbecoming an honest man towards my Cosens, and prevent my Sister and her

---

[1] The account promised by Samuel has not been found either in Greenwich or in the Rawlinson Collection.

[2] Greenwich MS.: 783. Secretarial copy. Printed: Tanner, *Further Corres.*, p. 305.

Children's meeting with any occasions of future Disputes, by my seeing all grounds of dispute removed, while I am in being, that may best see it done. The result of which Council I shall know in very few dayes, and shalbe then ripe, to give my owne opinion upon it, not doubting but if my Sister should bee prevented in this I shall be able by God Almighty's Blessing to make her Children as good a provision another way. Soe craving your Blessing, and with my kind love to my Brother, Sister, and Children I remaine

Your ever obedient and Dutiful Son
SP

Mr John Pepys

56. SIR JOHN BERNARD TO S.P.[1]

September 4th [16]77 Brampton

Sir

I find Mr Pepys your Father soe earnest in having his desyres and hopes accomplished by a settlement of your Lands in these parts upon Mrs Jackson, And knowing your great concernednesse to minister all the delight and ease you possibly can to the good Old man, I thought Fitt, upon the account of that true respect I beare to you Both, to give you this short intimation, how acceptable the hastning to perfect that worke would be to Him; you have formerly expressed to me the only rubb in the way, which seemes to be fully answered by the charges you have been att and payments you have made upon the account of the estate, which sett forth by a Bill in chancery will prevent all possible future reflections upon you, Att least in my opinion, which is submitted to a much better, and your pardon begged for this trouble occationed only by the affections I have to Mr. Pepys my exceeding kind neighbour, and that great esteeme which is due to yourselfe from

Sir
Your most humble Servant
J. BERNARD.

These to Samuell Pepys, Esquire Att Derby House in Cannon rowe, Westminster, London, Present

[1] Rawl. A. 191: 227. Original. Printed : Braybrooke, *Mem.* ii. 29.

57. S.P. TO JOHN PEPYS SENIOR[1]

15th September, [16]77

H[onoured] Sir

I doe in the enclosed to Sir John Barnard returne you my answer to your desires about our Brampton Affaire; which as I hope it will be satisfactory to you and my Sister, So I pray God it may have the good effect to the benefit of her Children which you designe. The reason of my saying this noe sooner, and writing now to you no larger, you will finde in my Letter to him: To which I therefore refer you: and begging your Blessing doe present you with my Duty, and my Brother and Sister with my kind Love and Blessing to their Children, remaine,

Your ever most obedient Son.

SP

Mr John Pepys

58. S.P. TO SIR JOHN BERNARD[2]

15th September [16]77.

Sir

As one most sensible of your kindness to my Father, and his whole Famely, I render you my most hearty thankes for the good will you are pleased to express towards us all in your Letter of the 4th instant. In answer to which I shall take leave only to say that having done my part in exposeing to you my scruples (one respecting what is just for us to doe towards my Cosen Pepys, the other what may be prudent to bee done in reference to my Sister's Children) I shall most implicitely resigne my selfe up to your advice and to my Father's Comand and without further insisting upon difficulties, which my other business will not suffer me to make my selfe full Master of, much less to resolve, shall intreat your advice by what steps we are to proceed in the obtaining what my Father desires; Wherein I shall most readily performe my part as one that place the first point of my own felicity in the contributing all I can to the satisfaction of my Father, especially when guided in it by advice soe fit to be relyed on as yours. I shall therefore waite your direction for my further proceeding in this Matter, and begging your excuse that by my attendance on His Majesty (who returned to Towne but this night) I have

---

[1] Greenwich MS. 788. Secretarial copy. Printed: Tanner, p. 308.
[2] Greenwich MS. 789. Secretarial copy. Printed: Tanner, pp. 308–9.

not been able to give you an earlier acknowledgment of the favour of your last, remaine

Your most obliged and most humble Servant
SP

Sir John Barnard

59. S.P. TO B. ST. MICHEL[1]

Derby House 14th January 1677/8

Brother

I have yours of the 13 Instant, and as Soone as you foresee certainly the departure of the Foresight and Assistance, or that your Busynesse with those two Shipps is over, I shall with the Privity of the Navy Board obteine you the Liberty you desire, but pray take not a chargeable Journey but upon occasions that are truely necessary, nothing being Less welcome to me then to See you in towne unemployed I give you many thankes for your Care about takeing acquittances for my money putt on board the Foresight, though I have not yet received them. Soe I remaine

Your truly affectionate
Brother and Servant
S P

Mr Michell at Deale

Post Script. Since my writing this I have a letter from Captain Willshaw which much troubles me he being a man of great worth, and one for whom I have an extra kindnes, while on the other hand I canot be less concern'd for any thing where you are. I therefore send you his letter, and a Copie of the answer I have sent him for you to guide your selfe by, which I leave to your direction to manage as you see fit, either by takeing, or not takeing notice of it at all as you shall judge the same may be done without widening the discontent between you if there be any. Send me his letter back againe.

60. S.P. TO B. ST. MICHEL[2]

17 January 1677[/8]

Brother.

I have yours of the 16th, and presumeing still that you will neither

---

[1] Adm. vi. 314. Secretarial copy. Marginal entry: 'sorry for his distemper.' The letter of Captain Francis Willshaw has not yet been found. The Greenwich MS., folio 805, contains a reply to Willshaw from S.P., written 14 Jan. 1677/8, sympathizing with his resentment if the affront were intentional, but suggesting that perhaps there has been a misunderstanding. Printed in part: Tanner, pp. 311–12.

[2] Greenwich MS. 806. Secretarial copy. Printed: Tanner, pp. 312–13.

conceale nor Disguise the Truth in a matter Soe much importing me as this, wherein I am now concern'd between Captain Willshaw and you, I cannot imagine what should lead soe sober a man as he to soe unanswerable a Degree of Passion and folly as he seemes to have rendred himself guilty of towards you.

For what you suspect of his being not soe well affected towards me (though that's noe new thing for me to meet with from Some Commanders); yet there can be nothing of that in this Case, there being not one Commander in the whole Fleet to whome I either really have, or have endeavoured to shew more reall Respect then Captain Willshaw. And therefore I have no other guess to make at the ground of it, then that the Company wherein you found him, might after your Departure either in mirth or mischief, enlarge upon your word (Busking)¹ and impose upon him that groundless and offensive Construction of your visit and Letter which he in his seemes to put upon it.

But be it what it will, though I cannot but approve of your warme Resentments of such usage, yet would I advise and doe conjure you to be cutting out noe sattisfaction for your self, but silently passing it over (at least for the present), leave it to me to see you righted, and in the meane time content yourself with a View of the enclosed Copy which I send you of my Letter to him this night. To which when I receive answer, I shalbe better instructed how to Advise you further. Soe

I remaine
Your truly affectionate
Brother to serve you
SP

Mr Michell at Deale

61. S.P. TO B. ST. MICHEL²

Derby House 22th January 1677[/8]

Brother

In answer to yours of the 19th I take very kindly your submitting the matter between your Selfe and Captain Willshaw to me, and yet your resenting of it as becomes you. Nor shall you suffer any thing

---

¹ Although the proper sense of *busking* was merely cruising about, or beating to windward, *O.E.D.* suggests a possible original sense of piratical cruising. Later, among seamen, the term carried a definite implication of reproach (i.e. pawning property not one's own, or disappearing).

² Adm. vi. 332. Secretarial copy. No signature.

that is unfit for you to beare in it; for as much as Captain Willshaw has sent me an answer to my Last, wherein he very franckly ownes his Errour, and his readynesse to make you any Satisfaction I shall direct. To which this night I make him a reply, a copie of which I send you as well as the originall of his to me, which last pray returne me. In mine to him you will find me shewing my friendship to him with much plainnesse, and doe hope with noe lesse care of what is due to you, and though I doe not thinke it soe proper strictly to prescribe what kind of Satisfaction he ought to pay you yet he will easily inferr what I would have by what I told him I would have seen paid him from you had the errour been yours. Wherefore let it be your part only to expect what he of his owne accord will doe, (giveing me an account of it) and if you heare from him either by a visit, or civill message suitable to this his Letter I would have you accept of his excuse, and let the matter dye friendlyly.

It being as much as you need, or can have, or is worth haveing from him: besides that he is a Comander in very good esteeme with the King and his Royall Highness and a person of great worth: however he light upon this mistake. Soe I remaine

Your very affectionate
brother and servant

Mr Michell

62. S.P. TO B. ST. MICHEL[1]

Derby House, 26 January, 1677[/8]

Brother.

I have your Letter of the 24, and doe take in very good part your acquiesceing in what I have done between Captain Willshaw and you, it being what is enough I think for you to expect on your part, and what became me to say to him on his.

And for the accident by which it is fallen out that my Last Letter to Captain Willshaw, wherein the whole matter between you was wound up came not to him, I would advise you to send it back to me, and I will take care to send it after him by the Phoenix under a fresh Cover.

Soe soone as you shall have mustered the Phoenix, I doe approve of your comeing up to Towne in order to your fitting yourself for

---

[1] Greenwich MS. 808. Secretarial copy. Printed: Tanner, p. 313. The Greenwich MS., folio 807, contains a letter (17 Feb. 1677/8) from S.P. to Captain Willshaw, enclosing one from St. Michel, and giving Willshaw opportunity to present further details, printed in Tanner, pp. 314–15. Here the incident fades from view.

your withdrawing from Deale,[1] you takeing care to have some person in the way to supply your absence for what Occasions the King's Service shall call for you there. Soe I remaine

Your very affectionate Brother and Servant
SP

To Mr Michell at Deale

63. ACCOUNT OF JOHN PEPYS WITH TRINITY HOUSE[2]

Trinity House
March 2d, 1677/8

Honoured Sir,

In pursueance of yours of the 31th of January last Wee have (by the Deputy Master and two Elder Wardens) perused the bookes of this Corporation, their Receipts and Payments of money, and by them doe find that your deceased Brother hath received of Mr Phillipson of Newcastle, and for Rent of the houses and land in Southwark, between the month of March, 1673/4 (the time he last accompted with this Corporation) and the day of his decease the summ of 593 £ 16s 3d.

On the other hand wee find reason to give Creditt on the said accompts for three yeares Sallary to your said Brother, which at 40 £ per annum amounts to   120. 0. 0

More to be allowed on the said Accounts for three yeares Sallary for a Maid at 4 £ per annum .   12. 0. 0

And for three yeares Candles for the House   .   30. 0. 0

And for what he may have paid of three Trinity Dinners within the said time (finding about 280 £ paid by us for those daies) the summ of   .   .   50. 0. 0

And for the Contingencies of the House in the said three yeares (although wee find severall Disbursements brought to account by the Maid Ann within that time) wee compute at   .   .   .   80. 0. 0

————————
292. 0. 0

Wee find by our bookes that fireing of all sorts and beere and ale for the House have constantly been paid for by the Wardens.

[1] St. Michel had just been appointed muster-master at Tangier, a position that he was unable to assume before 1681, by reason of his activities during the imprisonment of Pepys.

[2] Rawl. A. 191: 83. Original. Endorsed: 3d March 1677/8. Masters and Wardens of Trinity house about the debt due from his Brother. With their Receipt for 300 £ on accompt.

The Account by Estimate remaining in this State, wee are of opinion, that if your Honour depositt three hundred pounds, untill you shall have leisure to overlook and fitt for passing your deceased Brothers Accounts to the satisfaction of this Corporation, that summ may indempnify this Brotherhood from loss by the said Accounts remaining unadjousted.

And as your Honour hath in your said letter promised to secure this Corporation from any prejudice upon your Brothers Account his being in Debt to this Corporation, in case the summ soe deposited shall happen to fall in any wise short of ballanceing the said Account: Soe wee hereby assure and promise your Honour on our parts to repay you what surplusage shall remaine in our hands over and above what part of this 300 £ will make good the Debtor part of the said Account, and remaine

Honoured Sir

Your very humble servants

JOHN PROWS

THO BROWNE

ARNOLD BROWNE

JOHN BRADENHAM

ISAAC ... GREENE[1]

HUGH TILL

HENRY TEDDEMAN

ANTHO' YOUNG

WILL WILDE

THOMAS COLLYER

HENRY SHEERES

SIMION NICHOLLS

SAM CHAMBLETT

HENRY LOWE

JOHN NICHOLLS

THO: HEATH

| Received[2] then of Samuell Pepys Esquire Secretary of the Admiralty and one of the Elder Bretheren of this Corporation the Summe of Three hundred pounds upon the Accompt and conditions mentioned in the aforegoing Letter Witness my hande | £ s d 300: 0: 0 |

ARNOLD BROWNE WARDEN

Witnesse
Thomas Browne
John Bradenham

[1] Illegible.
[2] Rawl. A. 191 : 84. Also for John's receipts and disbursements see assorted papers in Rawl. A. 182 : 263–89; 290 ff.; 512.

64. S.P. TO B. ST. MICHEL[1]

26. September 1678.

Brother

His Majestie haveing given you leave to make a stepp over to ffrance to perfect all your busynesse there in order to your being at Liberty to betake your selfe entirely to the Service whereto you are now designed by his Majestie at Tangier I am in the 1st place to desire you to use all the dilligence you can in the dispatch of your affaires Soe as you may be speedily here to receive your Instructions for that Service and apply your selfe thereto without delay, the occasion thereof calling with all speed for you.

Next it falling out that Sir John Bernard a very worthy Gentleman, and my honoured friend, for whom I had Spoake to his Majestie for a yacht on purpose, is iust now goeing over with his Lady into France for their healths, Setting out hence to morow soe as to be at Rye on Saturday I shall desire you to Save the Sending of any other of his Majesty's yachts at a time soe full of Service for them all by your calling in your way towards Diepe at Rye there to expect the comeing of Sir John Bernard and his Company, who will be imediatly ready to embarque and give them the best accomodation your yacht can afford and shewing my Lady all the respect you can for the rendering her voyage to Diepe as easy to her as may be.

Lastly for the Spareing of another Yacht upon an occasion which his Majestie had given me his Comand to Send one expresse for, namely the bringing over our famous Ague-Doctor Sir Robert Taber who will be at Diepe on Tuesday next (as the same has been undertaken here by Mr Blaesethwayt, or within a day or two more at furthest) this serves to recomend to you the execution of his Majesties pleasure in this particular of takeing in the said Doctor Taber with his Company and Servants, and bringing him and them along with you at your Returne into the River of Thames Useing him alsoe on his passage, with all Curtesy as being a Person for whom his Majestie is pleased to have particular regard. But in case the state of your private concernment from Paris (upon which you goe) shall be soe soone dispatcht as that you shall be ready to returne sooner, you are not to attend at Diepe in expectation of the Said Doctor longer then wednesday or thursday next at furthest, but upon his failure to be at Diepe by that time, to repaire back for England with what speed you can. Leaveing the inclosed letter from Mr Blaesethwayt in some hand at Diepe, that may take care to deliver it safely to Sir Robert Taber when he shall come, leting him know your haveing attended him

---

[1] Adm. viii. 174–5. Secretarial copy.

two dayes beyond the time assigned for his being at Diepe (namely Tuesday). and that in case he chooses to attend there for the comeing of another yacht for him; he will doe well to give the Earlyest advice he can to Mr Blaesethwayt of his purpose to stay there in expectation of it. Soe with wishes of a safe, and speedy Voyage to you I remaine

Your very affectionate Brother to serve you
S P EPYS.

To Mr Mitchell

65. S.P. TO PAULINA JACKSON[1]

Derby-house, 5 December, [16]78

Sister,

This comes to thank you for your Letter of the 26th of November and to give my Father and you the satisfaction of knowing that I am (I bless God) in very good health, and in every other particular as well as it is possible for any one in my place to be at a time when things seem in so ill a posture every where else, I mean, with respect to the safety of His Majesty and the peace of his Government. In and for both which as all good men ought, so I in particular by many obligations cannot but be concerned with great care and anxiety of mind, but not without hopes that God Almighty will in due time dispell our fears and establish his Majesty and People once more in security of Peace and Religion and the enjoyment of the Blessings attending them.

One misfortune there is indeed which has created mee much trouble, namely, That by a most manifest contrivance one of my Clerks (Atkins)[2] has been accused and is now in Custody as a party some way concern'd in the death of Sir Edmundbury Godfroy; which (though most untrue) cannot be thought to pass in the world at soe jealous a time as this without some reflections upon me, as his Master, and on that score does occasion me not a little disquiet. But I thank God I have not only my innocence to satisfy myselfe with, but such an assurance of his alsoe as that I make noe question of his being

---

[1] Greenwich MS. 834. Secretarial copy. Printed: Tanner, pp. 328–9.

[2] On 11 Oct. S.P. left London for Newmarket to attend the king. On 13 Oct. Sir Edmund Berry (or Bury) Godfrey, an eminent Protestant magistrate, disappeared shortly after hearing privately the testimony of Titus Oates against the Catholics. On 17 Oct. his body was found on Primrose Hill, pierced with a sword, although death had apparently been caused by hanging. In an attempt to implicate Pepys in the 'Popish Plot', and to discredit thereby his patron the Duke of York, the king's enemies caused Atkins to be accused and arrested on perjured testimony, 30 Oct. He was not acquitted until 9 Feb. 1679. For an account of S.P.'s gathering the evidence to provide an alibi for Atkins, see Bryant, ii. 226–50.

able to acquit himself with advantage to him, and infamy to his Accusers; and that being done, the care which this accident occasions me will soon be over.

In the mean time, pray desire my Father to give no way to any fears concerning me, for that I bless God I have liv'd so carefully in the discharge of my Duty to the King my Master and the Laws I live under both towards God, and towards men, that I have not one unjust deed or thought to answer for, and consequently neither am myselfe, nor would pray him to be under the least doubt or care what can befall me, it being of no use to any man in my Place to think of supporting himselfe by any other means that has such an innocence as mine to relye on; and there, I bless God, lies my comfort, whatever befals me.

Which having said I have nothing at present to add but to pray you to continue your care of my Father all you can, and though through the muchness of my business I may fail you, pray do not you fail to let me know once a week how he and your Family do. So with the tenders of my most humble duty to my Father, and kind Love to yourselfe, &c, I remaine,

Your most affectionate Brother.
SP

Sister Jackson

66. S.P. TO B. ST. MICHEL[1]

Tower June the 19th 1679.

Brother Balty,

My restraint here preventing my seeing you before your going, and consequently my being able to give you any Advice in that Affair of my owne, wherein, under the direction of my Worthy Friend Mr Brisband,[2] you may dureing your stay at Paris (which I wish as short as may be in respect to the Occasions there May be for your presence here in your owne behalfe) be of great use to mee in your diligent attendances upon him, and your Sollicitations in any matters he shall committ to you upon the Subject of my Late desires to him, in reference to the matters wherein I stand maliciously accused by Colonel

[1] Rawl. A. 194: 14. Draft in hand of secretary, corrected by S.P. A copy of this same letter was evidently enclosed in a letter to Mr. Brisbane from S.P. in the Tower, 19 June 1679, acknowledging letters from Mr. Brisbane of 17 and 21 June N.S., discussing the propriety of approaching M. de Seignelay for evidence, and asking Mr. Brisbane's guidance for St. Michel's investigations in Paris. It carries the postscript: 'I beg you once for all to Excuse that from the Infirmity of my owne Eyes I am fain to Imploy another's hand.'

[2] John Brisbane was then secretary to the English Embassy at Paris; later, 1681, he was made Secretary to the Admiralty.

Scot.¹ I send this under Mr Brisband's Cover to let you know that referring you for more particulars to my next (as being prevented in time for saying more tonight) I give it you as my desire that you will apply yourselfe with all Industry from day to day to Mr. Brisband for his Directions in ought wherein hee shall think your Care may be Serviceable to mee, praying you also not to attempt any Thing in my Affair otherwise or further then as he shall approve; And this I the rather say, least you may otherwise proceed to the Execution of any thing that may have been hinted to you by way of advice in my Concerns by Will Hewer, I haveing had severall Considerations before mee relating thereto different possibly from what occur'd to him, when he spoke to you. All I have to add is, the recommending it to you to avoid all unnecessary Occasions of exposing your Selfe or name to Public Notice, or your being imploy'd in any matters relating to mee, which onely accidentally fall in with those occasions of your owne which call you thither.

Be also as good a Husband as you can, and be directed by Mr Brisband whether you shall attend Mr Savill² or not before you have a Letter of mine to accompany you to him, which you may expect by the Next, though your going hence without my Seeing you may (if it be needfull) give you a full Excuse for it. So wishing you health, and with my blessing to my Godson, I remaine

Your very affectionate Brother to Serve you
S P

To Mr. St Michel

67. SAMUEL ST. MICHEL TO S.P.³

Ce 22e Juin 1679

Monseigneur mon tres cher oncle

Si je suis coupable comme je n'en doute point d'avoir tant vielly sans me donner lhonneu[r]⁴ de vous ecrire ie vous Supplie de me pardonner apres que vous aurez pris la peine de lire mes excuses vous priant de croire qu'ayant lhonneur destre allié dune personne aussy

---

¹ The introduction to this volume summarizes the career of this professional adventurer. See also G. D. Scull, *Dorothea Scott, Otherwise Gotherson*, privately printed, Oxford 1883.

² Henry Savile, English Ambassador to France. Pepys had written to Savile, 26 May 1679, explaining the accusation against him, and requesting Savile to confer with M. de Seignelay 'to detect the truth or falsehood thereof'. Rawl. A. 194: 1–2. Savile's reply of 10 June, Rawl. A. 188: 141, promised cordial co-operation as soon as de Seignelay returned to Paris.

³ Rawl. A. 181: 114. Original. Holograph. Extremely tiny and perfect Italian hand.

⁴ Page cut.

illustre que vous je ressens en moy meme tant dhonneur de coeur
et de generosite que ie nay Jamais voulu faire paraitre mes im-
perfections aux yeux d'une personne que ie revere comme vous mon
tres cher oncle je scay bien que ie ne vous propose que de foibles
raisons pour mexcuser de ma negligence et que tout est encore foible
en moy excepte la resolution de vous obeir toute ma vie et de vous
cherir plus que moymeme, mais iespere qu'ayant touiours eu toute
sorte de bonté pour notre famille en general vous aurez encore
en mon particulier celle de me pardonner la faute dont ie mexcuse
puisque c'est la premiere fois que je prens la liberte de me dire
Monseigneur mon tres cher oncle
Votre tres humble tres obeissant et
tres affectionne Serviteur
Chevalieu St Michel

Je mets par lautre costé quelques mots francois et latin que jay com-
posé sans aucun ayde, pour vous montrer que iemploie mon temps le
mieux quil m'est possible Si ie pouvois faire un petit tour de danse
dans cette lettre vous y verriez toute ma Science
Quand je Suis venu dAngleterre en france Jay passe par plusieurs
villes que iay admire et ie me Suis arresté a paris dans la plus belle ville
de leurope. je Scay bien que ie dois tous ces bienfaits aux tres Sages
conseils de mon tres cher oncle ei aux fatigues de mon pere lesquels
ie remercie tres humblement a dieu
quando venj ex Anglia in galliam transivi per multas urbes quas
miratus Sum et commoratus Sum lutetiae in urbe pulcherrima
europae. non ignoro me debere haec omnia beneficia Sapientissimis
consiliis charissimi auunculi mei et laboribus patris mei quibus gratias
ago humillimas   vale

Monsieur Monseigneur Pepys premier Secretaire du Roy pour la
Navalle a Derby House A Londres

68. S.P. TO B. ST. MICHEL[1]

King's Bench. June the 26th 1679.

Brother Balty,

    Not doubting but that this will find you at Paris, and that there you
are met with what I wrote you of the 19th Instant under the Cover
of Mr. Brisband; this comes to tell you that I having not yet been able
to obtain a Copy of the Affidavit made by Colonel Scot against mee

---

[1] Rawl. A. 194: 19. Secretarial copy.

(which I hoped to have had a day or 2 since) I am prevented in being able to draw out those Quaeries, which would be necessary for me to send to you out of it, relating to the Court of France, and Consequently cannot send you what I in[1] my last promised to do by this post. But being assur'd of being Master of that affidavit by the next, I shall then give you what you might have expected from mee now, and in the mean time pray you in Case Mr Brisband shall give you any Commands in my Affair that you will use all diligence in the execution of them, remaining,

Your truely affectionate Brother and Servant
S P

To Mr St Michel

69. S.P. TO B. ST. MICHEL[2]

[King's Bench] July the 3d 1676.

Brother Balty,

I have this day had your Letters of the 27th, of June S.N. communicated to me by Will Hewer Wherein, as I am very glad to understand of your health, so does it bring mee matter of great surprise to find my Friend Mr Brisband expressing any dissatisfaction in your attendance on him in the matter which concern's my Selfe about Colonel Scot; Not but that I hope I have by this Post Satisfied him in his doubts both concerning my not being Interested in the Business of the Katherine,[3] and your being in France to avoid your giveing satisfaction to Justice in relation thereto; Netheless I do not thinke it becoming me to judge the reasons upon which in his Public place [he] may think adviseable for him to avoid his appeareing with you, and therefore doe desire you to comply with his advice therein, in forbearing any further visits to him, and so Soone as your own affairs shall be done, to make the quickest repaire back to England that you can in order to your doing right to your Selfe and the Law; as Sir A. D[eane] and Captain More are prepareing to doe in what (if anything) you are concern'd in relation to the Charge brought in by Captain Mohun touching the Hunter and the Katherine, and this I have in my Letter this Post told Mr Brisband I had directed you

---

[1] *by*, canc.

[2] Rawl. A. 194: 20–21. Secretarial copy.

[3] The *Katherine* was one of the English ships captured by the privateer *Hunter*. John More and Sir Anthony Deane were among St. Michel's partners in this unlucky venture, as outlined in the Introduction. S.P.'s full account is to be found in the Mornamont Collection in the Pepysian Library, Cambridge University, i. 1. 5–7. His letter to Mr. Brisbane is Rawl. A. 194: 21–23.

to doe, and would for the same Reasion have you do it without offring at any unwelcome visite to Mr Savill, whose Friendship and Mr Brisband's I have had too many past proofs of, that I should Entertain any present doubts concerning it, and think it of too much weight to me in this occasion to offer any thing to them of offence that may interrupt it.

However pray fail not to wait upon Monsieur Trenchepain[1] with my most humble service, and acknowledgment of my humble thanks for the trouble he is taking on my behalf at the request of my worthy Friend Mr Houblon in reference to his Inquiries touching Mr Pellissary[2] and one Captain Piogery[3] or Fiogery or some such like Name said to have been a Commander of note in the French fleet; How long either or both of them have been dead, their Religion as to Papist, or Protestant, and what other Intimations can be found touching the present State of Mr Pellissary's family, In whose hands his Bookes and Papers are, or from whom any Information can be gott concerning them, whether any of his Servants to be met withall that served him in 1675 about August, when Sir A. Deane[4] carried the 2 yacks into France, and was Entertain'd by Mr Pellissary at his House in Paris, and lastly what familiarity Colonel Scot was knowne to have had in Mr Pellissary's Family, and for how long backward, and whether it could be remembred whether Scot was upon that very day at his house at dinner-time, when in that month Sir A: Deane was entertained there; all these Circumstances going very farr towards the detecting the falsity of Colonel Scot's villanous Accusations against Sir A: Deane and mee; But, pray see that what you doe gather in this matter be truth and nothing Else, for I would not be beholden to any lye of my owne for a defence against another man's. But your Inquiries herein ought to be made with as little noise as may be, and therefore I recommend that in particular both to Monsieur Trenchepain and you, and that as to your Selfe you will consider the making

---

[1] A French merchant through whom S.P.'s friend, the merchant James Houblon managed the exchange of currency for St. Michel's trip.

[2] Former treasurer-general of the French navy, deceased.

[3] Capitaine de La Piogerie, deceased officer of the French navy. Letter 78 reports that he may have been 'Major de la Marine'. Bryant calls him Priogery (ii. 285). Rawl. A. 194: 52–55 contains several letters in French referring to him as M. le Major Heroward dit la Piogerie.

[4] In August 1675 Sir Anthony Deane, assisted by W. Hewer, had delivered to the King of France two yachts which Deane had built to order. It was during the festivities on this occasion, Scott alleged, that Deane carried maps and other secret naval documents from S.P. to M. de Seignelay, then secretary to the French Admiralty. In fact, however, poor Deane was trying to gather a bit of information about the French navy in the interests of his own government. In William Hewer's account to S.P., 2 Aug. 1675, Rawl. A. 185: 11, the Frenchman appears as 'Lord Marquis de Sinley'. Printed: Smith, i. 163–8; Howarth, pp. 51–53.

your return home as Speedy as you can, and your Journey as Easy as may be in the Expence of it, you knowing how many wayes of charge a Business of this kind, which relates to so many Severall Countries,[1] must lead a man into, and therefore calling for all good Husbandry to be executed therein. So, with wishes of health to you and my Blessing to my little Godson, I remain

Your most affectionate Brother to serve you
SP

To Mr St Michell

70. S.P. TO B. ST. MICHEL[2]

King's Bench July 7th 1679

Brother Balty,

I give you many thankes for your Letter of June 29th/July 9th and doe hope you have, or will suddenly receive mine of the 3d Instant, to which referring you for so much as I then had before me to mention, I now come to observe how welcome the Contents of this of yours are, in bringing me advice of the fruits of your first Conference with Monsieur Landry Secretary to Monsieur Pellissary which I am Extremely glad of your having an opportunity so timelily given you for, by those two Gentlemen Monsieur Trenchepain and Mr Pelletier[3] to both of whom as I do by you return my most humble Service and thankes, so do I (according to your advice) do it to the latter by a Line or two Inclosed from my Self as I shall more particularly to the former by the hand of my most Worthy Friend Mr Houblon on whose account onely it is, that I receive from him this kindness, as being my Selfe wholly a stranger to him.

Mr. Brisband having by the last post given mee an account of his Intentions of leaving Paris very suddenly I perceive I shall have no[4] opportunity of his further Assistance in this matter at Paris. However I have under the same Cover with this writt to him,[5] giving him

---

[1] Through James Houblon, S.P. carried on extensive investigations of the career of Scott in Holland. Through some of his maritime friends he was able to get reports of Scott's villainies in America.   [2] Rawl. A. 194: 24–28. Secretarial copy.

[3] S.P. had known M. Peletyer of Paris since his tour of the Continent in 1669. Rawl. A. 174: 335–6 is a letter of compliment from him to Mrs. Pepys, with internal evidence that he is caring for the shipment of her purchases, and that he is also in correspondence with S.P. and St. Michel (1669). Rawl. A. 174: 333–4 is a letter of condolence to S.P. on the death of his wife, dated 4 Decembre 1669. Both are in French. The enclosure mentioned to St. Michel, a letter of thanks in French from S.P., is found in Rawl. A 194: 28, a secretarial copy.   [4] *an*, canc.

[5] S.P. to Mr. Brisband, Rawl. A. 194: 28–29. Copy. S.P. requests that M. de Seignelay be put right on his confusion of S.P. with Matthew Wren, his predecessor as secretary to the Duke of York.

thanks for his last, and the Account I therein Received of the Success of his Late Conference with the Marquis de Seignelay[1] which was the Marquis's Renouncing upon his honour in most solemn manner his haveing had any Correspondence, good or bad with mee since his being sent into England by the King of France to adjust matters relating to the Conjunction of Our two Fleets against the Dutch, when he seem's to remember that upon that Occasion he had Conferences with me about the Business of the Navy. But in that he will appear to be in a mistake by taking mee for my Predecessor in my Imployment, Mr Wren, for as much as Mr de Seignelay's Being in England upon that affair was in the year 1671, and I find severall papers of Mr Wren's of that Date relating to Mr De Seignelay's being here, and the Business he came upon; whereas I came not into the Admiralty till Midsummer 1673, without having Ever had any occasion of business with him, or remembring that ever I spoke to, or saw him. Which I tell you the more particularly that you may know not onely how farr you may be satisfied in your private Judgment of the Indisputableness of my Innocence in this matter, but also how much I may be at ease in that onely one point, wherein I had any reserves of fear, which was that Monsieur De Seignelay might be induced to think the Removall of mee from the Service of my Master to be of so much moment to his as to give way to my ruine so farr as his avoiding to give testimony to my Innocence might contribute to it. But I thank God I find him a man of Honour and Justice suitable to the Character, which upon my late Inquiries, I had receiv'd of him, and upon which I was incouraged in my last to Mr Brisband to press him without further difficulty to the applying of himselfe plainly and openly to Monsieur De Seignelay in my affair, and have received this happy Issue to it, which I shall for a little while Suffer to remain, without offering at any further advances in it by any applications to Mr Savill, or otherwise till the Arrivall of Mr Brisband which (by what I hear) may be expected every day in Company with My Lady Cleveland,[2] for whom the Katherine Yacht wait's at Deep. This onely I would leave with you to advise with our two forementioned friends upon, viz Whether Mr De Ruvigny formerly Embassadeur in England may not be a proper hand to make use of in the French Court when it shall be expedient to make another Step there with Mr De Seignelay; Monsieur De Ruvigny not onely having a reputation of a Person of good Interest in that Court, but being also a Protestant and a man of great probity, and consequently

---

[1] Secretary to the French Admiralty.

[2] Barbara Villiers, Lady Castlemaine, one of the king's mistresses, figures often in the *Diary*.

one more to be relied upon for his Justice in this affair, he knowing mee to be of the same profession in Religion with him selfe, (we having frequently met in Our Devotions at the Savoy) and to be one who value my self upon the faithfulness and diligence of my service to my Master then any can be thought to be, that is wholly a stranger to me in the lesser Consideration, and less Inclin'd to do me right upon the former, respecting Religion, And let me have assoon as you can their opinion and yours in this particular, or what other better hand they think there may be of applying my self by to Monsieur De Seignelay upon his having thus far already discover'd his Justice to me.

Which having said in relation to that part of my Care it remain's, that I give you what I have to observe upon the other which respects our Inquiries after Mr. Pellissary, and his family, wherein you have also made a very satisfactory step in your Discourse with Monsieur Landry by which it appear's that Scot has not had any Long or notorious Conversation with that family as also that Mr Pellissary's having any such Draughts or Models as Scot charges Sir Antony Deane and me with the furnishing Monsieur de Seignelay with was not so public as to be known to [one][1] who, by your description should be thought as likely to be made privy to them, as Mr Scot, unless his Intimacy with Mr. Pellissary had been much more Noted then it seem's to be. But however as to this part of the Draughts, Mapps, and Models, I will admit it possible that Mr. Landry may have missed the knowledge of them, if sent to his Master upon terms of Secrecy from M De Seignelay. But in that Case it is a very proper matter for your Inquiry what kind of correspondence there was between Captain Fiogery (of whom I wrote you in my Last) and Mr Pellissary, about that time when these papers are said to have been sent to Mr Pellissary from Mr De Seignelay to be shewen to the said Captain, which was about August and September 1675.

But then, as to the other part of what Mr. Landry saies that there was no acquaintance between Colonel Scot and Mr Pellissary that ought to be extremely well examined, as being of mighty moment to me to have well searched and prov'd. For no man can Imagine that Monsieur Pellissary should communicate to a stranger those papers and Draughts, which are said to be of so much value, and privacy as to be thought fitt to be kept from the knowledg of Mr Landry, who (you tell me) was his Secretary, and Confident. Pray therefore let this business of Scot's being, or not being more then ordinarily acquainted with Mr Pellissary and Conversant in his Family, be well Inquired into, and what proof (upon occasion) I may be furnished

---

[1] MS. *me*, secretarial error.

with of it, and confine not those Inquiries only to Mr Landry, but make use of helps from what Inferiour Servants, who lived in the Family about that time you can light of. And that you may the more fully understand the matters you have to Inquire into, I do herewith send you the Substance of Scot's Information against mee, which you may impart to those Gentlemen in order to their assisting you in the Collecting Such points as may be fitt to be inquired after, for disproving all or any part of the said information. In which I hope for the better success, because I understand Mr Pellissary himself was a protestant, and I presume his Family and Servants were generally such, and particularly Mr Landry) and consequently as they may be thought the more Inclined to do right in this matter to my Innocence, who am of the same Profession, so will their Testimony in what they shall give it, be of the more authority among us here when it shall be produced. And if any proper meanes can be found of access to Madam Pellissary the Widow it were very adviseable that she be spoken with in this matter, as being (in all probability)[1] the best able to direct us to the Discovering of the full truth herein, and other then the truth (as I told you in my last) I am very farr from desiring you to make any search after, for as much as that alone is all that I need for my defence.

I hope you have not omitted to make use of the Courtesy offer'd you by Mr Landry of visiting the house of Mr Pellissary and its furniture, that you may the better compare what you see there with what, in the Inclos'd paper you will find alleg'd by Scot, to have been sent by me to Mr De Seignelay, and particularly the five Mapps or Draughts herein specified, which being also said to be very large, and in parchment they can the less be thought to have Escaped being seen by Madam Pellissary, Mr Landry and others of his Family. And if it should fall out, that any Mapps or Draughts of those Places, or ought belonging to the Coasts or Ports of England shall be found to have been in his House, ordinarily hanging up there, pray fail not to give me a particular Account of them and the names of the Authors that made and drew them.

And for as much as it seem's very uneasy to have these Inquiries of yours Effectually carried on without being more open therein then Our Friends and you did in prudence think it at first convenient to be to Mr Landry, I leave it to them and you (now you have had this generall Declaration of Mr. Landry's touching Scot's being a stranger to Mr Pellissary) to be as clear not onely with him, but with Madam Pellissary and where else you think it necessary as shall be by you joyntly thought fitt, letting them know the true grounds of your Inquiries. And this I the rather propose upon this Consideration,

---

[1] *possibility*, canc.

Namely, that this false information of Scot's seemes no less to reflect upon the Honour of Mr De Seignelay and Mr Pellissary in exposing of mee, then upon me in betraying of my Master, and consequently it ought to incite them to give me all just assistance in the Detecting his falsity. But then, pray let me caution you that you proceed with all the uprightness and circumspection that you can in the menaging of these your Inquiries that no occasion may be taken of charging you with any indirect Method therein, which I am sure our Adversary will be apt enough to Suggest, though there be no cause for it, and therefore will not fail to Improve anything that shall beare the least Semblance of a Cause.

If Mr Brisband should be come away before the arrivall of this you shall not need to returne it, but are at Liberty to peruse it for your own Information.

As to your own affairs, I understand that the triall of the Business of the Hunter, which was designed to be held at the next assizes at Winchester in the Countrey where the pretended Offence of her being sent to sea with the King's Stores was committed, is putt off, and consequently the time for the doing of it now left wholly uncertain. But care shall be taken for the giving you timely notice of it, so as you may be here to attend it, and thereby do right to your Reputation as well as to the Law.

One thing I must note to you in order to the enabling you the better to understand the Clause in the Inclos'd paper touching what pass'd between Mr Pellissary and Scot when Sir A. Deane was in the Garden, that Sir A. Deane was once, and but once at Mr Pellissary's house at Paris, vizt in August 1675, when he carried the two Pleasure-Boats over to the King of France, at which time there was a very great Entertainment made for Sir A. Deane and his Company, and before Dinner Mr Pellissary is said to have passed some little time walking in the Garden with Sir A. Deane, and (as Scot reports it) did leave Sir A. Deane there, and went in to the house to him, and had that Discourse with him makeing him dine privately in the house that Day by him selfe that Sir A Deane might not see him. But Sir A. Deane does affirm this whole thing to be untrue of Mr. Pellissary's Leaving him in the Garden and it seem's not Improbable, but it may be found out by Mr Pellissary's servants whether Scot did use to eate often with him, and whether they remember (this day's entertainment for Sir A. Deane being very remarkable) any time that Scot did thus dine there alone by himself or with his Lady and Children as he seem's to insinuate.

And lastly, since by the Coming away of Mr Brisband the whole sollicitation of this Affair will lie on your hand; I must desire that during your stay at Paris, and your Concernments therein you will be as assiduous in the same as may be, not omitting any fit means of furnishing your Self with Information, even from the lowest helps, by Inferior servants or others, in the finding out any part of the Truth that may be of use to us, letting me have an Account of your proceedings by every post under Mr Trenchepain's Cover to Mr. Houblon, or Mr Pelletier's to any Correspondent of his here, in case of any occasion of making use of both. Which recommending to your utmost Care, and thanking you againe for the proofs you have already given me thereof, I remaine

Your truly affectionate
Brother to serve you
SP

To Mr St Michell

71. S.P. TO B. ST. MICHEL[1]

Yorke-Buildings July the 14th 1679

Brother Balty;

I have this day received yours of the 8th Instant, for which I thank you not doubting your haveing done the like by mine of the 7th ditto, in which I not only inclosed one to Mr Pelletier acknowledging his favours, but made mine to you very long and particular in reference to all things wherein I could then, or can yet think of ought that might be matter for your Inquiry, and which haveing made the most of your inquiries in, I should think it would be of most use to me that you should prepare your selfe for, and hasten your returne. For as to Monsieur De Seignelay, I am still of opinion to expect Mr Brisband (who is hourely lokked for) before I doe any thing towards making any further applications to him, and therefore desire you to forbeare it, till I shall say more to you about it. In the mean time, So much of the falsehood of my accuser has already appear'd that I have my Liberty againe upon Bayle to appeare 3 or 4 monthes hence next term and So has Sir A Deane and Captain Moore as to their Business of the Hunter and Katherin, So that I trust in God you will not need to apprehend any further trouble in relation thereto. But of that (as I advised you in my last) you shall heare from me as there shall be occasion, you preparing your affairs for your returne, for mine will not (I hope) give you occasion of staying much Longer.

I am now with Will Hewer at his house, and have receiv'd from him all the Care, kindness and faithfulness of a Son, on this occasion, for which God reward him, if I cann't.

[1] Rawl. A. 194: 29–30. Secretarial copy.

To B. St. Michel

Being at this time driven to use my owne hand I cannot be longer because of my Eyes,[1] and therefore shall add no more but my most humble Services to Mr Trenchepain and Mr Pelletier, and my desires of your makeing your Enquirys into the History of Captain Piogerie as perfect as you can, what Ships he commanded and when, and where he was in August 1675, and of how much acquaintance with Monsieur De Seignelay and Monsieur Pellissary; remaining

Your most Loving Brother to serve you

SP

To Mr St Michell

72. S.P. TO B. ST. MICHEL[2]

York-Buildings July the 17th 1679.

Brother Balty,

Since mine of the 14th I have received yours of the 12th Instant, for which I give you my very kindest thankes, it giving me a very full account of your Care and diligence in my affair, as also of the great instances you meet with of the Friendship and Civility of Mr Trenchepain and Mr Pelletier to the later of whom haveing lately wrote, I give you now a line or 2 to the same purpose to the former[3] in acknowlegment of his great favours, and pray make both the one and the other understand how sensible I am of them, and particularly of the last good Office which I find done me in theirs and your Conference with Le Picard and Mr De la Valossiere and the Attestation, which you have Sent me thereof under their hands and the hands of the 2 Publick Notaries Which as to my own private Satisfaction I esteem of great moment to me, though my misfortune is, that the Law of England will not admitt in Criminall Cases any written Evidences, but requires all to be given personnally vivâ voce in Court, at least I am as yet informe'd so; but will indeavour to understand it a little more distinctly, and in the mean time desire that you will labour to gett what further intelligence you can touching Captain La Piogerie, and particurly in these points following, Vizt Where? When? Upon what Service and in what Command he was kill'd? Whether he understood English or not; whether he was in Command

---

[1] Mr. Arthur Bryant interprets this passage to mean that Pepys was too low in funds to afford an amanuensis (ii. 285). The very existence of this letter-book in the hand of a secretary confutes the hypothesis. Pepys probably means that his secretary is absent at the moment.

[2] Rawl. A. 194: 30–31. Secretarial copy.

[3] S.P. to M. François Trenchepain, in French, a polite acknowledgement of his aid to St. Michel. Rawl. A. 194: 30.

under Mr Destrée in the French Fleet that joyn'd with Ours against the Dutch in the last warr, and what Ship he Commanded, I finding in one List, which I have, one La Vigerie in that Fleet, and would be glad to know whether it be the same with La Piogery, whom you mention. Pray also endeavour to learn where your La Piogerie was in August 1675, Colonel Scot having said that he was then at Rochefort and that he was since kill'd at Tabago. Which possibly may be true and will be of no prejudice to me if it be so; but if you shall find it not to be true, may be of advantage to me. It may also be of use to understand in whose hands his papers now are, and whence it is that he should be the man of all the Sea-Commanders of France that Scot should pitch upon to have the Mapps sent to him from Monsieur De Seignelay through the hands of Mr Pellissary. In a word you will doe well to indeavour to gain as particular an account as you are able of this Gentleman by any of his Relations or acquaintance which you can find at Paris.

Pray also make your selfe certain whether Mr Pellissary spoke any English or noe.

I doe observe what you write of your Expectation, that by the Friendship of Mr Vallossiere you might have acces to Monsieur Colebert,[1] and Monsieur De Seignelay to obtain a declaration of the truth in this matter immediately from themselves. But having just now understood, that Mr Brisband is arriv'd, and the time not pressing me, I doe rather choose to forbear the giving you any advice touching that particular, untill I have the opportunity of seeing him, which you may depend upon my giveing you some account of by the next post.

I am sensible of what you observe touching the Interception of Letters, and very reasonably, but as for those 2 of yours you mention I am apt to beleeve it was onely my forgetfulness to acknowledg to you my receit of them.

I am in no doubt of your good Husbandry, though those Infinite expences, which this fellowes Villany puts me to, in my inquiries, through So many Nations after him, make my Earnest in my Cautions to you about it.

Very sorry I am for the Indisposition you have been under in your health, and no less gratified with the advice you give me of your recovery, which I wish perfect to you, and remaine

Your truely affectionate Brother and Servant

S P

To Mr St Michell

---

[1] Either Charles Colbert de Croissy, Secretary of State for Foreign Affairs in France, or his brother, Jean Baptiste Colbert, Minister of Marine.

73. S.P. TO B. ST. MICHEL[1]

York-Buildings July the 21th 1679.

Brother Balty,

I have this day receiv'd yours of the 16th instant, as I hope you have, e're this, mine of the 14th. Since which (by Mr Brisband's departure out of Town to the Court at Windsor immediately upon his arrivall here, and his not returning since) I am not yet instructed, as I would be, what to offer to you in relation to Monsieur De Seignelay, but doubt not to have my desire therein before the next Post (he being expected back this Night) and then shall give it you. In the mean time this Serves onely to give you my kinde thankes for the Continuance of your Care in my affair, and to let you know that I am very sensible therof and the good Effects I expect from it to the Justification of my Innocence and honour, and to the Reproach of the Villain that has thus indeavoured to traduce them. I am also very sensible of the favour I receive on this Occasion from my Worthy Friends Monsieur Trenchepain and Monsieur Pelletier to the former of whom I have prevented your desires by writting to him in my Last, and do by you returne my very faithfull thankes to the later for the Letter you have sent me from him in this. To which I shall at present add nothing but my desires of the Continuance of your Diligence in the getting satisfaction in what others particulars of my Demands you have not yet had opportunity of obtaining it, and the assuring you of my being

Your truely affectionate Brother
S P

To Mr St Michell

74. S.P. TO B. ST. MICHEL[2]

York-Buildings. July the 24th 1679

Brother Balty,

I have your wellcome Letter of the 19th instant and wrote you under the 21th Ditto.

The Contents of your Last give me additional satisfaction to what I have received from you before and am in great Expectation of the fruits of your next visite to Mr De la Valossiere wishing that you could obtain such an ample Certificate (as you speake of) from

[1] Rawl. A. 194: 32. Secretarial copy.
[2] Rawl. A. 194: 32–33. Secretarial copy.

Madame Pellissary and her Family; for it might be of present great use to me, however the Court, when it shall come to a Triall, may require Somewhat more. Pray therefore be indeavouring to obtain it as Large and particular as you can in the Circumstances which I have afore noted to you, and let me have it as soon as you are able.

Pray also, remember what I have desired of you touching Captain La Piogerie, for I am in doubt but upon inquiry, he that has been so bold in his lyes relating to Monsieur Pellissary may be found no less guilty of the like with him. Therefore pray be as inquisitive as you can in all the circumstances I wrott to you concerning him, and if (with the advice of Our Friends) it shall be thought convenient that Madame Pellissary her Selfe Should bee Spoken withall, and that you could obtain a good opportunity for it, I think it might not be unusefull.

I cannot yet despatch what I would do with Mr Brisband, he being still out of Towne; but at his first appearance here I shall doe it, and be then able to come to some positive Directions to you touching your Return to England, which you may be sure of my indeavouring to hasten all that may be.

In the mean time I am extremely glad of your recovery and pray heartily for the like to my Worthy Friend Monsieur Trenchepain, to whom, and Mr Pelletier I give my most humble services; Remaining

Your truely affectionate Brother to serve you
S P

To Mr St Michell

75. S.P. TO B. ST. MICHEL[1]

July the 28th 1679.

Brother

I kindly thanke you for yours of the 21 and 22th instant, and the great instances they give me of your diligence in my concerns, praying you to go on with your purpose of obtaining Madame Pellissary's and her family's Attestation in all the particulars depending touching Mr Scot, and to let it be as particular as you can, and vouched per as many of her Family great and small (besides her self) as you may. I being willing that this be done onely before a Notary as you are advised for her Ladyship's Ease though if more shall be hereafter judged necessary I may come againe to her to desire more [,] I shall not

---

[1] Rawl. A. 194: 33–34. Secretarial copy.

(I hope) need to repeate any thing of the particulars to be mention'd in the Attestation my former Letters having been very plaine therein.

Nor am I against your having a Copy of so much of Mr Pellissary's Inventory as concerne the Charts, Globes and Mapps, though I must pray you to remember that the things of that kind which Scot mention's to have been Sent to him from the Marquis De Seignelay were not for him to keep by him, but to be sent by him to Captain La Piogerie So as I am not to expect to find them remaining among the Meubles of Mr Pellissary.

Another thing I must pray you to note in what I already heretofore wrote you which is, that it imports me mightily to make as little use as I can of any Papists for my witnesses, and that therefore if a protestant can be gott, of which you may consider, it will be of much more Benefit and Security to me then to depend upon the Evidence of a Papist Such as I take our worthy friend Mr Pelletier to be, though a man of the utmost integrity, and one to whom I am infinitely bound for his Generous Offer of coming into England, on my behalfe and I pray you to returne him my most humble thankes accordingly, but Such is the Captiousness of Our Age against any thing that is not Protestant.

I have at length spoken with Mr. Brisband, but cannot be ready to give you my opinion touching your applications to Monsieur De Seignelay at present but I presume I shall make use of Monsieur De Ruvigny[1] about it and write to you in it by the Post on monday the 4th August I being obliged to go out of Towne for so long tomorrow.

Heartily grieved I am for Mr Trenchepain's Sickness whose recovery I pray for, and beg you to present him with my most humble Services and the like to Mr Pelletier.

Pray pursue your getting of Mr Le Goux's Evidence as particularly as you can in the points you mention. My Sister[2] and her Family were well last night, and full glad I am that you are so, hoping that one post or two more will put an end to your absence from home.

Lastly, pray find out what you can of Scot's Ever having been in the King of France's Service where he has heretofore bragg'd of his having been a Major Generall under the prince of Condé after his having deserted the Holland's Service, and indeavour also to Learn any instances of his having been or pretended to be of the Church of Rome as I am told he has to one of the English Nunneries in Paris

---

[1] Former French Ambassador to England.
[2] St. Michel's wife Ester occupied apartments in York Buildings at this time.

about the year 1673 and was very civilly treated by them and others on that Account, as I doubt not but you may upon inquiry (if you could find out any of his haunts) discover.

So being driven to make use of my own Eyes in writing this, I bid you heartily adieu, and am

Your truely Loving Brother to serve you
S. P

To Mr St Michell

76. S.P. TO B. ST. MICHEL[1]

York-Buildings August the 7th 1679.

Brother Balty,

I doubt not but you may be under some Surprise at my Silence to you from ever Since the 28th of July. But it has a reason from having had an extraordinary occasion of going into Oxfordshire, from whence I am newly returned and find my self in arreares to you for 3 Letters Vizt One of the 25th and another of the 29th July with a 3d dated the 2d instant, mentioning your receit of my last before exprest. For all which I returne you my very kind thankes, as also do with my most humble Services to Mr Trenchepain and Mr Pelletier to whom I will not fail by the next under my own hand (as you advise) in acknowledgment of their great favours to me, especially that last of theirs so freely offering to take the trouble of a voyage into England if the Justice of my Cause should be so unfortunate as to need it. But pray take care that Monsieur Pelletier do not misunderstand what I wrote you about the necessity of my making as little use as I can of popish Evidence, for such is the present Complection of the age that instead of doing good a popish witness were enough at this time to prejudice the justest Cause in the world. And therefore though I am not sure I shall have occasion of using it, yet you have done very well in making provision for another Protestant of Credit to joyn with Mr Trenchepain if it should be necessary.

Your last put's me in expectation of so much further usefull light in this matter as leaves me little more at present to say to you till I see what new Considerations will arise from it. This onely in generall I shall observe, that the most, if not the onely, thing materiall which is behind, is that of Mr De Seignelay, which truely I cannot yet come to any determination how to proceed in. Not that Mr Brisband gives

[1] Rawl. A. 194 : 35–36. Secretarial copy.

80

me any difficulty concerning it, but it goes against me to make use of
any Forein hands to approach Mr De Seignelay by, in a Case so
innocent as mine is, (it being enough for others whose cases need it to
take those Extraordinary Courses to justify themselves) and therefore am Some time in the mind of writting to him directly my Self
without making use of any other hand Especially Since he is reported
to be a person of so much Honour and Justice, and has given so full
a proof of it in what he has already said upon the first mention of my
Affair to him by Mr Brisband. But then on the other hand his
Quality being such as requires his being treated with all respect,
I would be loath my applications to him should be in any wise defective in that particular, and therefore am thoughtfull what [hands] to
make use of for the presenting of my Letters to him, in case yours or
those of my Friends with you should be thought too little. Wherein,
pray let me have theirs and your Advice as soon as ever you can while
I am also considering of it with others here, there being no time, as
I think, lost in it, as holding it expedient to perfect the rest of my
Intelligence as farr as I can before I address my selfe to him.

I am still of the mind to give Mr Savill no trouble in this matter,
till I see further use of it, then I yet doe, and therefore continue to
forbeare any applications, or appearances to him till I write you to
that purpose.

Pray make your Selfe more perfect in the Story of Mr La Piogerie,
for it will be of use to me to find that he was not a Sea-man, but a
Land-Officer onely or that at that time his Command was only
Major of the Land forces. This, I say, would be of great use to me if it
could be made appear. But let me tell you I am afraid there is some
mistake in it, for if La Piogerie be the same as La Vigerie then I can
assure [you] that from some printed Lists which I have of the Commanders of the French Fleet La Vigerie commanded the Hazardeux
under Mr Destrée in the year 1672 and the Bourbon in 1673.
Besides that I find the same in the printed Mercure Gallant of the
year 1672. But I must confess neither of these Commands were such
as should lead me to think him the onely man to be pickt out by the
marquis De Seignelay to communicate these extraordinary Papers
to. However pursue your inquiries after this Gentleman so as you
may obtain the full truth of his story in Each of the particulars I have
afore given you, it being my full perswasion (as it seems to be Mr
De La Vallossiere) that Scot's Choice of these Gentlemen Mr Pellissary and La Piogerie was chiefly grounded upon their being dead, and
therefore out of the way of denying any thing that he should father
upon them.

But one thing I must observe to you out of the Copy of Manning's challenge[1] which you send me, and that is, that in his threatning of Scot he saies among other things that Pellissary ne fera jamais avancer cet ouvrage &c. Which would imply that Scot had something depending before Mr Pellissary, and consequently was more or less known to him. Therefore pray labour to inform your selfe what the meaning of that Expression was, and also who that Manning and Sherwin were that I may be the better guided in my understanding of the one and Inquiry after the other. In the mean time I do not see how that use is to be made of that Paper which you would draw from it of Scot's being a Roman Catholick, though I have reasons given me to beleeve that from the English Nuns or Fryers you will find him to be or to have pretended to be of that Religion. And as to his having been in the king of Frances Military service a Gentleman of great worth tells me that Scot has declared it very openly to him that after his Leaving of the Dutch Service he was entertained by the King of France as a Major Generall and was in particular to attend the person of the Prince of Condé.

I take notice of your desires of being call'd home, which I shall indeavour to hasten all I can. But Our matters being now drawne so neare a head I am willing you should see an end of them rather then leave it to be done by another hand, or impose more upon Mr Trenchepain and Mr Pelletier then Either their Quality and business will admitt or my respect to them ought to offer at, but I do hope that a little time more will doe all. In the mean time my sister and your family are very well I thank God, and though my Friends must be contented to share with me in the Change of my present Fortune, yet I hope I shall not, by the King's Goodness and Justice, be bereft of opportunities one way or other of making provision for you and your family by some imployment wherein your Diligence and health may make up what the change of my Condition may (at least for a time) be of some disappointment to you. So I remain

Your truely affectionate
Brother to serve you

To Mr St. Michell   S P

[1] 'Colonel Scot

   Jay Escript a londres Comme vous avéz debauché Sheruuin du Service du Roy, Jay Escrit aussy en angleterre pour faire arrester vos ouvriers. et pelissary ne fera Jamais avanser cest ouvrage a moings que vous me donniés de largent ei des habits, vous ne vivres pas trois Jours, moy et mon amy avons faict serment de vostre destruction, et Sy vous estiés prince vous nen Eschaperes pas adieu Edouard maning

   Judy matin aupres de la place ou je vous ay Escript que ie Seray.' (Rawl. A.188: 180.)

   This document is entitled: Autre letre escripte en anglois par le mesme maning audit sr colonel Scot Traduitte en langue francoise de mot amot.

   It is endorsed in St. Michel's hand: Augt 1/11 1679 Coppy of a Letter of Challenge from one Edwd Manning to Coll^r Scott given me by M^r le goux before Mr Peletier and Mr Tranchepain.

82

77. S.P. TO B. ST. MICHEL[1]

York-Buildings August the 11th 1679

Brother Balty,

My last was of the 7th instant, whereof I inclose you a Copy, least by some irregularity in the method of it's superscription, it should happen to miscarry, and concerning which I intreat you to inform me in your next; and in the mean time doe acknoledg to you the receit of 2 of yours of the 5/15th and 6/16th instant. For both which I returne you my very kind thankes, and am not wholly without reflexions of the same kind with those you have of the Providence of God Almighty in my meeting with so large and Easy a Concurrence of testimonies of all sorts towards the evincing the truth of the matters depending between the Lawe and me upon the information of Colonel Scot and am accordingly desirous of giving due praise to God for it.

And now in reply to these 2 last of yours I observe what you write touching the Character given to Scot by Mr Chavo the Prince of Condé's Secretary, and that Scot never had imployment under the Prince. But I am apt to beeleve from Common fame that though he may not have been in the Prince's Service, yet he has been within the knowledg and under the patronage of the Prince.

I should be glad to know what Platt that was that Mr Courville saies was shewen by Scot at the Prince's house at Chantilly, whether it was a Platt relating to England or not.

Though I do not see it practicable to have any of the Fathers Benedictins come over into England, upon the Consideration that I have more than once mentioned to you, vizt That I must, by no meanes (if it can be avoided) make use of any popish Evidence, though it be never so innocent and true, yet I could be very glad to have some testimony authentically drawne and signed by those Fathers giveing a just account of any of those villanous Practises wherewith they charge Scot; and more particularly of those Mapps and Charts of the English Coasts which he shewed them, as made by him for the King of France, and would have borrowed five hundred pounds upon, of them; and the precise time when this happened, as also of the Scandalous Expressions he has heretofore let fall touching His Majesty.

I will speedily visite Dr Chamberlaine and deliver him the Letter inclosed in Mr Trenchepain's to Mr. Houblon from Monsieur St Helene. For which favour of Mr Trenchepain's, though I cannot do it my self under my owne hand till the next Post (I being suddenly

---

[1] Rawl. A. 194: 37–38. Secretarial opy.

interrupted) yet I will pray you, for the present to deliver my most faithfull acknowledgments to him as being an additionall instance of his great kindness to, and concernment for me.

I do greatly long to receive the Effects of Madame Pellissary's Justice and her Family's, but do most readily Leave it to be obtain'd by you, with such dispatch as you shall find convenient with respect to her.

Pray pursue your inquiry as farr as you can in relation to Scot's Religion, for (as little as I agree with those popish Fathers in other matters) I am much of the same mind with them in their belief of his Religion vizt That he passes for a papist in France as he desires to do of a protestant in England; and from the Course you are taking among them and the Nunnerys I doubt not but the truth may be discovered.

And if you find it not so convenient, and easy as I could wish, of having the testimony of the Fathers themselves touching the aforemention'd particulars which they have declared to you and the other 3 Gentlemen, pray get it well certified and sworn too by them; and the Like (in particular paper) of what Butterfield the English Mathematicall Instrument-maker at Paris [said] to the Same Effect, touching Scot's having a Large Chart of the Coast of England.

The like I desire, if it Can be obtained, of the English Watchmaker's Testimony[1] of Scot's Mapps &c and his Running away in his Debts, expressing the precise time of Scot's Lodging at his House, and when he went last away.

And perfect as farr as you can the Inquiry you are making of the Same kind with Mr Point the Mapp-seller there as soon as he comes to Towne. And if any thing be to be purchased that will appear to be of Scot's making or providing, pray get it.

I thank you for the Copy you send me of Sherwin's Paper, which does give me some further Light towards the interpreting what you last sent me under Manning's; and may be of great use to me, if Sherwin can be found out, which I shall indeavour. In the mean time pray take care of the Originall of Sherwin's paper, and if you can obtain any further information touching him or Manning let me have it.

Which, with referring you, in other particulars, to my Last, is all at present from

Your truely affectionate Brother to serve you

S P

To Mr St Michell

---

[1] James Joyne, something of a scoundrel in his own right, attempted for years to extract money from S.P. Many of his letters are preserved in the Rawlinson Collection.

78. S.P. TO B. ST. MICHEL[1]

Brother Balty,   York-Buildings August the 18th 1679

I have receiv'd yours of the 13/23th instant, for which I thank you, and am in the first place to let you know that mine under the 7th being seal'd and sent away by one of my Servants in my absence, it had not my seale, but for want thereof was seal'd by him with a peece of money the same that you have sent me over; so as I do not find that the Letter did meet with any ill hands; Nevertheless your Inquiry was very reasonable and I thank you for it, and the truth is when I came home and found in what an unusuall manner he had addressed it I was discomposed at it, and jealous of some miscarriage as you will find by my Inquiry after it in my last.

Next I am to thank you for the care I see you have taken in the obtaining and dispatching of the Severall Declarations of Mme Pellissary and her Family, wherein I acknowledge to receive great satisfaction as that which will direct me towards the gaining of a great deale more. This onely I shall note to you upon them that as I have heretofore observed to you the not finding of the pretended Mapps and Charts &c among Mr Pellissary's papers (which is so Industriously proved in these Declarations) is not a Circumstance of any great weight in my Cause, for as much as Scot does not pretend they were sent to Mr Pellissary to remaine with him, but to be by him sent to La Piogery.

On the other hand, though it still sufficiently appears by these Declarations that Scot did not dine at Mr Pellissarys nor was at his house the day that Sir A. D. dined there, yet I find by them that Scot was not so intirely a stranger to that house, as your Severall Letters heretofore lead me to think upon your first discourses with Mr Landry, and the Picard and I therefore could wish that you could gaine me some intelligence that might inform me a little more particularly how much (at most) Scot's acquaintance in that Family did amount to, viz whether he did come often thither, whether he had any Familiarity with Mr Pellissary, whether he did ever dine there and if ever how often, and whether at the table with Mr Pellissary and his Lady, and with any intimacy For in these particulars these Declarations you have sent me are as good as silent, and therefore it being those Declarations that we must found our present belief upon, and not upon what I am to gather out of your former Letters and private Discourses with these people it will be very necessary that I be made more clear therein; For otherwise it will be easy for him to magnify his Intimacy with Mr Pellissary and

[1] Rawl. A. 194 : 42–44. Secretarial copy.

his Family beyond the truth as much as he pleases (since it does appear that he was in some degree knowne to them) and I be wholly unable to disprove him, notwithstanding what in this Letter you say touching Mme Pellissary's Declaring that She never knew, nor to her knowledg Ever saw him.

I thank you for what you bid me expect by the next of further Informations touching Scot, and as to that particular you write me about his Discourse (at his last being there) with one Mr Foster I intreat you by all meanes to discourse further with him upon that subject, and if you can get his declaration of it before a Public Notary (as you did the rest) leading him to be as particular in it as you are able. For against a Lyar the best defence in the world is to obtaine the most you can of his Discourse; because let his memory be never so good, if he gives himselfe the Liberty of talking much he cannot avoid discovering himself. But that which I would more Especially recommend to you is the informing yourself from Mr Foster whether Scot did not let fall to him words of the Same Effect which I find he has to others vizt of his disgust towards me and design of revenging himself upon me by these accusations, for my arraigning him (as he imagines) in parliament of being a Jesuite, and of his running out of England upon the business of the plott; whereas I was indeed the occasion of pursuing a suspicious person about that time out of England upon notice given me of him from Mr. Pierce from Graves End. Which person proved at length to be this very Scott, but I was so farr from knowing it to be him, when the pursuite was made, that I pursued him by the Name of Godfrey that being the Name which he went by at that time at Graves End as at other times I finde he has gone by other Names. Besides that he is to me wholly a stranger as being one whose Name I never knew, nor his person till he came to the Barr of the house of Commons to accuse me. But this (as I understand) he has in some places said, and I beleeve to be the onely real ground of his takeing this Course of injureing me. And therefore pray See whether you can gather any thing to that purpose out of his Discourses to Foster, as also of the particular uses he has made of the D. of B.[1] or Lord S[2] his Names, or one Mr Wentworse's as to any Direction, Advice, Letters or Intelligence he has received from any of them relating to me or my Affairs, or his being Sent for by them over into England and the particular of the time when these Discourses between Scott and Foster did happen. Not leaving out what you say of Scot's telling him that he was carrying over to the D. of B. and Lord S Copies of S. P's Letters to Mr De Signelay.

[1] The Duke of Buckingham.
[2] Lord Shaftesbury, who had previously accused S.P. of having an altar in his house.

Next, for La Piogerie, I am greatly inlightened by you in relation to him, for Scot did, at his last appearance in Court declare that he was Major of the Fleet under Monsieur Destree, as I also find him to have then been in the printed Book of Ordonnances of the king of France relating to the Marine, where he is stiled Le Sieur Heroüard de la Piogerie Major de la Marine de Ponant 1672 Upon which it is of great importance to me to know what the Office of Major de la Marine is, it Seeming by your Discourse to appertaine more to Land then Sea Service, and then it seem's very improbable that Mr De Seignelay should direct these papers to one that was not a sea-man. And I the rather beleeve that if he was any sea-man he was no great one; because he is said never to have been a sea-Commander till the year 1676, and then commanded no bigger ship then the Emerillon which I find was but a Bruslot of 400 Tuns 40 men 24 Guns in the year 1673 commanded by One Monsieur Serpent under Monsieur le Comte Destree. Pray therefore inquire out this a little further, and whether she went in the same Capacity as a fire ship or as a Man of warr to Tabago, when La Piogerie commanded her in the year 1676.

For what you Note concerning La Piogery's not being at Paris in August 1675 Scot declares the same himself and there upon foundes his story of Monsieur De Seignelay's sending the papers to Mr Pellissary to be by him sent to La Piogerie at Rochefort. And yet methink's it should not be hard to find out at Paris some of the acquaintance of La Piogery that might give us some usefull Informations towards the further discovering this villaine's forgeries, by Circumstances relating to this Gentleman La Piogerie.

I take great notice of yours and our Friends opinion touching the Method of addressing to Mr De Seignelay, and shall govern my self by it as you shall find by my next or very suddenly.

Yours of the 6th instant with Sherwin's petition I have received as you will find by my last.

My sister and your Little ones were very well the last night.

Assoon as Will Hewer returnes (he being at this instant out of Towne) I will doe your desires to him.

My Blessing to my Little Godson; and Leaving to you the delevery of the inclosed,[1] I remaine

Your Ever affectionate
Brother and Servant
S P

To Mr St Michell

---

[1] Two notes of acknowledgement from S.P. to M. Trenchepain and M. Pelletier, both in French, dated 18 Aug. 1692 (Rawl. A. 194 : 42).

79. S.P. TO B. ST. MICHEL[1]

York-Buildings August the 25th 1679.

Brother Balty,

My Last was of the 18th in answer to yours of the 13th as this is to another I have this day received from you of the 20th instant with Severall declarations Enclosed of Mr Trenchepain and others, as your other was with those of Madame Pellissary and her family. Upon which latter haveing already given you my answer of thankes and observation in mine of the 18th (together with the like by particular Letters to Mr Trenchepain and Mr Pelletier) I am now to give you my fresh thankes for this of this day, and what further Light it brings me in relation to this Villain that has given me so much trouble. And in particular I observe with satisfaction what you take notice of touching Foster, and will make some inquiry after the Credit of his Evidence for he speakes very fully in a substantiall point about Scot's declaring to him his design of revenge upon me. And therefore as I hear more of Foster, you may expect to hear more of that matter from me.

In the mean time all that remains at present for me to add is, my agreeing with you in what you observe that the principall thing[2] now behind is the business of Mr De Seignelay, about which being now come to a resolution of writting to him myself you may expect the result thereof from me by the next post. Till which, as being just now going to attend his Majesty (who is under some present indisposition, by a feaver, which I beseech God remove) at Windsor, I bid you farewell, and, with my usuall saluts to Mr Trenchepain and Mr pelletier, remaine

Your truely affectionate Brother and Servant

S P

My sister and Little ones were well yesterday.

To Mr St. Michell

80. S.P. TO B. ST. MICHEL[3]

York-Buildings August the 28th 1679

Brother Balty,

My last was of the 25th in answer to yours of the 20th instant. Since which I have yours of the 23th giving me a large and very wel-

---

[1] Rawl. A. 194: 44–45. Secretarial copy.   [2] *point*, canc.
[3] Rawl. A. 194: 45–47. Secretarial copy.

come account of your finding and discoursing with Sherwin, and
your purpose of taking the substance thereof in writing before a
Publick Notary as the rest have been, hoping that you will do it as
expressly and particularly as you can in all matters of truth wherein
you can be informed by him not onely with reference to the matters
you have already from him but what further particulars he may by
his intimacy with Scot be inabled to inform you. Among which one
usefull one may be the business of his Gun-founding mentioned in
one of the last papers you sent me. For I have heard that among the
rest of rogueries one was his invegling some of Prince Rupert's[1]
workmen imployd in his new Invention about Guns and carrying
them into France, where he offer'd to discover and manage the same
for that King and made shift to cheate not onely those that imploy'd
him but the poor workmen that he carryed over with him. Of which
I know not how much is true, but would be glad to learn, and by my
finding his Name in Manning's Paper to guess that he may know
that Matter or, which is better, direct us to some others that doe,
For not onely a further proof of his knaveries will be obtain'd by it
but of his interesting himself in the Crime he would charge me with
of Serving the king of France.

And pray see whether he cannot direct us to persons that may in-
lighten us in any other parts of his infamous history, and let me also
know what stay he meanes to make in France, and whether I may
expect him here in England within a month or 2 at the furthest.
Which if I cannot, it will the more import mee to get his help in
directing me to any others that will be here upon the place able to
give any usefull evidence in this affair. Not that I shall omitt discoursing with Captain Gunman, but the Law puts little force upon any
report but those of the first hand.

Which having Said as to Sherwin, let me desire the Same of you as
to Foster, for he may also direct us to people that may be able to add
to our knowledge of Scott. But of this Foster, I beleeve I may say
more in my next, after I have had My Lady Pratt's account of him.

I could also wish that since nothing can be authentically had of
that of Scott's Conversation with the Benedictin Monks, it not standing with their methods to give the same attestations of matters of
fact, which Laymen do, and possibly it is never a whit the worse (for

---

[1] Prince Rupert's biographers are silent upon his dealings with Scot or Sherwin or this
French group. Eliot Warburton mentions: 'He also became a partner in several specula-
tions, one of which was the exercise of a patent for boring cannon by the agency of a water-
mill, and annealing gun-metal in glass-house.' *Memoirs of Prince Rupert and the Cavaliers*,
London, R. Bentley, 1849, iii. 494.

A holograph letter in French from Scot to Mlle Des Moulins mentions Prince Rupert
by name in connexion with the French project. 1675 (Rawl. A. 188: 168–72).

I know not what use I could with safety make of their attestations if I had them) yet for as much as the English Benedictins at Paris, as well as those here, are said to have been very active in this plott, I could wish (I say) that his Conversation and dealings with those Monks at Paris could (if true) be evidenced by any other hand, for I should think that better, then by the Monkes themselves, and if in truth he had any such dealings with them, I doubt not but the same must have come to the Observation of others as well as them.

What remains further for me to say to you at present (as not being yet enough prepared for Mr De Seignelay) is the praying that in order to the preventing any oversights on your part of any of the particulars which I have from the beginning of this affair recommended to you; and that you might have the whole in your view before your coming away, which I presume will not be long after your applications shall be made to Mr De Seignelay, you would once for all overlook all my Letters and (comparing the Same with the answers and papers which I have had from you) collect what you shall find to remain, either not at all (if there be any such thing) or imperfectly answered, and See the Same Supplied as soon as you can.

And for as much as it may behoove me that Some persons be gott hither, that their Evidences of the truth may be given Viva voce in Court (which from the chargeableness of it ought nevertheless to be as few as may be) I desire you to consider and give me advice who you think may be obtained on that account, and particularly in relation to Madame Pellissary's Family to justify Scott's not being intimate there, nor being there at all either in publick or private the day when the Entertainment was.

And it would also be of use to learn what English protestant Gentlemen now there are at Paris, who may probably be in England within 6 weeks or 2 monthes at the furthest; for it would doe mighty well, if some or other of them could be brought to discourse particularly with the people of that family, and thereby be inabled to evidence the truth of the Same at their coming into England. Which recommending to you I remain

Your affectionate Brother and Servant
S P

My just saluts to Mr Trenchepain and Mr Pelletier
To Mr St. Michell

81. S.P. TO JOHN PEPYS SENIOR[1]

London. August the 30th, 1679

Sir,

Though it pleased God to allow of my obtaining at length so much justice from the Court as to become Master of my Liberty upon bayle till the next Term; yet it does not give me such a freedom as to ease me of my Cares, for the defending my Selfe against what new attempts my Adversary and his Upholders may make upon me, when they shall receive fresh encouragement (as they Seem to hope) from the Countenance of some persons in the approaching parliament. Which I take notice of to you, not that either I have or would have you entertain any fears concerning the issues of any accusations that Either have or can be brought against me; for (I thank God) I have alwaies carried[2] about me Such a watchfulness and Integrity as will Support me, (with God's assistance), against any thing that the Malice of Mankind can offer to my prejudice; but onely to excuse to you my being yet no frequenter in my Letters, which nevertheless I should be if any thing of my Concernments or health should happen extraordinary to give me occasion of writing to you, which neither has nor does now, unless it be to let you know that during the great Sickliness of the present season, I am (I bless God) in a perfect state of health, and do think long to hear that you and your family are the same.

I doe not forget my undertaking to my Sister to make you a visite before the end of Summer, but will labour to order it so (if it be possible,) that I may do it when the King is at New-markett,[3] as being willing to save a double Journey if I can, and to be as little absent from hence as may be. And this I fully hope to doe; the King's Illness, which lately threatened the contrary, being, (God be praised,) in a great degree over, and he under the same purpose as before of going to New-Markett.

Which, with the Tender of my most humble duty to you, and true Love to my Sister and her Family, together with the begging of your Blessing, is all at present from

Honoured Sir
Your ever dutifull son
S P

To My Father

[1] Rawl. A. 194 : 47. Secretarial copy.   [2] *I am alwaies carrying*, canc.
[3] Charles II often required S. P. and other advisers to accompany him to the races at Newmarket.

82. S.P. TO B. ST. MICHEL[1]

September the 1st 1679.

Brother Balty,

My last was of the 28th in answer to yours of the 23th of August. Since which I have your other of the 27th for which I very kindly thank you as being a large and carefull summing up of the severall particulars of my demands to you and a Comparing of them with your replies. Which being many I shall not at present make you any other return to them then the telling you, that however I may seem in any point less satisfied then you might expect or could wish I doe assure it's farr from arising from any thoughts of your haveing done less or with less success then you might have done. For I am to the fullest degree satisfied with your Care, diligence and discretion exprest on this occasion. But when you consider the strictness of our Lawes, perfidiousness of my Adversary and the public prejudice my Cause and I doe at present lye under, you will forgive me, if I seem a little more importunate with you, then on another less important occasion I should and ought to be, and therefore as I have advised you to doe in my last I shall, according to your advice to me in this, overhall all that has past between you and me, and give you the result thereof in writting, wherein you shall have the plain and express terms, what ever I shall have to desire of you, beyond what you have already furnisht me with; observing this onely in the mean time, that though what Mr Trenchepain and the other Gentlemen doe testify, of what Sherwin and Foster tell them, of what they heard from Scot, may in our private Judgments convince you and me; yet so remote an evidence as that (which is only a hearsay of a hearsay) will never convince, or be suffer'd so much as to be read in Court.

And therefore though our Cause be in itselfe never so innocent it may never the less very well miscarry if we do not labour as much as we can to support it by witnesses of the first hand, and not Such as are so remote.

As for my delay in sending you letters to Mr De Seignelay I do not onely excuse, but thank you for your earnestness therein. But my friends and I are very doubtfull of the ill-consequences that may happen from my applying my Selfe to him at all, especially in a Cause wherein the right which I am labouring to obtain from him may be perverted to the doing me the greatest wrong. In so much that some of my friends are of opinion to let all Negotiation with Mr De Seignelay alone and trust God Almighty with the success of our other evidences onely. Do not therefore impute it to any delay or want of

---

[1] Rawl. A. 194: 48–49. Secretarial copy.

care of my owne concernments that I am so long in my determinations in this matter For I am at this very time at a stand againe about
it, and forbeare to send the Letters I had prepared for you by this post
untill I have further advised upon it.

Walbank tell's me that My Lady Pratt does owne Mr Foster for
her Brother and that he is supplied with monies from her and his
Friends here. So as you may make use of your relation to him in
getting what further informations you can from him.

Pray consider what I have wrote you touching your finding out
what English persons of credit (whether of the Court or others) are
likely to come for England within a month or 6 weeks. That I may
get some of them to hear some of the most valuable of our witnesses
declare the truth of their knowledge in this matter to them Viva
voce in order to their being able to evidence the same in Court, when
they returne hither.

Lastly, I am extremely sorry to find my little Godson infirme in
his health, and doe agree with you for your bringing him over into
England when you come, as being more perswaded of the necessity
of it, by the account you give me of the charge of keeping him longer
there, which I am sure the condition you are at present in, will not
be able to beare. Therefore you may be putting things in order for
his Coming with you, forbearing alsoe the trouble and charge of
looking out for a Tutor for him in France; for as much as I conceive
that that may be much better and cheaper provided for here, of which
I shall say more to you before your Coming away. In the mean time
letting you know that my Sister and your Little ones are in health
here, I remaine

Your truely affectionate Brother and servant
S P

To Mr St Michell

83. S.P. TO B. ST. MICHEL[1]

September the 4th 1679.

Brother Balty,

My last was of the 1st instant in answer to yours of the 27th of
August. Since which I have yours of the 30th ditto, and returne you
my kind thanks for it, it giveing me in the first place (from Mr. Foster's
naming Mr Wentworth and Sir Francis Rolls) to beleeve that he is
very well acquainted with Scot and his affairs, they being the persons

[1] Rawl. A. 194: 49–50. Secretarial copy.

that I did most suspect to be his patrons, and therefore I am in great hopes that you may prevaile with him to give you further informations concerning him, that may be usefull to me, and that he will let you have it in the same authenticall manner which others have done; it being hard to think, that in a Case where nothing but Truth is demanded, a Gentleman, and one to whom you seem to have some relation, should make difficulty of doing us that Justice which we every where meet with from strangers. Pray therefore use all fitting earnestnesses to obtaine a declaration from him of what he personally knows of truth concerning this villain, not omitting this of his having acknowledged his being Supported against me by the two Lords and the 2 Gentlemen you mention; observing to me whether Mr Foster be a Roman Catholick or protestant, and the like concerning the person you have last met with Monsieur Dallié, whose being a French-man makes me apprehensive of his being also a Romanist. However he being a witness not of my choice, but of Scot's owne making, I can not see that his Popery can be brought to prejudice my Cause, and therefore pray pursue your inquiries with him as farr as you are able. For if he has been such a privado of Scot as you understand him to be I make no doubt but he is able to unravle, not onely all his rogueries in generall but that which relates to me in particular, or at least so much of it, as may prove some thing and give me light into more. But then on the other hand, as this intimacy of his with Scot must have made him privy to his villanies so may it justly lead us to Some Suspicions of his own honesty; and therefore I doe greatly approve of the Caution you seem to have about you in your treatings with him. Wherein indeed you are to be alwaies upon your Guard indeavouring as much as you can to have creditable witnesses by of all that passes between you and taking the advice of our Friends in all your proceedings therein avoyding as much as is possible the making him any offers of reward or incouragement, either before or after the Cause shall be determined, otherwise then for a just satisfaction to be given him for the reasonable charges of his Journeys hither and home againe, and his time spent therein. Less then which no man can reasonably offer him. And more then that (if what he does, be out of a principle of honesty) he will not offer at the making condition before hand for it. And in this method of proceeding with him, and pressing him to nothing but the discovery of the truth (which I doe again conjure you, whatever be my fate, not to transgress in, either with him, or any other you shall have to deale with in this affair) we must trust God Almighty with the Event. For what is allowed for good in our proceedings upon the publick plott, cannot (I conceive) be excepted against in the Case of a private one, namely, to make an

honest use of one villain to discover the iniquity of another. I leave
therefore to your discretion, with the advice of our Friends with you,
to go on in your discourses with this man, and as you find his informations to be of moment answerable to what he pretends himself
capable of giving you, proceed to the incourageing him to come over
when it shall be required of him. Though, if it were possible, I could
rather wish I could myself have an account from you of the import
of his informations, before you imbark yourself into a bargain with
him for the charges of his coming over. for indeed the expence which
this fellowes wickedness has and is likely to put me to is very hard to
be conceive[d]; besides the trouble and reproach which at present
does also accompany it to my self and Friends.

My last gave you an account of the fresh doubtfulnesses I was
under touching what relates to Mr De Seignelay, which I am not
yet rid of. But will one way or other bring it to a finall issue very
speedily, and advise you of it. In the mean time referring you for
other matters to my former, I remain

Your truely affectionate Brother to serve you

S P

My sister and family (blessed be God) are in health.

To Mr St Michell

84. S.P. TO B. ST. MICHEL[1]

York-Buildings, September the 11th 1679.

Brother Balty,

My two last were of the 1st and 4th instant. Since which (vizt
last night) I have received yours of the 6/16th, and am indeed truely
sensible of your very great diligence in my affaire and do not doubt to
enjoy the Benefit which you design me by it, but hope I may be
again in condition of letting you and your Family receive some fruits
also therefrom to your advantage.

I am at a great loss what to advise concerning Sherwin, it being, as
you very well note, a mighty tender point, I meane, the furnishing
him with money, though upon never so just an account; it being so
liable to misconstruction. I therefore will respite the determining any
thing in it till I have better advice upon it, which I hope to have
against the new post; wishing onely that I had some plainer Characters given me of him, as to his quality, and manner of liveing, and who
there is here that could give me any knowledge of him. For as he has

---

[1] Rawl. A. 194: 51. Secretarial copy.

more or less the reputation of an honest man I should reckon my selfe the more Safe in our negotiating with him, it being not enough in this age, and in the company I am fallen into, to have the innocence of a Dove, without some mixture of the Serpent's prudence. Besides, that I finde Scot has his Spyes upon my inquirys in Holland, and I doubt not but he has Craft enough to have the Same in France.

And one thing more let me observe to you, that it is not Sherwin's, or any other man's Evidence of Scot's ill language towards the King, that will doe me good; but as it is joyn'd with proof of his villanous practices in this particular Case, which relates to me, and therefore to that point must principally be directed the forces of the Evidences we are to labour after. Not but that the others joyned with this will be also in some degree usefull; especially if his faults against His Majesty and the Government shall appear by deeds, as well as in the undutifulness of his discourses.

My Lady Pratt was very lately out of towne, but I will instantly inquire where she now is, and endeavour to get the letter you desire.

Though I have in my last said enough of my present thoughts and cares about Monsieur de Seignelay, and am no less impatient then you can be, till I come to some prudent issue concerning him; yet I cannot but note that your zeale therein seemes to be founded upon a very great mistake. For instead of the World's receiving their fullest Satisfaction from him; his evidence would (as the World is now bent) give me more prejudice in the opinion of the Publick, then any thing that could be offer'd; and the more, by how much that Evidence of his were more in my justification. That therefore which makes me think it of so much moment is the regard I have to the particular Satisfaction of the King my Master, from whom I may expect all impartiality of Judgement, and then I doubt not but the account I may expect from Monsieur de Seignelay will be such, and so cleare (if he be a man of that truth and Justice, which he is reported to be) as will doe me full right in the King's opinion, whose good thoughts of me, I had rather dye under, then live to have the good opinion of the rabble purchased by one ill deed, or thought.

As to the business of getting some witnesses to come over hither in person, I doe greatly approve of your care in what you say about Monsieur Trenchepain, and the other Gentlemen, who have been witnesses to the papers you have sent me; but I must pray you still to remember that one witness Vivâ voce is more then 50 hear-say; and that therefore it will be necessary to consider, whether any of Madame Pellissary's family, or the rest, whose Testimonies, you have Sent me in paper, can (if need be) be gott to come over. Which I recommend extraordinarily to you.

I greatly thanke you for your explanation of the business of Manning's Challenge, and would with all my heart know where Manning is, and whether he may become to be spoken with.

I also greatly thanke you for what you write about Mr Filding, whom I shall expect. As for what concernes my Nephew Samuell, concerning him I gave you my thoughts and Advice in mine of the 1st instant, whereto I referr you, and remaine

Your truely affectionate
brother to Serve you
S P

To Mr St. Michell

85. S.P. TO B. ST. MICHEL[1]

Westminster, September the 18th 1679

Brother Balty,

My last was of the 11th instant, answering yours of the 6/16th. Since which, being prevented the last post, I have 2 of yours to answer, namely, of the 10th and 13th, whereto, by the attendance I am at this time to give upon His Majesty and the Duke, as being just now come from Windsore, I Shall not be able to make that large reply which I otherwise might doe. Nevertheless without any unnecessary repetitions of my generall satisfaction in the dilligence and care you daily express in my concerns, nedding noe fresh professions of kindness on your part, I must in this express a more particular degree of satisfaction in the paper you send me from Mr Joyne under Scot's owne hand, which contain's severall matters very usefull and bring their owne Evidence with them. I wish to God we could gett some more such, they being (I say) very usefull and of credit without exception. Pray therefore cherish your acquaintance with Mr Joyne and improve it to my benefitt by getting him to look up any more papers he has of like kind in his hands, as farr as honestly you can. For as hard as you think of it, the Law is not to be disputed but obeyd, and therefore we must labour to gett such evidences as our Laws will accept of, among which Writtings are a principall. And such will Sherwin's testimony be if he comes over, as Mr Filding (who very civilly gave me your letter and a visite yesterday) tell's me, he very suddenly will; though others, I find, are of another opinion, as Suspecting that he dares not, upon the Score of his fowle play (as is said) with Prince Rupert, about the Guns.

Besides, I am told, that Monsieur Le Febure the King's Apothe-

---

[1] Rawl. A. 194: 55–57. Secretarial copy.

cary (a protestant) is at this time at Paris, and by a Letter, which I may possibly send you by the next, to adress you to him, I doubt not but he will be ready to doe me any good Office in company with you, that may inable him to give his testimony therein, at his returne hither, which, I am told, is likely to be time enough for my using it. As Mr Dulivier (whom I presume you know) a merchant of London, might and would have done, had it been thought on; he being lately come from Paris with an English Gentleman of my acquaintance; both of whom would most readily have done mee any Service. Againe, pray faile not, to recover (if possible by Mr Joyne, or from some Correspondent of his at Nevers, the precise time when Scot came from thence to Paris. For I find that he was at Nevers the beginning of August 1675 and in October following. Whereas, if his accusations be true, he must have been at Paris about the middle or 20th of August. Therefore, without declaring to any body the reasons of your inquiry, pray labour effectually, to collect the very time of his coming to Paris from Nevers, that it may certainly appear to us, whether he was indeed at Paris any time within the month of August 1675, and how much, it being of extraordinary importance to me to be able to know and prove it. And methinks either by Joyne, Mademoiselle De Moulins, or by some papers, letters or accounts the certainty of that particular may be found out.

And pray inquire too, whether Scot did appeare publicly and openly in Paris at his last being there; or whether he Sculked up and downe incognito; Some people telling me that his knaverys about the Guns and the multitude of his debts are such as would make him a prisoner, if he were know[n] to be there.

But that which I have principally to observe to you at this time is for the easing you of your paine about Monsieur Denize, his writting to Paris having been wholly in my favour, and done before I had opportunity, or indeed thought it necessary, to acquaint him with your being already at worke there. And so usefull I find him on this Occasion, that I am sorry with all my heart I thought no sooner of him, he being a Protestant, as well as acquainted with the Court of France, and the Officers of the French Navy, and in himselfe a very honest man, of very good Credit, and one whom upon these Considerations I should think the fittest for me to imploy into France if (as you seem to advise) it shall be judged necessary to send one. And I am greatly inclined to think that that will be much more effectuall, and in every respect better then to bring over such Gentlemen of business, as Mr Trenchepain, Monsieur Pelletier and others, to attend here for a time uncertain, onely to give Evidence of what they know from other men; and as to Mr Trenchepain I find by his letters to Mr Houblon that his affaires will in noe wise give him leave to come over. Therefore pray forbeare to putt him or any of the rest into any apprehensions of my being likely to desire it of them; it being a thing very unfitt for me to ask, Since it may as well (I beleeve) bee Supply'd by Sending one over from Hence to France; and if I can gett him, I doe[1] think Mr Denise will be the properest man I can send, he being personally acquainted with Madame Pellissary and her familly, and all [or] most of the persons I have yet heard named, from whom I am to expect information or aide. But of this I shall by the next say a little more, and in the meantime tell you, that having acquainted him with your being now at Paris before yours of the 10th came to me he expresst great Satisfaction, and of his owne accord brought me a letter from himself to you with Severall others he addresses you to for information upon his Score. Which having wrote, before (I say) yours came to me, you will finde that had yours come sooner, part of what he has wrote might have been Spared. However I send them all inclosed,[2] and commend them to your care to Seale and dispose of, as upon reading you shall find convenient. Onely let me advise you to respite the making use of anything that he has wrote Towards Mr De Seignelay, till you hear further from me, Which I now think, you may depend upon by the next. And that you may the better understand the grounds of his present writting, I doe here Send you, Copys of what he received from Monsieur De Brulis and Monsieur Houdan, in answer to his 1st to them on this affaire; by which you have all before you; it being very late, I cannot now say more, but shall supply it in my next, remaining

Your most affectionate
Brother to serve you
S P

To Mr St Michell

86. S.P. TO B. ST. MICHEL[3]

September the 25th 1679

Brother Balty,

My last was of [the] 18th instant in answer to yours of the 10th and 13th both which were very wellcome, and particularly the later[4]

---

[1] *doubt*, canc.

[2] Copies of letters in French from C. Denise to persons who had known either Scot or La Piogerie, the latter referred to as M. le Major Heroward dit la Piogerie: Mr. St. Michel, M. de Brulis, M. Houdan, M. De La Fontaine, M. De La Haye. M. Paul Sevenhuisen, M. de Gastigny. (Rawl. A. 194: 52–55.)

[3] Rawl. A. 194: 59–62. Secretarial copy.   [4] *last*, canc.

containing the originall Papers under Scot's hand, but yet not more wellcome then your last of the 20th bringing me the most satisfactory papers from Mr Joyne, with his particular letter to my Selfe, for which I doe by you returne him my very Serious thankes and will doe it under my owne hand by the next, my attendance on His Royall Highness,[1] who is imbarked this day back againe for Flanders (as the Duke of Monmouth did yesterday for Utrecht) not permitting mee to doe it now. Pray therefore doe you doe it (I say) in the mean time most earnestly, the evidence he gives not deserving it onely upon the Score of the benefit which may arise from it to Sir A D and mee, but from the frankness thereof without private interest or temptation, but upon the Single Score of his love to justice, which is a vertue at this time very valuable in England, whatever it is in France. And in particular pray let him know that I doe most thankfully owne and accept of his kind offer of coming into England for the evidencing of the truth here, and doe accept of it with the more satisfaction in the regard that the time he had proposed for his coming over with respect to his owne occasions, will agree very well with mine, that is to say, for his being in England about 3 weekes hence, when you alsoe will be upon your returne, by the Grace of God, with very good effects of your Journey to us, who are concern'd therein. In the mean time what I have now principally to Say to you is, that Sir A D and I have upon further thoughts judged it most convenient in every respect, to proceed according to your late advice in sending over Monsieur Denise, who, with Mr Joyne and you, will (if there be noe more) be sufficient witnesses in all that we shall have need of testimonies from abroad, touching onely reports. Not but that I feare there will be a necessity of bringing over one or 2, particularly Sherwin and some one of Mme Pellissary's Family to give their personall Evidence in what they can say of their owne knowledge. But on this and every thing else, you may expect my advice very largely by Mr Denise, who designes to sett out from hence with the Post on Monday next. By whom alsoe I will write to Mr Trenchepain and Mr Pelletier, to both of whom it would be a much greater trouble to be brought from their Occasions at this time of the year into England without any knowledg to be had before hand within what time they may depend upon being dispatch'd back againe, then is in any wise fit for mee to expect from them, or I could ever look to be in a condition of makeing them suitable ameands for. Besides the infinite care and

---

[1] James, Duke of York, exiled to Holland under pressure of the forces which had also caused the accusation of Pepys, had been recalled temporarily in August when Charles II was ill. Upon the king's recovery, it was found difficult to remove James. Finally he was made High Commissioner for Scotland and was persuaded to return to Brussels for his wife, on the promise that Monmouth would be exiled to Holland.

charge I should be necessarily involved in of treating them for soe long time here as their Quality and my obligations to them would require; which I must againe pray you to have some regards to; especially when the Office they are soe kindly to doe for me may be noe less effectually perform'd by others at much less Cost.

I observe what you say concerning Mr Wentworth and shall suspend my makeing any hard judgment of him till I see further into the truth and ground of his intimacy with Scot.

A most essential peece yet to be done is the getting Some thing declar'd from Mme Pillissary's family touching the little familiarity they had with Scot; all that has been yet vouch'd under their hands before a Notary as to that point (besides what has past between you in private talk) amounting to noe more then that he did not dine there that day when Sir A D did, which does not hinder but that it may be understood, he had din'd there often enough at other times.

And I find that Mr Joyne him selfe does owne that Scot and his Company of Gunfounders did once breakfast there together with Monsieur Pellissary him selfe notwithstanding what the Picard and others have told you of Scot's being wholly unknowne to them. Pray therefore when Monsieur Denise is come, who is very well acquainted with Mme Pellissary, and will, I doubt not, have my affaire recommended to her, and her Civilitys to mee acknowledg'd by Mr De Ruvigny, have especiall regard to the getting this defect Supply'd.

Monsieur Denise will alsoe bring with him my last resolution touching Mr De Seignelay, to which I shall referr you; it being a matter very nicely to be handled, especially where I need his assistance so little, as I now hope I shall be subject to, and that assistance of his soe hard to be securely made use of if I had it.

Pray be you your selfe very industrious in the considering the severall points of Mr Joyne's information in order to your understanding the whole history of them, as farr as you can learn it from him, in any circumstances either not at all, or not fully express'd in his paper, whereof I hope you have a Copy.

I long to heare of your recovering Some more originall papers of Scot's, from Mr Joyne, which pray intreat him to look for, with all the strictness he can, and if by any meanes he can, to find out (as I desir'd in my last) whether he was indeed at Paris the 21th of August 1675 (the Day of Sir A D's dining at Monsieur Pellissary's) it appearing under his owne hand, that he was at Nevers the 5th of that month.

Consider alsoe with Mr Joyne, whether there be noe way of recovering any of his Mapps and Charts and a knowledge[1] of what became of that large one, which Mr Joyne saw him carry to St

---

[1] Ms. *acknowledge of.*

Germains. Hopes alsoe I have that among Mr de la Piogerie's papers some thing of Scot's hand may be found, and possibly Mlle Des Moulins, may help you in that point likewise, there being nothing that will carry more evidence with it, then any thing that can be found under his hand. Bills alsoe and Bonds, Contracts, Acquittances, or ought else that he has sign'd to for money or on other occasions may be usefull to us, as I doubt not but Mr Joyne, as well as others, may have his hand to prove the Summs wherein he stands indebted to them. And very much doe I wonder, (as I observ'd in my last) how he has been able to appear at Paris, after the practices which I find layd to his charge by Monsieur Le Goux, Mr Joyne and others, and for which he is said to have been forced to fly.

Lastly, I doe again owne to you the extraordinary importance of this last business of Mr Joyne's Evidence, wherein you have given mee a noe less extraordinary instance, both of your Kindness, Care and good Conduct, and a God's Blessing to mee upon all; it being with the additions of what we have and are likely to have more, I doubt not, Sufficient[1] to confound this infamous villain, and doe right to Our innocences.

But one thing I must observe to you with a little wonder, that you should take noe notice neither to mee nor Will Hewer of the Summs of money that I understand from other hands you have been supply'd with to a considerable value, by Mr Trenchepain, besides what you have drawne upon Will Hewer himselfe. By which I have been wholly unable to make offer at repaying the Same as I ought from time to time have done. Whereof, pray faile not to give mee some account in your next, and consider againe what I have heretofore pressed you to of makeing this unfortunate Business as easy to mee in it's charge as you are able, in what concern's your management. Soe letting you know that my sister and her Family are in good health, I remaine

Your affectionate
Brother to serve you

To Mr St. Michell　　　　　　　　　　　　　　　　　　　　S. P.

87. S.P. TO B. ST. MICHEL[2]

September the 29th 1679.

Brother Balty,

My last was of the 25th instant wherein, among other things, I advised you according to your late proposall, that I design'd, by this

---

[1] A redundant *will . . . be* deleted here by editor.
[2] Rawl. A. 194: 62–63. Secretarial copy.

Post, to dispatch away Mr Denise[1] to joyn with you in the attesting such declarations as have already, and may further be necessary to have made at Paris in my affaire, and thereby not onely save a great deale of charge and trouble of bringing over Witnesses on purpose for that use, but be further assisting to you in compleating and perfecting all that is now to be done, and will require to be dispatch'd with all diligence in the business wherein you have made soe great and unexpected an advancement, to my extraordinary satisfaction, and alsoe of Sir A Deane's who recommend[s] him selfe in particular by mee to you with his thankes in an especiall manner for that which you lately mentioned concerning him, and in which he bid's mee tell you that you need not to be under any care in relation to that matter, for nothing ever passed, either in discourse or other wayes between Monsieur De Seignelay and him, that can give any rise to that suggestion, or can give either him or me any trouble.

Now, that you may know throughly all that remaines behind for Sir A D, or mee to desire from you, and wherein Monsieur Denise's assistance (who is a very honest man, a man of great diligence, discretion, and your Friend as well as Ours) may bee very usefull in regard of the muchness of the Worke, and Shortness of the time; wee have overhall'd the whole business in every parte of it, and collected into Severall distinct heads in writting all the Points, wherein wee desire Satisfaction; one Copy of Which[2] Monsieur Denise has, and we here inclose another to you; desireing (for your more strict execution thereof, and knowing from time to time your advancement therein) that you would each of you cause the Same to be forthwith transcrib'd with a blank left against each article; and as the Same are perform'd cause the performance thereof to be entred in the Said blank.

I doe alsoe send you a Copy of the heads of Scot's accusation against us, in French, in the termes wherein they have been delivered to the French Ambassador here and will be in the joynt letter, which Sir A D and I have resolved to send to Monsieur De Seignelay to be deliver'd by you and Monsieur Denise to him, without any letter from any other persons, as thinking it (upon long consideration) neither convenient nor necessary in the condition, which by your care, and God's Providence our business is brought into; we being under noe want (Nor could make use, if we had it) of any Justif[ic]ation from Mr De Seignelay him selfe (that is to say in the Court where our Cause is to be tryed) but that which we expect from him

---

[1] From S.P. to C. Denise, 29 Sept. 1679 (Rawl. A. 194: 70) a copy in English: 'In fine, I commit my whole affaire to you and my Brother, and both you, and it, to God Almighty.'   [2] *Such*, canc,

to be of any use to us is, the helping us to some other sort of Evidences, either by papers, or persons that may conduct to the clearing of our innocence without makeing any use of his Name. Wee therefore leave the Season and manner of delivering that letter[1] to him, and what others Mr Denise bring's from us to Mr De Ruvigny, Mr Colbert, Mr Mignon,[2] to you two, and the solliciting for the effects thereof. Which recommending to you, and referring you for other Particulars to another of this date, which I shall alsoe putt into the hands of Mr Denise before his departure. I remaine

Your truely affectionate
Brother to serve you
S P

To Mr St Michell

88. S.P. TO B. ST. MICHEL[3]

London September 29th 1679

Brother Balty,

I have already wrote you in another which you will receive herewith by the hands of Mr Denise. Whereto, haveing received nothing from you by the last post, what I have to add is in the 1st place to repeat to you my acknowledgments of the satisfaction which I have receiv'd from you in the whole Conduct of my affaire, and more particularly in your 2 last, which one would think (had I noe other evidence) were enough to render all that that Villain Scot can say, of noe credit among sober men. Such nevertheless is the Credulity of this unhappy Age to reports that are in any kind partiall to the side that prevailes, that noe accumulation of evidence can be too much to justify the most obvious Truth; and therefore I dare not let goe the Hint you lately gave mee, of sending one into France to joyn with you in taking, and bringing over the Attestations of such persons as cannot either at all, or without too much charge and trouble be conveigh'd hither Vivâ voce. To which end Mr Denise now comes, who has already given mee great proof of his Capacity and willingness to Serve mee in this Affaire; and has been the rather pitcht upon by mee, for the same, upon the score of his Credit here, and his being soe friendly a Wisher to, and soe well thought on by you.

---

[1] A long letter in French from S.P. and A. Deane jointly to M. de Seignelay, 29 Sept. 1679. (Rawl. A. 194: 63–64.)

[2] The Rawlinson Collection, vol. 194, contains letters in French from S.P. and A. Deane jointly to: M. de Ruvigny (65); Mgr Colbert (64–65); M. Mignon (65); and M. de Vauvre (66).   [3] Rawl. A. 194 : 68–70. Secretarial copy.

What the particulars are wherein Sir A D and I doe now expect the fruites of this your joynt care, I have given you most distinctly in my other, whereto I referr you, without any mention thereof againe here, more then the recommending to you most especially that which concern's the providing one or 2 Substantiall Witnesses (if possible) to prove the little acquaintance which Scot had with Mr Pellissary and in [his] family in generall, as well as that in particular he was not in Mr Pellissary's house, much less din'd there, either publikly or privately, upon the day soe much spoken of.

And here let me observe, that as I doe againe recommend to you and Mr Denise all good husbandry consistent with the well doing of the business you are about; soe I doe in particular desire you to express it as much as you can in the secureing those witnesses soe as we may have them when we need, and shall send for them, without bringing over more along with you (which I design may be before the 23th of October the 1st day of the Term) then what seem otherwise disposed to have come, if this occasion had not happnd vizt Mr Joyne and Sherwin. And I could wish that Mr Foster could bee here alsoe, that we might have two good witnesses to those words, of Scot's declaring his purpose of being revenged of mee for accusing him of being a Jesuite. For I doe not find that any body declares that particularly but onely Joyne and Foster, which would be of great moment to mee to have well prov'd.

The gathering alsoe (as I have elsewhere observed to you) of every Scrip of paper of Scot's owne writting that can be found, would be of great use, let it be almost of what Subject it would.

As to Mr Joyne, I cannot enough express the Content I have in the fulness of his report, and the ingenuity of his giving it, upon the onely consideration of doeing right to the innocence of one man, against the wrong done it by another whom hee knowes to bee a Villain. And this the more, in that upon inquiry I find his father to bee a man of Substantiall Credit in proportion to his quality, as you tell mee his Son alsoe is in reference to his. Pray therefore give him my very kind acknowledgements, with the letter[1] I inclose you to him, telling him that I have this day Spoken with Mr Browne, who answer's his desires very readily and respectfully, and seem's very desirous of seeing him here, that they might together entertain one another with the Historys of that fellowes villanies, which hee tell's mee, they have been soe often witnesses of.

As for Sir Elys Leyton, he is a person of such a fame, that though his acquaintance with Scot could noe doubt inable him to inform

---

1 Rawl. A. 194: 67. S.P. thanks Joyne for his 'love of justice' and his services, an makes plans for his coming to England to give evidence.

mee much concerning him; I am not very desirous of meddling with him, unless there were more need of it, then I hope there will be.

But among other of Scot's familiars, I find Dr Fitz-Gerald, (whom Mr Evelyn of Depthford, as you remember, recommended us to, when your poor Sister[1] and we were in France) is one, and being a Catholick, I doe not know but he may bee able to give you some light into the business of Scot's Profession in Religion, if not in other things; and therefore I leave it to you, to find him out, or let it alone as you see fit.

I shall by the next post provide some fresh Credits to Mr Trenchepain for money, upon occasion of Monsieur Denise his Coming over to you, by whom I have addressed a letter of acknowledgment to him, and another to Mr Pelletier, sending them both open, as I doe all the rest, that you may peruse them before delivery. Among which is one to Mr Savell without date, leaving it to you to give it that, when you shall judge it expedient to be deliver'd.[2]

Which haveing said as to my owne affaire, which I recommend to your diligence with a great relyance upon that, and God's Blessing for good success, I shall now as to your owne let you know that I cannot but still think it very great improvidence to imbark your selfe into the Standing Charge of bringing a Tutor for my Nephew from France (which is the uttermost Circumstance of Greatnesse that Sir John Bankes or any man of 5 or 6000 £ per annum can enter upon) before you can have a more certain view of the Condition you may be in to beare it, then under the present State of my affaires, I can give you. And therefore, though I would not have you despair of my Godson's being kept in such a manner as that he may not loose the benefitt of the Education you have hitherto endeavour'd to give him; yet soe farr I would have you to think of conforming your selfe for a Change in your fortune Suitable to what I doe in mine, as not to proceed further at present in the entertainment of a French Tutor, then to the finding out and treating with one upon terms that may be to your satisfaction, and his, in Case your occasions shall within any certain time (to bee agreed by you) invite you to send for him over after your and the Child's arrivall here. Which, with the assurance of my faithfull respect and affection to you and to your family, is all at present from

Your truely affectionate
Brother to serve you
S P

To Mr. St Michell

---

[1] i.e. S.P.'s wife.

[2] Letters mentioned are in Rawl. A. 194: to M. Trenchepain, in French (66); to M. Pelletier, in French (66); to H. Savile, in English (67).

89. S.P. TO B. ST. MICHEL[1]

London October the 2d 1679

Brother Balty,

My last were 2 of the 29th of September both by the hands of Mr Denise, which I hope will reach you long before this, and containing in them largely and distinctly all that I had before mee to Say to you upon the business that has given you and us all Soe much trouble I have nothing new yet to add as haveing had nothing from you by the 2 last posts. However, I will not omitt to give you the advice of Mr Denise's being gone towards you from hence on monday last, and I hope to see you both and him Shortly back againe to the compleating of that justification of mine which you have made so happy an advance in.

In expectation whereof I cannot at present think of any thing further to add, then the Supplying one thing which I find my last instructions were defective in, namely, your coming over very well able to prove what wee already know to be true viz that Mr Pellissary Spoke noe English and possibly Monsieur Denise knowes it himselfe, and then there will be noe need of it. But pray remember that you must have living witness of that as well as other matters to satisfy the Court.

Next it comes in my mind to hint to you that if Scot was soe extraordinary a Professor in France of the Protestant Religion as he would be thought to be here his Visiting of Charenton-Church and the receiving the Sacrament there must be very well knowne and not hard to find, there being, as I take it a Register kept of all their Communicants. Pray therefore see what can be learned of that kind from Mr Joyne or others of his acquaintance or some of the Elders of the Church, and if it should appear that in the time that he has been at Paris he has not frequented that Church or received the Sacrament there pray endeavour to get a good Certificate of it.

One thing more I have to add, Which is that My Servant Lorrain has out of his good will directed the two letters which are inclosed to two Protestant relations of his in Paris, one of which (Monsieur Blondel) hee thinkes is knowne to Mr Denise. Which letters I send you open for you (after perusall) to Seale and make use of, as you shall finde the Same may be usefull to you on my behalfe.

Since my writting thus farr yours of the 27th of September is come to my hand wherein I must confess I am not a little surprised to find you takeing so much paine to decry that peece of advice which I did then and doe still think in many respects as prudent as any thing that

---

[1] Rawl. A. 194: 71–75. Secretarial copy.

has come either into your thoughts or my owne from the beginning
of this unfortunate business of mine to this day. I meane the sending
of one over to you to joyn in the Witness in such cases where liveing
Testimonies cannot be gott hither and which would in noe degree be
worth the trouble and charge of sending for men of such Quality
over, as Mr Trenchepain and Mr Pelletier, the latter of whom being
a Catholick I have alwaies told you I should not dare to make use of
his evidence when I had it here. And for the former what ever he
might say to you or you fancy you saw in his lookes, I am sure I saw
a letter of his to Mr Houblon wherein he very earnestly acquaint[ed]
him with his being obliged to look after some pressing affaires of his
(being as I remember Such as would call him from Paris) for soe long
time as that he Should not be able without great inconvenience to
come for England in case I should desire it. Besides however you
come to think the Contrary were they two to come I could not
honorably by presents or otherwise make their coming soe little as
four times the Charge of sending Mr Denise (for though you are so
farr in the Right as to beleeve that men of their great dealing cannot
at any time want business enough to bring them into England yet I am
sure it would not become mee to tell them soe when they are here,
but must look upon their Journey as made on purpose for mee and
acknowledge it accordingly to them, especially after Mr Trenchepain's haveing wrote what (as I told you) he has done to Mr Houblon.
Which was in a stile soe earnest that I was almost out of Countenance
at the reading of it, he insisting soe much upon the pressure of his
affaires least you should have been too urgent with him on my behalfe
in your solicitations for his neglecting them to come over to mee, and
that very reflection it was that first mov'd mee to fall in with you in
the thoughts of Sending one over to you from hence to ease you and
mee of the Care and difficulty of bringing persons from thence, especially when I consider the uncertainty of the time that they would be
obliged to stay and I to entertain them here, and all for that which
may bee done as well by one who has nothing to doe but make a Step
to Paris, Stay there eight or ten dayes and come back againe, and bee
of noe more charge to mee.

Besides, too, when you see the list of particulars which Mr Denise
bring's with him; you'le find more work then I beleeve you would
easily have been able to have gone thorow with alone in soe short
time; Nor soe fitt for mee to have ventured upon my haveing answers
to upon the Success of one person, if any accident by Sickness or
otherwise should fall out, and I thereby want them at the time of my
Tryall.

Therefore pray let mee desire you (as I hope you will, from what you close with, of your being ready after all to submitt to my directions) to receive Monsieur Denise with the respect and kindnesse that is due to one who want's not business enough here, and therefore comes not at any request of his owne, but of mine, and upon very Small warning. And in some of the particulars of his instructions (whereof I have Sent you by him a Copy) I very well know you cannot expect to come to the knowledge soe well without, as with, him.

And for what you take soe much paine in to diminish the Creditt of his letters in Saying that they might have been spared, I told you that they might soe, but that out of the forewardness of his respect both to you and to mee, he had wrote them before your advice came touching your transacting with those persons to some of whom hee had wrote, and you have and may finde usefull, as low as you observe their Condition to bee. Which I presume you would have Spared, had you consider'd the quality of the person you are inquireing after, and who they are that are the likeliest to get an account of him from; and the quality of those who have given[1] you the best informations wee have hitherto been able to obtaine.

Nor doe I less wonder at your mistake touching the difficulty which Madame Pellissary's family may make, of being troubled to declare over againe the same thing before new Witnesses, which they have already done before others. For I don't remember that I have ever desired them to repeat againe any thing that they have declared to Mr Trenchepain, but to Supply that which you hapned to forget the getting them to declare before, touching Scot's haveing never dined there, nor had any familiarity in that Family. Which in discourse you tell mee, they had all professed to you; whereas in their Declarations before the Notary they onely denied his Dinning there that one day. True it is, that now Mr Denise is gone over, I could bee well contented, that the former Declarations could be renew'd in his presence; but rather then it should give the persons concerned too much trouble, I would not have you presse it, especially if some liveing Witnesses of that Family, can be gott to come over hither; which in my last I have desired; for as much as nothing but liveing Witnesses can stand mee in stead in Court. Which Had I been Soe well informed in at first (Some of Councell then being of another minde) I Should not have been soe sollicitous as I have been, for the obtaining the Declarations in writting, which you have with soe much care procured mee, not but that those Declarations may nevertheless bee of use to mee, though not in Court, vizt in the account which I doe in parte foresee I may bee driven to publish for my vindication. In

[1] MS. *giveing.*

which they will bee legible, where speaking Evidence cannot be heard.

And that is the reason, why I doe yet in some measure desire to get those written Declarations, though I tell you they will bee intirely useless to mee in my greatest concernment at my Tryall.

As to your desiring mee to read your letters all over, that as long as they for the most parte bee, and Soe ill as the Condition of my eyes is, I have not Spared to read every one of them my Selfe over and over, and with extraordinary Content (I assure you) every one of them but this, which I wish with all my heart you had forborne because I would bee very loath to have any reason of suspecting your thincking mee one of soe little judgment or justice, as to value your kindnesse and Care the less, for the haveing another joyning with you therein. And I cannot imagine what other Consideration Should lead you to the departing soe suddenly and with soe much earnestness, from a point I thought my selve soe much obliged to you for your advice in, as in this of my sending one over to you, and did alsoe think I should have given you alsoe soe much content in my choice of the person, as being one knowne to you for an honest man and one that on all occasions does express a great deale of personall respect towards you.

Wherefore I doe againe desire and conjure you to prevent (if it bee not too late) the inconveniences which may attend Mr Denise's observing any dissatisfaction in you towards him, upon the score of his Coming to you. For in the end, it is my Business that must suffer by it, which makes mee wish with all my heart, that you had not omitted writting to mee by thee last post; that what I know now from you, I might have done then before his goeing, and by that meanes have been able, to have given you the advice then, which I now doe, and hope you will follow. Which having said, and therein cleared my minde to you, I now come to say that which is matter of Some what greater pleasure to me vizt that it would bee to the utmost degree fortunate to my affaire, if it Should bee found that in truth this Friend of mine was not at Paris in the month of August 1675, nor in some time after. And if Sherwin bee able upon his Oath honestly to attest that, I doe recommend it to you by all meanes to inable him to come over into England; for that were a Demonstration that would ease us of all Care or Sollicitude for any evidence else. But pray do not goe soe easily away with it, or think that any body else will, if you should; that because hee appears to bee at Nevers upon the 5th, that therefore hee could not bee at Paris before the 31th. Nor is there any thing in the Contract between him and Joyne, that obliges him to stay at Nevers, all the time that the Worke mentioned therein was in doeing. And therefore as the thing in the World that can doe mee most

right, over and beyond all things else that we either have or can discover, when putt all together, I must recommend to you the care of
seeing this point fully cleared, in such a manner as may not bee liable
to any contradiction. For though I doe know it is enough for you and
mee to ground our belief upon, if Joyne should bee able in Court to
affirme that Scott was not then to his knowledge at Paris, and Sherwin
doe the like positively that he was then at that time with him at
Nevers; yet, I that cannot content my selfe to beleeve any thing
certain wherein there is any room left for mistake (as there must
needs bee in a passage of soe many years date as this is) and considering
that their being found mistaken in that particular would disparage
the Credit of their Evidence in every thing else, I cannot but give
you my advise, that notwithstanding their affirming this soe postively,
you will urge them to the recollecting themselves with all the strictness they can, in this point; it being almost impossible but some letters
or answers, bills or acquittances or other acts in writting or some
Circumstances else may be recover'd of that time, either at Paris or
Nevers, upon the score of moneys, lodgings materialls, Casting of
Guns, or something else, that may confirme their testimonies of his
being at Nevers all the Month of August, in case hee was indeed soe.
For letters and messages, must bee supposed to have been alwaies
going among them between Paris and Nevers, upon one occasion or
other, and I doe therefore above all things recommend to you the
finding out something of that kind for the putting this Truth (if it
bee a truth) beyond all fear of exception, remembring, that if you can
but prove where he Spent all August and the 1st 6th or 7th of September, it matter's not where hee was after.

Lastly for what you mention concerning Will Hewer hee is, I
thanke God very well, and one who from his heart wishes you soe,
it being not (I assure you) from any want of kindness, that you have
not heard from him, but from his haveing at this time Some cares
extraordinary of his owne, and his beleeveing you to have your full
load of mine. One thing indeed hee has taken notice of to mee, of
your haveing omitted writting to him, as you have likewise to mee,
in the point that requires it as much as any, namely, that of giveing
letters of advice to accompany bills of Exchange, you haveing drawne
upon him a bill of 46 Ł without one word of advice concerneing [it]
payable to Monsieur Pelletier, while you have done the like on the
same occasion to a much greater value upon Mr Trenchepain. Which
pray rectify by the next, as I lately desired in a former.

As to your owne affaires here, the occasion of your absence, I make
noe doubt but the king will be soe good to mee, as to hold it excusable
upon my Score, God Almighty sending the matter well over, who

(I trust) will alsoe continue you and your Family within His Care. With which prayer and the hope of seeing you now, very Speedily here, I bid you for the present farewell remaineing

Your true affectionate
Brother to serve you
S P

To Mr St Michell

90. S.P. TO B. ST. MICHEL[1]

London October the 6th 1679

Brother Balty,

My last was of the 2d instant, in answer to your[s] of the 27th of September, to which haveing left nothing to bee added but my hopes of it's giveing you full satisfaction in the principall matter of it's Contents and haveing nothing yet from you since that of the 27th all that I now have to give you is the notice of my haveing taken care by this post, from the hand of my Worthy Friend Mr Houblon, to provide you and Monsieur Denise fresh Credits[2] with Monsieur Trenchepain to the value of 50 Ł beyond what you have already taken up of him, which shall be follow'd by more as the necessity of my occasions shall require, and you advise mee of it. Hopeing that I shall not need to inculcate any thing of what I have already soe often pressed you to, of good Husbandry, and advertiseing mee from time to time of the Summs you are Supply'd with, the omission whereof for the time past haveing been matter of some wonder to mee. I doubt not but Monsieur Denise is e're this arrived Safe with you, and that you are applying yourselves to the improveing the little remainder of our time to the best advantage you can for the answering the Severall particulars of inquiry which hee brought along with him, and whereof I have sent you a Copy, with the addition of a point or 2 more in my last. Your progress wherein I shall most gladly receive Some account of from you, and in the meane time give this onely note, vizt that the greatest point to which most of my care is now reduced being (as you may observe in my 2 last) the grounds you have given mee to hope it will bee made to appear that Scott was not at Paris in August 75, and being therefore willing to offer you all the Scruples that occur

---

[1] Rawl. A. 194: 77–78. Secretarial copy.

[2] S.P. encloses the letter to St. Michel in one to Mr. James Houblon for the latter to peruse 'for the sake of that paragraphe thereof which respects the Credits I desire of you for him and Monsieur Denise, praying that it may run conformable to what I write about it.' (Rawl. A. 194: 79.)

to mee against it, I would have you to observe, that whereas Mr Joyne seemes to say, that the first and last time Scott ever ate or drunk in Mr Pellissary's house was in 76, I doe find Scot and his Consorts at Nevers in August, September, and October 1675 and does at that time in one of his letters to Mr Joyne mention Pellissary about his not paying of a bill for their use; Soe that it will bee adviseable that Mr Joyne doe recollect himselfe as particularly as ever hee can by papers or otherwise in the Circumstance of time through this whole affaire; for as much as if this one point could bee cleared at his and Sherwin's Coming hither that Scot was not indeed at Paris in August and beginning of September 1675 (as you seem to say those two Gentlemen are positive in) it would at once ease us of all further care, labours or expence in gathering of other evidences from Soe many difrant parts of the World, as I am now at the trouble and charge of. And therefore if the Sending an Express to Nevers it's selfe could contribute any thing towards the Discovery and fixing of this Truth, Sir A D and I should thinke it disbursement very well made. Of which pray bee very thoughtful together with Mr Denise, Mr Joyne, &ca.

I have againe satisfied myselfe by a 2d sight of Monsieur Trenchepain's letter to Mr Houblon, that you can have noe reason to doubt of his taking in any kinde ill from us our not makeing use of his Testimony in England (which I must confess I never from the beginning thought a fitt thing for mee either to desire or expect from a person of his business) that hee expresly takes notice to Mr Houblon with very much respect towards mee it would be wholly impossible for him by reason of his affaires to doe mee that Service in case mine Should call for it, unless it were to bee dispatched by his being here at the furthest by the 10th/20th instant. I doe therefore perswade my Selfe that My Sending Mr Denise to prevent that trouble of his can bee in noe wise misunderstood by him, I haveing endeavour'd in what I wrote him by Mr Denise to let him know how sensible I am of the interruptions I have already given him, without the addition of one which would bee greater then all, I mean the calling him out of his Countrey at this Season of the yeare.

I am to repeate by you my thankes to Mr Joyne, and though the frankness of his offer makes unnecessary as well as other Considerations unsafe to propose any matter of invitation to him to doe mee the justice hee seem's soe readily disposed to in this affaire, yet you may as you see convenient let him understand that the trouble this may occasion him will bee done for one that will bee very sensible of his kindnesse in it, letting him know that Mr Browne is very foreward in doeing mee the same justice, which hee does, both by himselfe, and those others whom hee has recommended to, whose testimonies, with what hee Shall bring along with him, will abundantly Shew the World the qualifications of this Villain that has attempted this wrong upon Sir A D and mee.

Let not this nevertheless Slacken the evidence I have desired you to provide from Mme Pellissary's family to bee ready to come over after you, when there shall bee occasion.

I thanke you for the further intelligence you putt mee in expectation of from Mlle Des Moulins, as beeing in hopes of hearing of some more of his Papers from her, Mr La Piogerie and others.

I cannot yet come by a letter from My Lady Pratt to Mr Foster, Shee being upon a sudden occasion gone into Wales, But I hope to have it suddenly. For I understand that Foster knowes a great deale of this Fellow, it being said that hee has upon some occasion or other heretofore writt Scot's life; but how farr this is true I know not, this being enough to mee, that hee does confirme of his owne hearing, what Mr Joyne declares of Scot's threatning to bee revenged of mee for accusing him of being a Jesuite.

What remaines, is the informing you of my Sister's health and her family, and that I am

Your truely affectionate
brother to serve you
S P

To Mr St Michell

91. S.P. TO B. ST. MICHEL[1]

London October the 9th 1679

Brother Balty,

Your last was of the 27th of September which I answer'd by mine of the 2d instant and another of the 6th without haveing any from you these 2 last Posts. Soe that haveing nothing of yours upon my hands to reply to, what I have now to say to you is in the 1st place to tell you how much I was surprised to finde Sherwin come over without any advice thereof from you. Nevertheless his Comeing is very wellcome, I haveing been conducted to him by Captain Browne, and receiv'd very good Satisfactions from him in many particulars though in the maine point of all wherein you seem soe assur'd in your Answer to my doubtings concerning it, I finde those doubts of mine were too reasonable, I meane, that of Scot's being in Paris in

[1] Rawl. A. 194: 80–81. Secretarial copy.

114

the month of August and part of September 75. For upon my conferring with those 2 Gentlemen, and Mr Harrison, and Compareing their Discourse with the Dates and Contents of the Papers you lately Sent mee from Mr Joyne, it appear's most cleare to them all, that though Scott was at Nevers the 5th of August, yet hee came to Paris very soone after, as by that very Letter of his of the 5th of August hee said he should. And therefore by the way pray learne of mee this one Lesson, which on this occasion I have Observed not onely you but others of Our Friends, not to have yet met with, vizt To bee most Slow to beleeve what we most wish should bee true; considering what the Consequences would have been of such a mistake as this should we have gone along in it to my Tryall, to the blemishing every other part of our Evidences; besides the generall and inward Shame that deservedly attend's the Guilt of an Untruth. Which therefore I trust in God I shall never be beholden to, though in the case of Life itselfe.

Mr Sherwin tell's mee of the extraordinary diligence you have used through this whole Affaire on my behalfe Which though I cannot bee more sensible of then I was before his telling it mee, yet I know not how to omitt the acknowledgeing it to you afresh, upon every fresh occasion I have of understanding it. And for your not adviseing mee of his Comeing, hee tells mee hee endeavour'd to take his leave of you, but not haveing the Fortune to meet with you hee presumes you might not have heard of his being gone when you last wrote.

I finde Harrison a very sober sort of [f]ellow; and though upon the whole I doe discover that in their dealings one with another there was none of the best Correspondents in their business of Gunfounding, nor I doubt too much honesty, yet I finde them all agree, that whatever the rest were to one another Scot was a villaine to them all and to all the World, and are most ready to give their honest assistance towards the Evidencing his being soe to mee as being by many Circumstances satisfied that hee is soe.

Here is alsoe Hastecote in towne, and Thomas Captain Browne's man. Soe that when Mr Joyne is here (which I now much wish for, and soe doe these poor men too) I make noe doubt of haveing this whole Fellowes wickedness made cleare, with the help of what else you and Mr Denise shall come furnished with, praying that you will let noe time bee lost in the gathering as much as you can, soe that I may have you here by the 23th of this month or at least one of you together with Mr Joyne in case you shall have any thing considerable to doe which cannot bee finished before that time. For though the terme begins that day, and consequently it will bee convenient for mee to bee possessed of as much of my Evidences as I can against that time, yet my Tryall cannot probably bee in less then a Week or 10 dayes after that; and soe if there bee a necessity for it, Either Mr Denise or you (as you shall agree between your selves) may bee at liberty to stay for the dispatching of any thing that shall bee behind, and bringing over any persons that shall bee judged needful, besides Mr Joyne and those which are already here.

Pray deliver my very humble services to Mr Denise, of whose safe arrivall at Paris, together with the Papers of Matterialls hee carryed with him I should be very glad to heare; praying you to Communicate to him what I here write, thereby to excuse mee of writting double.

My last brought you fresh Credits from Mr Houblon to Mr Trenchepain, and I hope will come safe to you.

One thing onely there is wherein I finde myselfe yet not fully clear'd, namely, the degree of Scot's acquaintance with Mr Pellissary and his Family. For I finde by these People here, that by the meanes of La Piogerie, Scot was introduced to the knowledge of that Gentleman, and Mr Le Goux, and was diverse times with him; but whether alwaies at his owne house I know not. But Mr Joyne is the best able (however he comes to mistake the yeare 1676 for 75) to cleare the whole matter. And therefore pray endeavour it while you are upon the Place. For it would look very oddly if these people here should allow of Scot's haveing any familiarity with Mr Pellissary himselfe (as some of them, methinks, seem to imply) while Mr Pellissary's whole Family, and particularly the very Porter, deny their haveing any knowledge of him. And pray remember that any defect on our side in this point would touch the very Essence of my Cause. Which with my repeating once more the business of lookeing out for Papers of all sorts, is all at present from

Your very affectionate
Brother and Servant

To Mr St Michell   S P

92. S.P. TO B. ST. MICHEL[1]

October the 13th 1679

Brother Balty,

My last was of the 9th instant, since which I have received yours of the 4th, and another this afternoone of the 8th ditto, for both which I returne you my very affectionate thankes, and in answer thereto,

[1] Rawl. A. 194: 84–86. Secretarial copy.

as fully and briefly as I can (as being at this time a little indisposed). I am exceeding glad of Mr Denise's being safely arrived with you, as not doubting of your joynt diligence and ease in the furthering of my Concerns according to the matterialls thereof brought you by him; the Time now drawing Very fast on, soe as (according to my last) I must repeat my desires of seeing one or both of you here, by the 23th, together with Mr Joyne leaveing it to you to determine which may be the fittest to remaine there in case, (as I then suggested) any thing should remaine undispatcht, that may need the stay of one of You to see done. Though by all that I can judge by here, I doe think it in many respects more proper and adviseable that in such case the part of staying, to see the whole done, should remaine upon you.

I am fully satisfied with what you write touching the Account I shall receive of your expence, and the manifold occasions of them, and therefore shall not need to say more on that head.

Nor can I think it in any degree needful, to repeat any thing of what I have been lately soe large to you, in reference to Mr Pellissary's family, and their perfecting their former Declarations in what they were defective in, about the small familiarity Scot had therein, all that they therein then said, extending onely to his not dineing there that one day. But I must confess that I should looke upon it as a great misfortune if [we] should not bee able to get some of them over hither at my Charge to give their testimonies here vivâ voce, if there should be occasion for it.

I must intirely alsoe leave it to you two to consider what is fitt to bee done as to the getting over of Mr Langley and Dally, and accordingly I doe soe, you being the best judges of the importance of their testimonies, and the meanes of obtaineing it. For I would not willingly want any thing soe matteriall as what you seem to think their testimonies to bee.

My last gave you an account of Sherwin's being here, but very ill in health, soe as not to bee able to goe out of his Chamber.

I doe observe your cautions and Cares about Mr Joyne, and (according to your advice) I doe by the inclosed[1] repeat my desire of his Comeing over with all speed. And as to what you write that his intention of comeing over should not bee published, you may remember that hee himselfe wrote word to Mr Browne of his intention of seeing him in England very speedily. Soe as Mr Harrison and the rest (whom Mr Joyne directed him to speake to) cannot probably but know it. But I will indeavour to keep it as little spoken of as may bee.

[1] S.P. to J. Joyne, 13 Oct. 1679, acknowledging afresh his favours. and pressing him to hasten to England to confer with his friends who are also to testify. (Rawl. A. 194 : 86.)

I wrote the Letter to Mr Savill for you to make use of just as you should finde it expedient. Therefore, doe as you thinke fitt about it, for I doe not depend upon any fruit from it. Onely if those to Mr De Seignelay, Mr Colbert &ca bee deliver'd, methinkes, as hee is the Minister from Our King, hee should not bee a Stranger to my proceedings with Mr De Seignelay and for those letters to him, Mr Colbert and Mr Mignon I see noe reason why they should not bee deliver'd; Mr Seignelay haveing noe doubt long e're this, been acquainted from hence by Mr Barillon, with the Contents of Scot's depositions, Mr Denise haveing given him a Copy of them a week or more before his departure from hence. Therefore I am clearly for the delivery of the said Letters to them; his being concerned in the accusations rendring it a respect to him (whatever bee the effect thereof to mee) that hee should bee acquainted with it.

I doe greatly thanke you for your care in gathering up of some more Papers, and hope you may[1] yet add to their number. Which I putt soe much value upon, as to bee unwilling to venture them, by the Ordinary Post, but rather chuse for safetys sake to respite my satisfaction in them, to your or Mr Denise's Comeing over. Nor doe I doubt, but Mr Joyne, when hee comes to peruse the Papers here, and discourse with Mr Browne, Harrison &ca will recollect matters more particularly then he can at this distance and alone.

I thanke you for what you write me from Mr Joyne about the Cooke. But not seeing how that can bee of any use to my cause at all, I think it will be best for mee to let that matter alone, at least for the present.

For My Lady Pratt's manner of writing, it is a little surpriseing; but for all that gives mee noe trouble. Since in whatever manner shee had wrote his Brother Foster's Case will not admit of his Comeing into England and soe his Testimony can bee of noe use to mee at my Tryall. However, you pressing mee soe often for a Letter from her, who then was, and is still out of Towne, I knew not what better hand to make use of to her, then that which you recommended mee to, I mean, My [Lady] Wallbanke's, though haveing since understood that Sir Timothy Terrell is relation to Foster, I did yesterday desire a line or two from him, which I herein send you, to make use of or not, as you shall see fitt.[2]

I doe wonder (according to my last) Mr Joyne should not yet recollect Scot's being at Paris in August 75.

Lastly, I am very Sensible of Mr De Ruvigny's Civility, and hope you will have some fruits of it, in obtaineing the Kindness and

---

[1] *might*, canc.
[2] No letters to or from Sir Timothy Terrell appear in the letter-book.

Justice of Mme Pellissary of haveing some body come over from her Family to attest the Truth here.

Soe hopeing e're long to see you here to both our Contents remaine

Your truely affectionate

Brother and Servant

S P

My very humble Service to Mr Denise

To Mr St Michell

93. S.P. TO B. ST. MICHEL[1]

Westminster October the 16th 1679

Brother,

My last was of the 13th, since which I have yours of the 11/12th, which finds mee in very good health, the last leaveing mee under some indisposition.

My former have e're this (I doubt not) told you of Sherwin's being here, and very well disposed to doe mee right, though his Sickness will (I feare) bereave mee of any benefit from his Evidence.

I finde Captain Browne a very good Witness of Mr Pellissary's speaking noe English, and Mr Harrison too.

Very sorry I am for the trouble you give yourselfe, though I doe kindly thank you for it, towards the finding where Scott was the middle or remainder of August and September 1675—it being most apparent, both from Mr Harrison and Captain Browne, and Mr Joyne's owne Papers, that hee must bee at Paris the later end of August, or else they are all confounded; and you may easily beleeve I should bee very glad they would prove soe. And therefore, since you are gone soe farr into that Enquirie, pray drive it as farr as you [can]. And yet if your Messenger bee not gone to Nevers about it, I am of opinion the matter would bee cleared without it, when these Gentlemen come to speake altogether here.

I thank you for what you write mee of your Observations from Monsieur La Pointe.

For the Account you give mee of the success of your applications to My Lord Colbert, I must confess I am much less dissatisfied with it then you seem to bee. For bee it what it would I expect as much benefitt from it one way as the other, and doe not wish I had moved one moment sooner or made any one step in it other then I have

---

[1] Rawl. A. 194 : 87–88. Secretarial copy.

done, or used any other hand. For I assure you I governed myselfe therein by a great many more Considerations then I either have, or doe now think needfull or expedient to bee putt downe in paper, and such as I think will render the usage I receive from [the] Court of France never a whit the less usefull to mee, for it's being of noe use.

And in like manner for Sherwin, though it falls out very well that hee is here; yet by what I see of him, I had rather have been without his Evidence, then by supplying him with the least summ of money to have put it into anybody's power, to say I bribed him for it.

I forgat that in the Clause of your Letter you tell mee you have wrote to Nevers.

The thing that remaines of most weight to bee done is the secureing one or two of the properest Persons of Mme Pellissary's Family to come over, if we should have occasion to call for them, and that I should think very severe to bee denyed. And therefore hope that Mr De Ruvigny (whatever Mr De Seignelay) will not see mee want that Justice. However, God's Will bee done.

As to the Marquise de Regny,[1] shee does very readily accord to Our desires, and will not faile, to write to the purpose thereof by the next Post, to Mlle Des Moulins, whose Papers, in particular and all others that you have or shall get are likely to bee Evidence, of as much use as any in my Cause; they saying a great deale, and leading us to the knowledge of a great deale more. Therefore, pray bee instant in that particular and methinkes Monsieur Le Goux should bee furnished for the giveing mee some Help therein.

I forbeare to write to Mr Denise,[2] because in his Letter to mee of the same date with yours, hee tell's mee of your purpose to send him back immediately for England together with Mr Joyne, which agrees with what you will finde of my desire therein in my last, and I thank you for it; hopeing that he will bring some of the Papers along with him, which you have lately mentioned your being possessed of.

Lastly I cannot possibly bee more sensible then I am, of the Condition of you and your Family; for next to the deliverance of my owne Person, I am concerned on your and their behalfe, and shall endeavour to express it, as soon as God Almighty shall inable mee; on whom, both you and I must depend. And I doubt not but his Mercy

---

[1] S.P. encloses a letter from M. Denise to Mme la Marquise de Regny, requesting her to induce Mlle Des Moulins in Paris to lend St. Michel certain papers in her possession relating to Scot, 16 Oct. 1679. Under the same date, S.P. writes to Mlle Denise, offering her a coach and the escort of 'quelque Personnes de Qualité' for the delivery of the letter to the Marquise (Rawl. A. 194 : 87).

[2] But S.P. does write to M. Denise, greeting him and J. Joyne at Calais upon their setting forth towards England, 16 Oct. 1679. (Rawl. A. 194 : 88–89.)

will bee Equall to his Justice towards us both. And as to the dischargeing, of my part towards you, you may relye upon my imploying all my Interests towards your Good, soe soon as ever God shall restore mee to a condition of imploying any for my owne. Which, with the adviseing of the health of my Sister and her Family, is all at present from

Your truely affectionate
Brother to serve you
S P

To Mr St Michell

94. S.P. TO B. ST. MICHEL[1]

London October the 23th 1679

Brother,

Your last to mee was of the 11th instant, which I answer'd in mine of the 16th ditto. Since which I have received nothing from you which I impute to the Crossness of the Winds which have hindred the Comeing over of the Packetts by the two last Posts. But wee doe hourely expect them, and with them I hope to see here Monsieur Denise and Mr Joyne. Till the arrivall of whom I have nothing remaineing upon my hands to give you answer to, or any new advice in, saveing that of the inclosed from Mme la Marquise de Regny[2] to Mlle Des Moulins, wherein shee has been pleased to send her desire to that Lady to put into your hands what Papers shee has either under Scot's hand or belonging to him that may give any light into the Truth of his Story and Practices. In which inclosed letter the Marquise does send her a Copy of a Promise I have made under my hand to returne the said Papers safely to her soe soon as the occasion is over, for which I desire them. Pray therefore bee carefull of them while they are in your hands, as I alsoe shall bee after their comeing to mine.

It remaines onely at present for mee to tell you that today being the 23th instant and the 1st day of the Terme Sir A D and I did make our appearance in the Court of the King's Bench, with hopes and Expectation of haveing a Time sett for our Tryall. But the Attorney Generall (who is the King's Councell in these cases) being lately removed, and noe other appointed to succeed to his Place and

---

[1] Rawl. A. 194 : 92. Secretarial copy.

[2] A letter in French from S.P. to the marquise, under date of 20 Oct. 1769, encloses a formal agreement to return to the hands of the marquise any papers lent to St. Michel by Mlle Des Moulins. (Rawl. A. 194 : 90.)

Business wee are and shall for some time remaine in the Darke as to
that Matter, but shall make it our Business with all the industry we
can to secure it, soe as that we may have an End of our troubles One
way or other before the End of the Terme, and I trust in God we
shall bee fully prepared for it. Whereof hopeing to bee able to say
more to you by the next, I remaine

Your truely affectionate
Brother to serve you
S P

To Mr St Michell

95. S.P. TO B. ST. MICHEL[1]

October the 30th 1679

Brother,

After long expectation I have yours of the 15th 22th and 25th
instant soe that in case you have received mine of [the] 16th wherein
I mentioned my haveing yours of the 11th I doe presume you will
finde that I have not wanted any of yours saveing that of the 30th
of September, which you mention but never yet came to my hands.
Therefore, pray recollect what it was, and advise mee what there
was of moment in it.

My last was of the 23th instant, since which through the Crossness
of the winds I have received together your said 3 of the 15th 22th
and 25th and the satisfaction of Mr Denise's safe and timely returne
to England, in Company with Mr Joyne, by whom I doe afresh
understand the greatness of your industry on my behalfe, and doe
give you afresh my faithfull thankes for it. I have had their Company
this Day and made an Entrance into the Matters wherein they
severally come prepared to informe mee, and shall from day to day
make further advance in it, The multitude of Particulars which I
have at present upon my hands from other Parts of the World, together with these from France, not permitting mee to doe it all at
once, nor indeed to give you at this Time full answers to severall
Points of these 3 letters of yours, but am forced to restraine my selfe
to 2 or 3 which call for present answer, referring the rest to the next
Post.

And in the 1st place therefore I am to tell you, that (as I feared)
I shall not have any Benefitt of Sherwin's Evidence, hee dying yesterday, and the truth is, had hee lived, I doe not see I should have had
any thing matteriall from him, in relation to my particular Case,

[1] Rawl. A. 194 : 94–95. Secretarial copy.

122

though enough concerning Scot's vilanies in generall, which I have sufficient witnesses of, though hee bee gone.

Next you are to know, that Scott has been withdrawne out of sight and heareing from ever since tomorrow will bee a moneth or 5 weekes (as I am informed) and is not yet to bee heard of, otherwise then As I have this day had some information of his beeing gone out of England with the D of B,[1] soe as for ought I know, hee may bee at this time at Paris. Which gives mee noe paine at all, I beeing as little fearfull of what hurt hee can doe mee there, as I would have you to bee of what can befall you from the D of B. This onely inconvenience indeed I may suffer by it, namely the beeing hindred of bringing our Business to a Tryall this Terme for want of Evidence to accuse us, and consequently doe not know when to foresee wee shall be able to bring our Affaire to an End. But we shall use all lawfull means to remove that Impediment, being bound in the meane time to remaine slaves to Our Accusers, and under an Endless expence in keeping of Our Witnesses together, which is very grievous.

Inclosed you have a letter from Mr Denise,[2] and in it one for Mr Colbert, giveing him advice of the reports of Scot's being at Paris.

Next I inclose you a letter from Sir A D to a kinsman of his and a Gentleman of good Quality, Mr Henry Timpeny, who is of late become a Benedictin Monck. Which we leave you to make use of as you see fitt, in order to the obtaineing (if possible) some Publick Attestation from that Colledge, touching those Rogueries of Scot's which they have heretofore given you soe full an account of. Which letter is left to you to seale, and deliver to him under the Title of Mr Timpeny, or Father Timpeny, as upon Enquiry you shall finde it proper.

By this Time you will, I suppose, have an answer from Nevers, though I must confess it does to mee seem very plain, from the Papers you have sent mee, that hee was at Paris, between the 20th and 25th of August 75.

Pray faile not to sollicite Mlle Des Moulins and Mr Le Goux for what Papers they have in their hands relateing to Colonel Scott, and particularly that of the Originall Contract between the 4 Parties, and what ever else can bee found of him, they being of very [great] use.

I shall not add any thing more this Time, but praying you to expect the remainder by the next, rest

Your truely affectionate
Brother to serve you
To Mr St Michell   S P

---

[1] The Duke of Buckingham.
[2] None of the enclosures mentioned is preserved in the letter-book.

96. S.P. TO B. ST. MICHEL[1]

London November the 3d 1679

Brother,

My last was of the 30th of October, giveing you the satisfaction you desired of knowing by Particulars that the severall Letters you had of late sent mee were safely come to my hand, there being none missing of any you mention, but that of the 30th of September.

This day I have received yours of the 29th of October, to which and what I omitted to say anything to in my last, I now come to answer, and 1st by telling you that I finde Mr Joyne a very ingenious, and I beleeve is a very just man, and seems greatly inclined to give mee proofs of it on this occasion which I have for his assistance. Soe as I reckon my selfe extremely happy in your lighting upon him, hee being soe thorowly acquainted with Scott's Story, and willing to give mee the satisfaction of knowing it. And as a further instance of it does send you the inclosed, by which you will bee directed to severall Places for further intelligence, and accordingly I intreat you to make the best use of it you can, and particularly in seeing whether you can meet with any body to whom Scott has been as open concerning his Design of revenging himselfe upon mee, as hee has been to Mr Joyne, and Mr Foster; Mr Joyne beleeving that if hee has to any body, it may have been to Monsieur Paris mentioned in his letter; this being a point of great moment to mee to bee able to prove, and therefore if this Monsieur Paris could attest it or any else that you can finde, I would bee glad it could bee done. But if not, then if you think it obtainable, try againe to get an Attestation of it in writting from Mr Foster. But if you doe think hee will not grant it (which were strange in a Gentleman, after haveing soe often said it) pray aske it not of him; though being confirmed by Mr Joyne, it would bee of use to mee to have it.

The postscript of Mr Joyne's letter is intended for the helping you to finde out Scott if hee should bee at Paris with the D of B. Which pray imploy to that use.

Next I inclose you a copy of Scot's Examinations at Dover at his last comeing over out of France. In which you will see the account hee gives[2] of his being a Pensioner to the Prince of Condé, his haveing had a Command in the said Prince's Regiment, his being sent for over out of England, about this time 12 monthes (when hee fled into France) by a letter from Monsieur Gourville to survey some Lands and Woods of the Prince's in Burgundy and Picardy, and his haveing

---

[1] Rawl. A. 194 : 97–98. Secretarial copy, much revised, apparently used as first draft.
[2] *of himselfe*, canc.

received severall Summs of money from the Prince, upon account whereof hee held himselfe obliged to gratifie the Prince in his goeing over. In the truth of every part of which, I would bee glad to bee very well informed, and doe not doubt but upon your applications to Monsieur Gourville, hee will tell you what thereof is true, and possibly give the same under his hand, which would bee a great kindness and Justice to mee.

It is not the Greatness of the Quality that I aim at in the Persons that should come over out of Mme Pellissarys's Family; but their Capacity of giveing the best Evidence in the Point wherein wee want it, namely, to prove Scot's[1] not being in the House or[2] dineing privately there that day. And as I doe think the Porter and one Servant more (such as the Buttler, or any other[3] whose business lay generally all over the House) would bee the most proper to satisfy a Court in this Matter: Soe the lowness of their [station] will, I presume, render them the more easy to bee had.

One thing I forgate to mention touching Foster, which is that I heare,[4] he is a very debauched idle Rascall, and therefore am the less willing to hazard the doeing wrong to my Cause by using soe scandalous an Evidence. Nevertheless hee being soe great a Confident of Scot's as not onely to know but to have wrote his Life, Scott will have the less reason to except against any declarations of Foster's, and therefore if you could get either that which I just now mentioned, or a Copy of that History of his, I should bee very glad.

For what you have soe often mentioned in former letters, and soe largely in your last, touching the extraordinary fortunes which others have raised to themselves, I need not name where, I have and doe still thinke it of noe use to you for mee to say any thing of it now, more then that at your returne you will finde your mistake, and I dare say be as sorry for it then, as at present I am.

For the Business of the Katherine, we have not heard a word spoken of it many a day, Moone[5] not appeareing, nor any word spoke of a long time touching any Prosecution intended[6] to bee of that Matter.

I hope e're this you have mine of the 23th of October, and that upon Mme La Marquise De Regny's letter inclosed therein, Mlle Des Moulins will bee prevailed with to let mee have the originall Contract about the Guns, it being a thing which my Councell tells mee,

---

[1] *his,* canc.　　　　　　　　　　　[2] *and,* canc.
[3] *Servant,* canc.　　　　　　　　　[4] *that,* canc.
[5] The same Moone, or Mohun, former captain of the *Hunter,* who had made damaging allegations against Sir Anthony Deane, St. Michel, and their partners, and who, according to Deane's reply, had swindled his employers out of all profits.
[6] *likely,* canc.

would bee of extraordinary use to mee. Therefore pray bee very Sollicitous to her in it.

I shall not faile to give you the earliest Notice I can of the Time of my Tryall, in order to your bringing over what remains of Mme Pellissary's Family. But as yet, Scott not appearing, I cannot gaine any Certainty therein, or indeed whether I shall have any Tryall this Terme or noe. And then pray consider upon what terms (as I heretofore observed) we should have ingaged Messrs Trenchepain, Pelletier &ca to have left their Business and[1] Country at this time of yeare, to doe nothing.

I shall satisfy Mr Houblon of the Summs you have taken up of Monsieur Trenchepain, and doubt not your good husbandry, though I cannot but lament the unfortunate occasion of soe great an Expence as this will bee, when all the Particulars are putt together.

Lastly what I have to add is the letting you know that my sister is very well (I thanke God) and her whole Family, my little Cosen Betty[2] haveing had some small indisposition, but is at present very well againe, and soe I remaine, in hopes of seeing you very shortly (for whether I have a Tryall or noe this Terme, you may depend upon my sending advice for your returne within a Week or Ten daies at furthest.)

Your truely affectionate
Brother to serve you
S P

To Mr St Michell

97. S.P. TO B. ST. MICHEL[3]

London November the 6th 1679 S.V.

Brother

My last was of the 3d instant in answer to yours of the 19th of October. Since which haveing received nothing from you, nor[4] any new mater to give you from my selfe, this serves onely to desire your takeing the first opportunity of Monsieur Le Goux's Recovery to obtaine from him what Papers of Scotts remained in his hands, and to doe the like with Mlle Des Moulins for the Originall Contract of Scott, letting mee know her answer about it, that in case Mme de

---

[1] *their*, canc.

[2] St. Michel's daughter Elizabeth, one of the scanty bits of evidence on the vexed question of the names of the children.

[3] Rawl. A. 194 : 101–2. Secretarial copy.

[4] *of*, canc.

Regny's first Letter doe not prevaile I may indeavour to doe it by a 2d, our Councell telling us that it will bee very necessary for us to see it here, and I have already engaged my selfe for the safe returne of it, and shall see it done, without letting it once goe out of my owne hands.

Upon discourseing afresh with Sir A D we doe thinke the Steward of Mme Pellissary's Family (Monsieur Desaunays) and the Porter to bee the 2 fittest of the whole Family to come over as being able to speake the fullest concerneing Scott's not being in their House at all the day of the entertainment, to which it might possibly bee desired that we had Mr Pavillon or any other of the Gentlemen that were there, and can positively attest that neither Mr Pellissary nor Sir A D were absent from the rest of the Company from the time of Sir A D's Comeing into the House to that of his Leaveing it. Which Sir A D does assure mee is true; and being soe it is impossible Mr Pellissary should have the private Discourse which is pretended, either with him or with Scott alone.

I have for some time omitted the mention of my humble Services to Messrs Trenchepain and Pelletier, but I hope you doe of course supply it, and desire you to doe it in particular to the later with my most respectfull thankes for his last Letter by Monsieur Denise, which I will speedily acknowledg under my owne hand, as Sir A D and I shall both of us to Mr De Ruvigny for his.

Since my writting thus farr I have yours of the 1st/11th of November wherein I am very glad to finde you soe secured of your haveing the Generall Contract from Mlle Des Moulins, which I hope Mme de Regny's 1st Letter will incline her to grant with the greater willingness. And if shee does, I am not very desirous of your ventureing it by the Post, but rather chuse to reserve it for your owne bringing, sending mee a Copy of it for my satisfaction in the meane Time.

Very glad I am to finde you designing the very same Persons to bee brought over hither for Evidence, which we had ourselves proposed as the most proper. And very right you are in your observation that they are, and must bee treated as Strangers. Nor doe we expect to have it done otherwise: But are at a perfect loss what to say to you at present by way of direction towards their Comeing in regard that it is impossible for us yet to foresee when we shall have our Tryall, or whether we shall have it at all this Terme, of which there is but 3 weekes left and noe indictment yet drawne against us, nor can bee till there bee Evidence, which there is not at present by reason of Scot's not appeareing. And less then 14 daies cannot bee allowed us for notice to prepare for Our Tryall because of our Witnesses being to bee fetcht from abroad. Soe that unless we can within a Week obtaine the appointment of a Time for Our Tryall, it will bee impossible for us to have it this Terme, without running too great a hazard of wanting some of our Chief witnesses. And if not this Terme, which ends the 28th of this month we can expect none till the next Terme, which begins not till the 23th of January, and then shall we bee under the same uncertainty for the day, which we are now; but with this Certainty (which we have not now) of being Tryed that Terme or discharged. Soe that all we can at present say touching these witnesses is to secure ourselves as farr as we are able of haveing the Benefitt of their Evidence when we shall need it within either this Terme or that and leave the Event of it to God Almighty. For more then this we know not what to propose, unless it were to bring them over presently and keep them here till then, which I presume would bee too much for us to aske, and more [then] their occasions (and especially Monsieur Pavillon's) would permit them to grant. Therefore we must leave it to you in this condition, to manage it as well as you are able; hopeing to bee able to say something to you about it by the next.

Next I wish you could get an attestation from La Pointe conformable to what hee declared to Mr Denise and Mr Joyne in your Company, touching Scot's acquaintance with Father Le Boue, and their workeing together upon the Mapp of the Coasts of England, as alsoe touching the 2 Dutch Charts which hee has belonging to Scott, from whence his Mapps were made; specifying the Time when this was done; this being a very usefull Testimony and such as I doe not know but it might bee worth the Charge of bringing him over if hee would bee willing to come. Whereof pray advise mee, but without comeing to any determination with him concerneing it, till you have sent mee his Attestation and received my advices thereupon.

There is something alsoe which Mr Denise informes of a Porter of Monsieur Gourville with whome Scott is said to have severall times left some of his Maps in his Lodge. Which (if true) I would bee glad you would examine into the Particulars of it as strictly as you can, and gett it attested before a Public Notary and sent mee. Which, with the assurance of the health of my Sister and her Little ones, is all at present from

Your truely affectionate
Brother to serve you
S P

To Mr St Michell

98. S.P. TO B. ST. MICHEL[1]

London November the 10th 1679.

Brother

My last was of the 6th instant, answering yours of the 1st/11 ditto. Since which haveing received nothing from you what I have now to say is onely to tell you, that Matters stand with us here as they did then, vizt, Scott seem's to bee still out of the way, and consequently little hopes left of getting an appointment of our Tryall this Terme, which is Matter of great trouble to us. But we must bee patient in that as well as in other things, hopeing that you will suddenly have Mme Pellissary in Towne; and thereby bee secureing us a promise from her of our haveing those Persons here whose Evidence you and we have pitched upon in our last Letters, when we shall need them, Whether it bee this Terme or the next. Of which I shall bee able to write you with more Certainty very suddenly; for as much as if we cannot get a Time for our Tryall within this weeke we shall not then (as I told you in my last) bee in Condition to have it within this Terme, because of the Time requisite for the sending for and bringing over those of our witnesses which remaine still in France.

In the mean time pray bee finishing that little which rests still to bee done there; and particularly the getting of Mr Le Goux's Papers; and the Originall Contract from Mlle Des Moulins.

And pray bee considering, what Correspondent you can provide at Paris to write upon occasion to, when you shall be called home. For noe doubt some little thing will bee still to bee done there, especially if by the want of our Tryall this Terme you should bee obliged to leave those Witnesses behind you. Therefore somebody must be thought on at Paris to continue a Correspondence with us here till the whole business bee at an end. And I feare it would bee too much for us to putt either upon Mr Trenchepain or Mr Pelletier, leaveing it to you to consider of.

Next, there is one little Matter which I'le pray you to doe before you'le come away which is that you will looke out for the Office of Intelligence at Paris where the Weekly Gazettes are writt which I thinke is stiled, Le Bureau d'adresse, and I am told is at present in the hands of Monsieur L'Abbé d'Angeau, alias Corcillon, to be heard of at the Court. My business wherein is this, vizt, In Aprill 1675 our Parliament in England then sitting, I was commanded by them, and accordingly did obey them, in presenting them with a very particular State of our Navy. Of which soe much notice was then taken that

---

[1] Rawl. A. 194 : 102–4. Secretarial copy.

in the French Gazette of Amsterdam, beginning Jeudy the 9th of May 1675, that Gazettier has these words

De Londres le 3d May

Le Parlement est tousjours assemblé. Hier l'on y fit un Acte pour la preservation de la Pêche sur les Rivieres; L'on y en fit encore un autre par Lequel il est ordonné qu'aucun Membre de la Chambre Basse ou des Commones ne poura exercer aucune Charge Publique; l'on y ordonna a Monsieur Pepys de faire un estat au vray de la Flotte, et de la communiquer au Parlement. From whence I am induced to beleeve it possible, that the Gazettier at Paris may about that Time have taken the like notice, of our Parliament's demanding this account of mee. Which if hee should, I should have a great deale of light to draw from it in my Business, that might bee of much use to mee, and therefore pray make it your Care to inquire it out if possible by searching the Register of that Office (where I am told the Copies of all Gazettes remaine entred) for any mention of this Matter or any thing else relateing to the Navy of England, between the 1st of Aprill and the last of May 1675, and purchase the Gazettes themselves, if they bee to bee had, or Extracts of soe much of them well attested. For I am mightily mistaken, if I was not told about that Time, that the French Gazettier did alsoe make mention of this Matter and Mee. Which with the assurance of the health of my sister and her Family is all at present from

Your very affectionate
Brother to serve you
S P

To Mr St Michell

Postscript

Since my closeing of this and being ready to send it away to the Post (it being late) I have received yours of the 5/15th instant, wherein I finde my selfe greatly surprised[1] at the Generosity with which Mme Pellissary and Family are pleased to express their desire of doeing Sir A D and mee Justice, by makeing such provision of evidence to testify the Truth here on our behalfs. And much the more surpriseing it is, by how much they appear more foreward in this good will of theirs then (by the villanous proceedings of Scott in absconding himselfe) we are in condition of makeing use of it. For (as I have already told you in my former letters and this) hee has withdrawne himselfe out of sight for 5 or 6 weekes past; soe as though the King himselfe has been pleased to bee soe gracious to us as to Signify His Pleasure with

---

[1] MS. *surpriseing.*

his owne mouth to Mr Attorney Generall (at my request) that our Tryall, after soe long delay, bee hastened all that justly it may, the Attorney Generall declares himselfe to bee yet wholly unable to doe any thing therein, or soe much as to draw up an Indictment for want of Evidence. And consequently we are wholly uncertain when we shallbe able to obtaine a Tryall, and noe less therefore unable what to advise touching those Gentlemen, who by this time are I doubt with you at Paris. This onely at present I can say that you would doe well to let them know justly how the Case stands with us, and the occasion of it, ariseing from Scot's not appeareing, expressing to them with all imaginable respect the sence Sir A D and I have of their great goodness and Justice to us, takeing to your assistance therein our Worthy friends Monsieur Trenchepain and Mr Pelletier, and pray the said Gentlemen Strangers to take in good part what we now doe in desireing their expecting our fuller request to them by the next post. By which time we hope to understand the Certain issue of our Affaire, as to our haveing or not haveing a Tryall this Terme. For as much as we should bee very loath to give them the trouble of a Voyage into England at this ill time of the yeare, unless they might bee assured of the satisfaction which they design to themselves of doeing us justice at our Tryall. Soe as out of respect to them in that Particular, we have chosen to forbeare the adviseing any thing touching their Comeing over for England or leaveing them at liberty from the same, till the next Post. Which pray, communicate with my most humble services to Mr Trenchepain[1] and Monsieur Pelletier, and with what I shall write on this Subject expect an answer in my Next to the other Parts of this your Letter which the time of night will not admit of my present replying to.

99. S.P. TO MR. HAYTER[2]

November the 11th 1679

Sir

    In answer to your enquiry touching my Brother Mr St Michel, His Majesty was pleased (upon my humble application to Him, on that behalfe) to give mee leave to imploy him into France, to looke after that unhappy Affaire of mine, in which my Life has been brought into question by the malicious information of Scot. The

---

[1] A courteous reply in French to a letter just received from M. Trenchepain, 10 Nov. 1679. (Rawl. A. 194 : 104.)
[2] Rawl. A. 194 : 105. Secretarial copy in letter-book.

importance of which Cause would not suffer mee to pitch upon any one for that imployment who was either less concerned for mee, or less qualified by his knowledge in the Language and Countrey then my said Brother, who (I thanke God) has soe succeeded therein, as that I hope within one Post or two to be in Condition of sending for him back, I wanting nothing towards it, but the assignment of a day for my Tryall, hee being ready to come over with my Witnesses upon the first Summons. Soe I doubt not of his being here to attend any Commands of the Honourable Commissioners of the Admiralty before the end of this Terme. And in the meane time I intreat you to let them know that I shall most readily waite upon them for their further Satisfaction therein, whensoever they shall be pleased to require it. Soe I remaine

Your very affectionate Friend and humble Servant
S P

To Mr Hayter

100. S.P. TO B. ST. MICHEL[1]

London, November the 13e 1679 V.S.

Brother,

My last was of the 10th instant whereto referring you for other Particulars, this comes principally in pursuance of my long Postscript to that letter in answer to yours of the 5/15th ditto touching the Gentlemen, which you were then expecting from Mme Pellissary, to tell you that after all the pains taken that Sir A D and I could imploy for the getting of a time appointed for our Tryall this Terme and as much readiness expressed towards it by the King's Attorney Generall as we could with justice expect from him; he has this day by Mr Hayes our Sollicitor sent us this positive and finall answer, That our Adversary Scott not being to bee found, nor any other Person appearing before him to this day to give in any Evidence against us &ca [he] is wholly unable to draw up soe much as [an] Indictment, and therefore much less in condition to undertake any thing in reference to our Tryall. Soe that we are in noe wise to expect that any thing can bee done in it this Terme. Which Declaration hee sends us in answer to our request made to him by our Sollicitor, that hee would let us know the certainty of what wee might depend upon concerning a Tryall, to the end we might save this which would bee the last Post we could make use of for the Summoning our Witnesses from France,

[1] Rawl. A. 194 : 106–7. Secretarial copy.

soe as to have them here with any reasonable assurance within the Terme, which ends the 28th instant.

Which being soe, and that consequently the next Terme beginning the 23th of January is the soonest (if ever) that we shall have opportunity of makeing use of our Evidence, I doe wholly concurr with you that it would bee in every other respect unadviseable soe would it bee noe less undecent towards Mme Pellissary and her Family and particularly to Monsieur Pavillon, for us to put him, and the other Persons designed to accompany him, to the trouble of an unseasonable and useless Journey into England.

Which being consider'd it remain's that this bee communicated to Mme Pellissary and those[1] Gentlemen in the most respectfull and speedy manner that we can; to the end that by how much the more satisfactorily they are eased of their present intended trouble they may with the least difficulty bee prevailed with to embrace the same againe in January, if we shall then have occasion for calling for it. To which purpose Sir A D and I have jointly wrote to Mr De Ruvighy[2] askeing his kindness therein, which we send open for you to seale and dispose of, after you have read and communicated it to our worthy Friends, Monsieur Trenchepain and Mr Pelletier,[3] to each of whom I have also singly wrote to the same purpose; praying you to conferr with them, and take their advice in your Proceedings with Mr Pavillon &ca for the putting a stop to their trouble of comeing into England, and acknowledgeing our great obligations to them for what they have borne with their Comeing to Paris on our behalfs. Which Sir A D joynes with mee in desireing and commissionateing you to see done, in the best manner you can to their Satisfaction, upon your adviseing with our two said Friends, that soe they may have the less reluctancy to doe us the same favour hereafter, which they now intended us. For though as the Proceedings of our Adversaries looke at this day, it seems too probable that we shall not have an opportunity of justifying ourselves to the World by a Publick Tryall, yet that is not soe to be depended upon as that we ought to discharge ourselves of any part of our Evidence, and therefore you are soe to leave these Gentlemen now, as if we were certain of our haveing occasion of calling for their helpe againe hereafter. But in the doeing of this pray see, that the Civilityes that you shall pay them on this occasion doe

[1] MS. *them.*

[2] S.P. and Sir A. Deane jointly to M. De Ruvigny in French, asking him to explain the postponement of the trial to Mme Pellissary. Marginal note: 'Memorandum That my Brother St Michell thinking upon very good Considerations with the advice of Messieurs T. and P. at Paris to be better forborne returned it.' (Rawl. A. 194 : 107.)

[3] Letters from S.P. to M. Trenchepain and M. Pellettier, respectively, asking each to assist St. Michel in making acknowledgements to Mme Pellissary and her household. (Rawl. A. 194: 108.)

not, upon any consideration, amount to ought that can beare the Construction of Bribery, for as the Justice of our Cause needs noe such things, soe would it bee exposed to the greatest injury in the World, should any such thing bee, or have cause given of it's beeing but pretended. And as this Caution was earlily prest upon you by mee from the beginning, soe I hope you have noe less strictly observ'd it, and will to the end.

Which haveing said, and referring you againe for other matters to my last, Sir A D joynes with mee in recommending it to you now to bee prepareing with all convenient speed for your returne for England, and with our kind acknowledgments of the Diligence and successfull industry you have exprest on our behalfs through this whole Affaire, we remaine

Your truely affectionate
Friends and Servants
A D   S P

To Mr St Michell

101. S.P. TO B. ST. MICHEL[1]

London November the 17th 1679.

Brother,

My last was of the 13th instant. Since which I have this day received together both of yours of the 8/18th 12/22th ditto, for which I thanke you, and doe in the 1st place referr you to my said last for answer to the principall point now before us concerneing the Persons designed from Mme Pellissary to come over for England, I being still of the minde, that not soe much for the charge of it (though that is considerable) as for the indecency of giveing them fruitless journey at this time of yeare into England, I think it by much the best and most obligeing to them, to stop them. For it is most certain that I cannot have any Tryall this Terme, and noe less uncertain whether I shall have any in the next, or ever any at all. For though since my last Scott is said to have appeared in Towne, yet from many considerations I am very fully perswaded that the Rascall will not know how to furnish himselfe with any further Evidence then what hee has; But that therefore, though hee has vilany sufficient yet hee has too much Craft and Cowardice to deare to stand a Tryall. Therefore as to that Point pray pursue the advice contained in my last wherein I communicated the same by particular Letters to Messieurs

[1] Rawl. A. 194 : 111–12. Secretarial copy.

Trenchepain and Pelletier and refer'd you to their kind assistance and Councell in the execution of it; and by hastning now from your returne expecting my positive and last determination therein by the next.

As for my little Cosen your Daughter shee is (I thank God) in a very good health againe and with the rest of your Family very well, my Sister onely Excepted, who labours of the Disease of the Season, which noe body at this time almost escapes, I meane a great Cold but I hope will bee soon well; Mrs Hewer[1] and almost every body in this[2] family being in like condition.

I am mightily bound to Mlle Desmoulins for her 2 new Papers you now send mee, and with a thousand acknowledgments of her favours in what shee has done must necessarily beg her to bee pleased to accommodate mee with the Originall Contract as being a thing that I would in noe wise bee soe importunate with her for, were it not that my Councell tells mee it will be one of the most important and essential evidences that I can have in my Cause, and that which I shall bee most carefull in the safe preserving and that just returneing of to her. Pray therefore bee as earnest with her as you can in it.

I shall acquaint Sir A D with what you write touching his kinsman Timpeny and advise you further concerning it in my next; in the mean time very well allowing of your Caution therein.

It was my misfortune to have the Letter I wrote last post to Monsieur Pelletier misse of his right delivery at the Post Office, by which means it has lost a Post, but I pray your excuseing it to Mr Pelletier by this, it being inclosed.

I thank you for what you observe of Mr Foster and Mr Gourville and am well satisfied with Mlle Desmoulins's reserveing the Contract just to your Comeing if you cannot get it sooner.

I am satisfied alsoe with what you write touching La Pointe and Mr Gourville's Porter.

I have seen 2 letters of the 18th and 22th instant from Mr Trenchepain to Mr Houblon, wherein hee speak's with very great care and kindness for mee about the business of the French Gentlemen's Coming over. For which pray return him my most faithfull thanks, and acquaint him with what I have now wrote you upon that subject, as being what I doe conceive to bee in every respect best with regard to them as well as to my selfe.

As to the last point concerning your further supplyes of money I doe not doubt your care of me in that respect suitable to what you shew mee in every other, and therefore though I have a great deale

---

[1] Mrs. Hewer, the elderly mother of William Hewer, in whose household in York Buildings S.P. was now residing.   [2] *the*, canc.

of reasons to bemoane the ill fortune of my being prest to soe great
an expence in this affaire, yet relying upon your good husbandry
therein, I have by this Post given order for Credits for you by Mr
Trenchepain for 50 £ and if the necessity of the business doe call for
it, of 50 £ more, but I intreat you againe to bee as thoughtfull on my
behalfe in this Point as you can, and being in hopes, as I have already
said to bee able to give you my last instructions for your returne by
the next post I bid you most kindly farewell, and remaine

Your truely affectionate
Brother to serve you
S P

To Mr St Michell

102. S.P. TO B. ST. MICHEL[1]

London November the 24th 1679.

Brother,

My last was of the 17th instant, I omitting writting by the last
Post in our expectation of some Letters from your selfe, that might
give mee some new matter. But it is now 2 Posts since I received any
thing from you, your last being of the 12/22th instant, at which
silence of yours I am under a loss what to impute to it, as being under
some impatience to know how you proceed with the French Gentlemen, least your good will to my Affaire should lead you to the hastning them away for England before your receit of my directions in
that particular by my letters of the 10 and 13th instant, for being
wholly prevented in my Tryall this Terme, and noe less uncertain
of haveing any the next, it would bee matter of extraordinary paine
to mee to have those Gentlemen hurried over hither to noe purpose.
Besides that since my last the French Embassadour has without any
expectation on my part or desire, or ever haveing spoken to him about
it, let mee understand from Monsieur Colbert the resentments hee
has of the injury done Sir A D and mee by this Rascall Scott, and has
promised that all just evidence shall bee ready to attend us from
Madam Pellissary's Family, whensoever our Cause shall require it,
in order to the doeing right to our innocence in this matter. About
which I shall bee able to write to you more particularly by this day
Senight at furthest, for as much as the Terme ending on Friday next
the 28th instant I doubt not but Sir A D and I shall receive soe much
right at least from the Law as to bee under some certainty what wee

---

[1] Rawl. A. 194 : 112–13. Secretarial copy.

may expect the next Terme, if we cannot obtaine our satisfaction this. And from thence it is that we forbeare till then the positive Orders I promised you in my last for your Comeing home, as not knowing what new thoughts or Councell that day may produce, but you are not to doubt but this day Senight will bring you our last advice, and accordingly you may expect it, and bee prepareing yourselfe for it.

Sir A D does concurr with me in approveing your forbearance to deliver the Letter to Mr Tempeny, and will finde out some other hand to deliver it by, if it continue necessary. My sister (thankes bee to God) is very well recover'd, and with her whole Family at this time in perfect good health, which wishing the continuance of to your selfe is all at present from

Your truely affectionate
brother to serve you
S P

To Mr St. Michel

103. S.P. TO B. ST. MICHEL[1]

London November the 27th 1679

Brother,

My last was of the 24th instant. Since which I have yours of the 19/29th ditto, with another of the same date from my most Worthy Friend Monsieur Trenchepain, which I doe acknowledge carry soe much consideration in them, grounded upon that of your haveing now none to come over but Monsieur Druillet and the Porter, that I doe perfectly concurr with Monsieur Trenchepain and you in the haveing of those 2 come over along with you without longer stay, in case we shall tomorrow (which is the last day of the Terme) have any prospect given us of a Tryall to bee had the next Terme, or ever at all. For unlesse more Evidence does come in against us, then has yet appeared we can never hope for a Tryall, and as the publick state of things is, I cannot promise myselfe that Our Judges will ever discharge us without a Tryall. But of this we shall be able, I hope, to make some tolerable judgement, soe as to understand what we may reasonably depend upon, and consequently send you our last and positive Directions by the very next Post. And till then I am not in condition of saying more, then that if ever we shall have a Tryall it will bee in the next Terme, and if we can bee assured of it then, we

---

[1] Rawl. A. 194 : 113–14. Secretarial copy.

shall give you our advice (as I have said before) for your present bring-ing over of these two persons with you.

That therefore being all that I can offer you upon [the] Subject, and haveing many things to take care for against my appeareing in Court tomorrow, I will pray you to excuse to Monsieur Trenchepain my not answering his till the next, assureing him of my most gratefull resentments of his kindnesse to mee and intreat him to assist you in your keeping these two persons under a suspense as to their comeing or not comeing over into England till you have what I now promise you by the next, it being matter of much trouble to mee to finde with what difficulty they are to bee brought to consent to their Comeing. And I pray to God, that the Cause of these poor Men's feare to come into England may not bee attended with as much reall danger to those of our Countrey-men who shall have occasion of goeing abroad, it seeming therefore to mee not unreasonable that these Per-sons have the satisfaction they desire for their being safe while they are here.

I wish with all my heart that you were once possessed of the Originall Contract from Mlle Des Moulins. Which being all that my present time will allow mee to say, saveing that my Sister and her Family Continue in good health, I remayne

Your very affectionate
Brother and Servant
S P

I shall answer this your last Letter more amply by the next, and particularly in writting to Mlle Des Moulins, whose letter is deliver'd to Mme La Marquise.

To Mr St. Michell

104. S.P. TO B. ST. MICHEL[1]

London December 1st 1679

Brother,

My last was of the 27th of November, since which I have yours of the 26th ditto with another of the same date from Monsieur Pelletier. Whereto I am to give you this in Answer, that our Terme is now over, and soe farr from giveing us an opportunity of Tryall, as that noe Evidence at all (though Scott bee in town) offer'd to appeare against us in Court; nor any intimation that any, unless it bee Scott, is ever likely to appeare. And yet such is the Law of Eng-

---

[1] Rawl. A. 194 : 114. Secretarial copy.

land, that we cannot obtaine a Discharge presently, but are constrained to waite for another Terme, and that, without any assurance of any Tryall then. Soe that in one word, we are yet as much to seek what to say concerning the bringing over of the 2 Persons you last mentioned, as ever we were, and[1] consequently cannot tell what to advise you about it; especially considering the unwillingnesse which they have to come, according to Monsieur Peletyer's Account in his Letter Which would render their comeing much more uneasy to them, in case at their comeing they should finde the Journey imposed upon them to noe purpose. Which in my private judgment I am apt to beleeve they would, for I am thoroughly afraid we shall never have the opportunity of clearing ourselves by a Publick Tryall; though I cannot nevertheless soe depend upon it, as to lay aside the care of my Witnesses. We shall therefore bee forced to waite yet another Post, to see whether we can by any means come to some clearer prospect of our Business; which we are daily useing means to obtaine, and by that time Mr Joyne will I presume bee in readiness to returne home, and with our Letters, bring you the result of all our deliberations in this matter, And to them therefore referring you, I in the mean time send my most humble Services and thankes to Messieurs Trenchepain and Peletyer, to whom I shall then give the trouble of Letters alsoe.

I shall alsoe at the same time return my most humble thankes to Mlle Des Moulins for that which I have now by your hand received from her, and which I hope will answer my occasions, without the Originall. What I have to add is, that I thank God my sister St Michell is in perfect good health againe with her whole Family, and that I am

Your truely affectionate
Brother to serve you
S P

To Mr St Michel

105. S.P. TO B. ST. MICHEL[2]

York-Buildings, December the 8th 1679.

Brother,

My last was of the 1st instant, wherein I answer'd yours of the 26th of November, without receiveing any from you since. Soe as what I have now to say to you is, that some thing relateing to our

---

[1] *by*, canc.   [2] Rawl. A. 194 : 116–17. Secretarial copy.

Affaire has prevented Mr Joyne's Dispatch from hence with this Post, it being Sir A D's and my earnest Labour to obtaine some certainty before hee goes, of what we are to expect the next Terme, which we cannot yet procure, nor can indeed tell how any Body can give us any perfect intelligence concerning it, but Scot himselfe, from whom we are not likely to learne it. This onely I can tell you, that hee does give out in his Coffee-house-talke, that hee has Eleven Witnesses to bring[1] from France against us, when the Parliament meets; that hee shall have the very Originall Papers which were deliver'd to Monsieur De Seignelay by Sir A D to produce to the Parliament; that hee will prove your haveing offer'd two thousand pounds to Foster, and (upon his Refusall) to some body else to informe you in some thing that may take away his Life, and that you would secure the true payment thereof to them by good Merchants in Paris. Of which, though every part bee (I am confident) untrue, and the greater part impossible; especially after soe much caution as I have given you touching the makeing of any Gifts or Promises, and the Evidences you have sufficiently given mee of your regard thereto in your dealings with Sherwin and Foster; yet I thought it not amiss to give you this intimation of it for your makeing such silent use thereof as in your Prudence shall seem fitt; and with particular respect to Foster, who (if hee bee a man of any degree of honesty) will make noe difficulty of giveing you some thing under his hand for the cleareing you of that Calumny, and the rather, because Scott has given out, that Foster himselfe has declared this. But I am of opinion you should respite the doeing any thing in this Matter till Mr Joyne comes, who will bee able to informe you more thorowly therein by discourse then I can this way; and I doe presume you may depend upon his setting from hence for France on Thursday next, soe as to imbarque at Dover on the Packett-Boat upon Friday the 12th instant, by whose hand you shall have a fuller account of all my Affaires together with the Letters I last promised you to Messieurs T and P and Mlle Des Moulins. But pray take notice, that though it may not bee amiss for you to acquaint Mme Joyne with the time of her Husband's purpose to bee comeing hence, yet upon considerations, which (for saveing time now) you will understand from Mr Joyne, the less notice is taken of your frequenting his house at this time the better.

You will alsoe from him fully understand the inducements for my respiteing your comeing from Paris till his returne thither. In the mean time you may depend upon that your stay will bee now very short, and that in case we shall still thinke it expedient to have those two French-men brought over by you, the later they come, the less

[1] *expect*, canc.

tedious their stay will bee here to the Terme, I longing in the mean time to heare from you of their being better fixt in their inclination and resolution to come over then they seemed to bee in your last account of them. Soe after adviseing you of the continuance of the health and Welfare of my Sister and her Family, I bid you kindly farewell and remaine

Your truely affectionate
Brother and Servant
S P

To Mr St Michel

106. S.P. TO B. ST. MICHEL[1]

London December the 15th 1679.

Brother,

My last was of the 8th instant wherein I told you of my haveing received none of yours since that of the 26th of November but have lately had one of the 6th/16th instant, for which I kindly thank you and particularly for the satisfaction it brings mee about the two Persons who are to come over. Concerning which I cannot yet for my Life obtaine information enough to direct mee what to advise; nor has Mr Joyne had yet opportunity of performing all that remains upon his hands to bee done here; though hee had bespoken a place in the Dover-Coach to have gone hence this day being Monday. But I doubt not but hee will bee able to depart hence on Thursday next, and I hope by him to be better prepared to send some finall Resolutions concerning those Gentlemen.

The Duke of Buckingham is not yet returned into England but said to bee still in France.

I doe thorowly agree with you, in it's being much better to have those 2 Persons come over of their owne good will, then otherwise. And therefore doe take notice of your care in that Particular.

I doe not blame your takeing soe heavily your haveing noe more intelligence from England. But you would doe it less, if you knew how little any man's head here is at leasure to write or doe more then just their owne business requires from them; I speake now, of your Friends and mine. For they have all their loads, though they doe not tell you of it; and some of them such as they must inevitably sink under. Therefore pray spare your opinion of them, and bee assured, that were there any thing extraordinary for you to bee informed of

---

[1] Rawl. A. 194 : 120–21. Secretarial copy.

in relation to your owne concernments, I would doe it myselfe, or at least take care to have it done by another hand.

My Sister and your Family I thank God is very well, and I hope a little time will put an end to this troublesome Affaire, that you may see them and your Friends with some satisfaction here againe.

In the mean time hopeing in God that you have taken care above all things to observe my caution to you against doeing any thing that might bee interpreted bribeing, or makeing of promises to any Persons from whom you have indeavour'd to gather informations, and particularly Foster and Dailié, I haveing heard that Scott has had the confidence to assert some thing very positively of that kind, in relation to those 2 men (which as I had rather my Cause should perish, then you should bee guilty of, soe I perswade myselfe you would choose alsoe) I remaine

Your truely affectionate
Brother and Servant
S P

To Mr St Michel

107. S.P. TO B. ST. MICHEL[1]

London December the 18th 1679.

Brother,

My last was of the 15th instant, since which I have yours of the 13th ditto, and am intirely at a loss what answer to give you to it. For as to the charge of bringing those 2 persons over, it is soe farr from haveing any weight with mee at this time (the Terme being now soe near againe) that the first thing that I not onely would, but ought to doe should bee to desire your comeing away forthwith to England and bringing those Gentlemen with you, had I the least ground to hope for my haveing a Tryall when they come (which I must confess I doe now wholly dispair of ever haveing, our Parliament[2] being prorogued till November next) or were sure that Monsieur de Ruvigny would not think a much greater slight to him to bee put to the trouble to get these People to come over and finde nothing to doe when they come, my doubtfulness in which puts mee under an uncertainty what would bee best for mee to doe. For rather then

---

[1] Rawl. A. 194 : 121–3. Secretarial copy.

[2] S.P. and Deane were not to be tried before Parliament, but, as the purpose of the accusation was political, the accusers were unwilling to produce their evidence in any court until such time as political capital might be made of the sensation they proposed to create. Charles II had prorogued Parliament.

give offence to Monsieur De Ruvigny Sir A D and I would have [them] come, whatever the Charge were though it was for noe other use, then to have the seeing and proveing the Good-will and Justice of Strangers, in reproach to what we meet with of the contrary in both from our owne Countrey-men and of our owne Protestant Profession. And it is onely from the want of Sir A D's Company at this present to give mee his personall Concurrence therein, that I doe not now send you peremptory Directions, to let them know positively that they are to come, but I perswade myselfe that unlesse I doe in the mean time receive something from you to hinder it you will receive such Order from us by the very next Post. And in confidence of that, I have taken upon Mee to stop Mr Joyne's Comeing away by this Packett; for if they come, I would not have him absent. But of this, you shall not need to take notice to his family, for I have not yet fully acquainted him with my intentions herein.

I hope you have 'ere this consider'd what Pretence (if any) Foster can have for the Discourse which I mentioned to you in mine of the 8th, and whether hee bee such a villain as to invent soe devillish an untruth, as my Confidence in your better integrity and Prudence assures mee that to bee; or to deny to give you something under his hand to his kinsman Sir Timothy Tirrell or some other Friend to vindicate himselfe against soe reproachfull a lye as some body has father'd upon him. But I must confess that I doe rather suspect that hee who values not the Truth in one thing will make very little difficulty to abuse it in another; as you will finde hee has done, in the Answer hee has lately given to the Letter sometime since wrote him by Sir T. Tirrell, a Copy of which Answer I doe here enclose you, leaveing it to your Prudence to make such use of it as (if possible) we may learne the very Truth of this Matter.

And that you may know who it was that this Intelligence came from out of France, which I gave you in mine of the 8th I have had the Good fortune to understand that it was wrote by that Person whom (not to name his Name) you told mee in yours of the 4/14th of October you wished to bee with mee, in company with Langley, as haveing been employed in writing upon the last great Chart. This I have from the Discourse of him that is best able to tell, and therefore doe recommend it to you to make the same use of it as of the former.

But this brings it into my mind to ask (if I never did it before) whether it might not bee of moment to have an Attestation of that Langley before a Notary, and to desire you to get it if it bee to bee had.

I likewise pray you to looke out for and bring over with you a Book or 2 if you can find them, viz one called La Police de la Mer, anothor upon the same Subject, respecting the Sea and Navigation writ by one Hobier, and any other you can finde relateing to the same Matters, as I am told there are Severall. There is alsoe another Book called L'Admiral de France printed, as I take it, about 80 or 90 years agoe, which I would bee glad to have. But if they bee bound up in Leather Covers, you must tear the Covers off or they will [be] in danger of being forfeited.

I wish we could hear something of Captain La Piogeries Papers before you come away. And [one] thing more (while I think of it) were to bee wished that if Madam Pellissary had any Friend here in England that shee does or could write to shee might bee prevailed with to write a few Lines to that Person (Man or Woman) signifying something to the Purpose of her former Attestation and her sending over these two Persons upon this occasion, nameing their Names, and the relation they had to her Husband's Service in the year 1675. By which alsoe somebody will bee here a Liveing Witness to attest her Hand, besides Monsieur Druillet who I presume knowes it. And this seems the more necessary for her to doe, as being a Protestant, since both these Servants of her late Husband's prove to bee Catholicks. Which and referring you for more to my next is all at present from

Your truely affectionate
Brother to serve you
S P

My Sister and your Family (blessed bee God) are all well.
To Mr St Michel

108. S.P. TO B. ST. MICHEL[1]

January the 1st 1679/80

Brother,

Being but newly returned to Towne without opportunity of giveing my selfe any recollection of my Matters, I should have respited[2] my writeing to you till the next Post were it not for the conveying to you the enclosed from Mr Joyne to your Selfe and Madam Joyne, and the owening to you my receit of yours of the 24th of December, my last being of the 18th ditto.

I am out of all doubt concerning your care in the Business you write of and am very glad of what you have received from Foster, I wish I had a Copy of it, and that hee would write a word or 2 to the same effect to Sir Timothy Tirrell or some other of his relations upon

[1] Rawl. A. 194 : 124. Secretarial copy.
[2] MS. *should have had respited.*

the Discourse hee has heard of Scott's report concerning him; I being in some hopes that even Dallié himselfe may bee abused in it, and doe pray you to consider whether by Foster or some other hand you could not come by the Truth of it. Which recommending and leaveing wholly to your Discretion is all at present from

Your &ca

S P

My Sister and her Family are all very well.

To Mr St Michel

109. S.P. TO B. ST. MICHEL[1]

January 5th 1679/80

Brother,

Hopeing you have received mine of the 1st instant owneing the receit of yours of the 24th of December this comes to give you Sir A D's and my finall Determinations for your Disposeing of your matters now for your returne into England and bringing with you the 2 French Witnesses you have now with you, and ordering it soe, as to bee here as near as you can about the last of this month English Stile. Not that I can foresee or hope we shall bee able to obtaine any Tryall, by which their comeing might bee render'd usefull to us, but principally to prevent the dissatisfaction which you seem apprehensive might bee taken by those Persons to whom soe much trouble has on our occasion been given in case we should seem to neglect their kindness therein by our not sending for these Witnesses over. To which may indeed bee added the Consideration of the Lowness of their quality, and consequently the less charge to bee contracted[2] by their comeing, whether we have any occasion to make use of them here or not.

Pray therefore bee prepareing for your and their Comeing accordingly, and expect what I may have further to say to you in any Particular about it, by the next post.

In the mean time I would desire you to remember to finish any thing that remaines yet to bee done; as particularly, that which I sometime since mentioned to you about Searching the Bureau d'Adresse enquireing after Monsieur Piogery's Papers, and buying the Bookes I named to you, and what (if anything) else you can recollect. And since Mr Foster has cleared himselfe to you under his hand (which I could wish hee would doe to the like Effect by a Line

---

[1] Rawl. A. 194 : 124–5. Secretarial copy.   [2] *collected*, canc.

or 2 to Sir T Tirrell) I could bee well contented you would by his hand (unless you could think of a better) endeavour to finde out whether Dallié will deny it too. For the Report is said by Scott to have been sent by one Dallié hither to one Willson to bee by him communicated to Scott (as I take it) about September, last, though I cannot bee perfect in the time. To which I am to add, that Dallié did not write to Willson in true, but fained, Names; Scott in particular being called by the Name of Artabane. Of all which you may communicate to Foster as much or as little as you shall in your Discretion thinke fit, and noe more. But indeed I am for findeing out the Truth, as haveing an imagination, that even Dallié in this Matter has been abused as well as Foster. And Foster may have reason enough to enquire after it in his owne Vindication as haveing been reported by Dallié to have told him that hee had had such an offer[1] made him by you. Soe referring you for more to my next, I remaine

Your &ca

S P

My Sister and her Family are well, and Mr Joyne who send's you his service, and did by the last a letter to you, and another to his Wife.

To Mr St Michel

110. S.P. TO B. ST. MICHEL[2]

London January 8: 1679/80

Brother,

The inclosed was what should have come to you by the last Post, but for the misfortune of it's comeing halfe an houre too late to the Post-house. But the Contents of it is such as will suffer noe great prejudice by the losse of 2 days, and therefore referring you to it for information in what Sir A D and I have at last determined on touching your Comeing Over and bringing Monsieur Druillet and Le Picard with you I shall only repeat what I therein said in relation to the time by which we desire we may see you with them here, which is by the last of this Month English Stile. The reason of our choice of which Time is that our Terme beginning here the 23th of this month, and ending the 12 of February (which wants a day of 3 Weekes) if you bee not here by that time, vizt. the 31th instant, we may run some hazard of wanting you, in case we should have the good fortune of obtaineing a Tryall this Terme; which though we

---

[1] The reference is to the false charge of bribing witnesses for S.P.
[2] Rawl. A. 194: 127–8. Secretarial copy with postscript in S.P.'s hand.

have little hopes of, yet it is not impossible, and therefore since you doe bring over those Gentlemen we would have them here soe, as not to want their Evidence, if we should have occasion to make use of it. Soe that if you can save any of these dayes which we have given you, it were soe much the better, and pray endeavour it, and expect the last that I shall write to you into France by the next Post, by which I shall send you my Letters of acknowledgments to Monsieur Trenchepain, Monsieur Pelletier and others of our Friends at Paris, as presumeing that by that time, you will have disposed of your Affairs, soe as to bee near your departure thence; I haveing nothing more of business from this moment that I design to trouble you with, and therefore will pray you to loose noe time in further Expectation of any from mee after you are ready to come away.

This onely upon a late discourse with Mr Denise I must committ to your care, which you will finde in one inclosed from him to Monsieur Le Comte d'Estrée and another to your selfe relateing to Scott's haveing offer'd to sell some Maps to the said Comte for the use of the K. of France, Mr Joyne confirmeing to mee that the thing is true, and another English Gentleman being here that can witness it. The matter I shall not need to repeat but[1] referr you to his said Letters for it.

What I have to add is to advise you that if you doe meane to make any attempt (either by Foster or otherwise) upon Dallié, to discover the truth of what I lately acquainted you with, of Scott's reports touching you, and that you have not already done it, you will doe well to make it one of the last things you doe before your Comeing away, and soe (if it might bee) as that Dallié might not understand that the Enquiry Comes from you. For if indeed hee does hold any correspondence with Scott, hee that has already had the villany to write one untruth (and soe bold a one) concerning you, will not omitt any occasion of inventing another. Which leaveing with you, it being now alsoe very late, I remaine

Your &ca

S P

My Sister and family are all well. Mr Joyne allsoe salutes you, and by the enclosed proposes to you one Enquiry more which may bee very usefull about the Count Monbas[2]

To Mr St Michel

---

[1] *must*, canc.

[2] This relatively unimportant postscript added in S.P.'s own hand corroborates the evidence of other emendations by his pen that these secretarial drafts in letter-books were really dictated original versions, from which fair copies were made to send through the post.

111. S.P. TO B. ST. MICHEL[1]

London January 12: 1679/80.

Brother,

My last was of the 8th, which brought along with it (by misfortune) another of the 5th instant, which should have come the Post before, but I doubt not but they will come both of them time enough by the last Post, soe as that this may finde you ready to begin your Journey, and that I may see you with Monsieur Druillet and Le Picard here by the time I proposed to you, namely by the last of this month English Stile, or within a day or two more, which I hope will bee time enough for the answering my occasions, in case we should bee soe fortunate as to obtaine a tryall the next Terme, which we still despair of.

It fall's out very well that Madam Colodon[2] is of the Acquaintance of Madame Pellissary that by her hand I may be able to aske what I have still to expect from Madame Pellissary; and much satisfaction it gives mee to hear how farr these two Persons are upon recollection, able to give their Testimony more particularly then before, for the evidenceing of the Truth.

I shall not need to repeate my desires in my last that you would try to get the Truth from Dallié, for I must confess I have severall reasons to think that Scott has in those reports made use of his as well as Foster's Name without their Commission. But if my good Nature does deceive mee therein, then the onely Remedy were to bee able to prove Dallié to bee soe great a Villain as you describe him to bee.

My meaning in what I writt touching Langley was onely the getting a Certificate from him of the Truth of what you learned from him in discourse concerning Scott, when first your Letters mention'd him to mee.

I thanke you for your Care about the Bookes.

I am very sensible of what you write touching Mr Joyne's absence from home, and hope to have a letter for his Wife by this, as I sent you one for her in my last.

I cannot imagine why you should apprehend it needfull for you to have the King's Warrant for your coming into England, there being not the least occasion I know of for it; there being noe body now appeareing, nor has for a great while, to prosecute the Business of Moon. Besides that had your departure out of England been censured by any body here (as I never yet heard it was) your returne to England

---

[1] Rawl. A. 194 : 128–30. Secretarial copy.

[2] Mme Pellissary writes to Mme Colodon of London in French, introducing her nephew, M. des Glereaux, and giving an account of the occasion upon which Sir A. Deane dined in her home. Original. Holograph. 27 Jan. 1680. (Rawl. A. 188 : 200.)

is the onely proper way to remove that Censure, I haveing long since in writeing under my hand acquainted the Commissioners of the Admiralty with your being in France by the King's leave at my desire and upon my occasion, and that you would bee in England againe as soon as the Condition of my Affaire would permit, which I presumed would bee against the Terme. Soe as I cannot in any kind conceive, that it is either necessary or soe much as expedient, to aske a Warrant from the King for your returneing to your home and to his Service. Neverthelesse I will immediately advise about it, and if I finde it otherwise, with respect either to your Selfe, or the 2 Strangers with you who are Catholicks, you shall certainly hear from mee, either at Calais or Dover. Therefore pray offer not at the makeing the least delay of your Comeing over, upon the Score of what you seem to think soe necessary for it, I meane, the King's Warrant. Besides, that if the worse came to the worse, if you should bee proceeded withall, as Captain Moore was when hee came from Sea and voluntarily surrender'd himselfe My Lord Chief Justice (though the Accusation was then fresh) never committed him to prison, but accepted of Bayle for him in noe greater Summe (as I take it) then 200 £. Which you shall not need to doubt the haveing Security for, if there should bee occasion. Bee therefore in noe paine upon this account, but take notice that if I finde it necessary to write to Calais it shall bee to Monsieur Molieres (the Person you propose) or if to Dover to Mr Bastincke or Mr Nephew. But pray let mee have as frequent notice as you can of your advancement upon the Roade towards England, and after your Arrivall at Dover, that if there bee occasion, I may know where any Letters of mine may meet with you, and at your Comeing to Towne either send mee word[1] to Mr Hewer's, that I may come to you, or come directly to Mr Hewer's; my Design being to lodge Monsieur Druillet and Le Picard at Monsieur Denise's house, (hee haveing offer'd mee accommodation for them) in case there bee not sufficient accommodation for them at your house, where I have had a Dutch Gentlewoman[2] lyeing at my Charge for above 2 monthes past, sent for out of Holland on the same Account.

Lastly, I send you the inclosed Letters[3] which after perusall I leave with you to deliver at your Discretion with my most faithfull

---

[1] *One*, canc.

[2] Deborah Egmont had apparently set out prematurely from Holland, without waiting to be called, in order to give evidence against Scot. (S.P. to Mr. Carr in Holland, 24 Oct. 1679, Rawl. A. 194 : 93.)

[3] Secretarial copies of four letters of gratitude, all in French: S.P. and A.D. to M. le Marquis de Ruvigny, including also acknowledgements to his son, M. de Ruvigny; S.P. to Mlle Des Moulins; S.P. to M. Trenchepain; and S.P. to M. Pelletyer. (Rawl. A. 194 : 130–1.)

acknowledgments and most humble Services due to Messieurs Trenchepain and Pelletyer as Persons to whose Justice and Generosity Myselfe and Friends must ever bee indebted. Which with hopes of seeing you at length and within or near the Time by mee proposed, in England, and assureing you of the health of my Sister and her Family, and with my Blessing to my little Nephew is all at present from

Your &ca

S P

To Mr St Michell

112. S.P. TO B. ST. MICHEL[1]

London January the 19th 1679/80

Brother,

   This comes to meet you at Calais in hopes that it will finde you and your Company well advanced soe farr towards England, and to give you a Copy of Soe much of my last of the 12th instant as I think of most moment to Supply you in case that Letter shall not have come to your hand before your departure from Paris. To which I haveing nothing now to add saveing that though the 2 Persons you bring along with you bee both of them Roman Catholicks, yet being Strangers and brought openly hither in order to the testifying the Truth in a case depending in a Court of Judicature, which I shall before your Comeing acquaint Mr Bastinck at Dover with, I have informed my-selfe from the Office of one of the Secretarys of State particularly by Mr Thinne that there will bee noe occasion of any Warrant from the King for their permission to land and come up to Towne. Where thinkeing long now to see you and[2] hopeing in a little time to enjoy the fruits of all that paines and Care which you have soe long been takeing for mee I remaine

Your &ca

S P

To Mr St Michel

113. S.P. TO B. ST. MICHEL[3]

January 26th 1679/80.

Brother,

   I have nothing to add of moment, to what (I hope) you have met with from mee at Calais, yet would I not omit to send this to meet

[1] Rawl. A. 194 : 132. Secretarial copy.   [2] *in*, canc.
[3] Rawl. A. 194 : 132–3. Secretarial copy with postscript in S.P.'s hand.

you at Dover, where, by your last, I hope you may suddenly bee, you telling mee therein, you expected to bee at Calais as this day. I have just now alsoe understood from Monsieur Trenchepain that Mr Druillet has fayled to come with you, and that another Gentleman comes in his Room. For which I am greatly bound to the Justice and Generosity of Monsieur De Ruvigny and Madame Pellissary, though (as I dreaded) I have this Evening received a finall Answer from Mr Attorney Generall, that we are not to expect the haveing any Tryall this Terme. Upon which Score I am driven to cancell some Letters I had provided to goe by this Post to call over some Witnesses from Flanders who wayte there in hourely expectation of it from mee, however you and those you bring along with you are very welcome and I hope to see you here in few dayes supposeing you will bring them hither to Mr Hewer's at your first Comeing to Towne, to bee conducted thence either to Mr Denise's or your house to bee lodged as at your Comeing shall bee judged most expedient. In the mean time I cannot but say to you, that takeing in all Circumstances of scandall Expence, trouble and hazzard noe innocent man was ever embarassed as I have been, and remaine at this day, from the vilany of one man of noe Acquaintance with myselfe nor Credit with any honest man else that knowes him. The thoughts of which, should I give much way to them, would distract mee. But God is above all. And soe wishing an end to your troublesome part in it, as well as my owne, I with most kind thankes bid you adieu, and remain

Yours &ca

S P

My Service to the Company with you, and to Mr Bastinck[1] under whose Cover this comes, and to whom I am very much bound. My sister and your family are in good health.

To Mr St. Michel

114. S.P. TO MR. BRISBANE[2]

February 20th 1679/80

Sir

    The Law haveing at length determined soe farr in the Cause of Sir Anthony Deane and mine, as to put an end to that part of our

---

[1] S.P. to Mr. Bastinck, 26 Jan. 1679/80, enclosing letter to St. Michel. Copy. (Rawl. A. 194 : 133.)

[2] Rawl. A. 194 : 136–7. Secretarial copy. John Brisbane, whom the diarist Evelyn calls ' a learned and industrious person', former secretary to the embassy at Paris, was now secretary to the Admiralty. Since the exile of the Duke of York, the office of Lord High Admiral had been vested in a commission.

Trouble which relates to our longer keeping of the Bearer my Brother Mr St Michel in France, where (through the Delays of our Prosecution here) hee has, by His Majesty's Allowance been attending for the bringing over our Witnesses, which we were encouraged by the Court to doe (in hopes of a Tryall) the end of the last Terme, but without the succes we expected, through the continued unreadiness of our Adversaryes to produce Evidence; I make it my request, that to the former kindnesses I received from you on this occasion at Paris (for which I pay you my most hearty thankes) you will add That of presenting my Brother to the honourable Commissioners hee being now in readiness to receive and observe any of their Comands, and particularly in what respects the Commission His Majesty was sometime since pleased to give him in relation to the Affaires of His Navy at Tangier, and which this Misadventure of Sir A Deane's and mine has given him this unexpected interruption in the execution of. I kiss your hands and am

Your obliged and most humble Servant
S P

To Mr Brisband

115. S.P. TO B. ST. MICHEL[1]

York-buildings, March the 4th 1679/80.

Brother,

This will, I hope, find you and our Friends well-arrived at Dover, and serves by your hand to give them my most faithfull Services and thankes for the Favours I have received from them all.

Particularly I intreat you to doe it with all Respect to Monsieur Des-Glereaux, and pray him to take the trouble of the three enclosed Letters[2] to Madam De Pellissary, Monsieur De Ruvigny, and his Son, with all possible Expressions of Sir Antony Deane's and my thankfulness to them, assureing Monsieur Des Glereaux that in whatever any interest of mine may bee employ'd to his particular Service in England, it shall be wholly at his Disposall.

Give alsoe my most kind Respects to Mr Joyne with the Enclosed

---

[1] Rawl. A. 194 : 138–39. Secretarial copy, with postscript in S.P.'s hand. The sheet shows no evidence of having been folded or sent through the post.

[2] The three letters entrusted to Mme Pellissary's nephew, all in French, are copied into one page, Rawl. A. 194 : 140. The letter to Mme Pellissary reports that the case is expected to come up again in June, at which time S.P. may ask the porter, M. Moreau, to return to testify,

to bee deliver'd with his owne hand to Monsieur Trenchepain,[1] with my most faithfull Services and Acknowledgements to him.

There is another Letter I intend, if I can dispatch it to night, to Mlle Des Moulins,[2] which I had designed to bee deliver'd her by Mr Joyne; And doe Still, if hee bee not of opinion with you, that it may bee better as carrying more appearance of Respect towards her, that it bee deliver'd by Monsieur Des Glereaux Mr Joyne accompanying him. This I propose as not knowing but there may bee some Acquaintance between Monsieur De Pellissary's Family and her. But being wholly ignorant therein, I leave it to Mr Joyne and you to doe, as you see fit, in it.

Pray let Monsieur Moreau have my particular Respect expressed to him, together with the Esteem I have of his readiness to doe Sir Antony Deane and mee the Justice, which his Place enabled him to, more properly then any other, in the Main Point of Scott's being or not being at Monsieur De Pellissary's, hopeing that if our Case should require it we may see him againe in England to testify the Truth therein.

Least you should not of your Selfe remember it, pray give Monsieur Des Glereaux's Servant a Guinny or what you judge fit, for the trouble, which has been given him on our occasion.

If it should fall out that the much other Business I have upon my hands to dispatch this night, should prevent my writeing to Monsieur Trenchepain, let Mr Joyne know that hee shall have one for him by the next post, which will bee at Paris, I presume within two daies, as soon as hee, if hee goes to Dunkirk along with Monsieur Des Glereaux.

Lastly, as for what concern's mee at Dover, it is, That you would deliver my very humble Service to Mr Bastinck, takeing his Advice touching what may be fit for you to enquire after from Mr Breams, Mr Nephew, or any other Gentlemen there, relateing to the Passages that hapn'd at Scott's last Comeing out of France, and his being seized at Dover.[3] In which pray forget not to deliver my humble Service to Mr Breams, Mr Nephew, and any other of our Friends there; and particularly see if you can the Originall Examinations of Scott then taken there, one before the Mayor and the other before the Commissioners of the Passage, observeing their Dates, and whether they were both signed by Scott. Discourse alsoe with Mr Breams about the Trunk full of Crucifixes, which Scott pretends

---

[1] S.P. to M. Trenchepain in French. (Rawl. A. 194 : 141.) Copy.
[2] S.P. and A.D. to Mlle Des Moulins in French. (Rawl. A. 194 : 141.) Copy.
[3] Copies of interrogations of Scot at Dover, 29 April 1679, are preserved in Rawl. A. 188 : 127–33, 137.

Mr Breams told him were sent him over from one Moulins at Calais, or Diep, and by him addressed to mee. Learn alsoe of Mr Nephew, who had the op'ning of Scott's Trunks at Dover, and seemed to bee under much conversation with Scott, what hee observed extra-ordinary therein, and particularly as to Mapps and Sea Charts. Other Particulars had I time I might possibly have collected, but these are the principall, wherein I desire you to informe yourselfe. And if it should bee your fortune at Dover to meet with one Mr Boltele, who is an Acquaintance of these Gentlemen and mine, pray deliver my humble Service to him, and ask his aid in anything hee can inform you in. Which is all at present, I designing to write to you againe tomorrow night, and remaine

Your truely affectionate
Brother to serve you
S P

Pray keep this Letter, my other Business not giveing me[1] time at present to copy it.

Not well knowing how to give the proper Adress to Madame De Pellissary and Monsieur De Ruvigny the Son I have put them under false Covers for you to get superscribed as they ought to bee, takeing notice for feare of mistake that That has a figure of 1, in the corner is to Mr De Ruvigny, and that which has a figure of 2 to Madame De Pellissary.

I have also enclosed a small Letter with a token, I beleeve, in it from Madame Houblon to Monsieur Trenchepain, which I pray you to deliver to Mr Joyne for him to deliver to Mr Trenchepain with his owne hand. But let him not deliver it till hee has another Letter from myselfe to him.

116. S.P. TO B. ST. MICHEL[2]

8 March 1679/[80]

Brother,

I have received yours of the 6 Instant from Dover, where I am very glad to finde you and our friends well arrived to whome I pray you to repay once more my most humble Service, and thanks, being very sorry on their score, as well as my owne, and yours for the hin-drance they meet with to their Passuage through the crossness of the

---

[1] MS. *my.*

[2] Rawl. A. 194 : 142. Secretarial copy. A comparison of this date with that of Letter 113, 26 Jan., indicates the length of time in which the foreign witnesses were lodged at S.P.'s expense.

winde; praying you to use as much good husbandry in it, as you can, and to make all the use you are able of your stay there to get Informations in the business I wrote you about from the severall Gentlemen I named to you, takeing the advice of Mr Joyne concerning the Mapps and what else Mr Nephew can remember, that he saw upon the opening of Scot's Baggadge. Enquire alsoe of his demeanour whilst in custody, and the Letter which Mr Bastinck wrote me word, he wrote to my Lord Shaftsbury from prison, and whither he ever let fall any threats or words concerning me.

As to your Stay there, or comeing away I confess I am loath you should leave them there. And yet if one winde should continue cross above a day or two longer I thinck you must of necessity get your selfe excused by them. Of which I shall write to you againe. And in the meane time it would not I suppose cost much for you to goe over to Deale, and goe on board the Foresight Captain Killigrew, and see the three Receits given by him to Captain Saunderson Comander of the Charlot Yacht, which sailed from hence on Saturday with Sir Palmes Fairborne and 8000 £ put in 8 severall Boxes for the Guarrison of Tangier. And this will be a Service to the King, and noe great time spent in it. Which with my very humble Service to all the Gentlemen my Friends of Dover is all at present from

Your truely affectionate
Brother to serve you
S P

Brother Mitchell at Dover

117. S.P. TO JOHN PEPYS SENIOR[1]

York Buildings. March 27th, 1680.

Sir,

It is long since I have express'd my Duty to you, and truely every day has follow'd one another with some new occasion of care, soe as that though I have been in a great measure restor'd to the Liberty of my Person, my Minde has continued still in Thraldome, till now that it has pleased God in a miraculous manner to begin the Worke of my Vindication, by laying his hand upon James my Buttler by a Sickness whereof hee is some days since dead, which led him to consider and Repent of the wrongs hee had done mee in his Accuseing mee in Parliament, which hee has solemnly and publickly confess'd upon

[1] Rawl. A. 194 : 145–6. Secretarial copy. Printed : Smith, i. 210–11; Howarth pp. 93–94.

the holy Sacrament to the justifying of mee and my Family to all the World in that part of my Accusation which relates to Religion, and I question not but God Almighty will bee noe less just to mee, in what concern's the rest of my Charge, which hee knowes to bee noe less false then this. In the mean time His Holy Name bee praised for what hee has done in this Particular.

What I have to add is the letting you know that I am commanded to attend the King the next week at New Market[1] and by the Grace of God will goe and waite on you one day in my goeing or Returne; which I presume will bee either Tuesday or Saturday next, I designing to sett forth hence on Monday, and shall rather chuse to call upon you in my Goeing (which will bee on Tuesday) for feare least I should bee commanded to accompany the Court to London, where the King design's to bee this day Sevennights. In the mean time trusting in God to find you in good health, and with my most humble Duty presented to your Selfe, and my kind Love to my Brother and Sister, and their Family I remaine

Sir

Your ever obedient Son
S P

To Mr Pepys of Bramton

118. S.P. TO LORD BROUNCKER[2]

Tuesday Morning
May 11th [16]80

My Lord,

The enclosed is Copy of the Paper I mentioned to your Lordship this morning, as it was given to the Councell in 1675. The issue of which was, that being left to the Law, my Brother gave 5000 Ł Bayle for his answering the Complaints of his Accusers, and nonsuited them. Since which hee never heard word more of them till May 1679, when by the Practises of Mr Harbord &ca the said Persons were excited to renew their Clamours, onely to add to the noise against Sir A D[eane] and mee. For in now I hear more they have never appear'd to Mr Attorney Generall about it, soe often urged to it in Court by Sir A D[eane]; nor soe much as offer'd at troubleing my Brother about it, since his returne out of France,

<hr>

[1] S.P. was not interested in the racing. In a letter to James Houblon half a year later, 2 Oct. 1680, printed by Howarth (p. 102), S.P. reports himself again at Newmarket to solicit the king for considerable arrears on his salary. Rawl. A. 194.

[2] Rawl. A. 194 : 155. Secretarial copy.

though it bee now severall monthes that hee has been publickly knowne to bee in Towne, and openly appearing on his occasions. In a word, if any of the Commissioners of the Admiralty will give your Lordship and the rest any reasonable assurance that my Brother shall bee prosecuted in this Affaire hee will bee soe farr from desireing, that nothing shall tempt him to accept of any Employment or other occasion for his being out of the way to answer it. Or if for want of That they shall nevertheless desire to have something to justify their Sending him abroad in case hereafter any Enquiry shall bee made after him, when hee is gone; I will undertake hee shall [give] 5000 Ł security more for his Answering by his Attorney here to any Demand that shall bee made concerning him on occasion of this Matter in his Absence. I leave the same to your Lordship's Application and am

My Lord, Your Lordship's most obedient Servant

S P

To My Lord Brouncker

119. DR. JOHN TURNER TO S.P.[1]

Eynesbury May 20 1680

Sir

I give you many thanks for your great kindnesse to me at London, I have bin at Brampton the old Gentleman and the rest of the Family have good health, and fewer complaints were made then I have bin accustomed to hear from them, I heartily wish that you also may have lesse trouble in that kind, your Father thanks you for the care of his Watch, Sir you may now iustly expect from me the promised account of Sixtus 5tus Bible which I have travailed in, but instead of answering your expectation, I am necessitated to request a troublesome favour of you which is that you will please to let some of your servants pack up that Bible in a box or case and send it to Mr Joseph Came at the Rose in St Laureance Lane to be sent to me, he is my son in Law and will be very carefull of my concerns

Sir I beseech you deny not this my earnest request, I doe promise the book shall in a little time be sent back and with it you shall have an account whither this be truly the Bible of Sixtus 5tus or of Clemens Octavus what makes that of Sixtus quintus of so great value and what advantage we make by it against the Romanists Sir you may easily think that I make not this request for my owne sake or to shew

[1] Rawl. A. 181 : 293. Original. Printed : Smith, i. 212; Howarth, p. 94.

any skill that I have to make such iudgment, but I am desired to doe it by a person for whome I have great reverence, and foreseeing no inconveniencie can ensue from it, I have spoken confidently that this request would be graunted me and I once more humbly beseech you to graunt it, Sir I hope in god to wait on you at London next October and give you a particular account of all circumstances about this matter, I pray God graunt you health and peace

Sir

Your most affectionate and humble servant

JOHN TURNER

For Samuell Pepys Esquire, at Mr Hewers house in York-buildings in the strand.

120. DR. JOHN TURNER TO S.P.[1]

Eynesbury June 10 1680

Sir

On Teusday last I waited on Sir Nicholas Pedley to your Fathers house where we sealed new writings so setling Mr Jacksons land on his wife and children that tis not in his power to make any alteration, and if they dye without Issue the inheritance to the survivor and their heires, Sir the old Gentleman desires you will please to consider the inclosed and if you think Fitt to doe anything about the settlement then some afternoon to call at Sir Nicholas Pedleys chamber in Lincolns Inn, Whenever you shall come to Brampton I hope [you] will find matters there more easy then last time, though not so wise or happy as we desire, I have all their writings of settlement in my keeping till there be an opportunity of delivering them into your custody.

Sir I again renew my earnest request that you will please to lett your Sixtus 5tus Bible be sent to me, for that which occasions my desiring it is again renewed to me and I could not but say that my friend whose the book was had not denyed my request, Sir you may be assured of its safe and very speedy return

Sir

Your most obliged and humble servant

JOHN TURNER

For Samuel Pepys Esquire, at Mr Hewers in York buildings in the Strand

[1] Rawl. A. 181 : 315. Original.

121. DR. JOHN TURNER TO S.P.[1]

Eynesbury June 21 1680

Sir

I received your Sixtus quintus very safe and have sent it where it must receive sentence, Sir I am very much obliged to you for this favour and when I tell you all the circumstances about it I dare say you will be very well pleased with graunting my importunate request, espetially when the book is safely returned which I will take care it shall be in a very short time, Sir Mr Jackson is now with me and saith your Father and sister have both good health and that they are very peacable at home and like to continue so I doe believe him for when I was last there I found things much better then formerly, some of his debts begin now to be called for and for the payment of them all he must presently sell his copy hold land which is yet unsetled he tells me he is offered 180 £ for it your sister hath a great desire that you would please to buy it, and they all desire that you will please to let them know whither you will or not, for if you like not to purchase it he must speedily dispose of it to some other chapman, Sir I hope you will see Brampton shortly and find things there much more to your content then you did the last time.

Sir

Your most affectionate and obliged servant
JOHN TURNER

For Samuell Pepys Esquire, at Mr Hewers house in York-buildings in the Strand

122. S.P. TO DR. JOHN TURNER[2]

August the 4th 1680

Sir

I doe truely acknowledge my selfe ashamed of my haveing noe sooner thanked you for your last Favour. But the truth is, the occasion of your trouble (I mean in reference to *Brampton*) is soe unpleasant to mee in the very contemplation, that for my owne quiet I suppress what I can the memory of it, and soe am with much difficulty able to bring myselfe to admit the care of it into my owne

[1] Rawl. A. 181 : 310. Original.
[2] Rawl. A. 194 : 182–3. Secretarial copy in letter-book. Terms in italics indicate blanks in the written text which S.P. has filled in with shorthand symbols. The present editor has transcribed the shorthand by reference to Shelton's *Tachygraphy*.

thoughts, and ought therefore much less to express any forwardness in makeing it the occasion of trouble to any other. Nevertheless my Father hath soe pressed me to doe something in it towards the reliefe of *my sister* and her *children*, as the only thing that can give him quiet, that I am contented to listen to my Sister's Desire of my secureing the Land of her Husband's at Ellington, and provided that my doeing it may bee effected without exposeing my selfe to any Loss, by not haveing a penny-worth for a penny) I will (contrary to what I had resolved to doe) buy it. But then I tell my Sister too, that as I will expect to have it done without losse to myselfe as before; Soe I will have her satisfy mee, by doeing it to you, that this will put her and him out of *debts*, and her into a Security against any further new difficulties that his folly or ill-husbandry can contract upon *her*. Now, Sir, I doe make it my earnest request that you will bee pleas'd to take the trouble of receiveing from my *sister* what Satisfaction *she* can give you in this Matter. For I would not give my selfe any further care about it if what *each* now desires of mee be only to *stop* a present *gap*, and have the same thing or more come with a Rebound upon *me again* a year or two hence; it being a thing that I should much better like to know the worse of it now, and will bee never a whit better for them to keep for mee to hear of hereafter. For the Opinion I have of *his* incorrigibleness makes me I confess fear some such Designe, *he* not seeming to mee to bee made of *stuff* capable of any *amendment*, and I can well satisfy my selfe (I thanke God) that I have already done too much, to have any more flung away upon *him*.

This, Sir, is my Prayer to you, and this the truth of my apprehensions Wherein nevertheless I should be most glad to understand from your hand that I am under any misreckoning. Nor shall I offer at giveing you any Method to order your Enquiries by, but wholly leave it to your owne direction, and have referr'd my Sister to it as shee shall learne it from you. And as you shall encourage and advise me I shall governe myselfe towards her, who will always bee bound to you for your good nature on her behalfe, and soe shall I on the score of *our desolate*[1] *family*, remaineing

Your most oblig'd and most humble servant
S P

To Dr Turner of Eynesbury

[1] Transcription uncertain. Shorthand apparently reads: *disol* or *desol.*

123. DR. JOHN TURNER TO S.P.[1]

[Eynesbury] August 26 1680

Sir

I have returned your Bible with most humble thanks I hope you will receive it safe, the person for whome I borrowed it saith that it is not the Bible of Sixtus 5tus but of Clemens Octavus with the title of Sixtus, this he knoweth very well having the Originalls of both by him, when Clemens had printed his translation a little more then two year after that of Sixtus, the protestants observing some contradictions and above 2000 varieties in these two impressions proclaim to all the world that one of these two popes must needs be a Fallible interpreter of the scripture the church of Rome sensible of this endeavour whatever they can to call in all the impression of Sixtus and in severall places cause that of Clemens to be printed under his name this makes the true translation of Sixtus 5tus which is very rare to be of so great price, I will adde much more that hath bin said to me on this subject when I next wait on you, which I hope to doe next November

Sir I have received your letter of August 14 and have bin at Brampton where this is the plain case Mr Jackson hath land unsetled part Freehold and part copy to the value of 13 Ł 18s 0 per annum, but when the quitt rent and charge of alienation is rightly considered I would not be willing to give him above 200 Ł for it and so much I think it is worth; there are two reasons which move the old Gentleman and Mrsis Jackson so earnestly to desire your purchasing this land one is for that the estate being dismembred of this part will not be convenient for a tenant whereas they hope by your being owner the whole may continue togather The other reason is that he may discharge his debts which I told them on Friday last might be don by the mony of any other purchaser as well as by yours, but by a closer examination I found that it would not be don by either, for they confesse him to be in debt 350 Ł when the land will not sell for above 200 Ł so that upon the whole matter I think that your buying the land at a iust valuable rate will not put an end to their trouble from their creditors or yours from them But if you please to give 350 Ł for that which is not worth above 200 Ł then Mr Jackson offers to have the whole estate both reall and personall so settled upon Trustees for the use of his wife and children that he shall not be able to receive any part of it whilest he lives but will be confined to an allowance of 8 Ł or 10 Ł per annum, Sir You are better able then

---

[1] Rawl. A. 181 : 337. Original. Excerpts printed in Smith, i. 233–4, omitting family matters.

I am to judge how same such settlement may secure your selfe or Mrsis Jackson from future trouble, ther nothing remains to be considered but your accepting or refusing the Dear purchase, Sir I shall be most ready upon all occasions to afford them what assistance or advice I am able being most thankfully sensible of your kindnesse and favours to me

         Sir

                 Your most humble and Faithfull servant

                         JOHN TURNER

they tell me that Mr Jacksons estate (if this purchase be made out of it) will be 65 Ł per annum for six years and then but 50 Ł per annum out of which Mris Jackson must maintain her selfe and children, and give him an allowance

For Samuell Pepys Esquire at Mr Hewers house in York buildings in the Strand

124. S.P. TO DR. JOHN TURNER[1]

                        London. September the 3d. 1680

Sir

     I am newly return'd from a small journey to Essex, and finde both your Letters of the 26th and 30th instant Of which though the latter puts some stop to my present consideration of the former; yet I cannot, nor ought to forbeare the returneing you my most faithfull thankes for your extraordinary Friendship exprest upon the occasion of it's contents. Which I must confess carry matter in it of very little satisfaction to mee; unless it be that it would have been yet less satisfactory, to have had my knowledge of it longer delayd. And since it has pleased God to put this Sickness of my Brother Jackson's in the way of my comeing to any determination concerning it, I shall respite the offering you any new trouble on that Subject till the Event of that Sickness appears; and at present only add my further thankes to you for the safe returne of my Bible, wishing only that it had better answer'd your trouble of peruseing it. Not but that though it's Title at the Beginning deceive us, the Table at the end does make good that greater Fallibility of the Popes, which we Protestants please ourselves with, from those different Translations of Scripture expos'd by Sixtus and Clemens; with the additionall Cheat of putting

---

[1] Rawl. A. 194 : 194–5. Copy in letter-book. Printed : Smith, i. 236–7; Howarth, p. 101. Both omit postscript.

the Title-Page of one Pope to the Text of the Other. Soe, respectfully kissing your hands, I remaine

Your oblig'd and most humble Servant
S P

To Dr Turner

I shall endeavour to look up that Assignment of my Brother Jackson's to my Brother John Pepys (in case I have it) with all speed I can.

125. DR. JOHN TURNER TO S.P.[1]

Eynesbury September 7 1680

Sir

   I received yours of September 3d Mr Jackson dyed on Thursday
last in the evening at the request of Mris Jackson I went over on
Friday morning and gave the best advice I could for his private buriall,
and Mris Jacksons behaviour towards the creditors I have also requested Sir Nicholas Pedley to afford her his advice upon all occasions
when it shall be needed, and I hope she will not meet with any diffi-
cultyes but the creditors will be content with what they have right
to without causeing trouble to the widow and Fatherlesse, Sir I wish
you all happinesse and am heartily gladde of any opportunity (though
it be to your trouble, of testifying my selfe

Sir

Your most affectionate and thankfull servant
JOHN TURNER

For Samuell Pepys Esquire, at Mr Hewers in York buildings in the
strand London send by Sayer at the green dragon within listofe gate
on friday

126. DR. JOHN TURNER TO S.P.[2]

Eynesbury September 14 [16]80

Sir

   I am iust now come From Brampton whither I went to meet Sir
Nicholas Pedley that Mrsis Jackson might have full information
what answer should be given to the creditors some of which are very
clamorous but she is fully instructed how to deal with them, and Sir
Nicholas hath shewed himselfe a very kind and Faithfull friend Sir

---

[1] Rawl. A. 183 : 33. Original.   [2] Rawl. A. 183 : 39. Original.

it will be absolutely necessary that the Assignment of Mr Jacksons lease of Ellington parsonage be found out, which he made to Mr John Pepys, and that you take out letters of Administration for the estate of mr John Pepys in order to dispose of the said lease as you shall think fitt, for if your title doe not hinder the creditors will immediatly seise on it, I know not of any farther trouble will at the present be put upon you about Mrsis Jacksons affaires Sir I wish you good health and allways remain

       Sir

           Your most affectionate and humble servant
                JOHN TURNER

Sir your Father is very well and sends his blessing

For Samuell Pepys Esquire, at Mr Hewers in York buildings in the strand London

127. B. ST. MICHEL TO S.P.[1]

               Downes Friday night
               September 24, 1680

Most Ever honoured Sir

After Assureing your Honour of the Continuance of my most humble dutey with intier resignation to your wills and comands, and the giveing you, as I Shall to my lives Einde trew proofes of my most Faithfull Services without any consideration but trew honour; which being from the very botome of my hart and Sowle, I humbly pray, and hope you will doe me that Justice to beleeve: and after my giveing your Dear honour millions of thankes (not Ile asure you for the present imployment I have, in soe much confusion, paine, disquiets, and discouragements it haveing by delay prooved as it doth soe much to my misfortune, and ruine; by the disapointements of those advantages your goodness designed me, and therefore (for which ware I not more then comon man I shoold Runn to dispaire) though I am sacrified, and towrne from the Bowells of my sweet litill famely; and from my five small babes whoe cryed after theire owne father, at my departure from them, and that to, after all my youth Spent in his

---

[1] Rawl.. A. 183 : 47–50. Original. Holograph. St. Michel is finally embarking upon his appointment as agent at Tangier. S.P. has anticipated St. Michel's needs in a letter to Thomas Hayter, 27 Aug. 1680, suggesting the propriety of his receiving recompense suitable to the complicated nature of his employment far from home, such as £250 per annum and 'allowance for necessary instruments . . . Upon the Whole, the Designation of my Brother to this Employment was intended by the King as an advancement to him in kindness to mee, who I hope shall not bee deem'd to deserve less then I did then, because I have suffer'd more.' (Rawl. A. 194 : 188–9.)

Majesty's Service in Ever and all dangers and trubles, which I have performed with trew faithfullness and honour both to your Dear selfe, and his Majesty's Service)[1] to have at last noe other recompence then to be sent to the Divill for a New yeares-gift. yet the infatigable and Generous Eagerness wherewith you ware pleased to Express and act on my late behalfe, besides the Ever obligations I have to your goodness, and which I cann never repay but with my blood; wherefore I say dutey, as well as my love, bindes me to give you those Millions and Millions of thankes I owe, haveing yet noe more to give, wherefore, pray your honour to accept them from one, whoe, I hope you know, is your most faithfull Creature, till the world, my good fortune in your Esteeme, and your owne goodness, may give me other oportunitys, to Shew, what one occasion, in great truth, faith, and honour, I then may and will doe for your Dear service. in the Meane while this only comes to give your honour truble, by acquinting you of my only bodely unfortunate proseedings since I had the honour last to kiss your hands at london. thus.

After I had tooke my leave of your Dear honour, and that after I had bine to doe the like with my pretey sweet famely and leave them (perhapps never more to returne) desolate which burstt my hart to thinke of theire pretious teares both of Mother and babes. Munday last at 3 the afternoon I went to Debtford, hopeing soe to have finished buseneses with Mr hosier, as to have bine after, that day, time Enough at Gravesend and soe by land tweasday night at Deale; but it hapined that wee could not have done, till 11 that night, and Consequently was forsed to lye there from whence next morning being tweasday at 6 i set forward for Gravesend where I was by one that afternoon, and where, when I was preparing to take horse to goe on for Deale aforesaid; a Gravesend boat, then there, tould me, that the Newcastell, and Gloster-flyboat ware noe farther then the boy of the Nowre, and that for Eight shillings, they woold put me on board that night, which being confermed by severall, and my owne thoughts that it must needs be soe if thay ware there the Morning, the winde being Easterly; and allsoe Cheefely for good husbandry (soe often by your dear honour recomended to me) I accepted of the oportunity; and putting my selfe in a Gravesend wherry at about 3 of the clock the Afternoon with a peece of bread and Cheese, i proseeded in the said boat, but by the time we ware gott as Farr as the lower Einde of the hope, Such a Fogg and Storme arose, at E, that our Cockell Shell tooke Every Sea over, and we like to perish not seeing one inch before uss nor knowing wheither to Steare, Soe that my Good husbandry

---

[1] *Diary*, 4 Dec. 1665, records admission of St. Michel on S.P.'s recommendation to the Duke of Albemarle's Guards.

had like to have made at once a poore widow, and five miserable
orphans, but god had marcy of them and woold not have it soe, for
it pleased him that from the Kentish shoare, (where we Judged wee
then ware, and that we knew there was noe place on that side to putt
in) we rowing over about 3 howers time, wee got onn the Essex side,
and feeling out the way (with our boat Ever full of watter) got in Cole
haven where at 11 at night wee arived, we got on shoare and drying
our Cloathes, refreshed our selves with what the house aforded, but
beads¹ they had none, soe wee resting on a bench with a house over
our head till 4 of the clock wensday morning, when the winde being
litell less, and suferings (though inosent) haveing bine my meat and
drinke for some yeares past, and besides my owne nature not to be
dashed out of Courage for dangers; I therefore resolved to proseed,
in hopes to have met the shipps as at first designed; but in vaine; they
ware gone; thus being in a small wherry in open sea as low allmost
as the Read-sand, and knowing not what to doe, (besides the per-
plexity of my Minde fearing if I shoold returne to loose soe mutch
time to returne to Gravesend and then by land, that before I could get
to Deale the shipps woold be sailed on theire voyage,) and the winde
freshening upon uss teribly, as the day before at East, at last on our
totering resolutions, god sent uss passing by, a small Ketch bound to
Margate namely the unity of that place Edward Tomlins Master;
whoe takeing pitey of uss, took uss upp, this was about 2 the Afternoon where I continued; but the winde still continuing fresh at E,
and we not able to make but one tide a day, thay falling out soe cross,
it was till this morning at about 10 before we got through the Boyes
of the Narrow, and at about 11 got in Margat Road, where the Ketch
being bound noe further, and when I thought to have gone on shoare
to have proseeded by land, Just as wee ware coming to Anchor an
other small Ketch which folowed uss throug the Narrow (we haling)
founde him to be a Chichester man, bound thether (her name the
Mary of that place Thomas long Master, on board which I went and
by 2 this afternoon wee ware off the N foreland wher (to my great
harts Ease (small things being soe to one made upp of payne and
sorow) I fearing the shipps ware sailed out of the Downes before) I
saw the New Castell off the Gulls, getting in the Downes, being
come by the Swinn, through the Kings-Chanall, then was I at Much
Ease (and like a wooman in labour after her deliverance) forgot my
former terible 4 days truble on board the ketches where wee had noe
meat nor drinke but stincking water bread and Cheese; in my said
last ketch, I got in the Downes this night about 7 when likewise
came in the New-Castell, but the fly-boat which came about likewise

¹ i.e. beds.

with her not yet in sight though Expected to Morow. I gott on shoare
by nine at night where in some litell rest I now wate her coming. What
therefor I have further to marke to your honour, and give you further
truble in, is to desier yow to take notice of the various steppes of My
life, since I have had relation to the Navey under your patronage,[1]
how full of thornes my life hath bine, and that I, and only I of My
age Ever had the like measure in this world, from my first Essay, in
Bloody fights, both at home and a broad, to all the dangerous imployments on shoare, wherefore I humbly begg your Dear honour not
to be angrey with me, if repeating I tell you that the obediance to your
wille (which to my lives Einde I will observe) is the only cause of
any content in, or consent of Myne to this Soe Cross intended voyage,
and that therefore your goodness woold please to Consider, and in
time lay hould of the occasion of Caling me home, to more happy
imployments, which by that time I hope, I may deserve and Claime as
My Due, from his Majesty, and your favour, that soe I may not have
Still, and Dye in imployments (only provided for me) full of Danger,
Great truble, and Noe gaine such as none but I, could be singled out to
have: (Lord why was I borne) shall I never have rest from fightgs and
stormes, but continue when My youth likewise and Greatest vigour is
past, oh My Essays and Continuances have, bine and are; and without
hopes woold be to cruell; and which is worse, the Slights the world,
of those creatures you have made, Show me dayley at the Navey office,
&c: beleeving me, most Ignorent in imployments, and of less sowle
then any other, or that Elce you woold before this have done for me,
as for others less related, had I deserved any thing Either, by Courage,
honour, or capacitey: wherefore I hope, when your honour shall have
made the Kinge sensible of the contrary, and of the unjust measure
hath bine meeted to me; and that he hath none in his navey, that after
such dangerous imployments all theire youth past, without reward;
is still soe zelously willing in his age to manifest to the world his duty
to his Prince, and not repine nor denye; his sending me still in more,
and more dangers and trubles and now at last, which imployment
I could neither have but Just now at this Juncture of time, when
nothing but ill is to be Expected, both of to bodey, Content, or incouragement, makeing me as litell considerate, as posible thay cann,
in soe much as a Master of Attendant (and at Tangeire to) is My
superiour. pray Allsoe[2] Dear your honour please to Consider that
my lost time, and places of imployment, from which I have bine
unjustely towrne, are detrimantall to me above 600 Ł which his
Majesty May know, besides what I have lost, by not haveing gained,

---

[1] *Diary*, 25 Mar. 1665/6, records S.P.'s securing post as muster-master at sea for
St. Michel.   [2] MS. *Allose.*

since the time of my dismisment, pray likewise Dear sir, Judge and Consider of My most Cruell and severe case, beyond any Mortalls, that had I not had Mr Hewers (My Most Dear and worthy freind whoome god Bless) his favour of advancements (in this my vacansey) for bread, I and famely Might have Starved, soe that now I worke for only to repay him; as when a man as is usuall to say hee workes for a Dead horse; wherefore pray your honour (since you have bine pleased to grant me the liberty and freedome of speaking to you, (which by my Ever dutifull respects I shall Never abuse of) give me leave to pray to continue your Esteeme, and favour of, and to your poore but most faithfullest creature; and that in time and times noe oportunity may slipp, to be tooke upp by others: that soe I may live to make all those lyers, that thinkes i deserve not your favour; which hopeing in god, and you, that you will sudenly performe, Either by imployments at home, at land, or sea, or Navey; to which latter, I pray your honour to beleeve I shall and May performe with halfe the Incouragement of any there, and that I am bawked at nothing in this world, or stand in awe of any, but your Dear selfe and Comands; by the admiration I have of your wisdome, but which is more the love I Bare, and shall to My grave, to the Dear Lord, and Cheefe-halfe, of my never to be forgotten Dear Sister. remember me and Myne Dear your honour while yet you may, that I may be in a Capasitey of serveing you (as none other will) when (as I forsee) you may not for your selfe, that soe then (as I will on my sowle in times and place) you may be revenged, of your Enemys by me, or your litell disiple Samuel when perhapps you may not your selfe. for tis for your sake your honour knows, I am hated, and being soe low cannot hold head against them, as when hyer I will to theire shame and confusion; and when incouraged but wherewith; oh lord how shoold the world then, feele, see, and know; whose freinde, and relation I have the honour to be, all which recomending to your honours Noble serious, and fatherly consideration; and with my most humble service and Millions of repeated thankes to our Dear, and Most worthy freinde Mr Hewers, and humbly begging the continuance of your honours and his favour and kindeness, towards all my poore fatherless famely, under whose protection next to god I have left them.

I remaine, with most Dutifull obedience
                    Your honours Most faithfull
                    and most humble Servant
                         B St Michel
pray to give my Dearest love to my wife and Blessing to my Children

128. B. ST. MICHEL TO S.P.[1]

Downes September 29th 1680

Most Ever honoured Sir,
haveing received a letter from the Lords of the Admiralty, of which I heerewith sende your Honour a coppy,[2] togeather with my answer thereto: and besides my haveing yett the Comfort of your counsell and advice while yet at noe further distance; I owne it my Dutey to signifie nothing to them, while I may Either by writeing or otherwise, without your aprooval to which I will Ever submitt; and hope (since you see by the perussall of it, how uneasey, and slaveshly litell (by theire mistrustefull proseedinges) thay will make me subordinate to Every one, and consequently barr me by degrees, of the oportunity and Nesesarys for the performeing my Dutey soe as at last to Ruine me, but that my hopes in your honour's favour at home, and my owne infatigable diligence abroad will protecte me from theire spight.) that you will acquiess to what I have write: which after perussall and that it is to your liking I humbly pray you will please to have delivered, and if it may not be to your pleasure, please to let answer of the same date be sent them, such as by your most wise Judgement you shall thinke Convenient, for which purpose I herewith alsoe sende you my signature to a Blanck which if made use of then please to sende me a Coppy, or if my owne letter hath your aprobation, then please to returne me my Blanck. which with, Millions of pardons for this truble, and My Dutifull Obedience, I rest

Your Honour's Most faithfull and humble servant
B ST MICHELL

To the Honourable Samuel Pepys These

129. B. ST. MICHEL TO S.P.[3]

Downes-October 2d: 1680

Honoured Sir,
haveing received this day a letter from the navey Board with a new method of a bond for me to signe, not likeing it seemes the first, or at least thay being resolved never to leave me in quiet, but turment me, and my freinds, to the very last: I have therefore humbly made bould

[1] Rawl. A. 183 : 45. Original. Holograph.
[2] Evidently S.P. did not approve St. Michel's letter, as the original, written by a secretary and signed by St. Michel, is still in the collection (183 : 40), together with the signed and dated blank (183 : 42), and the copy of the Lords' letter signed: 'Your Loving Freinds Brouncker, D. Finch, and Thomas Littleton.' St. Michel's unsent reply states that despite the Lords' giving him all the unease possible, he will comply and obey readily.
[3] Rawl. A. 183 : 283. Original. Holograph.

to give your honour more truble, and heere inclosed sende you the Coppy of theire said letter,[1] and with it (for looseing noe time) the Bond signed and sealed, and before those wittnesses as thay desired, to the Einde that if it hath your aproovall and Consent, you may please to have it delivered them, or if not, that after you shall have Canseled my name: you woold (per the very next if your leasure may permitt) please to signife to me your pleasure and advice therein which with My Dutifull Obedience is all at present from.

Your Honour's Most faithfull and humble servant
B St Michel

To the Honourable Samuel Pepys These

130. S.P. TO PAULINA JACKSON[2]

London October the 14th 1680

Sister Jackson,

I wrote you by the last Post, and since have received yours of the 12th with one enclosed from Mr Hewer: But still want another of his, which he directed to me at Brampton and sent by the Post on Saturday was Sevennights, which should have come to you at Brampton the day following. Therefore in case it did not come to your hand, pray let it be inquired after for I would not have it miscarry.

And pray present my Service to my Cosen Hollinshead, intreating her to accept of a peece of Cloath from me to wear for my Father, which I shall send to my Cosen her husband tomorrow for her, with the like for a Suite for himselfe.

I am takeing our Letters of Administration for my Father and endeavour to dispatch that and my other Businesses so, that (if it be possible) I may look over my Father's Papers relateing to Brampton, before the Terme begins and hope to that end to get downe to you againe the beginning of the next week to be able to take the advice of Sir Nicholas Pedley in anything wherein I shall need it, before he sets forth for London. Which is all at present from

Your truly Loving Brother
S. P.

To my sister Jackson

[1] The letter from the board complains that St. Michel's bond as stores' keeper at Tangier has been made out faultily and encloses another for him to sign before witnesses. 30 Sept. 1680. (Rawl. A. 183 : 285.)

[2] Rawl. A. 194 : 213. Secretarial copy.

John Jackson has died in September. S.P.'s father has died in October. S.P. has been in Brampton to care for his sister, who is ill, and to take over the management of her estate. He is temporarily in London.

131. S.P. TO SIR NICHOLAS PEDLEY[1]

Brampton. Tuesday. October the 26th. 1680

Sir

Being disappointed in the hopes given me from severall hands of your being in Towne on Friday last, I sett out thence on Saturday, and had the further misfortune of reaching Huntington yesterday morning just after your departure thence for London. So as I am driven to supply in this manner what my desire was of compassing (with less trouble to you and more satisfaction to my selfe) by my personall attendance on you in relation[2] to some affaires of my owne ariseing from the late Death of my Father, and others of my Sister Jackson's from that of her husband; in both of which I have many instances of your kindness already to acknowledge.

As to the latter she has since my comeing downe let me understand the favour of your late advice to her for the delivering up to him that has administered whatever remaines in her Custody of the Goods of her Husbands. Which I shall most gladly assist her in, as being very desirous (especially in her present ill state of health) of ridding [her] of all other cares relateing to her Husband's Concernments, then what immediately appertaines to the secureing of her owne Right and her Children's. Whereto I shall onely add, that I have found the Originall Indenture (beareing Date the 25th of March 1675) wherein my Brother Jackson assigned his Colledge-Lease from Peter-House to One Mr John Denn of Grays-Inn for the Summe of 200 Ł with a Declaration (which I have alsoe found) under the hand and seale of the said Denn, that the said Assignment was made to him in trust onely for my Brother John Pepys, and that the 200 Ł mentioned therein was my Brothers proper money. So as I hope I am sufficiently provided to answer any Demands that may be made touching that Particular.

And for what concernes the former the onely thing I shall at this distance trouble you with (hopeing in a very little time to have the honour of waiting on you at London) is the letting you know, that I am above all things desirous to discharge my selfe as soon as I can towards what my Father was so sollicitous with you in, before his Death, relateing to my settleing the Lands in Brampton and Buckden upon my Sister's Children in case of want of Heirs of my owne Body. In order whereto haveing taken out Letters of Administration, I have made this Journey principally to obtaine a Court for my takeing up the Copy-Hold-Lands, while Mr Jolley is here, he being (as I

---

[1] Rawl. A. 194 : 213–14. Secretarial copy in letter-book. Original was evidently enclosed to W. Hewer (Rawl. A. 194 : 215) to be delivered to Sir Nicholas at Lincoln's Inn.
[2] MS. *relatation.*

am informed) designed some time this weeke for London. Upon which I am humbly to request you, to let me receive your advice, what (if any thing) there is to be further done by me (while upon the Place) towards the putting that Settlement in Execution this Terme, according to which I shall govern my selfe both in my Proceedings here and in the time of my comeing up to waite on you. Which with kissing your Hands is all at present from,

　　　　　　　　Your most faithfull and obliged humble Servant.

　　　　　　　　　　　　　　　　　　　　　　　　S. P.

To Sir Nicholas Pedley

132. S.P. TO WILLIAM HEWER[1]

　　　　　　　　　　Brampton. November the 4th 1680.

Sir.

　I have yours of the 2d instant as I hope you have mine of the same Date, giveing an account of my receipt of yours of the 30th of October, and doe againe bless God on your behalf from the deliverance from your late danger of fire.[2]

　I told you in my last that I had laid aside my resolution of sending home the Coachman upon the promises he has given mee of his Amendment. In hopes of which I shall keep him, at least till my owne Coachman be in condition to supply his place; which for your Family's sake I am glad he is in soe faire a way of being in a little time able to doe, and that Catharine alsoe begins to be better.

　The Newes-Papers you send me, though very extraordinary are yet of great satisfaction to have. But for your ease-sake I wish them printed.

　I am beholden to the Ladys you mention for their Visite, and am still of the minde, that it were very fit what you and I agreed on should be done towards that Family; and to that purpose, if you still like of it you shall have against the next week a Letter from me thither to that purpose.

　I take notice of the whole Account you send me of My Lord Mayor's Show.

　The Weather has been here and is still soe stormy that under all his infelicityes I should be glad to hear that the D. and his poor Dutchess were safe on shoare.[3]

---

[1] Rawl. A. 194 : 223–4. Secretarial copy.
[2] There had been a fire in York Buildings, where the Hewer family resided.
[3] The Duke of York had embarked for Scotland.

I wonder I have noe answer to my late Letter to Sir Nicholas Pedley, because among other things my governing myselfe here, in reference to the hastening my returne to London depends upon it.

I meet every day with new Matter of dissatisfaction relating to the condition my Brother Jackson has left my Sister and her Family in, that gives me an occasion of care, which I did not expect, his Creditors being very many, her Tenants perverse, and herself by her present Sickness very helpless. Soe as I have her Business upon my hand to dispatch as well as my owne; the State of which later, is that I have to get two Speciall Courts called for the 2 Mannours of Brampton and Buckden, and prosecuted my determination therein, as far as the particular Customs thereof will admit; whereof more largely in my next. But the Charge thereof, and the Fines to the Lords of the severall Mannours upon every new admission, together with the funerall Charges of my Father and dischargeing of severall dribleing Scores has drayned me almost to the bottome of what money I brought along with me, which was neare three score pounds; Soe that I shall be forced to pray you to returne me 50 Ł further after I shall have informed you of the readiest way of doeing it, which I shall endeavour to learne against the next Post.

There are alsoe the 2 forreine Debts, which for severall reasons I would be glad to have cleared, the one of 15 Ł; for which Sir John Werden is concerned, and the other about 6 Ł to some body in Holland, whose Names and Letters in both Cases you may alsoe expect by the next.

You have very well rectified the mistake in your first.

You remember what it was, that I was thinkeing of for the 2 young Gentlemen in Winchester-Street,[1] I haveing two fair Ones I thinke of my owne. If not, others may soon be made in exchange for something of mine that is become unfashionable with some little Distinction to be made between the Elder and the younger Brothers. But if you can think of any thing else of Plate more proper pray doe it.

I thanke you for the satisfaction you gave Sir John Chichley, my Letters by each Post being (I hope) always sufficient to doe the like.

My last brought you a Letter and Paper for Sir Thomas Beckford.

Soe with my Sisters and my owne humble Services to Mrs Hewer, Family and Selfe, I committ you to God's Protection, and am

Yours most affectionately
and thankfully

S. P.

To Mr Hewer

[1] Evidently gifts for the Houblon children.

133. [Fragment] S.P. TO PAULINA JACKSON[1]

[London, December, 1680]

any thing of that Ceremony from you, till by more health on your side, and a little more ease and quiet on mine, it may be more Seasonable for us both.

Which praying God to grant, and wishing you and your Family a happy New-Year I rest

Your most affectionate Brother
S P

To Mrs Jackson

134. B. ST. MICHEL TO S.P.[2]

Tangeire December 13th 1680

Honored Sir,

With most humble dutey and presentations of my Ever faithfull Services this comes to acquinte you that after a most cruell pasage of above 2 munths without any Comfort but the deck during my pasage by the directions of that Beast Bothwick, the perticulars of which will in some time by all the shipps Company be avouched; but all this dear your Honour, is not comparable to the Torments of my Sufferings by your silence, of which I have only this to say that by my Small service though i have never done anything which might balance with those great and many favours I have received from you yett Sir I know your goodness is such and that you know me soe well to beleeve from your very Sowle, that when soever I did any thing for you, it was to the uttermost of my power from myne; and that my life it selfe, was never soe dear to me as when I might imploy it for your service, in which resolution (as god is my Judge) I shall Continue to my Grave; and in the meane time still pray his heavenly divinity for your preservation, health, welfare, and to sende you victory over your Enemys.

Now sir I come humbly to give you accompt how it is with me, since my arivall heer being the 9th instant you may please to know then, that there was noe Admirall Herbert, nor Master Attendant heer, thay being both gone over to the Spanish side, but I went to

---

[1] Rawl. A. 194 : 235. Secretarial copy. These lines represent not merely the fragment of a letter, but the fragment of a folio as well, for the letter book is damaged at this point, ten sheets being gone. The date is therefore merely inferred, partly from dates of folios preceding and following the break, and partly from the evidence of the last sentence of the letter.   [2] Rawl. A. 183 : 55–56. Original. Holograph.

great[1] Mr Sheares[2] and presented him (with all imaginable respect)
your letter the Efects of which I know not, but have not yett seen
or found any assistance or kindeness from him, more then Compli-
ments for that I have not yet where to put my head or doe my buse-
ness; neither by the Master Attendance his absence have I any Boat
or men to doe any of My Navall dutey on float, soe that if it be not
bettered by some suden order I am likely to be but in a very sadd
Condition to performe my Dutey.

yesterday came in the Admirall whoe sent for me on Board to
whoome I presented your Honour's service and letter, and though
hee be the lofteist man in the world, yet hee received both with soe
much respect, and seeming kindeness imaginable, which though you
may beleeve (for some reasons) to be but fained, yet give me leave to
assure your honour (I haveing had some time in my miserable life)
to wreede man, and by my perticular acquintance with him) that what
came from him was with honour and trew respect to you-wards. hee
is going againe this day over to the Spanish side to convoy over the
Spanish officers and in 4 or 5 days hee tells me hee is to returne, and
that the fly Boat with the stores shall then be ordered to Gibralter and
then what to doe with the stores heer, if hee have me there, and how
I shall performe my other duteys of Musters here, and survaying the
victualing Christ Jesus knows, for I am at My witts Eindes and
though I have this post given accompt allsoe thereof to the Navey
Board, yet I humbly pray, that you woold give my most Dear and
faithfull service to Mr Hewers,[3] and desire him to lay all theese my
Greevances before them, for theire giveing me theire fresh directions
in the perticulars; that soe thay may not ketch at my security for any
neglect of myne, perticularly for my Mustering, since I shall have
noe boat nor men, there being indeed noe boat heer at all. Oh lord
Jesus sende (that paradox to me) quickly your honour's saying to
come to pass vizt that the worse shoold be the better still, though I
beleeve my life will not least[4] to see it, gods will be done. I conclude
with praying the heavenly god to prosper and keepe you and remaine
as I shall Ever to the Einde of my life

        Your Honour's Most Dutifull and Ever Obedient Servant
                        B St Michel

I humbly begg the Continuance of your protection to my Poore
famely, and that you woold send My Dearest love to My wife and
Blessing to my 5 Dear babes

To The Honourable Samuel Pepys These London

---

[1] i.e. *greet*.   [2] Henry Shere, the engineer of the Mole at Tangier.
[3] William Hewer was now secretary to the Admiralty.
[4] i.e. *last*.

135. S.P. TO THE COMMISSIONERS OF THE NAVY[1]

March 24th 1680/81

Gentlemen,

Being very desirous of the benefit of your Justice and favour on behalfe of my Brother St Michell, in relation to what I sometime Since gave you the Trouble of my Waiteing on you about (vizt) Bills for the arreare of his Pay due by his present Commission; and haveing understood your desire of Sattisfaction touching the time by him spent in France after the date[2] of his said Commission and before his entrance on the Service whereon he is now employ'd at Tangier by vertue[3] thereof, I thought it fitt for me to lett you know, that upon the Charge which was with soe much artifice and Mallice brought against me in Parliament, and for which I was committed to the Tower in the Moneth of May 1679 and Lay for Many Moneths together under dayly Menaces of a prosecution for my Life, his Majesty (out of his gratious regard to me and the Justification of my Innocence) was then pleased at my humble request, to dispence with my Said Brothers goeing (with the Shipps about that time designed for Tangier) and to give leave to his goeing into France (the Scene of the Villanys then in practice against me) he being the only person (whome from[4] his Relation to me, together with his knowledge in the place and Language, his knowne dilligence, and perticular affection towards me) I could at that tyme, and in soe greate a cause pitch on, for committing the care of this affaire to[5] of detecting[6] the Practices of my Enemyes there. Which (by the favour of Almighty God[7] had its full Success, as in due tyme will appeare, not only to my particular advantage, but to the Incouragement of all Such as (like me) Shall expose themselves to the Same usage by a[8] more then Common Zeale in his Majesties Service. Through which occasion, and by the stay necessary for his bringing over Wittnesses against my expected Tryall, my Brother was prevented in returning to England untill the February following; from which time, I doubt not but both the Lords of the Admiralty and your Selves are well Sattisfied in the Closeness of his Attendance on his duty; Which, with the repeateing of this my Earnest Request to you on his behalfe (the present condition of him-

---

[1] Rawl. A. 183 : 22. First draft in the hand of a secretary with corrections by S.P.
[2] *thereof*, canc.
[3] *of his said Commission*, canc.
[4] *by*, canc.
[5] *for detecting*, canc.
[6] *enqui-*, canc.
[7] Altered from *God Almighty*.
[8] *theyr*, canc.

selfe and family greatly urgeing me thereto) I leave with all respect with you, and remaine

Your most affectionate Faithfull and most
humble Servant

S. PEPYS

These For my Honoured freinds the Principal Officers and Comissioners of his Majesties Navy London

136. S.P. TO MR. MATTHEWS[1]

March 26th 1681

Sir

My Servant Lorrain haveing given me an Account of his late waiteing on you and of the Condition he found my two Nephews in, in reference to their wants of Some Linnen and Cloathes, I take the Liberty of desireing your giveing your selfe the trouble of informing me by him, what things they are already furnisht with, the better to enable me to determine what more will be requisite to be provided for them, my Sisters Illness being such, as [to] render her at present wholly uncapable of being advised with either in that or any other of her affairs the most Important. But I trust in God her recovery may in a Little tyme Supply it. In the meane while though the weight of my owne affaires here have alwayes kept me (as they still doe) a Tottall Stranger to hers and even to my owne there. Yett soe farr I shall Interest my selfe there in on her behalfe dureing her present Illness as to see the Termes upon which her Children have beene by her committed to you made good to your full sattisfaction, and their wants supply'd as soone as ever I know them. Wherein againe praying your speedy advice I doe with all respect remaine

Your affectionate and humble Servant
S P

To Mr Mathewes

137. S.P. TO ROGER PEPYS[2]

March 26th 1681

Honoured Cos'n,

This comes to kiss your hands and my Cousen your Ladyes, with many thanks for her and your last, favours at Impington. Since which

---

[1] Rawl. A. 194 : 244–5. Secretarial copy in letter-book.
[2] Rawl. A. 194 : 245. Secretarial copy. Printed: *Mem.* ii. 47–48; 1848; 1854; 1879; Howarth, pp. 111–12.

it hath pleased God by a continued Sickness of my Sisters to prevent my comeing to any determination touching my House at Brampton; for that my thoughts therein would be much governed by my haveing or not haveing her to reside there for the better looking after my small affaires as well as her owne about that place my dependences here being still such as will not I doubt for some time give me Leasure to retire thether myselfe which (as publick matters goe, without any hopes in my view of their bettering) Is the first thing I could wish to compass. But my Sisters Illness being become such as our best Phisitians here (where she has for some moneths beene) can give me noe assurance of any Speedy recovery, I finde it inconvenient for me to delay any Longer my takeing some resolutions in that matter and therefore remembring (though imperfectly) a Motion you were pleased to make me about this House when I last waited on you I thought it becomeing me to advertize you, Soe farr of it as may give me the Sattisfaction of knowing whether in my proceeding herein I can have any opportunity of Serving you.

I remember also the little things you were pleased to bespeake of me I meane my moddell and two Pictures, which however I may happen to dispoze of the House I shall with greate pleasure make good to you my Promise of, by preferring them to a place with you at Impington, whenever a Convenience shall offer it Selfe for their conveyance thither. Soe with my desires alsoe of understanding how it fares with you in your health and my Cousens, I remaine, Both her and

Your most affectionate kinsman and
Humble Servant
S P

Cosen Roger Pepys

138. B. ST. MICHEL TO S.P.[1]

Gibralter, Aprill 21th: 1681

Honoured Sir,

Though my grievances, misseryes, Torments, and Disincouragments; hath beene to such extremitie, passing the Expression of Tongue, Since my being in this parte of the World, by nott onely my continuall labour, and Slavery: Ocationed by the Sevearest injustice crueltie and unkindness of fortunate fopps; as in time will be manifestly made knowne by many here, as well as else where, besides

<hr>

[1] Rawl. A. 183 : 184–5. Original.

great Impositions wants, and misseryes, Indevoured to be burthened one me, to my utter ruine all which to prevent, as well to my owne Honour as friends, though I grone under: yett with the helpe of my god, I Doe nott Doubt but to labour through in Dispight of all mallice; Sir all theise with millions more of misseryes, which I howerly Suffer without rest or justice, as most comanders if they live to come home will aquaint you: is nott comparable to the griefe of spirit I have for your Silence, and although they boldly Dare tell me at this Distance, and friendless helpless and moneyless, what were the[y] Caesares they should nott Dare Else where, that they onely plague me thus, to be revenged of you; yett Sir though I have never for almost this 20 years past in his Majesty's Service, which I have executed in all Imployments which by your favour I have been putt upon, with uttermost Dilligence and Honour eate my meate butt with bitter-Sauce, yett Doe I Kiss that rodd, and will Still to my lives End Obey cherrish, and love, my Deare benifacter. Sir it is nott a quire of paper, can give you an Exact State of my condition, nor the full height of the missery thereof; it may please onely to Suffice you that I Say as the world and others will like wise joyne that if I Stay longer here I shall be tenn times worse ruined (if my life cann beare the burthen out longer) then should I (as a cast away) have at home Newgate for the reward of my well Serveing my prince and honouring my friends, in all which that just god which I adore, I am sure will revenge my cause and those inocent ones which will by my ruine grone, and bring your Deare Honour to a time to Show ingretts theire Duties.

The chiefest Ocation of my giveing you trouble at this present, is to aquaint you that this Day Died in this roade Captain William Coleman late Comander of his Majesty's Shipp the james-Gally, who dureing his life had besides that advantage of goeing abroad, by the Dukes onely favour the place of Collector at Plymouth which being now voyde by his Death, if your goodness woold be Such as that Imeadiatly (This being the very first advice and noe Doubt butt that Speedy Sollisitations will follow) you woold please to gett from his Majestie, Duke or lords of the Treasury, or whosoevers Station Else it is to grant itt, that place for me it woold not onely (as formerly it was to Captain Coleman) be a parte of a reward for my long and zealous Service, butt alsoe a quiett and happie being in that cheape place for me and mine the Remnant of my Dayes, and god I hope will reward you for itt, and I to the last of my blood acknowledg itt. I have only to add, and repeate the praying you that nott one minutes time may be Deferred while if, by (as I Said before) the Speedy Solisitations which will from all partes be made for the Same, will baulke my hopes, and Null your Honours Indevoures. butt if one the contrary by your Justice and Kindness I may be soe Happie as to gett it, you will have the prayers of all your Humble little creatures that his Divine Majestie give you in this world many happie Dayes of prosperity, health, and welfare, and in that to come life eternall: which is alsoe the Dayly Petitions to the father of heaven from Sir

Your Honour's Ever Obedient and Dutyfull Servant
B S<small>T</small> M<small>ICHEL</small>

My most Humble service to Mr Hewers and family with the Dearest love and blessing to mine.

B S<small>T</small> M

I being very Sick in bed with the Greefs and wants I Suffer, in a Strange place, without any Creditt, friendless and Comfortless and reduced for the wants aforesaid to bread and water theise Six Dayes past and Sometimes (when I Could have Creditt for itt) a little raw milke till a friend of mine by Chance a Captaine of Tangeire namely Captain Trelaney hapened to be here and lent me five Pistolls and a frenchman here five more otherwise I might nott have beene in a Condition to have given your Honour any trouble at all; the reasons aforesaid and Consequently my Disabillity of wrighting hath ocationed my present makeing use of another hand

B S<small>T</small> M

I hope that Deare Mr Hewers Kindness and friendship to me and the memory of yours and mine will nott prevaile with you or any others to my prejudice in favour of his unkle Blackborne butt that with the same faithfull Assistance which I have Ever Received from him and his goodness he will Rather joyne with you for my aide and with usuall Honour and Kindness to me wardes value true friendship and ballance it Equall with Intrest or blood which I most Humbly pray you to begg of him on my behalfe as I doe from my very harte with Humble Request nott Doubting butt that one day yett as I have more then any of his Relations Soe shall I be in a Condition Some way, yett nott Knowne to make him Senceable by some Emenent Service that he hath not befriended an Ingrate B M

139. S.P. TO MR. LOKE[1]

Saturday April 23th 1681

Mr Loke,

   The reason of my noe sooner thanking you for your Letter of the 10th instant has been the expectation I had from you in that Letter

---

[1] Rawl. A. 194 : 245–6. Secretarial copy in letter-book.

of receiveing some further advice touching my Sister's Affairs upon your speaking with Mr Mosely, which I pray you to let me have assoone as you can. For my Sister being still out of a condition of giveing me any information therein herselfe, I must desire to receive it from you, and pray you to that purpose to informe your selfe all that you can in it, that I may know [how] far it may be fit for me to clear that Mortgage; I neither knowing the value of Land, nor the Summe which it is mortgaged for. I intreat you alsoe to dispose of her Pastureground to the best advantage that you can for her, and to doe me the like favour in reference to any concerne of mine at Brampton, and particularly about the Close I leaveing it wholly to you to doe what you judge convenient in it. My maid is alsoe at a losse for Direction about two Cowes and a Calfe, wherein I have directed her to be advised by you and act accordingly. I hope to have opportunity to visit you e're long, and in the mean time giveing you my hearty thanks for the kindnesses on this I remaine,

Your truely affectionate Frend and Servant
S. P.

To Mr Loke

140. MR. HUNTER TO S.P.[1]

Gibraltar 14th July [16]81

Sir

    This comes to kisse your hand and to pay my Duty to you by the hands of Mr St. Michel, whom, I am sensible by what he will be able to tell you, you will finde to have so much reason for his Comeing home, that itt will appeare that, without prejudice to the King's service and Ruine to himselfe, he could hardly avoyd itt; I am too sensible of the many Difficulties he hath mett with, and the Miserys he hath Indur'd, since the Admirall, as much as itt may be to Gratifie his owne humour and revenge, as to forward the King's service, thought fitt to Remove the Stores hither; I will not Sir trouble you with perticulars, since the Bearer will be able att Leasure to Recompt them to you; I will only Sir presume to give you all Imaginable assurance, that, during his absence, my Duty to your selfe, the trust Mr. St. Michel hath reposed in mee, and the perticular respect and Kindness I have for him, together with an absolute Impossibility in my Inclination to doe otherwise, cannot butt obleidge me to use so much care, diligence, and honesty in the Execution of the Imployment he

<hr>

[1] Rawl. A. 183 : 266. Original.

hath Left me the Charge of, that I cannot butt hope that he will finde no Cause to Repent that hee had too much Confidence in him, who aimes att nothing beyond your good opinion and esteeme, which bounds the ambition of

Sir

Your most obedient and most humble servant

S HUNTER

To the Honourable Samuel Pepys These most humbly Present

141. S.P. TO MR. SPENCER, BURSAR OF PETER-HOUSE IN CAMBRIDGE[1]

Brampton June 29th 1681

Sir

I send this in discharge of my duty to your honourable Society, to whome by the death of my Brother in law Mr Jackson I am become Tenna[n]t for their Parsonage at Ellington; letting you know, that being very lately come into the Country I made it yesterday my first business to visitt my Tennants at that place, in order to the seeing how they had answered my expectations in their timely paying you in their last halfe year's rent, which to my greate surprize and noe less dissatisfaction I finde they have not done, notwithstanding your early Letter to Goodman Gates on that subject.

Their excuses for this faylure (however I may) I doe not expect your receiveing any Sattisfaction from, and therefore shall not trouble you with their mention.

That which alone I thinke becomes me to tell you, is, that they have given me a preremtory promise of paying it within a Fort-night from yesterday, and this I will see punctually made good; purposeing in the meane time to kiss your hand at Cambridge on munday or tuesday next, to supply what (if anything) this shall want of giveing you and the rest of my Honoured Land Lords present Sattisfaction. I am

Your most humble servant

S. P.

---

[1] Rawl. A. 194 : 253. Secretarial copy. The tenants at Ellington, as far as is known, were not relatives. S.P. was doubtless in Brampton for the purpose of looking in on St. Michel's family, who were tenants there.

142. ESTER ST. MICHEL TO S.P.[1]

[Brampton] August 28th [1681]

Honored Sir

your Letters I have received and your good instructions for frugality
and good huswifry I shall to the utmost observe. And indeed the
straightnes of my condition allong hath forct me to it, (if my Inclinations had bin otherwise I being A stranger as well to my husbands
estate as Actions, always in a worse condition then the meanest
servant he kept, not haveing the liberty of asking for my necessaryes,
without the fear of a rewd denyall. his privat wayes known only to him
selfe, tell by their great expences brocke[2] forth: his family never having
so great an allowance as since my being at york buildings, which well
considered I think was managed with great frugality, if your honour
will be pleased to consider the quantity and quallity which I must of
necessity practice being ther, we having nothing but what necessity
required and At Deale I had som times presents which was of great
use to the house: otherwise my life would have bin more tiresome.
but when I chuse for my ease it shall not be an husband, with home[3]
I never had any &c. Sir the reason why I did not use Sam so hardly
was the Infirmities of his Eye. his Edication his father managed as
all other things: His first going to France was not known to me 2 days
before I was commanded to waite on my mother in Law thither with
the Child which I did. I confesse I was remanded home 5 months
before I Came; but mother and Child returned at the same time.
I having no desire att all ever to returne; had not my husbands
coming to Paris required it: although I did not com back with him
but 4 months after. when I Came to Callis I found my mother with
Sam: and a maid: wondering att the sight: I asked the reason. answer
was made It was your Honour's order: comeing to Deale with them,
my miserable Abode was ther 7 months after which I returned to
Callis Againe and stayed ther 11 months all Against my desire and
will my husbands promises wer such as I wished but performances
which are yeat to come. After which we all returned to deale wher
I was a bove a yeare time tedious indeed seeing ruin tumbling on us
apace; which by all the arguments I could use was not great enough

---

[1] Rawl. A. 183 : 177–8. Original. Holograph. Part of first paragraph quoted by
Bryant, *Samuel Pepys: The Years of Peril*, p. 361. While St. Michel was in Paris on S.P.'s
behalf, the latter evidently maintained the family in York Buildings. Later, during St.
Michel's service at Tangier, the arrangement seems to have continued under the thin
disiguise of a loan from William Hewer. Naval pay was customarily in arrears. Early in 1681,
when the illness of Paulina has necessitated that she be removed to London and her two
boys be placed with Mr. Matthews, Mrs. St. Michel and her brood have evidently been
installed in Brampton for economy.   [2] i.e. *brought*.   [3] i.e. *whome*.

to doe any thing but reap my self unquietnes, which was so tiersom to me that I Left it, when Mr Michell was at London, wher in 6 weekes he spent enough like as att other times. his Son being at London with him to have the honour to kisse your hands. I came to London to but not to my husband, hoping that my leaveing his family might worke some reformation, but did not prevail at all. Afterward knowing wher i was I was advised to goe to Deale Saying that Sam: was to goe to france which I did to litle purpose. After to york buildings in as great ignorance as before. At my husbands goeing awaye I asked him if he owed Mr Hewers mony. his Answer was that Mr H. owed him some pounds I have forgot the sum. I desired I might se that which he promised me but never performed, he goeing out every day only gave us leave to conduct him to york staires; but he tould me that Mr hewers did promise him that his salary did goe on at 300 lb a year and upon those words he depended, I having a 100 lb per yeare a great while 2 yeares or near that time. After I had 150 lb per annum Mr hewers paying 32 Ł a yeare for the house; which continued for Another yeare which is all I knoe i ever had of Mr Hewers: but Mr. Hewers promised to pay me the same allowance by my husbands order at his parting. Is I said before Mr Hewers letting him beleve that he had 300 lb a yeare coming to him from the time of his Commision to his going awaye which is now retrenched to 250 Ł per annum. I confes Mr Hewrs hath toald me that my husband was 700 lb in debt to him: but when my husband hath presed concerning his employ which he had Commition for Tanger in my hearing his Answear was, what need you trouble your selfe as long [as] you have 300 lb. a year. ought you not to be contented. if I had so much to doe nothing I would not be unsatisfied, is not England as good as Tanger. att which my husband was contented: but Mr Hewers hath don like a wise man to get his own which he ses is 700 lb. but if my husband should dye, or to pay his debt, living, he deny me competency to live then I must, wher I se another loock to my selfe, which if I could finde a way to provide for my family he might seize on all. I could make a shift. I am sure if Mr Hewers had not assured my husband of his Salary during the time of his Comission his Ignorance would not have gon so far, as to have Leaft us to Spend 200 Ł a year wher should Mr Hewers be paid; but he depended on the salary which Mr Hewers assured my husband in my hearing 3 times Elce with out being stark mad a man would not have left shuch a ruin on his Children. I speake not this, as if there were no necessity of saveing, were it not for Mr Hewer's mony. no I ought to doe my endeavor to use in all things the greatest frugality: neither did I desire to have bin left in such a necessity of expence: but all wayes

thought it needlesse looking upon the necessity of the Cheldren.
Which Sir, you are pleased to mention in their being healpfull on to
Another: I doe not know how that may be, the biggest of 10 yeares
is far from healping herselfe

your humble sarvant Sam. the badnes of his Eye hath bin all along
a great hinderance to him, and is still, but I hope your affection to
him will still be his encourgement as one, whome he doth much
honour and respect and upon whome he doth wholly depend

Honored Sir I canot beleave you thinke me unsencible of my condition because I doe not bemoane it. To the world In deed I doe not;
but in my one private thoughts enough, and to much, since I doe not
find it ads on mite to my Comfort, but to the contrary destroyes my
health and Confounds my understanding, leaving me fit only to talke
to my selfe, for, if to an other they would not know whatt I meant.
Is it possible to forget 700 £ to pay, and know not how nor out of
whatt but 250 lb a year and so many to be kept out of it and that
depending on so many unceartaintyes.

Sir as to my expences here, I have only set downe the greatest, but
every lettell thing I thought would not have bin required; but since
it is shall henceforth make it my buisnes, that Sir you may be satisfyed
in that and all other thinges, that I can. As for the ill manners of my
Childern I know there age tells me they have enough to much, and
shall endeavour to correct that fault.

thus with my hearty prayers for your wellfare and prosperity I
remaine Sir your humbell sarvant

to Command   ESTER ST MICHELL

I beg your pardon for not answering your letter sooner waiting for
som thing wherin I might render you Servis. To Samuell Pepys
Esquire att Mr Hewers's house in yorke Buildings nere the New
Extchange London

143. S.P. TO ESTER ST. MICHEL[1]

Saturday September 24 1681

Sister,

To make my first letter less unpleasant to you I told you I should
trouble you but once on that subject and in that kind and I will be

[1] Rawl. A. 183 : 160. Holograph. First draft in shorthand. A cutting from some un-
identified journal lies between the sheets of the Rawlinson MS. at this point. The article,
titled *Pepys Again*, summarizes a lecture given by J. E. Bailey, and includes transcriptions
of two shorthand drafts of letters to Mrs. St. Michel, this one and number 145. The lecture itself reveals ignorance of some of the family circumstances now made clear to
readers of the present work.

The editor, however, has differed in several passages from Dr. Bailey's readings, making as good as my word it being at all times unwelcome to me to be giving unwelcome counsel specially in a case like yours where no room is left for hope of receiving any fruits from it but censure instead of thanks, as to my trouble I see poor Mr Hewer is likely to do. But I say I shall not give you or myself the trouble of any second expostulations, having or rather choosing to reserve them for my brother your husband whom I daily expect here.

What then I have to say is in particular to what you lately wrote to Mr Hewer about money, which is that the time being out for which I designed the money I left with you at the rate of 20 s a week which is what with frugality may very well suffice for your and your family's support in that place (where you are freed of the charge of house-rent and may live as sparingly as you please) I have here enclosed a letter to Mr Loke to pray him to supply you with 10 Ł more which I expect and doubt not your making to last at that rate for 10 weeks more. If Mr. Loke should happen either not to be at home or not to have sufficient money by him, let me know by the next post and I will return you it by the next coach.

When you consider the greatness of the debt your husband has already contracted to Mr. Hewer without any penny paid or in likelihood speedily to be and such a family as you have to provide something for, you will not think the going on in trusting him further as far as 50 Ł a year more either a small kindness [or] that in your condition you ought to spend more. I am sure I say this out of perfect regard to your welfare, and hope you will take it. If not I fear the consequence of it on your and your children's behalf. Adieu.
Sister St M.

144. ESTER ST. MICHEL TO S.P.[1]

Brampton, September 24 [1681]
honored Sir
yours I have with the Inclosed to Mr Loke, A supply of 10 Ł Intendid ten weekes suficient, Provicion for my family. that Canot be. since Eaight Pounds with fifty shillings Creditt hath but provided for

---

her own transcription from the shorthand, and using the 1641 edition of Shelton's *Tachygraphy*. Although it is the 1691 edition which is found in the Pepysian Library, we know that Pepys was using Shelton's system at least thirty years before 1691. We also know that it was Pepys's custom to replace books in his library by later editions. It should be mentioned, perhaps, that Shelton's system underwent definite changes with the years.

[1] Rawl. A. 183 : 169. Original. Holograph. A few phrases are quoted by Bryant, *Samuel Pepys: The Years of Peril*, pp. 361–62.

8 weekes, and my sarvants waggis yeat to pay. Sir you doe not Consider that Although I am In the Country althings are as dere here As att London, and some derer Except Chickins, or piggions, which Are not for me—therefore of noe profit. As for Buchers mett, bread, bere, and Routs, as turnops, Carrots, onions, In fine All Gardinage is derer here A peny in too pence. then for sope, starch, ote mele, Salte, peper, Candels, thread, tape, &c Shouse, Stockins, gloves, Cloath, mending tabs, and A great many more things to many to troble you with, or Ever before sent in A letter by me. thearefore know not how to rite them, Sir for foretene days I have not had one penny, being unwilling to troble Mr hewrs, untill I Could not resist my necesitys Longer. which I thoaft was Sevelity, to him and my duty, far from that you Are pleased to taix me with, (sencure)[1] as all my indevors will Clere me in, and when I left my house, quite Against my husban[d's][2] Commands, and Councill, in order to searve Mr Hewers, Came to Brampton, without making Propocials, or Ashewrencis, of A Livelihood when there all of which were necesary, and should have bin by me yoused, to Ani other then to your selfe and Mr Hewers. But I Contrary Layed my Cheldrens and one life down to your mursise, which I thoaft would have gon as far as great frugality, but not to Imposibelitys. the maner I finde you Are pleased to youse me with, for Acording as you Intendid 8 lb. for 8 weekes, if I had nether mony, nor Creditt, it was resolved, noe further supply, as to My husbands return the mening I Canot Geas, but Am Joyed at the newse, since my Condition is soe unsertaine hoping by his presence I may be A lettell Esed, Althoe noe great Incoragments I confes. if my husband should not be here before this ten pounds is gon Sir be pleased to lett me know what i shall trust to. which is All from your humble

Sarvant
Ester St Michell

Mr. Loke sends you his humbell sarvis and desiers your honor to beleve him Ready to obey your Commands, upon all ocashions. Sir the worke men which were Imployed About your honers stare Case are in great distres for want of there mony and desiers to be remmebred.

To Samuell Pepys Esquire att Mr Hewers's house In yorke Buildings, nere the New Extchang London

---

[1] i.e. *censure.*

[2] Edge of paper. Mrs. St. Michel is of course implying that her husband had told her to remain in York Buildings until his return from Tangier.

145. S.P. TO ESTER ST MICHEL[1]

Saterday October 1 1681

Sister.

Your desiring to know what you are to trust to is the reason of my writing to you again I having determined to restrict any further writ[ing] at least till my brother your husband comes which I hourly expect and therefore doubt not his being here long before the 10 weeks are out. What then you have to trust to from me and Mr H is what I told you in my last namely after the rate of 20s per week and no more this being as much as I and my wife had for several years to spend and yet lived so as never to be ashamed of our manner of living though we had house rent and tax to pay which you have not and this in London too and yet [safe] from ruin upon that score. The truth and surety[2] of which do appear in the daily account she kept of every issuing of her family expense even to a bunch of carrot and a ball of whiteing which I have under her own hand to show you at this day. Therefore do not expect that any profession of frugality can be of satisfaction to me but what appears in an account. Not but that I could wish with all my heart that my brother's condition and yours would afford you a larger allowance. But where every farthing of what he and you spend is to be taken up upon credit as it is without any surety[2] of prospect when you will be in a condition to repay it and yet (besides all this) a numerous stock of children to provide for you ought not to think any degree of sparing too much to be exercised at least that is my opinion and that will not let me be guilty of encouraging you in any unnecessary profuseness by lending you beforehand more then what I think sufficient for you and that I take 20s a week (as I have said) prudently to be, and more then will be reasonable of you to expect from me also unless you can bring yourself to receive it with greater appearance of acknowledgement then you yet do, specially after saying that you went into the country only to serve Mr H to whom your whole family owes its having a bit of bread to eat at this time and for several years backwards and his real ayme for prevailing with me to send you down to my house was to preserve you as much as he could from being undone by the chargeableness of your living here, and particularly under so great a house-rent. Which that you may be the better convinced of, if you do indeed find as little benefit in the charge of living by being where you are but if all things are as dear and many dearer than they are at London you shall be at

---

[1] Rawl. A. 183 : 165. Rough draft in shorthand. Holograph. See note on letter 143. Spelling of Saterday is correct, as heading is written in longhand on original.
[2] Transcription doubtful.

liberty to return to town and have the same allowance of 20s a week for your use, here or where ever you please till your husband be here to provide otherwise for you. And this I am at heart willing to offer you because I will by no means have you stay an hour longer where you are then you not only take it as a kindness from me but do really find and by your accounts shall convince me that you c[an][1] live more cheaply[2] there then here. Therefore I do with all kindness desire you seriously to think of it as being the utmost you have to trust to, and rather more then less, unless it shall please God to give both my brother and you more thoughtfulness of your and your family's condition then to my great trouble I fear you have ever hitherto had.

Adieu

If the workmen come again pray direct them to Mr Loke to whom I will write about them this or the next post in order to his looking over their work and paying them for I do not love to have any scores of my own and do depend upon your not letting me hear again of any of yours.

146. ESTER ST. MICHEL TO S.P.[3]

Brampton october 5th [1681]

Honoured Sir

yours I have datte october: 1st:, wherein you Are pleased to exspres the dissattisfaction you have received by my Indevors. in order to your Commands and Charitable Counsils. mainly frugality, alsoe the Emtines of my Acknowligments for those innumirable favors you have and doe soe frely bestoe one my sealfe and family. the first I have and doe youse my utmost efforts, haveing tistified the same in those letters which I have given my selfe the honour to rite unto you. the Latter I thought the vollome of A sheat of Paper to small to Containe whatt I have to Saye one that subject. therefore only expresed my Redines in following your honours Counsill which to the utmost of my power and Capasity have done. which is the only thing I doute Since I know the Conduct of one of your goodnes and experience to Just to mention or Command Any thing which is imposible. but to those hose Lettell Capacity makes itt soe.

Sir, give me Leave to mention the Commands of my husbands, first that I should not Leave the house; wheare I was at his parting from England. and that if I did, it wold not only disapoint him, in his porposis, but that I should Incur his great displeasur. 2 ly to make noe

---

[1] Transcription doubtful.   [2] MS. *cheaperly*.
[3] Rawl. A. 183 : 279. Original. Holograph.

Alteration in his family, Ether in Lescining it or yousing Any other methods then them he had Alredy Acustomied his famly to. thirdly the Education of his Son Leaving A tutor in the house as A settelment for that Porpose. untill by him or by his order to be removed. thirdly the other Children which are Able to be kept at scoule, forthly that the Agrement was made betwen M Hewers, and himselfe, for sufitient to Entertaine all these his Comands. 5 ly he defending[1] me Letting one Chamber althoe to what Advantage soe ever I mout thinke it. which was the first of his Commands I broke, then all the reast, wherein I have not only Porchased your honour's Ill openion, and Mr Hewers's dissatisfaction in managing of that Alowance you Are boath Resolved to beleave Añufe, but to Ad to all my husbands tcheckes and reflections which I Canot expect to be of small number and of Longe life.

Althis I have done to Advance the Payment of Mr Hewers, debt, which I thought was in order to searve him haveing noe other power to put in youse one this ocation. your humble sarvant to Comand

ESTER ST MICHELL

Sir Mr Loke desires to Lett your honour know that his goeing oute of town is the reson that he Could not return An answer to your letter by this Post but by the next hopes he may

To Mr Samuell Pepyes att Mr Hewers's house in yorke Buildings nere the New Exchange in the Strande London

147. MR. MATTHEWS TO S.P.[2]

Huntingdon October 20th 1681

Sir

That which put's me upon giveing you the trouble of these lines is the great need which your Kinsmen have of clothing, those which they wear being soe bad, that I am almost ashamed they should be seen in them; wherefore I humbly intreat, that you would be pleased either to send them some, or give me your commands, and I will be both carefull and frugal in providing for them: they are both (I bless God) in good health, continue good boys and observant of my commands, the youngest will infallibly make a Scholar, the other (I question not) an Honest well-temper'd man; the utmost of my regards shall be toward them: you were pleased (when in the Countrey) to speake of some single Basses (which you had at London) proper for one voice, one or two of them obteined at your hands would adde a

---

[1] Mrs. St. Michel uses the word in the French sense of *forbidding*.
[2] Rawl. A. 178 : 99. Original. Holograph.

greater weight to those many obligations which I already ly under,
of being
Sir
Your devoted Servant
JOHN MATTHEWS

Your Nephews present their dutys.

My wife begg's your acceptance of her Humble Service.

These For the Worshipfull Samuel Pepys Esquire att Mr Hewer's
House in Yorke-Buildings neer the Strand London

148. MR. MATTHEWS TO S.P.[1]

[Huntingdon] November 6th 1681

Sir

　　I not receiveing any answer to a Letter which I made bold to
write unto you about a fort-night since, fear it hath miscarried, and
therefore I am forc'd (by your Kin's-men's great want of Cloths) to
write this second time: I humbly intreat you, Sir very speedily either
to send them some, or to give me your Commands, and I shall be
very carefull in providing for them: those cloth's which thay have
indeed are soe bad, as that they are both dangerous (by reason of their
thinness) and almost disgracefull: they are very good boys, observant
of my commands, and diligent at their books: my tender regards are
not, neither shall be wanting towards them: my wife beggs your
acceptance of Her Humble Service, your kins-men of their dutys:
I am

Sir
Your ready and obliged Servant
JOHN MATTHEWS

These For the worshipfull Samuel Pepys Esquire att Mr Hewer's
house in Yorke buildings neer the Strand. London:

149. S.P. TO MR. MATTHEWS[2]

London. November 12e 1681

Cosen Matthews,

　　I give you my very respectfull thankes for yours of the 6th instant,
and am no less sensible of your reguards to, and care of my Nephews,
then glad of the Characters you give them.

---

[1] Rawl. A. 178 : 97. Original. Holograph.
[2] Rawl. A. 194 : 259–60. Secretarial copy.

If it be indifferent to you to have your last Quarter paid here, I will see it immediately done upon letting me know the hand I shall pay it to: But if not; I will find the first convenience I can for it's being done in the Country.

I take notice of your advice touching their wants of Cloaths, and am desirous of their being instantly supply'd therewith. To which purpose, since you are contented to take the trouble of it, I shall intreat my Cosen and you to consider what is necessary to be bought for them; not doubting your good management in the price thereof. Nor will you (I suppose) think it of any use to make them overfine (especially for Winter) provided what you buy be such as will keep them warme and cleane, and last well. The charge of which and of what other Expences you have been at for them, since my last waiting on you, I shall upon your sending me an account thereof, see instantly made good to you, my Sister (though I thank God in a good state of recovery) not being yet fully in condition to take that care againe upon herselfe.

I pay my Cosen and you many thankes for your continu'd care of them, and the Civilitys I received my selfe from you both, when last in the Country. I remember too my promise about some Bases for a single voice. And will performe it some time the next week, by sending you a couple of short Anthems to begin with Which when you have you will from the proof of them, be better able to say what you would have the next to be, as to more or less difficult, whether English or Latine, serious or more gay: For I think I can accommodate you every way. Onely the hand that ordinarily pricks for me, is not just now with me; and my owne Eyes being under some present indisposition will not suffer me to prick them myselfe now. But I doubt not of doeing it the next week.

When I was last at Huntington I left (I doubt) a small thing unpaid for at Dr Fulwood's. As I remember it was an ounce of the Leave of Asarum finely powder'd. If it were soe, pray doe me the kindness to see it satisfied, and bespeake two ounces more of the same to be prepared for me, and sent up when done; putting it into your other Notes of Disbursements which you shall have to send me. Which with the tenders of my very faithfull respects to my Cosen and your Selfe, and my kind Loves to my Nephews is all at present from

Your very humble servant
S P

To Mr Matthews

150. MR. MATTHEWS TO S.P.[1]

Huntingdon November 21 1681

Sir

I can doe noe less than return my most Humble thanks for your kind and welcome Letter, and likewise for your candid resentments therein expres't of my regards towards your Nephews: I will endeavour what I may, Sir to serve you in them: and to form them such, who may deserve your benigne aspect and smile:

According to your direction and order, I will likewise take care to see them well and warmly clad, in the management whereof I will be as faithfull and frugal as I am or can be in any proper affair of my own:

I should be ungratefull did I not before hand make payment of thanks even for the promise you are pleased to give of Honouring me with some of your Basses, I confess it was impudence in me soe boldly to crave the favour which I never deserv'd, neither had reason to aspire to: but your Humanity and goodness made me presumptuous and promp't me on: if at any time I may be capable of serving you in that narrow Orb wherein I act, command, and you shall experience me both ready and sincere.

I have bespoke (according to your desire) two ounces of Asarum at Doctor Fulwoods, but it is not yet prepared, and therefore cannot be sent up, untill another opportunity: my wife crave's your acceptance of her Humble services, your Nephews of their dutys: I am

Sir

Your obliged and devoted Servant

JOHN MATTHEWS

These For the Worshipfull Samuel Pepys Esquire at Mr Hewers House in York-buildings nere the Strand London Carrier paid

151. MR. MATTHEWS TO PAULINA JACKSON[2]

Huntingdon November 21 1681

Madam

I received your Kind Letter the last weeke for which favour I desire by these to return my Humble thanks: Your Son's (I bless God) are moderately well, they both of them have a tertian-Ague, which Handle's them very softly and gentlely, and I hope will prove noe long or tedious Companion to them: my wife's tender regards

[1] Rawl. A. 183 : 235. Original. Holograph.
[2] Rawl. A. 183 : 233. Original. Holograph.

are not wanting towards them: they are very good boys, observant of my commands (which are not grievous:) and diligent at their books: I hope they will prove your comfort, my credite: I and my wife unite in presenting our Humble Service to you, your Son's begge your acceptance of their dutys: I am

Madam

Your obliged and ready Servant

JOHN MATHEWS

These For Mrs Paulina Jackson at Mrs Hollingshead's house at the black Swan in Woodstreet nere Cheap-side: London: Carrier paid

152. ESTER ST. MICHEL TO S.P.[1]

Brampton November 29th 1681

Honoured Sir,

I humbly make bould (with presentasion of the humble duty of Littel Samuell whoe prays your Blessing, and the ever dutiffull servis of all the rest of my famely) to acquaint that I should have given my selfe the honour to have inquired after your health (which god Longe preserve) before n[ow][2] had not my owne indisposition (haveing bine very ill theese 3 weekes past) hindred me, this now comes to give cover to the inclosed not which was lefte for your honour [not] at your house, but at the Post house, and further to advise you that I And famely are now redused to the Last and wate your further directions. and orders assuring you that to the uttermost of my power I have managed Every mite with the best huswiferye as posible I could humbly praying to hear Speedely from you I remaine

your Ever Obedient and Moste Humble Sarvant

ESTER ST MICHEL

To Mr Pepyes att Mr Hewers's house In yorke Buildings nere Charring Cross London

153. S.P. TO B. ST. MICHEL[3]

London Saturday 7 January [16]81/2

Brother,

I had your Letter of the 24th of December and am very glad to understand that your Family is in health and to hear from Mr Hewer

[1] Rawl. A. 178 : 73. Original. Holograph. The enclosure mentioned has not been found.   [2] Edge torn.

[3] Rawl. A. 194 : 262. Secretarial copy. St. Michel has returned from Tangier without permission and, laying his grievances before the Navy Board, has gone to his family at Brampton to await developments.

the account you give him of the considerations you are under towards the better Settlement of your Family, Wherein I wish you all good success. What principally occasions my now writing is the telling you that I find by my Discourse with the Officers of the Navy, and in particular also with My Lord Brouncker, that nothing to this hour is done in the Business you are attending on, relating to your charge at Gibraltor, since your leaving this Towne, Nor (for ought I hear) is likely to be unless some body be here to solicite it, none now looking after it. So as it will bee necessary that you do prepare your selfe to be here in a little time; My Lord telling me that he otherwise fears advantage may be taken by one or other to impute it the delay in this Matter to your absence. And indeed it will be thought your onely proper Worke (as being in the King's Wages) to look after it; Especially since you have no written License for your non-attendance. Wherefore pray be disposing your selfe as soon as you can to come up, for fear of any inconvenience; and let me know when you are ready to come. In the mean time for the present satisfaction of the Officers of the Navy, I have employed the Blank you sent Mr Hewer in a Letter to them, to acquaint them with your readiness upon Comand to returne (in the forme enclosed) and to communicate to them Extracts of Mr Hunter's 2 last Letters[1] to you from Gibraltor. Which with the wishing the Comforts of a happy New Year to you and your Family is all at present from

Your truely affectionate Brother and Servant
S P

To Mr St Michel

154. S.P. TO MR. MATTHEWS[2]

London Saturday 7 January 1681/2

Good Cosen,

The Holy Days calling me a little out of Towne has prevented my answering yours of the 3d instant by the last Post. I receive great Satisfaction in the account you give me of my Nephews, and returne you and my Cosen my very kind thankes for the continuance of your

---

[1] These extracts, copied by a secretary under the title, *An Extract of 2 Letters of Mr. Hunter's from Gibraltor to Mr St Michell, one dated 21th the other 25th of October, 1681* (Rawl. A. 183 : 199), record that Admiral Herbert, Commander-in-Chief in the Straits, who had hampered St. Michel in his work at Tangier, had now seized letters and supplies directed to St. Michel, and, refusing them to the latter's appointed deputy, Mr. Hunter, had given them over to Captain Beverly, the master attendant at the port of Gibraltar. The reports detail the unbusinesslike manner in which stores were being issued.

[2] Rawl. A. 194 : 262–3. Secretarial copy in letter-book.

cares of them. I will give order for the payment of the Bill you send me, the next week, and send you a Receipt from Mr Goodday for Mr. Farside's use. When also I will make good my word about some Musick, Which I have been unfortunately till now prevented in, by not being able to come to my Musick-Papers through their having been in a late removall of my Books and some of my Papers pack'd up by my Servants, so as I know not readily where to turne to them. But I now have them and so shall you what you expect of them.

As I am under good assurance of my Nephew John's continuing to do his part in reference to his Studies; so I should be very glad to hear that Sam betakes himselfe, as I formerly advis'd (and your Bill mentions) to his Writing and Arithmetick; because the Spring will shortly be comeing on, when I have it in my thoughts to put him forth in som condition suitable to his Genius. Which with the Wishes of a happy New Year to you and your Family is all at present from

Your most affectionate and humble Servant
S P

My kind Love to the Children

To Mr Matthews

155. S.P. TO MR. MATTHEWS[1]

London Thursday 12 January 1681/2

Sir

According to my Letter by last Saturday's Post (which I hope you have received) I herewith send you a Receipt from Mr. Goodday by the hand of his Servant (himselfe not being home) for the Money. Wherein after my coming home I found a mistake, the young man haveing drawne his Acquittance for 22 ⅃ 11s, whereas I paid him but the just summe mentioned in your Bill, and Mr Farside's note viz 22 £ 2s 11d. Of which pray take notice to Mr Farside that he may do right to Mr Goodday.

My Servant is just copying out a couple of Anthems for you, and I doubt not will have done them time enough to send with this by the Carrier. My owne Eyes not serving me to do it, and he being no Latinist, you will (I doubt) find the words none of the best written; but I pray you to excuse it.

I give you many thanks for the trouble you took for me about the Asarum-Powder.

[1] Rawl. A. 194 : 263. Secretarial copy in letter-book.

Upon second thoughts, the best way of rectifying the Enclosed-Receipt, will be by your dividing the 8s mistaken between my 2 Nephews, as a token from me, and I will pay so much more to Mr Goodday: and then the Acquittance may stand as it does, and Mr Farside may make him Debtor for the whole Summe of 22 ₺ 11s Which with my true respects to my Cosen and yourselfe is all at present from

Your affectionate and humble Servant

S P

To Mr Matthews

156. B. ST. MICHEL TO S.P.[1]

Dover March 5th: 1681/2

Most Ever honoured Sir,

I hope your honour doth beleeve that from the very botome of my sowle (I am sure) I am truely sencible, and most humbly thankefull for your most Dear and Generous favours to me-wards; but most perticularly I shall to my lives einde Ever remember your late kindenesses, by the resentements I soe visibly saw, your goodness was pleased to have for the late hardshipps imposed on me, by the[2] soe cruell and bitter proseedings against me: but god reward them according to deserts, however I shall still to the last of My life, first observe in all perticulars your wise Comands, and next shew the world by it, that I have the honour to obay and serve you; and doe not doubt by gods helpe and yours but that eare longe the worst wilbe the best still and that I may live to over come all your and My Enemys to theire owne Confusion.

This further comes in Obedience to your Comands in order to your Drawing from it, what you shall please to have the lords of the Admiralty know of My obedience to theire (Noe)[3] order for my repare to the Tigar in the Downes. Thus the night I lefte your Dear, honorable, favours and kindeness, to see your only creature at Billingsgate (a soe great an honour and kindeness which I Blush to thinke that I shall never be able to repay) where I last kissed your honour's hands, I imediatly (the boats being all gone) hired an Express on which I were all Night in bitter Could the wind very fress at (NE) by which reason and My Not putting of till ¼ Ebb wee Could

---

[1] Rawl. A. 178 : 11–12. Original. Holograph.   [2] *late*, canc.
[3] i.e. *now* or *new*.

save our tide but as low as Eriff[1] at allmost 12 I there went a shoare
and though sleepe hath forgott my Eyes (thay being to busey in my
Brayne to accompany my maney afflictions) yet lay I downe one a
bead till next tide which was yesterday Morning by ½ past 5 when I
proseeded for gravesend, and where I was by 8, thence (it being the
Crossest day for all Cariages of traveling) however with Much a doe
I gott conveinecess at very Great Charge, as well as tedious (Espetially in the Eager desier I was of Speed, that the Admiralty Lords
Might know I cann obay in any truble and danger when for my
kings service, what thousands cannot paralell if thay had had the like
triall) to Canterbury where traveling all Night without any rest I got
by 2 this Morning and thence heither by 8 where noe sooner arived
but the winde came to the (SW) and heard that the Tigar was still
in the Downes on board which I shall god willing to moroe mor[n]-
ing goe after (if my Eyes will Joyne with what my Body requiers) I
have gott this Nights rest I not haveing bine out of My Cloathes
since I last saw you to this hower Now 3 the Afternoon, I humbly
pray your honour that what you shall please to have presented to
theire Lordshipps and the Navy Board May be the same night you
have this that thay May be sencible of My care and hurey to comply
with speed with theire (noe) directions and Espetiall that My Lord
finch may find faulce what my Enemys woold persuade him, vizt that
I woold not goe in which further please pressingly to note to them
that I hope they will finish, and give other more momentall and
authenticke orders, and directions to redress those grivances I groned
and shall still grone under without theire relife in all the perticulars
of the late proposalls which lies before theire Lordshipps for which I
have herewith sined to Blancks for your honour's pening what you
shall please to them and the officers of the Navey both or Either as in
your wisdome you shall thinke fitting. I have Noe time to enlarge
being pressed by the post only humbly Begg you woold please to give
My Most faithfull and ever zealous service to that Most worthy
Gentleman Mr Hewers whose favours and kindenesses I shall Ever
acknoledge and owne to my grave being to him, and your Honour
A Most faithfull and Ever humble servant
B St Michel

If by the list your Honour may know that still wee are in the Downes
pray give my Droopeing speritts the Cordiall of a line from you and
lett peeter be sent for upp with speed soe that now the windes are at
(SW) againe it May soe happen that hee May come to me before we
saile.

[1] i.e. *Erith.*

For the Honourable Samuel Pepys Thees

Memoriall for Mr Hewers to be pleased to give order to some of his, to have the perticulars gott for me vizt.

holland Shirtes of about 4d a Ell and 3 ells in a Shirte the sleeve⎫
to be but 2 thirds of a yard wide a litell lace at the sleeves of about⎬
4d a yard to save Cuffs ⎭

a reaime of Best Horne paper and a hundred of pens and 2⎫
blanck books of 3 quires Each Covered with parchement with⎬
noe other ruleing but a large Merget ⎭

2 pare of sad[1] Coulered Gloves of kid
one pare of Muske Culered silke stockins
2 pare of thread stockins
a good white or gray bever hatt the bigness in the head of that Mr Hewers had from me which I thinke his Man wears now Peter Cloathed with a darke Coulered Cloath lined with Read sarge, and white pewter buttons and 2 pare of read woolen stockins for him and 2 pare of shows, and 2 Course shirtes.

157. B. ST. MICHEL TO S.P.[2]

Plymouth March the 9th 1681/2

Honoured Sir,

I hope you have Safely received my last from Dover of the 5th instant, whereby, by what you Shall please (in my name) to Signifie to the Lords of the Admiralty thay may See that my Speedy and redy obaying theire noe[3] comands (howsoever Cruell and bitter as I thinke the whole world cannot be but sensible thay ware to order not only my returne, with that hurrey of but 7 howers warning, but which is worse, without provision directed, for redress to those greevances, which forsed me to come home) goes still paralell with all my Ever rediness in my Dutifull Obediences to his Majesty's Services, and that never dangers, or adversiteys by sea or land, abroad or at home, in warr or peace Could Ever hinder me (as I am bould with comfort to say) and that though I have Spent all the prime of my youth for allmost theese 20 yeares in never other then such, I Ever performed my dutey with faithfull zeale to his Majesty's Service, and honour to my Dear Patrone, Protector, and Benefactor, which I am sure I will Ever continue dooing to the last of my breath.

[1] Johnson's Dictionary gives: *sad*, dark coloured.
[2] Rawl. A. 183: 302–3. Original. Holograph. One paragraph quoted by Bryant, *Samuel Pepys: The Years of Peril*, pp. 372–3.   [3] i.e. *now* or *present.*

This now comes againe with my most humble dutey and service to your Dear Selfe, and my most worthy freinde Mr Hewers (to whoome pray give my Ever faithfull service) to further acquinte you both, that (though in my foresaid last, I advised you of the wind being then at SW, and that therefore I purposed to lie at Dover that night, to rest my wearied speritt and body till next morning 10 or 11, when I was resolved to goe to the Downes with the fludd, which woold be about that time)[1] before I went to bead, about 9 night the winde being come about farr to the N, thence to the N b E, and NNE I was in noe litell paine, fearing that the shipp might way in the night, and pass by which againe hindred my needful rest, wherefore I kept a man watching all night on the Peer-head, whoe by 4 next morning munday 6th (the winde continuing still fare) brought me notice, that hee spied some vessells about the foreland coming out of the Downes, and that I might sudenly Expect the Tiggar; which news at that time of the Morning quickly turned me out of bead, and imediatly riseing hired a boat, put my things in, and my selfe wated redy, watching on the Peer-head her coming about the S foreland till 10; when she apeared, then I imediatly putt of [,] mett her, and boarded her; in Dover Road about 12 Noon, soe contin[u]ing sailing on, on Board her with fare weather and winde sometimes vearing betwen the NW and NbE wee this morning b[y][2] arived safe heer, of all which I humbly pray that with your usuall wise method and favour to me-wards you will (with adition to my advantage,) please to give the Lords of the Admiralty advise of as from me, in the Enclosed blanck, which I herewith humbly send to your honour Therefore signed by me.

I hope still (with a great faith) in god, and your Dear goodness to me-wards, that when you next see the Duke it will not be longe now, how I shalbe Eased from theese soe maney Throuldomes of miserys I growne under, (only Cutt out for poore me) and remooved according to Justice, to some other imployment at home, of more honour, and profiet, but perticularly of more capacitey of service to you wards; when I may with my dear poore famely pass the remnant of my days in comfort, for otherwise, I fearme me for theire sakes (god is my Judge) and not for my owne, and am allmost sure, that in this, I shall worey,[3] my life and days out, to my infinite loss and ruine, in an imployment, and in a place, which will not hardly give me bread now, much less gaine, for my suport, in my age hereafter with my small (great) famely: however i in the fullness of Anguish of Speritt, will wate still with patiance, trusteing in your honour's profeceys, vizt:

---

[1] *on being to my desire*, canc.   [2] *day, night, late*, canc. in turn.
[3] *whorey*, canc.

that the worst wilbe the better still; which I hope againe in my god, and your favour will be, that when the next Occasion falls, of better preferment for me, I may not doubt to reape the benefiet of your Continued Kindenesses, and that soe, some Enemys (if I shoold not say fooles) may see that what you have done for them, shoold not have bine rewarded by ingratitudes: which with my Ever prayers to the allmightey for your preservation, prosperity and welfare

I remaine

with my repeated humble service and

thankes to Mr Hewers

Sir

Your Honour's Most faithfull and obedient

servant

B St Michel

I most humbly pray that I may have the Comfort of often hearing from you, or Mr Hewers, when you shall thinke it fitt; and if heather[1] you woold please to sende a line or two, it wilbe but a letter lost shoold we be sailed, wee (it seemes) being only to call heer for some Shipps bound to the straites, Except the winde shoold (by turning) stay off longer which if you doe pray direct for me, on board the Tiggar Prise, in Plymouth Sound.

158. B. ST. MICHEL TO S.P.[2]

Plymouth Sounde March 12th 1681/2

Honoured Sir,

My last of the 9th instant from hince, acquinted you of my arivall heer in the Tiggar; last night the winde being indiferant fair or N. westerly wee wayd, and sailed in order to the proseeding on of our voyage; but wee hardly gott the lengthe of foy, but the winde shifteing betweene the S.b.W. and S.b.E., with much winde and raine, wee ware forsed to bare upp againe, and about 2 this afternoon we againe returned and at Anchor heer; where if (as it still doth, and is likeley) the weather contin[u]es, wee may continue yet some time heer, soe that I hope I may have the hapiness of hearing from you and mr Hewers, however I though[t] it convenient (as well for the presenting my Most Dutifull and thankefull service to You, as for that, you might please on my behalfe to make what use you shall thinke fitting to tell the Admiraltys, or Navey Board in the Enclosed blanck) I say I therefore though[t] it my dutey to advise you of the

---

[1] i.e. *hither*.   [2] Rawl. A. 178 : 9. Original. Holograph.

same, as I shall allsoe of my Next departure, in the Meane while with my most humble service to you and mr Hewers I remaine
Your Honour's Dutifull and Ever faithfull Servant
B S᷊ᴛ Mɪᴄʜᴇʟ

Captain Elmore whoe is the most obligeing person to me in the world, and a perticular respect and honour for you, desiers you woold please to accept of his humble service

For the Honourable Samuel Pepys at Mr Hewers house in Buckingam Street in Yorke buildings in the Strand These London

159. ESTER ST. MICHEL TO S.P.¹

Brampton: April the 4th 1682
honoured Sir, I have received yours of the 1st Instant wherein you are pleased to Lett me know, of Madam Jacksons, return to your one house at Brampton, (which she is Mistris of were it mine) it will be noe troble to me or straitnes, if it proves not soe unto her; to finde your Lodgings Crowded with popell, which hath not had the honour ever of Madam Jackson's Aquaintance, besides the meneness of ower Capasity, one all respects, Espesially that of Entertainment, (according to her Merrits and your sister) but to that I shall say noe more since your honour hath mencioned it all ready: whatt I have to say to Madam Jackson, I shall Omit untill her return to Brampton, in the mene time I wich her A good and speedy Journey and safe prograce in her Afares, with the dutifull services of my family and selfe
I remaine your honours Obedient Servant
Eꜱᴛᴇʀ S᷊ᴛ Mɪᴄʜᴇʟʟ

160. DR. JOHN TURNER TO S.P.²

[Eynesbury] Aprill 13th 1682
Sir

This morning I received yours of Aprill 11th and with Gods help tomorrow I will wait on Mrsis Jackson and carry all her writings which are safe in my keeping, I shall then also wait on Sir Nicholas Pedley and contribute all I can towards the bringing her affaires to an easy and quick composure, Sir I am obliged to this by the respects

---

¹ Rawl. A. 178 : 29. Original. Holograph. Printed incorrectly: Smith, i. 283–4.
² Rawl. A. 183 : 203. Original. Holograph.

I have for Mrsis Jackson, and the memory of her good Father and particularly for the great favours your selfe have pleased upon all occasions to conferre upon
> Sir
> > Your most affectionate and humble servant
> > > JOHN TURNER

For Samuel Pepys Esquire at Mr Hewers house in York-buildings in the Strand.

161. S.P. TO PAULINA JACKSON[1]

Aprill 29th 1682

Sister Jackson,

I have received your Letter of 22th; which came to my hand but on Wednesday last which was 26th.

I am extreamly Glad of what you tell me is offered you by Mr. Herbert, for if he makes good his word, most Certainly Mr. Sharpe will have noe right at all to the obligeing you or any body elce but the Executors who have Administred to the Payment of the Bond, and now it is apparent that whence it was that Sharp was Soe forward to take up the Land, in order to his hedgeing-in the Bond. Therefore you may lett Mr Herbert and Your Tenants know, that upon his delivering-up all the Writeings, and Surrendring back the Copy-hold-Land, which sharpe has taken up; The mortgage mony shalbe payd. But pray take care to have Sir Nicholas Pedleys and Mr Loke's advice, as also your freinds at Ellington, how the Same may be done Safely.

The reasonable charges of Court must also be allowed him, and soe shall what Intrest remaines unpayd upon the money. Which I will looke over your husbands' papers about. But one thing lett me tell you, which is fitt for you to know and consider with yourself, that as I remember when Sharpe shewed me his papers at Huntington to prove the mony lent by Mr Herbert, he did shew me a Declaration entred upon the back syde under Mr Herbert's hand, that the money lent was not his but Mr Moseley's. Some thing of this kinde I doe remember, tho I am not very perfect in it. And therefore I doe a little wonder how Mr. Herbert now comes to say that the mony was his owne, and that he has your husbands' Obligations in his hands.

But be it how it will; if he will see[2] them delivered-up to you, and the Land Surrendred back, the mony shalbe payd.

---

[1] Rawl. A. 194 : 271. Secretarial copy, evidently the rough draft.
[2] *Surrender*, canc.

Pray returne my Services to all the kinde Gentlemen you mention, and the like to my Sister St Michell. Soe with my Blessing to your Children I remaine,

Your assured Loveing Brother
S PEPYS

162. ESTER ST. MICHEL TO S.P.[1]

Aaugust: 1st: [1682]

honoured Sir

this with my duty Aquainte you with my speedy return to London, which my Ocasions requires. therefore intreat your honour to return me that note of what goods you were pleased to intrust me with in your hous at Brampton, which, when I have peruseed shall acordingly deliver them into the hands of Madam Jackson, home god bethanked is in perfect health, if your honour pleas's to give Leve and Leberty of my familyes, remaining in your hous, untill I Can other wayes provide for them, which shall be with as much speed as posible, you will ade to the rest of your Charityes which shall ever be Acknowlidged by your Humble Servant

ESTER ST MICHELL

163. B. ST. MICHEL TO S.P.[2]

Tangier June 27th: 1683:

The aflictions of my Spirit are Soe many and my Griefes and Torments soe passing unsufferable; to Thinke that him whose life was never Deare nor vallued (together with the hazard of his Reputation and fortunes) longer then (by all) he could be Serviceable to [his][3] Deare Though most cruell Benifactor to clearly thus forg[et][3] and

---

[1] Rawl. A. 178 : 135. Original. Holograph. It is not clear on what business Mrs. St. Michel returns to London. As early as May of the same year, S.P. and Hewer had been corresponding about a possible situation for her as rocker in the household of the Duchess of York. These letters have been printed by both Smith and Howarth (132–3, 139–41).

[2] Rawl. A. 190 : 42. Original. Written by secretary, signed by St. Michel. No salutation. On 10 Aug. 1683 Pepys set sail for Tangier with Lord Dartmouth and a large party under sealed orders. When the orders were opened at sea, it was learned that Dartmouth was to destroy the English-built mole and to supervise the evacuation of the city; Pepys was to assist in evaluating property there as a basis for compensation of the evacuees. The expedition returned to England in March 1684.

When we again hear of St. Michel, he is commissioner at Deptford, and S.P. is secretary to the Lord High Admiral, the Duke of York.

[3] MS. torn.

leave in afflictions, in a hellish Torred-zone, a Creatur of your Owne makeing, who never yett Dishonoured you, Though you are Still pleased (by this your long Silence &c) to leave him without your usuall formerly Soe wholsom Counsells or give him hopes of Speedy Redemption from this hell, this hell of Brimston and fire, and Egipts Plaugues; (which god Eternally Curse) I say my true unsufferable Torments are Such, that were it nott to Enquire after the health and welfare of him who I ever loved Honoured and Respected (if nott more) Equall with my owne father I Should never give you the Trouble I by theise doe by the hands of this most worthy Gentleman Docter Morgan who with my Humble Service, will alsoe give you my Everlasting Duty: which with my Eternall well wishes and the Continuall Prayers of a Poore Desolate aflicted-Soule, for your Prosperity health and welfare I Remaine.

Your Ever Dutifull and most Humble Servant

B St Michel

164. S.P. TO B. ST. MICHEL[1]

December 11th 1686

Brother St Michel,

I cannot but thank you (though in few words) for your kind enquiry after my health by yours of the 7th instant. It was not without very much ground, that in one of my late letters of generall advice to you, I cautioned you against depending upon any support much longer from mee, I then feeling what I now cannot hide, I mean, that paine which I at this day labour-under (night and day) from a new Stone lodged in my Kidnys and an ulcer attending it, with a generall decay of my Stomack and Strength, that cannot bee playd with long, nor am I sollicitous that it should.

This satisfaction I have as to your owne particular that I have discharged my part of friendship and care towards you and your Family, as farr as I have been, or could ever hope to bee able, were I to live 20 yeares longer in the Navy; and to such a Degree, as will with good Conduct, enable you both to provide well for your family and at the same time doe your King and Country good Service. Wherein I pray God to bless you soe, as that you may neither by any neglect or miscarriage fayle in the latter, nor by any improvidence (which I must declare to you I am most doubtfull of and in paine for) live to lament your neglect of my repeted admonitions to you touching the latter.

[1] Rawl. A. 189 : 226. Secretarial copy.

This I say to you, as if I were never to trouble either you or myselfe about it more, and pray think of it as such, from

> Your truly affectionate Brother and Servant
> S Pepys

Commissioner Navy at Deptford

165. B. ST. MICHEL TO S.P.[1]

Deptford January 24th 1686/7

I returne your Honour my most humble and harty thanks for yours of the 22d instant and for your great goodness and kindeness, in Stopeing the clamours of that nastey wooman about the Sadle, conserning which, ware it worth the giveing you truble of the Perticulars in the Sircomstances of Soe insignificant a matter, I humbly beleive you woold not blame my delay of payment, though I owne it a debt, which ought Justely to have bine paid eare this (as now it is). wherefore to the rest of your letter, with all humility, I begg leave to Say, that besides those many reasons, by which more prudent persons then my Selfe, with such a famely, might (by the Occasion of intervalls from Employments, first between the yeares 78, and 80, then from 83, to 86, and many other griveous causes, duering those times;) have contracted debts to greater value, then I am Sure by any extravagancy, or otherwise, i ever did; espetially when groneing, (both at home and abroad) under those circomstances of evills, and afflictions, both of boddy and minde, which then most grievously oprest me; and Such as i much question if any other could have waded through, or borne the burthen of, (which I humbly referr to your consideration) from which indeed I ought as a man, and a Gentleman longe before to have found a remedie, without addeing Oyle to my woonds in giveing truble and paine, to the person in the world next to god, I most honoured and respected, as I Shall to my lives einde. it is therefore extreame grievous to me, to have from Such a beloved person, Such an expretion as on the begineing of your Said letter, though i doe and Shall, make it my Studie all my life, to make it good, by giveing you the least truble I posible cann, more then by the respectfull duteys of me and Mine; and although you are pleased to Say, that you heer of my continued extravagant expences, I hope it is but the efects of your generous and kinde conjectures,

---

[1] Rawl. A. 189: 224–5. Original. Holograph. Endorsed: 'Mr St. Michel to Mr Pepys and Mr Pepys's Answer thereto; giveing him his generall and finall Advice for the good of his family.' A draft of Letter 166 appears on the bottom of the sheet.

being confident that (by my constant attendance on, and diligent execution of my present dutey) none but the blackest envy or malice (on
which curses attend) cann accuse me; I haveing god, and the world,
my witnesses of the contrary.

as to my Childrens (great and Small) knoledge of your goodness,
that theire present bread, and future hopes hath Sprung (under god)
from it only, thay have bine tought that from theire Cradles, and will
owne to theire graves. but as the changes of times of which, in your
usuall great goodness, and kindeness, you are pleased to advise me,
to reflect on; I have to Say (as I Said before) that I shall performe my
dutey (in the post I am in) with care, diligence, faithfullness, and
Industry; to the uttermost of my power for the Kings Service, as well
as my benefactors honour, and I shall be as frugall, and industrus in
all my owne domestick consernes as posible I cann, after which, if
malitious fortune unjustly be my ruine, I must rest content, though
heavey revengefull woe will attende the black pride of the authors
thereof, and bring theire famelys lower then myne. I most humbly
begg your honour's pardon for this truble, and to conclude (with
praying the heavenly god to prosper and preserve you) is only to most
hartely begg, the continuance of your favour and kindeness, to him,
whoe more then any one liveing esteemes it, being

Your most obedient and humble Servant

B St Michell

I longe to kiss your hands, if you will permitt it, and not be angrey
with me.

166. S.P. TO B. ST. MICHEL[1]

Thursday noon January 27th 1686/7

Brother,

I have received your Letter of the 24th, and have sayd my Say.
Upon your owne head bee it, if in deceiving me, you at length finde
the Effect of it to the ruin of your Family. I am sure I have nothing
to lead mee to these Jealousys concerning your Conduct, but my
feares on their and your behalfes, and desires of your Good. Nor have
I my information but from them that beare you good Will; besides
that your runing on the Score for this Sadle seemes very little to con-
sist with the good husbandry you would bee thought to walke by.
But I have done; and shall bee glad to see you and without Anger as
you call it, though it deserves another Name; it being too painfull a

[1] Rawl. A. 189 : 225. First draft, dictated on bottom of sheet of Letter 165.

thing to mee to write at all, and much more upon a Subject soe un-pleasant to mee as this is, would my care for you have suffer'd mee to bee silent. But you have sayd and Undertaken for soe much in this your last Letter, that it ought to putt mee at full ease concerning you, and therefore trusting God and you for the Event, and your Family to the Consequencies of it, you may rest secure against my ever giving either you or myselfe any more trouble of this kinde either by Penn or Word. Soe that you may freely visit mee, when ever your businesse will permit it, and bee wellcome.

Your truly affectionate Brother and Servant
S. PEPYS

167. MR. TILGHMAN TO S.P.[1]

Deptford February 9th [16]86/[7] 4 a Clock
Honourable Sir
Whilst Comissioner St. Michell is Drowned in Tears, and his Spirrit Sinking under the Sence of so heavy a Loss, I am by him Commanded to acquaint your Honour That this after noone about one, his Lady fell in Travell, was about two Delivered of a Son; but the Birth of the Child became the Death of the Mother, for within a quarter of an Houre after, her Soul expired; And hath left a Husband and numerous Family bleeding under (I think) the Saddest Accents of Sorrow I ever Saw.

I most humbly beg Leave to Subscribe
Honourable Sir
Your Honour's most Obedient and most
humble Servant
ABRAHAM TILGHMAN[2]

168. MR. TILGHMAN TO S.P.[3]

Deptford 10th February [16]86/7
Honourable Sir
In all Dutifull Obedience, I return your Honour my most humble thanks for that great Favour you have condescended to vouchsafe

---

[1] Rawl. A. 189 : 312. Original. Printed: *Mem.* ii. 74; 1848, p. 322; 1854, p. 234 misdated; 1879, p. 151 misdated; Howarth, p. 174.
[2] Endorsed: Mr. Tillman, Mr. St. Michel's Clerke.
[3] Rawl. A. 189 : 314. Original. Printed: Smith ii, pp. 64–65; Howarth, pp. 174–5.

me, by owning your acceptance of my yesterdays Letter acquainting you with the Afflicted state of the Comissioner and his Mourning Family, thro Decease of his Lady; An Honour Sir which I could in no reason expect, for the doeing only my Duty.

I did in Obedience to your Honour's Comands, by the first oportunity I could discerne of any relaxation from that Grief he groans under, Deliver him your Honour's Letter; And have in Command (for Answer) only to say, That he returnes your Honour Millions of Thanks for your great kindness and Generous Favours therein expressed, which he will own to his Lives end, and endeavour strictly to observe and obey those excellent Advices you are pleased to Administer; which haveing said, a deluge of Tears againe overwhelming him, could Add no more, than humbly to beg your Honour's pardon that he can not at this time farther enlarge. With great Submission, I subscribe

Your Honour's most obedient and most humble Servant
ABRAHAM TILGHMAN

To the Honourable Samuel Pepys, His Majesties Secretary for the affaires of the Admiralty York Buildings London Humbly Present

169. B. ST. MICHEL TO S.P.[1]

Deptford February 14th 1686/7

Honoured Sir

After my haveing paid the Last devoirs to my Dearest Wife, and as Soone as Soe great a greefe for Soe great a loss could permitt, I have thought it my dutye in the very next place to returne you my most humble thanks, for your Soe generous and Kinde letter of the 9th instant which Ile asure you (most Dear and Ever honoured Sir) was (in the depth of my bleeding harts-sorow) the greatest comfort and Cordiall, that could ever be given me, which being the Efects of your allwise usuall goodness and favours, I shall to my lives einde, with the uttermost of power ever Studye to obay your Comands and folow every [one] of your counsells, not letteing the least hinte of your wise[2] advices Slipp my most exact observation; I am Sir Stopped with a Torent of Sorofull Lamentation, for Oh god I have lost, oh I have lost such a loss, that noe man is or cann be Sensible but my Selfe: I have lost my wife, Sir, I have lost my wife; and such a wife, as your Honour knows has (may be) not lefte her felow, I cannot say any

---

[1] Rawl. A. 189 : 316–17. Original. Holograph.
[2] *counsells and,* canc.

more at present being overwhelmed, wherefore I most humbly begg
your pardon and excuse for theese ill, and nonesensicall lynes, as well
as for the giveing you truble therewith: and concludeing with my
continuall prayers to the Heavenly God for your Dear health, prosperity, and welfare; beseeching the Continuance of your favours I
remaine

Your Most Dutifull and Obedient Servant

B St Michel

170. JOHN JACKSON TO S.P.[1]

Cambridge 24 February 1687

Vir Nobilissime et Amplissime!
Animus herclè meus in verecundiâ atque pudore usque antehac
attentus fuit, qui totiès me ingratitudinis maculam sustinuisse coegit;
tanta autèm tua jàm in me beneficia redundant; ùt in ipsam justitiam
peccem sì tacendo, diutiùs tàm inhumanitèr a me actum esset; gratias
igitùr haberem, nèc me penes est; quantum enìm (Vir Illustrissime!)
tibi debeam, exprimere stupet lingua, depingere calamus; hoc autèm
mihi negotii (dùm in vivis agam) credam potissimùm dari, ùt gratum
erga te animum ostendam; jam verò nihil amplius in me est, nisi
vitam longam, omnèque tibi beatitudinem precari, èt meipsum sub-
scribere

Observantissimum Nepotem èt ad
omnia tua imperata paratissimum

Johannem Jackson

Dedi e Museo meo Cantabrigiae Vicesimo quarto die Februarii
1686/7

These For Samuel Pepys Esquire at the Admiralty office in York
buildings in Buckingham Street London humbly present

171. B. ST. MICHEL TO S.P.[2]

Deptford 23 May. 1688.

Honoured Sir
　　Your humble Servant Samuel being just return'd from Ham-
brough in the Fubbs yacht, comes with this to wait on you, and with

---

[1] Rawl. A. 189 : 294. Original. Holograph. Endorsed: 'Cambridge 24th February
1686/7 My Nephew John Jackson's first Letter to mee after his going to reside at Magdalen Colledge in Cambridge.' Printed with endorsement: *Mem.* ii. 80.
　　This is, of course, Paulina's second son, engaged in fulfilling the predictions of Mr.
Mathews. See Letter 147.

[2] Rawl. A. 179 : 117. Original. Dictated, signed by St. Michel.

his humble Duty to kiss your hand, as also to present you my most humble thanks for your late, as well as ever favours and kindnesses, for which I give you my most Dutyfull acknowledgments; Sir He hath been more than Sixteen Months in the said Yacht, and very assiduously attending each Voyage for his improvment both in Winter and Summer, but being desirous of finishing his two years Voluntiership in a larger Man of Warr for his further Experience, that soe on its determination he may be Qualified against the next Voyage for a Midshipman in order to his future preferment; I therfore humbly make it my request on his behalf (Captain Hopson being my particular friend and old acquaintance ever since the warr in 1666) that you would please to procure his Majesty's Letter for Samuels being Voluntier on board the Bonadventure; for although I have an Infinite Esteem for Captain Loyd and doe heartily thank Mr Atkins for his proposall to you of sending Samuel to him in the Streights by some Merchant Ship, yet have I some reasons which at present inclines me to the contrary as I am almost confident you will approve of, when next I have the Honour to wait on you and shall acquaint you, besides that it may be hoped with your favour which I heartily wish, that Captain Hopson with the Bonadventure may ere long goe to the Streights.

I am still very weak of my late Indisposition, yet make I a shift dayly to craul about this Yard, for the Seeing dispatch'd his Majesty's Naval Services, and this day being an indifferent faire one, I am just going to Woolwich. I therefore humbly take my Leave, and remaine
Your Honours' most faithfull humble Servant
B St Michel

I humbly refer to your Honour's favour if you shall think fitt, on this subject to have Samuel wait on you for presenting him to the King. B St M.

For the Honourable Samuel Pepys, His Majesty's Secretary for the Affaires of the Admiralty London

172. S.P. TO B. ST. MICHEL[1]

Admiralty 7th June 1688
Brother.
I will as you desire, both by a letter and word of Mouth, recomend my Nephew Samuell to his Captaine before his going. And if you will bring him up any morning the beginning of the next Week to be here

[1] Adm. xiv. 214. Secretarial copy.

between 9 and 10 I will present him to the King. I cannot well appoint a day, because I cannot undertake to keep appointments of that kind, as not being soe much Master of any part of my time, and therefore leave it to you to take what morning you please, all being alike probable for me to be in the way. Adieu

Yours &c
S P

Comissioner St Michell

173. SAMUEL JACKSON TO S.P.[1]

From on board the foresight
this 20th Day of July
in the Downes, 1688

Honored Sir

This Day we Arrived At the Downes from the wrack[2] tho with the Losse of our Commander Sir John Narborough who Dyed upon the 26th of May Last and As though fate had Decreed him to Lye there After he had setled all his Matters with the Masters of vessells who were permitted to worke on the wrack upon Certaine Conditions we had orders to saile upon the 25th of the same may And as wee where weighing our Anker the smale Bower Cable broke and all the Arguments Captain Stanley: Levtenant Hubbard and the Rest of our officers Could use proved Altogether Inefectuall for Sir John was Resolved not to Leave the Anchor behind him: though unfortunately Left him where upon we plyed to windward All Day and at Evening Came to an Anchor As neer the bouy as Conveniently wee Could: And gote It Abord But at 3 of the Clock next Morneing: Death put A peryod to his Life And In the Evening we Celebrated his obsequies In A manner as suitable to the occation As the place and Company would Admitt: Honored Sir I hope I have made such A progresse In the Art of Navigation by the Assistance of one Matthew Jane: the yeoman of the powder Roome to who I am very much Engaged for his voluntary paines and troble In instructing of mee that I Doe not Doubt but to give your honor Ample satisfaction therein: May It please your honour the presente Gunner Christopher Mercer: who was Appointed by Sir John: to act in that station Is A person to whome I am Extremly obliged for his kindness and Civility

---

[1] Rawl. A. 179 : 70. Original. Printed: Howarth, pp. 191–2. Samuel Jackson is one of S.P.'s godsons, the elder son of Paulina.

[2] A treasure ship, off St. Domingo, which Sir John had been sent to salvage.

Dureing the tyme of this voyage: he was seven yeares Gunners Mate
Abord the James Galley under the Command of Captain Shovell and
hath A very Large Certificate: whom If your honour Is pleasd to
vouchsafe your favor: I Doe not Doubt but he will give you sufficient Satisfaction Concerneing his sobriety Loyalty and Abilityes,
for that Employ: As may render him Capable thereof: and which I
Humbly Request: Sir I should not have Dared to have given you
this trouble had not your honour's transcending goodness and to
Avoyde the Sin of Ingratitude been the Cheife Motives that Encouraged me thereto: humbly Craveing your pardon: for this bold
presumption And hopeing that your Honour will put A favorable
Construction upon these Lynes and fearing Least by too much
prolixity I should become troublesome I subscribe my selfe:

SAMUELL JACKSON

This to the Honorable Samuell Pepys Esquire Att the Admiralty
office In the stran[d]e London presente

174. S.P. TO B. ST. MICHEL[1]

Windsor 14th September 1688.

Brother St Michell,
    Tho I doubt not but you will be advertised otherwise Thereof
from the Navy Board, yett I thought it not amiss to tell you, that the
King is at this time under a determination to go down the River
towards Chatham on Tuesday next, in Order not only to the viewing
His New Fortifications in the river of Medway, but for his satisfying
himself in his way touching the forwardness of his shipps now fitting
forth, both in the Thames and Medway. Concerneing which, though
by the Encouragement I have received from the Officers of the Navy,
the King has been assured by mee, of the readiness of every one of his
said Shipps and Fireshipps, as to their Hulls, Furniture and Stores
(the Guarland only Excepted; which came up to Deptford but yesterday) yet forasmuch as either by oversight or otherwise, something
may be left undone, It will be needful in the first place, that you use
all the Care and Inspection that you can, for the preventing or
removeing any such; and that tho in strictness nothing more can be
expected from you, in the dispatch of Shipps forth, then what relates

---

[1] Adm. xv. 43–44. Secretarial copy. The days of James II as King of England are drawing to a close. This letter and the succeeding reveal not only the urgency of preparation
against an expected Dutch invasion, but also the fear of disaffection at home. In Rawl. A.
186 : 257–8, William Hewer reports to S.P. a satisfactory tour of ships in company with
St. Michel.

to the Worke to be dispatched, by the Officers of the Yards under your direction; I cannot but privately observe to you, that in a larger sence, they may be reckon'd to be within your Enquiry and Observation while they remaine within the reach and inspection of any one of your under Officers, and soe they must be allowed to doe while in the Checke of your Clerk of the Checque, and that I take to be as low as the bottome of Longreach. And this being soe, you will be looked upon as accountable for the preventing as much as may be by your advice and authority, or to report dayly to me for his Majesty's own Information and Correction, any Neglects that you can discover in any the Comission or Warrant Officers of the said Shipps in their Attendance by Night or day, and their performances otherwise of all that they are able towards the dispatch of their Shipps, As to their Manning and getting their Provisions, Gunns and Gunners Stores on board; and keeping their men in good discipline there, after they are Entered for the better and easier doeing of the said Workes.

I know very well, that It will be somewhat a new thing and consequently ungratefull to them) for Comanders to find themselves Chequed for their Absences like common Men, and would indeed be some lessening to them should it be by the Clerk of the Checque in comon with their under Officers and Shipps Companys. But forasmuch as the King's Service will be subject to inconveniencys of infinitely greater consequences (at the rate that I find Comanders at this time generally disposed) should they look upon themselves as wholly secured against any Comptroll or Inspection as to their Attendances, there is an absolute necessity of haveing some provision made for it, and that (as I conceive) can in no wise be more proper or decently done, than by the Commissioner of the Yard from whence their Shipps are fitted. And in that consideration I begin with recomending this matter to you, and shall by this very next post, do the like to your Brethren of the other Yards; desireing you will use some meanes of haveing this Effectually and Cautiously done; it being a miscarryage much to be lamented, to see all the effects that can be wished of industry and dispatch from the Office of the Navy and else where in the fitting of Shipps forth, and at the same time find that Industry rendred' ineffectuall to the King; by the Supinness Ignorance or want of good affections in those upon whome the latter part of the said Shipps dispatches doe depend. I am

Your &c
S. P.

Commissioner St Mitchell at Deptford

175. B. ST. MICHEL TO S.P.[1]

Deptford 18th September 1688.

Honoured Sir

I found here on my returne from Windsor your letter of the 14th. and doe most Respectfully thank you, for that Intimation given me, of his Majesties intentions to be down the River as this day; and tho he is not yet come, I shall take due Care, that all matters within my precinct of both Yards, be in good Order against his passing by, or puting on shoar at either of them: That assurance you have given his Majestie of the Readines of his Shipps and Fireships Ordered hence, I doe affirm is no other than Truth, soe farr as it respects their Hulls Riging and Stores, for a full, and ample satisfaction wherein, I did but yesterday singly Examine the respective Comanders of each of those which are not Sailed, and doe not find them speak anything wanting to compleat in those particulars: To what followes in your said letter, I never thought it other then my Duty, and it hath also been my practice, to inspect the Attendance, and Dilligence of Commission Officers in Forwarding the Fitting forth their Shipps (for I say nothing of the Warrant Ones, since they in this matter are under strict known Rules of Duty, and any neglect in them is easily punishable if not Reform'd) yet must Confes I find too much cause to wish that some way might be found of bringing them to a stricter complyance, with their own Instructions in that particular than generally they have given, and therefore whatever the consequents may be to me, I shall not fail of a Vigorous (yet Wary) endeavour to prosecute what you Advise thereon; only I entreat leave to pray, you will please to explaine somewhat more clearly your pleasure, as to those shipps only which now are, or hereafter may be Rideing in Longreach, whether you mean, that I my self goe dayly thither to Muster, or by my Authority and Direction have a private Account thereof from the Clerk of the Checque, and my self to goe now and then at times unthought of; and yet in either of these somewhat of Objections will arise, for If the former, besides the Infinite hardships 'twill bring me under to goe dayly soe far (especially in the Winter season) those other his Majesties many Workes incumbent on me, at both the Yardes, must inevitably be neglected; and if by the later way, (I finding nothing in the Clerk of the Checques generall Instructions directing them to Report the absence of Comanders or Lieutenants) doe question whether they may not require some better Authority, to begin

[1] Rawl. A. 186 : 187–8. Original, dictated, signed by St. Michel. A comparison of the style of this letter with that of the earlier florid compositions by the same writer suggests that frequent correspondence with Pepys may have influenced the force and dignity which begin to show themselves here.

their so doing; than the Single Hand of a Port Comissioner: Let me beg your farther patience in offering one thing (of near relation to this) being what I have often observ'd to be a very great obstruction to that Dispatch generally aim'd at, in Fitting his Majesties Shipps to Sea, to wit, The very late Appearance of Comission Officers (after the ship is Ordered) at the place from whence she is to be Fitted, many Daies are often spent, in getting ready the Hull before her Comander is known, at length it may be by that time she is Graved,[1] the Captaine appears (to take a view of his Ship) yet brings not one Hand to Enter on her, tho if he had, all her Company she is at this very day ready to receive them, and they would be of excellent use in the speedy geting of her Cables, Anchors, and those heavier kinds of Stores on board, the bringing too of Sailes &c, whereby the ship would quickly break Ground, and fall into Deeper Water for takeing in her other Stores and Victuals, but ere her Men can be gotten, there is much time lost which passeth undiscern'd, under a notion, or pretence that the Ship is not ready for them, when in truth the Company are not ready for the Shipp; This Sir I doe assure you is a very frequent Case, and would, in my humble opinion be remedied, if the Comanders were appointed when the Shipp is first Ordered, (especially, since now the Hulls of all his Majesties Shipps are kept in such constant readines, with their Riging and Stores layd apart) and they directed, to get ready their Men against the time their ship shall be Graved, and soe the time of her Fitting would by the Sailers be employd in furnishing themselves with Beding [,] Cloathes and necessaries, for doing of which time cannot be denyed them tho after the Ship is ready and stayes for want of them only; All which I humbly submit to your juditious consideration, and remaine

Your Honour's most Obedient Servant
B St Michell

176. S.P. TO B. ST. MICHEL[2]

Admiralty September 19th [1688]

Brother

    I thanke you for your Letter of yesterday's date, it containeing Severall Considerations of very good moment in the matter it related to; But that which is to bee said further upon it being not so properly

---

[1] 'Grave a ship, to make her lye drie a ground, and to burn off the filth with stubble. Phillips, *New World of English Words*, 1658.
[2] Adm. xv. 15. Secretarial copy.

for handling in a Letter, I shall respite it till Our meeting. Recomending it only in the mean time to make your own Observations as farr as you Can doe it with your own Eye in the places where you are, and privately give mee Intimation where you see any thing worthy of it, either for the doeing Right to an Officer, where his Extraordinary Dilligence requires it, or to the Thing[1] where the like degree of Negligence may make that necessary. And for what Concerns the use of the Clerke of the Checque, I will think further of that, and (as you propose) shall probably write something to them my selfe. I am

Your &c

S P.

Commissioner St Michell

177. B. ST. MICHEL TO S.P.[2]

Deptford 21th November [16]88

Honoured Sir

His Majesties Ship the Phoenix having laine at this place 9 or 10 daies after she was compleatly ready (on our parte) for Sailing, through want of a Winde for it, the same having hung for the most part between E N E, and E S E; Yesterday it pleased God to bring it about to the SW, very favourably for makeing use of the morning Tide, on which I was not a little joyd, as heartily wishing for his Majesty's Service those severall Shipps Ordered might be with the Fleet; But when I rose which was at half past 6 morning, finding the said Ship not Sailed I was in noe little paine therfore; soe presently sent to know the reason (as I thought became the Duty of my Post) and what Officers were on board, the Clerk Checque return'd me, that neither the Comander nor Lieutenant were nor had lain aboard the night before, but the rest of the Officers were on their Duty; Then imediatly the Master came to me, I askd him why the Ship was not Saild, and told him I was much troubled to see soe faire an

---

[1] King? Possible secretarial error.

[2] Rawl. A. 186 : 18–19. Original, dictated, signed by St. Michel. This letter and the two following furnish testimony to the disorganization of the last weeks of the rule of James II. Tanner (*Private Correspondence*, i. 24–27) prints an account of the king's flight, from an account in John Jackson's hand. The Rawlinson MS. contains four original letters from Captain Gifford: His assurance to S.P. that his ship is ready and his promise to sail as soon as wind is favourable (186 : 12); his defiance to St. Michel, laying upon him the blame for the delay (186 : 20); his report to S.P. that he has arrived at Long-reach, by which he makes it appear that he left Deptford a day earlier than St. Michel credits him. By this time he has involved himself in a dispute with one Captain Ellmore (186 : 16). Finally, he writes from the same place in amazement over St. Michel's complaint, inasmuch as he insists that he has complained previously of the negligence of the pilot and requested St. Michel to do likewise (186 : 23).

opportunity for it, lost, especially the season of the Year, and late unsettlednes of the winds considered, with inclination to Frost, which might give us cause of feare 'twould quickly be about againe to NE; he replyd that his Captain nor Lieutenant were not aboord, the later on his Duty pressing Men, and the Captain at London whome he hourly expected, and that the Pylot was not come, on which my Zeal for his Majesty's Service could not but move into some passion for such a Neglect and Excuses, asking him why he had not sent for the Pylot who Lives but at Greenwich he told me he had promised to come without sending for, (but I conceive had the Captain been aboord he would have sent for him in time) After this just trouble of mine, and dispatching some other buisnes at my Office, I at 10 a Clock went for London to joyne Sir Anthony Deane and Mr Hewer (as usually each Tuesday) on his Majesties Navall Affaires relateing to our charge with whome I was till two, and then returned to Deptfor[d]¹ hopeing to find the Wind Stand till next Tide, which seeing it did, I at 7 sent off to know if the Captain or Lieutenant were yet come downe, thereby to prevent a like Slip of this mornings Tide if the wind should favour which I hoped it would, whereon the Lieutenant quickly after came to me, (the Captain not being come downe) I pray'd him to be very circumspect in Sailing with the said Ship the morning tide, he told me he assuredly would, and soe I left him goeing to buisnes in my Office, where was till past ten then being very weary I went home to Bedd, wherein had not been half an houre, but rar rap at my Doore comes the Globe Boy, bringing the Inclosed Note with express Order to deliver it me presently which accordingly was done, The Contents when you see I leave you to judg, whether sufferable from Captain Gifford to One who hath the Honour of Serving the King in my Station especially while I am pressing for his Majesties Service; Oh how soon will all Government and Rule in the Navy be violated and trampled on, if the Commissioners thereof may thus be used by every Captain; Wherefore I leave the matter to your prudence, for considering thereof as may best stand with your leasure, knowing this a most busy juncture of time with you: tho doe most humbly conceive (under correction of your peirceing Judgment) a gentle reprimand to the said Commander may be necessary now, and herafter severely to be called to accompt; with out which neither the Navy Board, Port Comissioners or the Subordinate Officers can be capable of doing the King that Service incumbent on them; tho at the same time doe tell you Sir this comes from One who dares doe his Duty, and will against all discouragements; I have been too tedious, but this is a growing Evill, and ought I think to meet with a Strenuous

¹ Edge of paper.

opposition least it become universall and destructive to all good Government.

I thank God my well wishes for a faire winde and eager pressing, has now had the desired effect, the wind being still faire Westerly, and the Phoenix th[is][1] morning is Sail'd to Longreach.

And in a day or two more the Mermaid may, if a Master can be gotten for her, which as well Captain Loy her Comander as myself has often wrote to the Board for but none is yet come downe. I am

Your Honour's most Obedient Servant

B St MICHEL

The Tyger prize might also have sailed this morning, but her Comander (on my pressing him to be gone) tells me his Men run from the Ship soe fast, he can not get Strength enough to Venture on Sailing.

B St M

To the Honourable Samuel Pepys, His Majesty's Secretary for the Affaires of the Admiralty, London

178. B. ST. MICHEL TO S.P.[2]

Deptford 23d November 1688

Honoured Sir.

In Answer to yours which came to my hand last night; Tho I must ever, and will, with all thankfulnes Acknowledg your regards towards me have been expressd with great tendernes, Yet doe assure you Sir my Temper is not soe overweening and soft, as on any such ground to have offered you the least trouble in relation to Captain Gifford's ingentile, and I may well say Rough, if not Rude, returne to my Zealous discharge of that Duty and Trust incumbent on me, for hastening to Sea all the Addition of Force possible at such a time as this, when the King and Kingdome are under the highest Dangers (probably) thro a Foreign Invasion; But with what Temper and circumstances of decency or indecency this my resentment might be exprest, or whether not prompted by some personall disrespect or private peique to the Threatning or Useing unhansome expressions toward the said Comander, is the subject of your now prudent enquiery; Whereunto I shall with all open heartednes, plainnes and Sincearity, tell you the very Truth, whole truth, and nothing more

[1] MS. torn.
[2] Rawl. A. 186 : 21–22. Original. Dictated, signed by St. Michel. Endorsed : 'Comissioner St Mitchell to Mr Pepys—History of his Difference with Captain Gifford—prays notice may to bee tooke of it.'

or lesse, and this doe assure you Sir I will closly keep to, on the Faith
of a Christian and word of a Gentleman; Captain Gifford is a person
for whome through the course of many years acquaintance I have
borne a very greate Esteeme and Respect, and which as well while at
Tangier, as since our returne thence when wee have happend to
meet, I have ever been ready on all occasions to cherrish, particularly
dureing the time of his present Shipps Fitting from hence, wherein
I have streined my Cares and my Authority too to Oblige him, not
only in point of Dispatch, but that of Accomodation; And I must at
the same time justly owne that till this One Instance I never found
the least flaw in a reciprocall returne on his part; Soe that Sir I hope
you will from hence be sufficiently Satisfied there was noe former ill
blood betwixt us, nay I was heartily vext to find him for whome I had
such Regard, to fall under soe greate a neglect, Yet thought my self
in Duty bound roundly to resent it, as well with respect to the other
Shipps getting away as to that of the Phoenix, however this I only did
by telling her Master that his Commander deserv'd to be written
against for this default, whereto he replyed, that he the said Master
had Orders, and would have Saild but that the Pylot disappointed
him; and to that I made Answer that then himself deservd to be
severely handled for not sending for the Pylot in time; This with
what I have said in my last, of my sending for the Lieutenant that
night, is the whole in matter and manner of what has past from me
on this Occasion; And certainly Sir had there any other cause of
provocation been given him by me, you would have found it charg'd
home on me in his Note, which is exprest (as you well observe) with
soe much heat as to overshoot himself in blameing me touching his
Pylot, who neither could be, nor was appointed by me, but is a Trinity
Man, and was sent him by Captain Wilshaw, being the same person
who carryed most of his Majesties Shipps lately fitted from hence,
and whose capacity, it Seems, has never been doubted, but if wanting
in Dilligence, they should have taken the more Care to have kept
him on board while they had him two or three daies before, which had
the Captain been present might easily have been done; thus much for
the Pylott; and for my self whome he joynes in fault with the Pylott
for his not Sailing, or divides the same between me and him I know
not what he means, being conscious to have done indeed all that lay
in me for his dispatch, but never any thing to retard it: I most readily
acknowledg (with you) that all due respect is to be given those persons
who bear the Character of his Majesties Commission; but must say
too, the reason is as strong at least, that they ought to doe the like by
others in a Station above them, and of the two I humbly conceive the
consequence to his Majestie must be far worse that a Comander may

at his pleasure Slight or Huff the Board or a port Commissioner, then it could be for the later soe to doe by the former; but as I ever have and shall carefully avoid any thing of this in my practice, soe if suffered in them will soone draw greate Disorders with it on his Majesties Service, which is the only Subject of my regard in thus Speaking or Acting: I know you will be tender to guard and protect the Trust care and Charge committed to Our Board, yet this is but One Instance and some other Commanders (especially the Courtlike Finer sort of 'um) who endeavour to lessen us, by shooting these little Arrows thro me (a Member) at the whole Body.

I have informed my self into the Occasion of the Said Captain Giffords sending me his Note by the Globe Boy at that time of Night, and find it was from the said Captaines being then at that House just returnd from London, who after he had there wrote and sent me the said Note continued about one houre there in Company of Captain Smith of the Tyger Prize, his Lieutenant, Captain Loy of the Mermaid, and Mr Edisbury, and soe he went on board. Thus beging your Pardon for this tedious trouble I remaine

Your Honour's most faithfull and obedient
humble Servant
B St MICHEL

179. B. ST. MICHEL TO S.P.[1]

Deptford 25th November 1688.

Honoured Sir

In Obedience to your Comands of yesterday I here returne to those Quaeries you made while I then Waited on you

1st Quaery— What was the Date of the Navy Boards Order for Fitting out the Phoenix?

Answer— The Second Instant.

2d Quaery— Was her Comander in Drink at the time of Writeing his Note?

Answer— I have enquired of the Master at the Globe who was Drinking with him, and sayes he seem'd to be Sober;

[1] Rawl. A. 186 : 25. Original. Dictated, signed by St. Michel. There is not unreasonably a hiatus in S.P.'s family correspondence at the time of the abdication and flight of James II in December 1688. Rawl. A 186 contains much of the correspondence of James with Lord Dartmouth, who was in charge of his forces at sea, and a few brief notes from the king to S.P. on naval matters. No personal note from James to S.P. survives from this period, however, despite a family tradition that James was sitting to Kneller for a portrait for Pepys, at the very hour when the Prince of Orange was landing on English soil. Rawl. A. 186 also contains the correspondence of Dartmouth and S.P. after the arrival of the Prince of Orange.

but I am apt to believe, (the time of Night considered) he might be somewhat warm'd with Wine, without which he could not have soe wrote.

3d Quaery— How long time the Pylott has been Ordinarily employed for carrying his Majesties Shippes?

Answer— Captain Wilshaw acquaints me he hath been a practic'd Navall pylott for between twenty and thirty years.

4th Quaery—Was this Pylott ever complain'd against for Disability or Negligence?

Answer— Not as I can learne.

I remaine, with Dutyfull Obedience

Your most Obedient and faithfull Servant

B St Michell

To the Honourable Samuel Pepys, His Majesties Secretary for the Affaires of the Admiralty Present

180. B. ST. MICHEL TO S.P.[1]

Deptford January 25th 1688/9

Honoured Sir,

T'is possible I may Err in the timeing of this my Aplication to you, but being well assured not soe to doe, in the person for whome it is made, I cannot but hope it well meet with your favourable reguards, espetially, Since I well know it to be your chiefe Aime and care to have in the Navall Service, Able Sober Experienced persons;

Mr Tilghman my Cheife Clerk being one, whoe by his universall knoledg in the practice of the Navy and Yards, from an Experience of Seaventeen yeares of Clerkship in them, almost three whereof hath bine with my selfe here; through which time, I have in all Cases found his abilitys such, as indeed render him (without Exception) duly qualified for better Employments, Doe therefore humbly presume (with as much ardency as may become me) to recomende him to your Justice kindeness and favour, for a Pursers Employment on any such of the men of warr, as may fall Vacant through decease of Mr Browne late Purser of the Royall Prince; and permitt me Sir to add, that Since Mr Tilghman left an Employment in Chatham yard (and thereby may be quited if not disobliged some of his former freinds) to Embarque his fortunes with me; 'twold afford me matter of great

[1] Rawl. A. 179 : 53. Original. This is the last letter exchanged between S.P. and St. Michel in their respective official capacities, as the reorganization of the navy under the new régime naturally provided for the replacement of such staunch adherents of James II as Pepys. That St. Michel was for some time continued as Commissioner at Deptford is attested by the address of Letter 186.

truble Shoold my owne Circumstances hapen to alter with theese
Changing times, soe as to leave him destitute, or compell'd to ask an
Employment of both your and my profest Enemys;
    Sir from this Consideration I am Zealously desirous of his now
obtaining Somewhat by warrant which may be to him of more certainty for the future, then what hee enjoys under me; I need not put
you in minde, of what favour the other port Comissioners' Cheefe
Clerks have bine all a longe vouchsafed in this particular, mine only
excepted; wherefore being well assured (for which I will be respon-
sable) of his making a very Inteligent, usefull and Extraordinary good
officer, Such (as I said before) as you might wish ware Generally in
the Navy for the welfare thereof; I doe againe with much humble
earnestness comend him to your goodness, being very well assured,
that the Navy Board have soe good an Esteeme for him, as that thay
will give theire redy and zealous recomendation of him, on this, or
any occasion. I remaine
                    Yours Honour's Most faithfull humble servant
                            B St Michel

he hath very good and well handed Certificates, besides a General
Recomendation from the Navy Board, the Originalls whereof are
with mr Atkins in your office, but for less trouble in repairing to them,
I here Enclose theire Copyes. B S M

To the Honourable Samuell Pepys Secretary of the Admiralty These

181. B. ST. MICHEL TO S.P.[1]

Deptford, May 28th 1689

Honoured Sir
    After my late haveing groaned under Some trubles (on my private
Account) which at this unfortunate juncture of time have prooved
extreame heavy and Grivious to me; I understand that by the mali-
sious inventive ill Offices of a female Beast,[2] which you keepe, I am
like allsoe to lye under your Anger and disgrace (to me more in-
suportable then the former) but I hope, and humbly pray, (though
she tould me impudently, and arogantly, you Scorned to see me) that
with your Generous Usuall goodness, wisdome, manhood, and
former kindeness you will not damm him Unheard whoe Shoold Joy
to hazard (as in duty bound) his dearest Bludd for your Service. The

---

[1] Rawl. A. 170 : 62. Original. Holograph. No papers have come to light explaining the
difference between S.P. and St. Michel which must have come about in the interval
between January and May of 1689.
[2] Probably Mary Skinner, whom biographers usually call Pepys's housekeeper, although it is certain that a paid domestic of that title headed his household staff. Since the

meane while, returning your honour my most humble and harty thanks for the Petition[1] you sent me, and for all other your many favours I remaine

Your Ever Dutifull and most faithfull humble Servant
B ST MICHEL

For the Honourable Samuel Pepys Esquire at his house in Buckingam Street Yorke Buildings These

182. S.P. TO SIR R. HADDOCK[2]

Sunday, Aprill 21th 1689

Sir Richard Haddock

I have understood soe much from my brother St. Michel of your frequent Significations of your respects towards mee, and your kinde reguards to him, that I cannot but (by this) owne the same to you with a great deale of thankfullnesse, and the more, from the Circumstances of the time wherein you give mee occasion of doeing this, rendering very unlikely my being any more in a Condition of returneing you any Services or other acknowledgements for it; at least as a Navy-Man, however you may give mee oppertunity (which I should bee very glad of) of doeing it otherwise. And since I have this Occasion of takeing notice of the present Circumstance of time, pray give me leave to make this further use of it.

I understand that the Lords of the Admiralty are upon the point of comeing to some Settlement in the business of the Offices and Officers of the Navy; Wherein (as little Sollicitous as you see mee in any thing that relates to my selfe) I cannot but owne a deep concernment for what may fall to the Shaire of my Brother St Michele to beare, unless some reguard be had to him and his Numerous Family, after neare 30 Years Service in the Navy, without Reproach, through many Offices of Trust, though none of a Sufficiency to enable him to lay up any thing, till this last wherein his time has been soe short.

What his dilligence and paynes have been in it, and the Effects of those paines to the good of the Service, I had rather leave you to be

death of Elizabeth, Mrs. Skinner had lived with Pepys, treated by him and his nephews with tenderness and by his most respectable and learned friends with respect and affection. Evidence of the dignity of her status may be found in the Codicil to S.P.'s will, Wheatley, *Pepysiana*, appendix I, pp. 251–70; Hanford, 'Pepys and the Skinner Family', *Review of English Studies*, July 1931, vii. 257; and the numerous references to her in S.P.'s letters to his nephew in Tanner, *Private Correspondence*. That Mary Skinner regarded herself as a recognized member of the family is evident from her own will. (Whitear, *More Pepysiana*, pp. 149–50.)

[1] Evidently S.P. had drawn up for St. Michel the petition which elicited from the new king the recommendation reprinted in this collection.   [2] Rawl. A. 170 : 138. Copy.

judge of, then offer any thing about it my selfe, especially in the case of soe neare a Relation. Nor can I thinke it naturall for mee to appeare a Sollicitor to my Lords for the keeping another in an Employment, who am myselfe soe lately out of one. But being soe long acquainted with his Qualifications fitting him for Employment, the circumstances of his fortune needing it, and his Principles of faithfullness to the Trust (whatever it is) that he undertakes, I cannot but with great earnestnesse bespeake your Advice, furtherance, and Friendshipp to him at this Juncture, that he may not at this time of day bee (with such a Family, as God Almighty has given him) exposed to the wide World. Wherein you shall to the last degree have your good Offices towards him owned by

Your most faithfull and humble Servant
S.P.

183. S.P. TO SIR J. LOWTHER[1]

Yorke-buildings May 9th 1689.

Sir

I have not beene in a Condition,[2] since your late favour to mee in your kindenesse to my brother, to wayte upon you with my thankes on that behalfe, nor indeed yet am, but shall doe it at my very first goeing abroad. In the meane time I take the liberty of doeing it by him, who allsoe prays leave to doe the same for himselfe, and[3] repeteing to you my most earnest desires of the continuance of your advice and support to him in the calamitous state whereinto without it hee and his family must inevitably fall,[4] after soe long a Service to the Crowne. I doe with greatest respect kisse your hands and rest

Your most faythfull and obedient Servant
S PEPYS

184. THE KING TO THE COMMISSIONERS OF THE NAVY[5]

At the Court at White hall
the 11th of July, 1689
Present
The Kings most Excellent Majestie
in Councill

Upon reading the Petition of Balthazar St Michel Gentleman late One of the Commissioners of his Majesties Navy, Setting forth, that

---

[1] Rawl. A. 170 : 126. First draft. Holograph.   [2] *nor yet*, canc.
[3] *and humbly with*, canc.   [4] *cannot avoid falling*, canc.
[5] Rawl. A. 170 : 95. An elaborately flourished and scrolled copy, among S.P.'s papers. No endorsement. No seal.

his Office of Commissioner for his Majesties Yards at Deptford and Woolwich hath been lately discontinued. That he hath served in the business of the Navy, for 29 yeares past, and praying some Employment Equall to what he hath lost, to Support himselfe and his 7 Children; or such allowance, as by the knowne practise of the Navy has allwayes been, and is at this day made in severall Cases of Officers meriting by their longe Service therein, as in the said Petition hereunto annexed is more at large sett forth, his Majestie out of his Gracious Intentions towards the Petitioner, is pleased to Referr his Case to the Right honourable the Commissioners for Executeing the Office of Lord high Admirall of England, to examine the Alligations, and report to his Majestie what may be fitt to be done therein for the Petitioner.

WM. PLAITHWAYT

185. B. ST. MICHEL TO S.P.[1]

July 22d 1689

Honoured Sir

I Being Consious to my selfe That by neither thought, word, or deed, I Ever did you wronge what soever my Enemy-Stars might bring on me and myne.

That with honour, faithfullness, Diligence, and Capasitey; I Ever performed what soever your favour putt on me Either in publick or private.

That my soule loveing you, above any male freind in the world, I shoold have Joyed (as I still Ever Shall) in Ventureing my Dearest Bludd for your service.

That consequently the misfortune I groane under, noe ways affecteing you, being (as you have bine pleased to have it tould me) under noe manner of obligation to me wards; though I will Ever owne myne to you to my lives Einde, with all the Gratefull acknoledgements I Ever may be Capable of. These Considerations most honoured Sir if not retreeved, by the returne of your favour and Countenance, will of nesesitey hasten me a pace before time to where I shall never truble you more, to se, that I, whoome the world thinkes have your kindeness by my haveing tasted the bread thereof theese many yeares, shoold now lye under your disgrace, to the Slight of your very Servants, I, I say whoe have drawne my sword, with

<hr>

[1] Rawl. A. 170 : 93. Original. Holograph. Endorsed: 'Mr St Michel to Mr Pepys, upon occasion of Mr Pepys's present Displeasure towards him.'

honour [in] severall Bluddy fights though I have never Caused the Trumpet to be sounded for it. I must add that the love I bare you is Such that did not I dayly passeing by your house heer of your welfare, my hart (which will not longe last) woold Eare this have burst; Soe god of heaven Bless, keepe, and preserve you.

and now, What I have further to make bould to give you truble in, is the Enclosed Coppy of K W Referance, on perusall of which if you shall please, (with all Imaginable Speed) to speake to Sir John Lowder, before thay returne theire Report, I may hope by your Pleading my Cause, to have a more favourable one, then otherwise, which most humbly begging of your goodness to doe; I remaine
Your Honour's most Dutifull and humble Servant
B. St Michel

I gave the Referance but last night to the Lords but nothing is yett done.

For the Honourable Samuell Pepys These

186. SAMUEL ST. MICHEL TO B. ST. MICHEL[1]

Hyleck Road near Leverpole
August 2d 1689

Honoured Sir

After our Busking up and down the Irish Coast Wee arrived this morning at Hyleck where wee Ride till the first Opertunity of Conveying the Army over that lyes here (of about 24000 Men as Reported) for Ireland, and thought it long till I writ to you, in hopes of our lyeing here a weeke or there abouts to gett an Answer of your health and my Sisters which I soe long for: as to the knews I can tell you is only that London-Derry in ireland holds out still bravely against the Seaze[2] of their Enemy in great hopes of Our Army Comeing over quickly to assist and Eade them, and that Major Generall Kirke with his Army has been over this great while and has landed his army in a small Iland Called Inch which they have fortifyed; and Many of the Prodestants in Ireland Comes every day to them, where they have had Some Small Combatts with the Enemy. and gott alwayes the Advantage much: I have noe more to say but pray that it may not be our Station this Winter to Cruse in St George's Channell it being the wo[r]st place Imaginable for

---

[1] Rawl. A. 170 : 96. Original. Printed: Smith, ii. 224–5, incorrectly; Wheatley, *Pepysiana*, p. 279, correctly.
[2] i.e. *siege*.

Tempestuous cold Wather wee having had this yeare noe Summer
to speake of but Winds and Raines. I Remain
　　　　　　　Your Dutyfull Son
　　　　　　　SAMUELL ST MICHELL
I desire I may have one Line or two from my Sister Elizabeth

To Balthazar St Michell One of the Commissioners of their Majesties Navy att Deptford nere London Kent with Care delivered

187. B. ST. MICHEL TO S.P.[1]

August 6t 1689
Honoured Sir
　Whatsoever your pleasure, or displeasure is twords me; I Shall
never faile of my duty to you-wards while I live, being (besides my
naturall Inclination) thereto Obliged, by all the deeds of Gratitude
I cann Ever be capable of, which I will show to the hazard of my life,
whensoever your Service, or Comands may call for the same; the
meane while I haveing Just now received the Enclosed, which (after
above 4 months absence, and silance) being very infinitely welcome
to me, and beleeveing your Ever generous goodness to be still such,
that it is noe less allsoe to you have therefore, thinking it my duty,
made bould to give you the truble of its perusall; and remaine
　　　　　　　Your Honour's Most dutifull
　　　　　　　　faithfull and humble servant
　　　　　　　　B. ST MICHEL
For Mr Samuel Pepys at his house in Buckingam Street Yorke
Buildings these August 6t, 1689 per peny post payd

188. B. ST. MICHEL TO S.P.[2]

March 20 1691/2
Most Eever Honoured Sir,
　Ever since the knoledge of your Generous goodness, favour,
Kindeness, and Charity, Signified to me by Mr. Boudler, it hath

[1] Rawl. A. 170 : 99. Original. Holograph. Printed: Smith, ii. 223, incorrectly. Endorsed: 'Mr St Michel to Mr Pepys, enclosing one from his Son from Sea.'
[2] Mr. Arthur A. Houghton, Junior, of Corning, New York, has graciously allowed me
to transcribe and reprint this letter from the Pepys-Cockerell MS. in his private collection. (i. 60.) Original. Holograph. Endorsed: 'Mar. 20. 1691/2. Mr St Michell to Mr.
Pepys. An acknowledging and Begging Letter.'

pleased god soe to have afflicted me with Such Sickness, and torment-
ing paines all over my body, with the adition of the Yallow-Jandis,
and other distempers (, which the wants, and hardshipps, my late
misfortune hath ocasioned my Groning under,) as but two days agoe,
it was thought, I Shoold never more have Seene light in this world:
but this being the first day (since my foresaid terible illness) that I
have bine able to hold upp my head, and penn, I could, nor woold not
lett Slipp the oportunity which (by this littell respite I have) God hath
bine pleased to afforde me that Soe I might with trew gratitude, give
your Honour my most dutifull and humble thanks for the Same,
which I doe from the very Bottom of my hart and Soule, and
Assuring your Honour that tho (to my last breath) I will Ever owne
to have had the best part of my life, Suport, and bread, by your only
favour and goodness; yett this late Generous Act of yours hath (to
me-wards) out done all the former, for that at this pinch, in this my
latter age, and Groneing under Such Circomstances of Afflictions,
and miserys of boddy and minde, which none but the Great Divinity,
and my Selfe knows, & indeed Such, as I am Sure hath noe paralell;)
you ware pleased to releave me: for which as I againe, returne your
Honour my Everlasting Dutifull thanks; soe shall allsoe my Dayly
Prayers, be ever to the Heavenly God, not only to repay you 1000-
fold, but allsoe that his divine Majesty woold Ever Keepe your Dear
Body and Soule to Everlasting life and Glory.

   I am
    Your Honours Poore afflicted
     but most faithfull Humble and
     Dutifull Servant
      B St Michel

if you have an old Spare Cast-off Morning Gowne, Peruiques, and
Some like Cast off large Cloake-Coate, which things you could
Spare without the least inconveniency to you, if you woold Spare
them to your Afflicted Servant they woold be very welcome and with
Milions of thanks, and to have a Bundle made upp, and by a porter
to have it privately left for me, at Trinity House watter lane at Mr
Hunters

For Mr. Samuell Pepys at his house in Buckingam Street in yorke
buildings neer the Strand these London

CALENDAR OF OMITTED PAPERS

THE items calendered in this list, while not all family letters or papers of sufficient pertinence to be included in this edition, shed light on or corroborate details in some of the letters and papers printed in this volume.

1. Apollo Pepys to John Pepys, Sr. 19 July 1630. Egerton MS. 2716: 13. (Br. Mus.)

   Written from Hinchingbrooke and addressed 'To my much respected good cosen Mr John Pepys at his house in Salisbury court neere fleete Cunditt', this letter concerns the licensing of alehouses in Huntington and some unspecified matter of business in Brampton between Apollo and J. Pepys and Cosen Nann, perhaps involving the estate which later caused much correspondence.

2. Inventory of the Estate of Thomas Pepys. 13 April 1664. Rawl. A. 182: 319.

   'An account of soe much of the value of the Inventory lately given into the Court by Mr. John Pepys Administrator to Mr Thomas Pepys, as hath yet come into his hands.' (S.P.'s hand.) Items total 32–15–04.

3. Funeral Expenses: T. Pepys. 13 April 1664 Rawl. A. 182: 305.

   'An account of disbursements already made & debts payd by Mr John Pepys as Administrator to Mr Thomas Pepys, vizt . . .' listing various items including "4–14–00 payd to his Son Samuel" . . . bringing total to £32. 15s. 3d. Although the coffin cost but £1. 9s., the "bisket for the funerall' came to £4. 11s. and the wine £2. 2s. 6d.' (S.P.'s holograph.)

4. Funeral Expenses. 13 April 1664. Rawl. A. 182: 318.

   This is a fair copy, also in S.P.'s hand, of Rawl. A. 182: 305.

5. M. Peletyer to Mrs. Pepys. 26 October 1669. Rawl. A. 174: 335–6.

   M. Peletyer writes at some length in ceremonious French, hoping that Mrs. Pepys has had an enjoyable voyage on her return from France, and reporting that he has packaged and dispatched the purchases she ordered sent after her.

6. M. Peletyer to S.P. 4 December 1669. Rawl. A. 174: 333–4.

   In French, M. Peletyer condoles with S.P. over the death of Mrs. Pepys, expressing his own sorrow and that of Mme Peletyer.

7. Bill for a Coat: J. Pepys. October 1670. Rawl. A. 182: 154.

   Entitled 'Mr John Peeps a Blk Cote' and receipted: 'Received october 1670 in Full of thes bill by me Nicholas Penny', the itemized bill totals £4. 1s. 6d.

8. B. St. Michel to Commissioners of the Navy. 16 March 1671/2. Rawl. A. 184: 235.

   This is a very early and humble letter from St. Michel, in which he reports acting on his own initiative in assisting the captain of the *Diamond* to repair his ship.

9. B. St. Michel to Commissioners of the Navy. 2 April 1672. Rawl. A. 184: 237.

> St. Michel volubly requests one more man for his boat's crew for attending muster on board ships in harbour, and also protection for all the crew from being pressed into the navy.

10. B. St. Michel to Commissioners of the Navy. 8 April 1672. Rawl. A. 184: 231.

> St. Michel refers to the granting of his requests made in Rawl. A. 184: 237, and gives an account of restoring a lost anchor to Captain Ball.

11. B. St. Michel to Commissioners of the Navy. 14 April 1672. Rawl. A. 184: 229.

> St. Michel sends the names of the men of his boat crew and mentions a disbursement of nine pounds for which he wishes to be compensated.

12. B. St. Michel to Commissioners of the Navy. 23 May 1672. Rawl. A. 184: 227.

> St. Michel requests orders about recompensing certain salvagers at King's Down and about selling at auction some worthless hulks on the beach at Deal.

13. B. St. Michel to Commissioners of the Navy. 28 May 1672. Rawl. A. 184: 270.

> St. Michel reports that the noise of a sea-battle has been heard at Deal and repeats his requests of 23 May. A memorandum in S.P.'s hand indicates that a reply was sent on 30 May.

14. B. St. Michel to Commissioners of the Navy. 2 June 1672. Rawl. A. 184: 266.

> St. Michel reports names of the ships in the Downs and recounts the passage of a small vessel from Holland bearing a flag of truce.

15. B. St. Michel to Commissioners of the Navy. 8 June 1672. Rawl. A. 184: 249.

> St. Michel has collected and paid for the salvage at Kings-Downe, and again requests directions about the old boats on the beach at Deal.

16. B. St. Michel to Commissioners of the Navy. 6 July 1672. Rawl. A. 184: 241.

> St. Michel encloses the receipt for four booms delivered to the *Ruby*.

17. B. St. Michel to Commissioners of the Navy. 30 October 1672. Rawl. A. 184: 272.

> St. Michel reports delivery of an anchor to the *Phoenix*, promises to send two anchors to Chatham, inquires again about selling the old boats on the beach, and reports what ships are now in the Downes. A notation in S.P.'s hand indicates that a reply was sent on 2 November.

18. B. St. Michel to Commissioners of the Navy. 14 November 1672. Rawl. A. 184: 239

> St. Michel reports that orders for the *Dragon* arrived after she had sailed, but that he will get a boat at once for the *Phoenix* as directed.

Calendar of Omitted Papers

19. Appointment of John Pepys. 18 June 1673. Rawl. A. 180: 189.

'Copy of a Warrant to Thomas Hayter and John Pepys to bee Clerks of the Acts, signed: 'By his Majesty's Command, S. Pepys.'

20. S.P. to B. St. Michel. 12 August 1673. Adm. ii. 70.

S.P. advises St. Michel to postpone his coming to town because of a possible naval engagement [Battle of Texel, Third Dutch War].

21. S.P. to B. St. Michel. 18 September 1673. Adm. ii. 173.

S.P. conveys the king's permission to issue British stores to the Count d'Estrée, Vice-Admiral of the French fleet.

22. S.P. to B. St. Michel. 22 September 1673. Adm. ii. 155.

St. Michel's courtesies to the Count d'Estrée are acknowledged briefly.

23. S.P. to B. St. Michel. 21 October 1673. Adm. ii. 246.

S.P. authorizes St. Michel to come up to London as soon as he secures the approval of the principal officers and the Commissioners.

24. S.P. to B. St. Michel. 8 January 1673/4. Adm. iii. 20.

S.P. acknowledges receipt of a list of the ships now in the Downs.

25. S.P. to B. St. Michel. 3 March 1673/4. Adm. iii. 136.

This formal letter encloses copies of the Treaty of Westminster, closing the Third Dutch War.

26. S.P. to J. Pepys, Jr. 27 March 1674. Rawl. A. 180: 115.

S.P. requests his brother to give the bearers a copy of a naval report about past payments due to them.

27. Duties of the Trinity House. 1675[?] Rawl. A. 178: 214.

This is a detailed listing of the powers and responsibilities of Trinity House, filed among the papers of John Pepys.

28. Bills of Fare: Trinity House. 1675. Rawl. A. 180: 287–8.

Endorsed: 'Bills of Fare for Upper and Lower Tables, Trinity Munday, 1675,' this sheet gives elaborate two-course menus for the upper end of the first table and the lower end of the second table. Filed among papers of John Pepys.

29. Disbursements of John Pepys. 1675. Rawl. A. 180: 295.

This small sheet in a fine secretarial hand contains two lists: one of nine items of clothing, and the other, entitled 'Sent aboard the Barge', of nine items ranging from food and wine to books and a gown.

30. A Bill for John Pepys. 1675[?] Rawl. A. 180: 274.

Entitled 'Sqyer Pyepes bill', this itemized account for mending linen, for wrist bands, and for caps comes to 8s. 8d. It is a tiny soiled shred among the papers of John Pepys.

31. S.P. to B. St. Michel. 24 February 1674/5. Greenwich: 703.

S.P. acknowledges St. Michel's letter about official reimbursement of Mr. John Evelyn for his care of the sick and wounded.

Calendar of Omitted Papers

32. Scott's Contract. 27 May 1675. Rawl. A. 188: 235.

This is merely a later copy of an agreement between Colonel Scott, M. Pellissary, Mlle des Moulins, and Sieur de la Piogerie concerning the plan of Scott and Sherwin for casting iron. See also originals of Scott's letters to Mlle des Moulins, Rawl. A. 188: 168, 170, 172.

33. S.P. to B. St. Michel. 29 May 1675. Greenwich: 710–11.

S.P. authorizes St. Michel to facilitate correspondence among certain ship captains: Captain Wright, Sir Robert Holmes, and Captain Cotten.

34. Scott-Manning Contract. 4 June 1675. Rawl. A. 188: 167.

'Originall of Manning and Scott's contract about gunns. 4 June 75.'

35. S.P. to B. St. Michel. 25 June 1675. Adm. iv. 158.

S.P. repeats the news of his letter of the previous day, he says, that the King will come to the Downs to set sail for Portsmouth.

36. S.P. to J. Pepys Jr. 19 August 1675. Greenwich: 715.

S.P. encloses a letter drafted by himself to accompany certificates being granted to boys completing the mathematical school of Christ's Hospital.

37. S.P. to B. St. Michel. 19 August 1675. Adm. iv. 217.

S.P. provides for courtesies to be extended to Edmund Sheffield, Esq., in his crossing from Dieppe to England.

38. S.P. to B. St. Michel. 21 August 1675. Adm. iv. 220.

S.P. acknowledges St. Michel's care in delivering a message to Captain Sanderson.

39. S.P. to B. St. Michel. 24 August 1675. Adm. iv. 221.

S.P. encloses a packet for the frigate *Guinea* en route to Tangier.

40. S.P. to B. St. Michel. 27 September 1675. Adm. iv. 266.

S.P. authorizes St. Michel to inspect the *Katharine*, confer with the captain and crew, and report on points specified in connexion with a pass. S.P. also gives directions for a cask of sea-water to be sent to town for the king.

41. S.P. to B. St. Michel. 9 November 1675. Adm. iv. 278.

St. Michel is directed to inspect the ship *Nativity of Christ*, bound from Amsterdam to London, and to report the particulars before a pass can be granted.

42. S.P. to B. St. Michel. 15 November 1675. Adm. iv. 288.

S.P. encloses documents for the masters of several ships soon to arrive from the Straits and from Tangier.

43. S.P. to B. St. Michel. 13 December 1675. Adm. iv. 315.

S.P. directs that an enclosure be put on a ship bound for Malta. The enclosure (Adm. iv. 312), addressed to Sir John Narborough, concerns his shortage of victuals as well as the negligence of certain other commanders.

44. S.P. to B. St. Michel. 16 December 1675. Adm. iv. 318.

S.P. enjoins St. Michel to be sure to deliver a packet of letters to Captain Andrews of the *Katharine*.

45. Scott's Contract. 17 December 1675. Rawl. A. 188: 250.

This is a later copy of a contract between Colonel Scott and one Latour for casting of cannon.

46. S.P. to B. St. Michel. 24 December 1675. Adm. iv. 327.

S.P. encloses an important letter to Captain Davis of the *Foresight*.

47. S.P. to J. Pepys. 18 April 1676. Adm. v. 7.

S.P. directs J. Pepys to secure an able pilot for the yacht *Portsmouth* on the king's voyage to Danzig.

48. S.P. to B. St. Michel. 2 May 1676. Adm. v. 22.

S.P. appoints St. Michel and Captain Clements to settle an unfortunate incident connected with the detention of a French prize ship.

49. S.P. to B. St. Michel. 9 May 1676. Adm. v. 25.

S.P. counsels St. Michel and Captain Clements in the solving of the diplomatic entanglement concerning the French prize ship.

50. S.P. to B. St. Michel. 29 May 1676. Adm. v. 40.

S.P. encloses an order for the captain of the *Foresight*.

51. S.P. to J. Pepys. 31 May 1676. Adm. v. 41.

S.P. urges the selection of an able pilot to guide the yacht *Cleveland* on the king's trip to Jersey.

52. S.P. to B. St. Michel. 31 May 1676. Adm. v. 43.

S.P. acknowledges St. Michel's courtesies to Mr. Shere, engineer of the Mole at Tangier.

53. S.P. to B. St. Michel. 2 June 1676. Adm. v. 45.

S.P. reminds St. Michel that the ship in command in the Downs shall hoist a larger red pennant than any other.

54. S.P. to B. St. Michel. 26 June 1676. Adm. v. 63.

S.P. encloses letters for Captain Killigrew and Captain Griffith.

55. S.P. to B. St. Michel. 1 July 1676. Adm. v. 70.

S.P. acknowledges a letter of information from St. Michel, dated 29 June.

56. S.P. to B. St. Michel. 4 July 1676. Adm. v. 73.

S.P. thanks St. Michel for personal courtesies extended to his friend, Sir James Houblon, the wine merchant.

57. J. Pepys Jr. to S.P. 30 October 1676. Rawl. A. 180: 320.

J. Pepys has called a court, in accordance with S.P.'s wishes, for discussing the administration of the almshouse at Deptford.

58. S.P. to B. St. Michel. 2 November 1676. Adm. v. 211.

S.P. gives St. Michel the responsibility of getting to Captain Clements, either directly or indirectly, a warrant for a convoy of horses.

Calendar of Omitted Papers

59. S.P. to B. St. Michel. 4 November 1676. Adm. v. 214.

S.P. gives St. Michel responsibility for seeing that certain orders of the king shall be delivered in one way or another.

60. S.P. to B. St. Michel. 22 November 1676. Adm. v. 248.

St. Michel has reported his energetic attempts to carry out the directions in the letter of 4 November, and S.P. assures him that he need concern himself in carrying out the orders only if the ships arrive in the Downs.

61. S.P. to B. St. Michel. 23 November 1676. Adm. v. 250.

Some misfortune having occurred to the ship *Rose* and to her commander, Captain Ashby, S.P. signifies the king's pleasure that the packet directed to Captain Ashby be given to Captain Temple to open and to carry out the orders therein.

62. S.P. to St. Michel. 28 November 1676. Adm. v. 260.

St. Michel is authorized to muster the land forces *en route* to Virginia, with due respect to the officers of those forces.

63. S.P. to J. Pepys Jr. 1 December 1676. Adm. v. 262.

J. Pepys is to assure a pilot for the *Garland*, now waiting at Sheerness, laden with goods for the King of Sweden.

64. S.P. to B. St. Michel. 2 December 1676. Adm. v. 266.

St. Michel is to show all English commanders the enclosed order forbidding their capturing French privateers.

65. S.P. to B. St. Michel. 22 December 1676. Adm. v. 293.

S.P. acknowledges a letter of 18 December from St. Michel recounting dangers and difficulties in delivering a packet of much importance for the king. He encloses a letter for delivery to Lady Berkley.

66. S.P. to B. St. Michel. 17 January 1676/7. Adm. v. 316.

S.P. encloses three letters for delivery to the commanders of the *Swallow* and the *Adventure* and to Captain Kenning.

67. S.P. to B. St. Michel. 6 February 1676/7. Adm. v. 334.

S.P. encloses orders to be sent aboard the *Quaker* as she passes through the Downes.

68. S.P. to B. St. Michel. 19 March 1676/7. Adm. v. 362.

S.P. encloses urgent orders for the *Yarmouth* to stop in the Downs when it arrives.

69. S.P. to B. St. Michel. 20 March 1676/7. Adm. v. 365.

S.P. encloses an extremely important letter to Captain Sanderson of the yacht *Portsmouth*, for his taking up at Dover instead of Rye a passenger for Dieppe.

70. Abstract of Proceedings of House of Commons. 22 May 1679 Rawl. A. 193: 38–39.

Mr. Harbord reports for the committee appointed to examine into miscarriages in His Majesty's Navy, and introduces the complaint against Sir Antony Deane, Mr. Samuel Pepys, and partners on the testimony of Captain Moon.

71. Speaker's Warrant. 22 May 1679. Rawl. A. 188: 31.

A copy of the Speaker's warrant for the arrest and detention of Sir Antony Deane and Mr. Pepys.

72. S.P. to Mr. Savill. 26 May 1679. Rawl. A. 194: 1–2.

From the Tower S.P. summarizes the predicament in which he and Sir Antony Deane find themselves and requests the help of Mr. Savill in getting information and in treating with the distinguished French witnesses. Mr. Henry Savill's reply is dated Paris, June 10, 79, Rawl. A. 188 : 141.

73. S.P. to Mr. Brisbane. 26 May 1679. Rawl. A. 194: 2.

A brief letter encloses the epistle to Mr. Savill, Rawl. A. 194: 1. Mr. Brisbane's reply, Rawl. A. 188 : 143–4, is dated Paris, 10th June, 1679 st. n.

74. S.P. to Mr. Brisbane. 2 June 1679. Rawl. A. 194: 2–3.

This letter merely encloses copies of the previous letters of 26 May to the addressee and to Mr. Savill, in case of their loss in transit. Mr. Brisbane's replies are Rawl. A. 188 : 145–6, dated Paris, 17th June, 1679 st. n., and 21 June, 1679, Rawl. A. 188 : 147–8.

75. Scott's Deposition, dated 7 June 1679. Rawl. A. 188: 36–39.

In this English translation Scott deposes that M. Pelissary, treasurer of the French navy, had invited the deponent to his home, where he showed lists of English ships and maps and charts of English harbours, purportedly brought from Mr. Pepys in England by the hand of Sir Antony Deane. He also quotes M. Piogery as referring to S. Pepys as 'that Traytor Pepis'.
The French version of this deposition (Rawl. A. 188 : 32–35) is dated three years earlier, 7 June 1676, and is so endorsed as well. Both English and French versions are witnessed by Fr. Pemberton.

76. S.P. to Mr. Brisbane. 12 June 1679. Rawl. A. 194: 6–7.

S.P. asks his correspondent to find out whether Scott was actually in Paris at the times he has claimed, and whether Scott ever sold maps or draughts to the King of France, especially maps of English fortified towns. Mr. Brisbane's reply is dated Paris, 28 June, 1679 st. n., Rawl. A. 188 : 149–50.

77. S.P. to Mr. Brisbane. 19 June 1679. Rawl. A. 194: 12–13.

From the Tower S.P. refers to helpful information concerning Colonel Scot, discusses the mental reservations of M. de Seignelay, and suggests Mr. Brisbane's advising and directing the operations of B. St. Michel in Paris. In a postscript S.P. apologizes for the use of an amanuensis, because of 'infirmity' of his own eyes.

78. S.P. to Mr. Brisbane. 26 June 1679. Rawl. A. 194: 18–19.

Acknowledging Mr. Brisbane's letter of 28 June (new style, apparently), Pepys discusses the delicate possibility that M. de Seignelay may actually have been in conspiracy with Scott, and announces that B. St. Michel will soon be in France to pursue the investigations.
Mr. Brisbane's reply is dated Paris, July 2/12, 1679, Rawl. A. 188 : 151–2.

79. S.P. to Mr. Brisbane. 3 July 1679. Rawl. A. 194: 21–23.

In reply to Mr. Brisbane's 'dissatisfaction' in being involved with St. Michel, who was accused jointly with Mr. Deane in the matter of the *Katharine*, S.P. gives assurance that he himself was in no wise involved in that transaction.

80. S.P. to Mr. Brisbane. 7 July 1679. Rawl. A. 194: 28–29.

Acknowledging Mr. Brisbane's letter of 2/12 July, Pepys explains that M. de Seignelay is confusing him with his predecessor, Mr. Wren.

81. Deposition of Scott. 8 July 1679. Rawl. A. 183: 60.

Colonel Scott deposes that, while on a visit to his friend Lord Allington in the Tower, he was abused and threatened by a prisoner, Colonel Roper, for having given evidence against Mr. Pepys. Another copy of this same deposition is Rawl. A. 188: 42. Colonel Roper's accounts of the same incident, with widely varying detail, are found in Rawl. A. 188: 46–47, dated Feb. 1679/[80].

82. Deposition of F. Trenchepain and A. Peletyer (Paris). 20 July 1679. Rawl. A. 188: 153–4.

This deposition details the entirely formal and official dealings between M. Pellissary and Sir A. Deane (French).

83. Edward Manning to Colonel Scott. Copy dated 11 August 1679. Rawl. A. 188: 180.

'Coppy of a Letter of Challenge from one Edward Manning to Colonel Scott given me by Mr. le Goux before Mr. Peletier and Mr. Tranchepain.' Endorsement is in S.P.'s hand. A note explains that this is a literal French translation of the original, evidently of earlier date, which was in English. See also Rawl. A. 188: 176–83, for Sherwin's accusations of Scott as an impostor.

84. Edward Manning to Colonel Scott. August 1679. Rawl. A. 188: 179.

This is a later French translation of an undated letter of much earlier date in English, which in both body and postscript proposes a duel.

85. Depositions of French Witnesses. 29 August 1679. Rawl. A. 188: 155–8.

MM. Trenchepain, Peletyer, and others give testimony respecting Scott's exhibition of charts of the English coasts (French).

86. S.P. to the Duke of York. 6 January 1679/80. Rawl. A. 194: 126–7.

Pepys, in this letter of gratitude to his Royal Highness, reveals the personal interest which the king and the Duke of York have taken in helping him in his defence against Scott. In particular they have sent him a Mr. Milburne, who has been able to reveal some of Scott's former operations.

87. Deposition of Captain Browne. 9 January 1679/80. Rawl. A. 188: 160–6.

The deponent testifies that he aided Scott and Sherwin in casting cannon for the King of France, and that Scott urged him to give false testimony concerning Mr. Deane's relations with M. Pellissary.

88. Mme Pellissary to M. Durel. 27 January 1679/80. Rawl. A. 188: 202.

Mme Pellissary deposes in French that her deceased husband entertained Mr. Deane only once, an official dinner, and that Colonel Scott did not come to the house that day nor dine privately with her, as he has averred.

Calendar of Omitted Papers

89. Mme Pellissary to Mme Colodon. 27 January 1679/80. Rawl. A. 188: 200.

Mme Pellissary avers that Scott's boasts of secret intrigues with her deceased husband are false, that she has never dined privately with Scott, and that she believes that she has never even seen the man (French).

90. Deposition of M. des Glereaux. 3 March 1679/80. Rawl. A. 188: 204–6.

M. des Glereaux, nephew of Mme Pellissary, authenticates the letters and depositions of his aunt, affirms that his uncle, the treasurer of the French navy, never served upon the sea, and that the sieur de la Piogerie was an army officer with no voice in naval affairs. He also witnesses to the Protestantism of M. Pellissary. The English translation of the same text is Rawl. A. 188 : 208–10.

91. M. de la Tour to S.P. 2 April 1680. Rawl. A. 188: 248–9.

M. de la Tour recounts in French his shady dealings with Mr. Joine and Mr. Manning and Colonel Scott in making iron cannon; he includes also an account of the Scott-Manning duel. Rawl. A. 188 contains many other depositions, only the most pertinent of which have been included in this calendar.

92. S.P. to Cosen Pepys [1680]. Rawl. A. 194: 173.

By the hand of Cosen Allcock, S.P. sends Cosen Pepys of Martin Abbey a brief notice of his acquittal and an acknowledgement of her kindness and loyalty during his persecution.

93. S.P. to Sir Thomas Littleton. 5 August 1680. Rawl. A. 194: 179.

S.P. requests Sir Thomas to give explicit directions to St. Michel concerning his duties in his new post in Tangier.

94. Lords Commissioners to B. St. Michel. 23 September 1680. Rawl. A. 183: 43.

'Coppy of . . . letter . . . requireing the Issuing no stores without Admirall Herbert's order', signed 'Your Loving Freinds, Brouncker, Thomas Littleton, D. Finch.'

95. B. St. Michel to Lords of the Admiralty. 28 September 1680. Rawl. A. 183: 40.

St. Michel acknowledges receipt of instructions on his future duties at Tangier and promises obedience, at the same time accusing the Lords of giving him 'all the Unease in the execution thereof as possible'.

96. Navy Board to St. Michel. 30 September 1680. Rawl. A. 183: 285.

Dissatisfied with the form of the bond executed by St. Michel as stores-keeper at Tangier, the Board encloses an acceptable form to sign and seal.

97. M. d'Allais to S.P. 30 November 1680. Rawl. A. 188: 262.

M. D. V. d'Allais (the Dallié of St. Michel's correspondence) gives an account of his agreement with Scott for the production of cannon.

Calendar of Omitted Papers

98. Mr. Hunter to B. St. Michel. 21, 25 October 1681. Rawl. A. 183: 199.

One of S.P.'s secretaries has copied extracts from two of Mr. Hunter's reports to St. Michel, reports which tend to confirm St. Michel's accusations of unbusinesslike transactions among his Majesty's servants at Tangier and Gibraltar.

99. John Vernon to S.P. 5 December 1681. Rawl. A. 178: 81.

Some years ago, John Pepys Jr. gave his bond for £500 for a Mr. Randall, Collector of Hearth Money, who has since defaulted. The creditors are now claiming the money from S.P., as heir of his brother's estate.

100. Mr. Feilding to S.P. 17 March 1681/2. Rawl. A. 178: 45.

Mr. Feilding reports the sailing from Plymouth of the Tangier-bound St. Michel, 'the thoughtfullest and Melencolliest man I ever saw Contrary to the humor then when I was honoured with his Company at Parris'.

101. B. St. Michel to the Officers of the Navy. 7 May 1682. Rawl. A. 178: 141.

St. Michel sends muster rolls and vouchers, and requests authority to move from Gibraltar to Tangier, to buy or rent facilities for storing supplies, and to secure a boat for his naval duties.

102. S.P. to William Hewerr. 19 May 1682. Rawl. A. 194: 276–7.

In the fourth paragraph S.P. relates some negotiation with Lady Peterborough concerning a post of rocker [of infants] in the household of Ann Hyde, Duchess of York. Apparently a fee or bribe will be required. The biographer Charles Bryant assumes that this post is desired for Elisabeth, St. Michel's wife.

103. S.P. to B. St. Michel. 12 July 1686. Adm. xii. 161.

St. Michel is to direct the pursers of the *Portsmouth* and the *Saphire* to return to their respective ships, as the latter has been ordered to sea.

104. S.P. to B. St. Michel. 10 August, 1686. Adm. xii. 195.

S.P. thanks St. Michel for his minute account of the projects now under way at Deptford and Woolwich, and asks for a continuance of such reports weekly. St. Michel is now Commissioner at Deptford; S.P. is secretary to the Lord High Admiral, the Duke of York.

105. Will Spencer to S.P. 15 November 1686. Rawl. A. 189: 300.

The Fellows of St. Peter's College remind S.P. that his eighteen-year lease of the Ellington property has expired, and that they will give him first consideration among the several who have already applied for the property.

106. Will Spencer to S.P. 18 December 1686. Rawl. A. 189: 298.

Mr. Spencer, bursar of Peterhouse, refers to a letter from S.P., requesting time to consider the Ellington property. The Fellows have set a minimum of £500, for the property has been evaluated at £700.

107. Will Spencer to S.P. [January 1686/7.] Rawl. A. 189: 302.

Referring to the lease of the Ellington property, Mr. Spencer mentions a minimum figure of £500 acceptable to the Fellows of Peterhouse, Cambridge. The writer mentions a previous letter, on the 18th of the preceding month, as yet unanswered.

Calendar of Omitted Papers

108. S.P. to B. St. Michel. 8 March 1686/7. Adm. xiii. 1.

The king has postponed the testing of a new type of pump. Also, a petition from one of the parish officers has been submitted in the wrong form and must be rewritten.

109. S.P. to B. St. Michel. 17 March 1686/7. Adm. xiii. 18.

The king has chosen the following Saturday to come down to see the newly invented pump tried out in competition with ordinary chain-pumps.

110. S.P. to B. St. Michel. 11 April 1687. Adm. xiii. 42–43.

S.P. promises to investigate the complaint of a sawyer in the shipyard who alleges unlawful arrest.

111. S.P. to B. St. Michel. 13 April 1687. Adm. xiii. 44.

The carpenter of the *Swallow* is to be allowed to assist Sir Robert Gordon in setting up the pumps for the experiment.

112. S.P. to B. St. Michel. 16 April 1687. Adm. xiii. 48–49.

The aggrieved sawyer (11 April) has been found not to come under the king's protection from arrest, as he is a piece-worker and not a contract labourer.

113. S.P. to B. St. Michel. 28 April 1687. Adm. xiii. 77–78.

St. Michel is to use care and dispatch in making the *Isabella* yacht available to the Duke of Grafton, although proper orders cannot be issued at the moment.

114. S.P. to B. St. Michel. 30 April 1687. Adm. xiii. 82.

John Martin, carpenter, is to be allowed to go to Chatham for a few days for the convenience of the Duke of Grafton.

115. S.P. to B. St. Michel. 2 May 1687. Adm. xiii. 84.

St. Michel is to make arrangements for the launching of a new ship, waiting the king's pleasure for the name of the ship and the hour of the ceremony.

116. S.P. to B. St. Michel. 19 July 1687. Adm. xiii. 199–200.

St. Michel is requested to answer a set of queries concerning the exact condition of the residence of the Navy Treasurer at Deptford, for the settlement of a petition before the Council Board.

117. S.P. to B. St. Michel. 25 July 1687. Adm. xiii. 210.

A further query is added to those sent in Adm. xiii. 210, this one regarding Wise the gardener for the Navy Treasurer's residence.

118. S.P. to B. St. Michel. 15 February 1687/8. Adm. xiv. 43–44.

St. Michel is directed at the king's pleasure to re-employ a naval cook, Grey, but to warn him that the next neglect of duty will incur permanent suspension.

119. S.P. to B. St. Michel. 5 April 1688. Adm. xiv. 114.

St. Michel's advice is requested on a petition concerning overland transportation of fresh water for the king's ships.

Calendar of Omitted Papers

120. S.P. to B. St. Michel. 8 April 1688. Adm. xiv. 119.

St. Michel is commended for his watchfulness when the *Lark* was afire, and is requested to report the names of officers absent from duty.

121. S.P. to B. St. Michel. 13 April 1688. Adm. xiv. 149.

S.P. promises to try to relieve the citizens of Deptford from the burden of an excessive number of soldiers quartered upon them. (The gathering of troops doubtless reflects James II's preparations to defend his crown.)

122. S.P. to B. St. Michel. 3 May 1688. Adm. xiv. 160.

Certain shifts are ordered in the commands of various yachts.

123. S.P. to B. St. Michel. 14 May 1688. Adm. xiv. 169.

S.P. inquires concerning possible delay in provisioning the *Garland*, which has been ordered to Ireland.

124. S.P. to B. St. Michel. 22 May 1688. Adm. xiv. 184.

Thomas French, gunner, is to be allowed shore leave by the king's express permission.

125. S.P. to B. St. Michel. 4 June 1680. Adm. xiv. 206–7.

St. Michel is directed to settle peacefully if he can a dispute between Mrs. Shish, widow of the late master builder, and one Thomas Nicholls, an employee in Deptford yard.

126. B. St. Michel to S.P. 23 August 1688. Rawl. A. 186: 252–3.

St. Michel gives a long and detailed account of the degree of readiness of all ships in the several yards, in response to a request from the king.

127. W. Hewer to S.P. 23 August 1688. Rawl. A. 186: 257.

William Hewer reports on the readiness of the various ships which he has been inspecting with Mr. St. Michel and others, with a view to hastening their dispatch.

128. S.P. to B. St. Michel. 11 September 1688. Adm. xiv. 409.

St. Michel is directed to secure a report from each ship commander concerning the muster of men on board. The figures are to be sent by messenger to S.P. at the Admiralty Office for him to report to the king within 24 hours.

129. S.P. to B. St. Michel. 22 September 1688. Adm. xv. 28–29.

St. Michel is directed to make detailed inquiry about one Cowley, a gunner, a former pirate pardoned by the king, who is now apparently a deserter.

130. S.P. to B. St. Michel. 6 October 1688. Adm. xv. 100.

St. Michel is requested to send Captain Wiltshaw at once to speak with S.P., pursuant to his reporting immediately at the Nore on the king's business.

131. Captain Gifford to S.P. 11 November 1688. Rawl. A. 186: 12.

From Deptford the captain notifies S.P. that the *Phenix* is ready to sail into the Long-reach.

Calendar of Omitted Papers

132. S.P. to B. St. Michel. 15 November 1688. Adm. xv. 375.

St. Michel is to have the yacht *Katherine* refitted for sea with all possible dispatch by orders from the king.

133. S.P. to B. St. Michel. 19 November 1688. Adm. xv. 387.

Certain Dutch vessels are to be set free at once.

134. Capt. Gifford to B. St. Michel. 20 November 1688. Rawl. A. 186: 20.

The captain, having heard that Commissioner St. Michel intended to report him for not sailing that morning, lays the fault upon his pilot or upon the Commissioner himself. This note is enclosed by St. Michel in his letter to S.P., dated 21 November 1688. (See Letter 177.)

135. Capt. Gifford to S.P. 21 November 1688. Rawl. A. 186: 16.

The captain, having settled a dispute with Captain Ellmore over certain seamen, has just sailed from Deptford into the Longreach and now awaits guns and other stores.

136. Capt. Gifford to S.P. 23 November 1688. Rawl. A. 186: 23.

Captain Gifford blames the pilot for his not sailing from Deptford on 20 November and accuses St. Michel of injustice.

137. S.P. to Sir John Lowther. 13 November 1689. Rawl. A. 170: 124.

In a letter on behalf of his kinsman, Charles Pepys the joiner, S.P. refers to his own many previous importunities on behalf of B. St. Michel.

APPENDIX I

Peddegree From my Grandfathers Grandfather William Pepys, Cottenham[1]

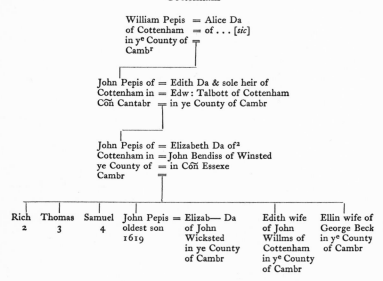

William Pepis = Alice Da
of Cottenham = of . . . [*sic*]
in ye County of ⟊
Camb^r

John Pepis of = Edith Da & sole heir of
Cottenham in = Edw : Talbott of Cottenham
Cõn Cantabr ⟊ in ye County of Cambr

John Pepis of = Elizabeth Da of[2]
Cottenham in = John Bendiss of Winsted
ye County of = in Cõn Essexe
Cambr ⟊

| Rich 2 | Thomas 3 | Samuel 4 | John Pepis oldest son 1619 | Elizab— Da of John Wicksted in ye County of Cambr | Edith wife of John Willms of Cottenham in ye County of Cambr | Ellin wife of George Beck in ye County of Cambr |

---

[1] Rawlinson A 185 : 443. Endorsement in Samuel Pepys's hand.
[2] *John*, canc.

244

APPENDIX II

Family Tree

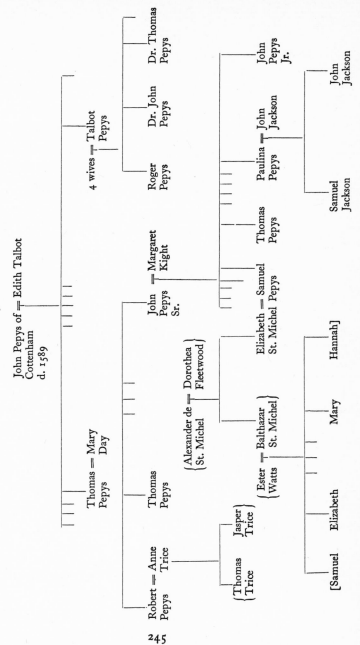

PREVIOUS EDITIONS OF
THE LETTERS

Memoirs of Samuel Pepys . . . comprising his Diary from 1659 to 1669, deciphered by the Rev. John Smith, . . . and a Selection from the Private Correspondence. Edited by Richard, Lord Braybrooke. Two volumes. London, 1825.

Memoirs of Samuel Pepys . . . comprising his Diary from 1659 to 1669, deciphered by the Rev. John Smith, . . . and a Selection from his Private Correspondence. Edited by Richard, Lord Braybrooke. Second edition. Two volumes. London, 1828.

The Life, Journals, and Correspondence of Samuel Pepys . . . including a narrative of his voyage to Tangier. Deciphered . . . by the Rev. John Smith. Two volumes. London, 1841.

Diary and Correspondence of Samuel Pepys. With a life and notes by Richard Lord Braybrooke. Third edition. London, 1848.

Diary and Correspondence of Samuel Pepys. With a life and notes by Richard Lord Braybrooke. Fourth edition. Four volumes. London, 1854.

Diary and Correspondence of Samuel Pepys . . . with a Life and Notes by . . . Lord Braybrooke. Deciphered, with additional notes, by Rev. Mynors Bright. Six volumes. London, 1875–9.

Private Correspondence and Miscellaneous Papers of Samuel Pepys. Edited by J. R. Tanner. Two volumes. London, 1926.

Further Correspondence of Samuel Pepys. Edited by J. R. Tanner, London, 1929.

Letters and the Second Diary of Samuel Pepys. Edited, with an introduction, by Robert Guy Howarth, London, 1932.

Shorthand Letters of Samuel Pepys, from a Volume entitled 'S. Pepys' Official Correspondence, 1662–1679'. Transcribed and edited by Edwin Chappell. Cambridge, 1933.

INDEX

Artabane, *see under* Scott, Colonel John.

Atkins, Samuel, clerk to S.P., xiii, xiv, 63, 223.

Banbury, 6.
Barillon, M., 118.
Barton, John, 12, 42, 45.
Bastinck, M., 150, 151, 153, 155.
Bernard, Sir John, 36, 52, 55, 56, 62.
Blasethwayt, Mr., 62, 63.
Blondel, M., 107.
books: histories, 14; Fuller's *Worthies*, 27; Book of *Ordonnances* (of the King of France), 87; concerning navigation, 143–4, 145, 148; the 'Sixtus 5tus Bible', 157–8, 161, 162–3.
Bothwick, Captain ('that Beast'), 174.
Bowles, Mr., 35–36.
Brampton (Hunts.), estate of, xix, 1, 3, 4–5, 6, 8, 9, 11, 12, 17, 43, 46, 52, 53, 56, 158, 159, 163, 170, 171, 173, 178, 183, 187, 189, 194.
Breams, Mr., 153, 154.
Brisbane, John, 64–65, 66, 67, 68, 69, 70, 73, 74, 76, 77, 78, 79, 80, 81.
Brough, Doctor, 6.
Brouncker, Lord, 30, 156.
Browne, Captain, 105, 113–14, 115, 117, 118, 119.
Buckingham, Duke of, xi, 86, 123, 124, 141.
Bugden, estate of, 171, 173.

Calais, 37, 38, 149, 150, 151, 154.
Carverth, Captain, 50, 51.
clothes, 7, 9, 10, 170, 177, 190, 191, 192, 199, 229.
coffee-houses: 'Coffee-house-talk', 140; the *Globe* coffee-house, 218, 221–2.
Colebert, M., 76, 104, 118, 119, 123, 136.
Coleman, Captain William, 179.
Colodon, Mme, 148.
Condé, Prince of, 83, 124.
cost of living, 60, 187, 188, 192, 194;

greater in London, 188–9; *see also under* servants.

Dallié, M., 94, 117, 142, 145, 146, 147, 148, 239.
Deal, 17, 24, 31, 49, 60, 155, 165, 166, 183, 184.
Deane, Sir Anthony, xxv, 67, 68, 71, 73, 74, 85, 100, 101, 103, 105, 113, 114, 121, 123, 125 n. 5, 127, 131, 132, 133–4, 135, 136, 137, 140, 142 n. 2, 143, 145, 146, 152, 153, 156, 236.
debts, 1, 8, 34, 54, 84, 163, 173, 184; 'clamorous' creditors, 163; *see also under* Jackson; Pepys; St. Michel.
Denise, M., 98, 99, 100, 101, 103, 104, 105, 106, 107, 108–9, 112, 113, 115, 116, 117, 118, 119, 120, 121, 122, 123, 127, 128, 147, 149, 151.
Destrée, M. le comte, 76, 81, 87, 147.
Dieppe, 62, 70, 154.
Dover, 17, 124, 140, 141, 149, 150, 151, 152, 153, 154, 155, 197, 199.
Druillet, M., 137, 144, 146, 148, 149, 151.
Dulivier, M., 98.

Egmont, Deborah, 149 n. 2.
Ellington, estate of, 16, 17 n. 2, 36–37, 41, 43, 53, 54, 160, 161, 182, 203, 240.
Elmore, Captain, 202.
Ensam, Matthew, 47.
Ensam, Robert, 47.
Evelyn, Sir John, Commissioner for the Care of the Sick and Wounded, 23, 24, 25, 38 n. 3, 40–41, 233, friend of the Pepys family, 106.

Fairborne, Sir Palmes, 155.
Francklin, Samuel, 25.
funeral expenses: of Uncle Robert Pepys, 7; of John Jackson, 163; of John Pepys (senior), 173.
furniture, 13–15, 178.

Gibraltar, 175, 181, 195.
Gifford, Captain, 219, 242.
Glereaux, M. des, 152, 153.

Index

Godfrey, *see under* Scott, Colonel John.

Godfrey, Sir Edmund Berry, murder of, xiii, 63.

Gourville, M., 124, 125, 128, 135.

Goux, M. le, 79, 82, 102, 116, 120, 123, 126, 129.

Gravesend, 33, 86, 165, 166.

Haddock, Sir Richard, 49, 224.

Harbord, Mr., 156.

Harrison, Mr., 115, 117.

Hayes, Mr., solicitor to S.P., 132.

Hayter, Thomas, xii, xv, 29, 131.

Henson, Thomas, 43, 45–46.

Herbert, Admiral, 174, 181, 195 n. 1.

Hewer, William, 15, 32, 54, 65, 67, 68, 74, 87, 102, 111, 149, 151, 168, 175, 188; good friend of the family, xii, xiii, xxii, xxxi; lends money to the St. Michel family, 184, 186, 187, 188; fire at his house, 172.

Hewer, Mrs., 135, 173.

Hollier (Holard, Holyard, Hollyer), Dr. Thomas, King's Physician, 13, 54.

Hollinshead, Mrs., cousin to S.P., 170.

hospitals, 22.

Houblon, James, 68, 69, 74, 83, 99, 108, 112, 113, 116, 126, 135, 154.

Impington, xix, 177, 178.

inventory of the tailor shop, xix, 7, 8, 9, 10, 11, 13–15, 25, 231.

Jackson, John (senior), xxiii; nephew of lawyer at Brampton 11 n. 1; married to Paulina Pepys, 16; leases Ellington from Peterhouse College, 36–37, 47; sees about lands at Brampton, 45–46; has trouble with his farm, 41, 47; made Assessor of the Tax in Ellington, 54; lands settled on wife and children, 158–9, 162; goes to London, 42; sends food to his father-in-law, 42; his debts, 159, 161, 173, 203; incapacity, 160; falls ill, 162; death of, 163, 170, 171, 182; is buried privately, 163.

Jackson, John (junior), xxix, xxx–xxxi; bequeathed property by his grandfather, 18; heir to S.P., 52 n. 5; is 'very ill', 42; in good health, 190; mildly ill, 193; needs new clothes, 177, 190, 191, 192; 'will infallibly make a Scholar', 190, 196; schooling paid for by S.P., 191; is obedient and diligent, 191, 194; writes S.P. a Latin letter from Cambridge, 210.

Jackson, Paulina, xxii–xxiii; acknowledges gifts from her brother John, 17–18; father bequeathes her a silver tankard and a share of his estate, 18–19; promises to repay S.P., 37; wants him to buy land for her at Ellington, 159, 160, 161; is 'very ill', 42; well and happy, 159; ill, 171, 173, 174, 177, 178; is well again, 204; wants repairs done at Brampton, 43; finds Ellington 'unworthy', 43; has disposed of this 'troublesome parsonage', 53; S.P. promises to visit her, 91; her behaviour towards her creditors, 163; her management of her estate, 171, 173, 181, 203; left badly off, 173; returns to Brampton from London, 202; *see also under* Pepys.

Jackson, Samuel, xxviii–xxx; receives hat from his uncle John Pepys, 17; is 'very ill', 42; in good health, 190; mildly ill, 193; is heir to S.P., 52 n. 5; good character, 190; obedient and diligent, 191, 194; schooling paid for by S.P., 191; must specialize in 'Writing and Arithmetick', 196; describes life on board the *Foresight*, 212; recommends friend to S.P., 213.

James, John, butler to S.P., xv; his false testimony, 155–6.

Joyne, James, 84, 97, 100, 101, 102, 105, 107, 111, 113, 116, 117, 118, 120, 121, 122, 128, 139, 140, 144, 146, 147, 148, 152, 153, 154, 155.

Killigrew, Captain, 155.

King Charles II, 2 n. 3, 33, 56, 59, 62, 82, 88, 91, 96, 97, 149, 156, 167.

King James II, 213, 220; *see also under* York, Duke of.

King William III, 225.

Kingsmill, Sir Francis, 20 n. 3, 27.

Landry, M., 69, 72.
Langley, Mr., 117, 143, 148.
legal procedure, 75, 89, 90, 93, 94, 96, 97, 109, 121–2, 123, 126, 127–8, 129, 131–4, 137–9, 146, 151–2; *see also under* witnesses.
letters, viii, 85; conveyed by carrier, 12, 163, 196; interception of, 76; enclosures, 83, 107, 121, 149, 154, 228, 236; sealing of, 85; left open for perusal, 107, 123; delayed by weather, 121; gone astray, 122, 170, 191; distrust of the ordinary post, 118, 127; post missed, 135, 146; cancelled, 151; redirection of, 154.
linen, 13–15, 177.
Lock, Mr., 186, 187, 189, 203.
Lodge, Mr., 34–36.
Lord Mayor's Show, 172.
Lorrain, servant to S.P., 107, 177.
Lowther, Sir John, 225, 227, 242.

Manning, Edward, 81–82, 84, 89, 97, 238.
maps, 83, 143; as decoration, 14, 72; of the English coast, 83, 84; alleged to have been stolen by S.P., 71–72, 76; and by Scott, 79, 83, 85, 101–2, 147, 237; Scott's two Dutch charts, 128; left by Scott in the porter's lodge, 128; in his baggage at Dover, 154, 155; Mr. Point the Mapp-seller, 84.
Matthews, John, schoolmaster in Huntingdon, 177, 190–4.
medicine, 192, 193, 196.
Merritt, Mr., 43, 45, 46.
Mignon, M., 118.
Militia, 43, 46.
Mohun, Captain, xxv, 67, 125, 148, 236.
Monmouth, Duke of, 100.
More (Moore), Captain, 67, 74, 149.
Moreau, M., 153.
Moulins, Mlle des, 98, 102, 114, 120; 121, 123, 125–6, 127, 129, 135, 138, 140, 153.
music, 190, 192, 196.

navy: lack of men for, 34, 219; sickness reduces numbers, 50; officers take too much shore leave, 48, 214; S.P. reports on the state of, 129–30;

Lords of the Admiralty, 169–70 200, 201; ships refitting in Thames and Medway, 213, 214, 215, 216; *see also under* Jackson, Samuel; and St. Michel, Samuel.
Navy, French, 81.
Nephew, Mr., 153, 154, 155.
Nevers, 98, 101, 110, 111, 113, 120, 123.
Newmarket, 63 n. 2, 91, 156.
news: the *Weekly Gazette*, 129; the French Gazette of Amsterdam, 130; no intelligence from England, 141; newspapers sent to S.P. by W. Hewer, 172.

Pavillon, M., 127, 128, 133.
Pearse, James, Surgeon General to the Navy, 21, 22, 40 n. 3, 86.
Pedley, Sir Nicholas, 158, 163, 170, 171, 173, 202, 203.
Pelletier, M., 69, 74, 75, 77, 78, 79, 80, 82, 88, 90, 98, 100, 106, 108, 111, 127, 129, 131, 133, 135, 138, 139, 140, 147, 231.
Pellissary, M., xiv, 68, 69, 71, 73, 76, 78, 81, 82, 87, 107, 127, 237; speaks no English, 107, 119.
Pellissary family, 68, 72, 78, 85–86, 90, 96, 99, 100, 105, 109, 113, 114, 116, 117, 125, 126, 129, 130, 133, 136, 144, 148, 151, 152, 153, 154, 239.
Pepys, Elizabeth, wife of S.P.: visits Brampton, 12; correspondence with S.P., xviii; their visit to France, xi, 106; his 'late deare Consort', 20, 168; her early life, 26–28; attractive appearance, 28; frugality and careful housekeeping, 188; death of, xi, 69 n. 3.
Pepys, John (senior), xix, xx; receives advice on housekeeping from S.P., 1; given allowance, 3; admonished by Dr. Thomas Pepys, 8–9; finds him 'troublesom', 10–11; has paid funeral expenses of Uncle Robert, 7; administers estate of Thomas his son, 10; is worried concerning lease of Ellington, 38; anxious for S.P. to buy land for Paulina, 160, 161; his debts, 8, 9; promises to repay S.P., 23; concerned about S.P.'s heirs, 55; thanks S.P. for looking

Pepys, John (senior) (*cont.*)
after his watch, 157; quarrels with his wife, 2; memorandum for his will, 18–19; declares the inventory is true, 11; visits London, 42; goes to live at Ellington, 38; S.P. promises to visit him, 91, 156; is well and happy,159; dies,170; funeralcharges, 173; S.P. his executor, 170, 171.
Pepys, John (junior), xxi–xxii; Thomas his brother expected to make him an allowance, 6 n. 6, 8; father plans to bequeath him a gold ring and a share of the estate, 18–19; urged by S.P. to apply for clerkship to Trinity House, 16; instructed to call a court of Trin. Ho., 45; is owed 3 years' salary by Trin. Ho., 60–61; sends his father oysters and lends him money, 17–18; sends wine and offers money, 29; sends him a bottle of spirits and box of sweets, 41; has lent money to John Jackson on security of Ellington, 163, 164, 171; arranges legal business of Ellington, 38, 47; helps St. Michel family with 'manyfould Favours' and loans of money, 30–31; dies in spring of 1677, 51; his estate, 60; S.P. goes through his papers, 54.
Pepys, Paulina ('Pall'), xxii; to be placed in service abroad, 3; a suitor for, 6; has allowance from brother Thomas, 6 n. 6; *hereafter, see under* Jackson.
Pepys, Robert, xi, xx, 1 n. 4, 2 n. 4, 7, 11, 12 n. 1, 53.
Pepys, Roger, 8, 47, 177–8.
Pepys, Samuel (S.P.): lends money to his brother Thomas, 15; named administrator of his father's estate, 18–19; is concerned about his heirs, 52–53; 54–55; sends his father wine, 53; gives bail for St. Michel, 156–7; buys land at Ellington for Paulina, 160; gives presents to Jackson boys, 197; writes to Navy Board on behalf of St. Michel, 176; still paying John Jackson's debts, 203; his illness, July 1664, 12–13; Dec. 1686, 205; his eyesight, xi, 52, 64 n. 1, 75, 80, 110, 192, 196; accused of being a Papist, xiv, 26, 153; vindicated, 156;

professes Protestantism, 70, 72; endangered by arrest of Atkins, 63; supposed to have supplied maps, &c., to French Navy, 71–72; is 'maliciously accused, 64; protests his innocence, 63, 70, 72, 77, 91, 102, 115, 151; repudiates use of false testimony in his own defence, 68, 72, 86, 94; prefers Protestant witnesses, 79, 80, 83, 94, 143; suspects Scott of being a Papist, 79, 82; praises M. Denise as a witness, 98, 104; also Mr. Joyne, 105, 124; withdrawal of charges against him, 152, 155–6; intervenes in quarrel between St. Michel and Captain Willshaw, 59; deposits £300 (on contingency) with Trinity House, 61; attendance on the King, 97; at Newmarket, 63 n. 2, 91, 156; at Windsor, 88; released from the Tower on bail, 74; stays at Will Hewer's house, 74; stays with the Jacksons, 91; visits his father upon his release, 156; *see also under* Jackson; Navy; St. Michel; Scott, Colonel John.
Pepys, Thomas, brother to S.P.: merchant tailor, xix, xx, 6 nn. 3, 6, 7 n. 1, 11 n. 3, 13 n. 2, 15, 23, 54.
Pepys, Doctor Thomas, 7, 8 n. 3, 10–11, 39.
Pepys, Uncle Thomas, xi, 1, 2, 5, 52, 53.
Pepys, Thomas, son of Uncle Thomas, 29 n. 3, 52, 53, 56.
Perkins, Aunt, 1, 5, 29 n. 2.
Peterhouse College, Cambridge, 37, 41, 47, 182, 240.
Picard, M. le, 75, 101, 146, 148, 149.
Piogerie, Captain Heroüard de la, xiv, 68, 71, 75, 76, 78, 81, 85, 87; 102, 116, 144, 145.
Plymouth, 179, 199, 201.
Pointe, M. la, 119, 128, 135.
poor relief, 44, 46.
Portsmouth, 33.
Pratt, My Lady, 89, 93, 96, 114, 118.
prisons, xii, 34, 74, 179.

Regny, Marquise de, 120, 121, 125, 126–7, 138.

Rolls, Sir Francis, 93.
Rupert, Prince, 87, 97; the 'Original Contract', 123, 125, 126–7, 129, 135, 138.
Ruvigny, M. de, 70, 79, 101, 104, 118, 120, 127, 133, 142, 143, 151, 152, 154.

St. Michel, Balthazar, ('Balty'), xxiv-xxviii; Muster-master at Deal, 17, 19 n. 2, 60; goes to Calais, 37, 131; to Dieppe, 62; condoles with S.P. on the death of Elizabeth Pepys, 20; sends lamb and fish as present to Charles II, 33; warned and admonished by S.P., 19, 34, 36, 57, 102, 205–6; urged to economize, 69, 76; and to keep accounts, 112, 117; blamed for extravagance, 102, 106, 111; financed by S.P., 120–1; thanked, 57; and commended, 40, 51, 102; for his diligence and care, 92, 115; for 'good husbandry', 136, 155, 165; makes good resolutions, 206; and acknowledges favours, 207; plans to revise finances, 195; quarrels with Captain Willshaw, 57–59; with the Admiralty, 169–70; with Captain Gifford, 219–21; with 'that Beast Captain Bothwick', 174; about a saddle, 206, 207; is thwarted by Admiral Herbert, 181; quarrels with Mary Skinner, 223; and S.P., 223; hopes to return to his favour, 226; instructed to arrange for transport of witnesses, 100, 145; is jealous of M. Denise, 109, 110; returns from France, 149, 150; told to buy books there for S.P., 143–4, 145; appointed Muster-master at Tangier, 60, 175; ready to set out, 152; departs, 164; arrives, 174; comes home, 188, (without permission) 194 n. 3, 195; returns, 197; trouble concerning the privateers, 156–7; *see also under* Ships; sorrow at parting from his family, 164–5; now has 7 children, 226; his tribulations, 167, 168, 174, 178–80, 199–200, 229; complains of illness, 211, 229; wants to be made collector at Plymouth, 179; wishes for better post, 200–1; is made commissioner at Deptford, 204 n. 2, 206; S.P. recommends him to Sir R. Haddock, 224; and to Sir J. Lowther, 225; wishes to be given clothes, 199, 225.
St. Michel, Elizabeth ('Betty'), xxvii-xxviii, 126, 135, 228.
St. Michel, Ester, 79, 82, 87, 137, 139; general incompetence of, xxvi; has moved to Brampton, 183; complains of plight, 183, 184, 189–90; 194; has had to borrow money from Will. Hewer, 184, 186, 187, 188, 190; her children are ill-mannered, 185; S.P. gives her an allowance, 186–7, 190; and urges her to keep accounts, 188; returns to London, 204; dies in childbirth, 208; grief of Balty, 209–10.
St. Michel, Samuel, xxviii; 'Littel Samuel', 194; the 'littell disiple' of S.P., 21, 22, 168; goes to Calais, 32, 38, 183; S.P. gives advice concerning his upbringing, 40, 93, 97, 106; writes French letter to his uncle S.P., 65–66; S.P. sends him his blessing, 87; 'infirme in his health', 93; recovers from his cold, 137; has trouble with his eyes, 183, 185; his tutor at Brampton, 190; has been sent to sea, 210; about to become a midshipman, 211; Balty wants him presented to the King, 211; S.P. agrees, and recommends 'my Nephew Samuell' to his captain, 211–12; describes cruise off the Irish shore, 227–8.
Saunderson, Captain, 155, 234, 236.
Savill, Mr., 81, 106, 118.
Saville, Henry, English Ambassador to France, 65, 68.
Scott, Colonel John, xiv; 'This Rascall', 136; alias Godfrey, 86; alias Artabane, 146; 'maliciously accuses' S.P., 64, 68, 72, 73, 131 makes affidavit against him, 66–67, 103; accuses S.P. of selling 'draughts, Mapps, and Models' to the King of France, 71–72, 76; accusations due to desire for revenge, 86, 88, 105, 114, 124, 155; his false testimony, 76, 83, 92; accuses S.P. of bribing witnesses, 142, 146; 'villainous accusations' against Sir

Scott, Colonel John (*cont.*)
A. Deane, 68; his 'coffee-house-talk', 140; his patrons, 93–94; friendship with M. Dallié, 94; and with the Pellissary family, 68, 72, 73, 78, 85, 90, 101, 109, 113, 116, 117, 125, 127; accused of stealing charts, &c., 79, 83, 85; of being a Papist, 79–80, 82, 84, 89–90, 106, 107, 114; challenged to a duel by Manning, 82, 96; his debts, 84, 98, 113; his ill language towards the king, 96; involved in gun-founding for Prince Rupert, 89, 92–98, 101 111, 115, 123; his papers, 102, 105, 123, 126; Mr. Foster writes his *Life*, 114, 125; his examination at Dover, 124–5, 153–4, 155; is absent, 123, 126, 129, 130, 132; reappears, 134, 138; *see also under* Rupert, Prince, *and* Nevers.
Scott, Cozen, 7, 8.
Seignelay, M. de, 68, 70, 71, 72, 73, 74, 76, 77, 79, 80, 81, 86, 87, 88, 90, 92, 95, 96, 99, 101, 103, 118, 120, 140.
servants: wages, 7, 8, 60; tips, 153; clothes for 'Peter', 199; of the Pellissary family, 68, 72, 73, 116, 118, 125, 127, 137; of S.P., 85, 157, 172, 181, 196, 226; in the St. Michel household, 183, 198–9; *see also under* James, John, *and* Lorrain.
Shaftesbury, Lord, 86, 155.
Shere, Henry, engineer of the Mole at Tangier, 175.
Sherwin, Mr., 82, 84, 89, 92, 95–96, 97, 105, 110, 111, 113, 114, 115, 117, 120, 122, 140.
ships: in the Downs, 33, 48, 49; privateers, 36, 37; *see also* St. Michel, B.; H.M. yachts, 62; yachts for French King, 68, 73; Dutch pleasure boat, 17; merchantmen outsail the Navy, 49; packet-boats, 140; a Gravesend wherry, 165; *see also under* Navy *and* Trinity House.
Adventure, 51.
Assistance, 57.
the *Charlotte* Yacht, 155.
Dartmouth, 49.

Dragon, 21, 32, 232.
Falcon, 17.
Foresight, 57, 155, 211, 235.
Francis, 51.
Greyhound, 37.
Henry, 17 n. 1.
Hunter, xxv, 36, 67, 73, 74, 125 n. 5.
the *James* Galley, 179, 213.
Katherine, 67, 70, 74, 125, 234, 237, 242.
Mary, 166.
Mermaid, 219, 221.
Newcastle, 165, 166.
Phoenix, 59, 217, 220, 221, 232, 241.
Speedwell, 17.
Spragg, 50, 51.
Tiger, 197, 198, 200, 219, 221.
Unity, 166.
sick and wounded, care of, 21, 23, 24, 38 n. 3, 40–41, 233.
Skinner, Mary, xxvi, 223.
Spencer, Mr., Bursar of Peterhouse College in Cambridge, 182, 240.
Stankes, John, 4.
Stankes, Will, 1, 11, 13.
Sturtlow, estate of, 1, 2, 41.

Taber, Sir Robert, ague-doctor, 62.
Tangier, xvii, 60, 62, 152, 155, 167, 170, 174, 175, 176, 180, 220, 239.
Temple, Captain, 49–50.
Thinne, Mr., 150.
Tillman, Abraham, clerk to B. St. Michel, 208–9, 222–3.
Timpeny, Father Henry, O.S.B., 123, 135, 137.
Tirrell, Sir Timothy, 118, 143, 144, 146.
travel: by cart and wagon, 22; the Dover coach, 141; a bad Channel crossing, 154–5; ship delayed by contrary winds, 155; St. Michel's journey from Gravesend to the Downs, 165–7; from Dover to Plymouth, 197–201.
Trelaney, Captain, 180.
Trenchepain, M. François, 68, 69, 74, 75, 77, 78, 79, 80, 82, 83, 88, 90, 92, 96, 98, 100, 102, 106, 108, 111, 112, 113, 116, 126, 127, 129, 131, 133, 135, 136, 137–9, 140, 147, 151, 152, 154.

Trice family, xi, 12.
Trice, Mrs., xi, 46.
Trice, Tom, foster-son to Robert Pepys, xi, 1, 12.
Trinity House, 16, 29, 31, 39, 43, 45, 60–61, 233; erection of lights, 43–44; pilots, 218, 220, 222.
Turner, Dr. John, cousin to S.P., 157–8, 159–60; 163–4, 202.
Turner, Sir William, 39.

Valossière, M. de la, 75, 76, 77, 81.

Walden, Sir Lionel, 46, 54.
Wentworth, Wentworse, Mr., 86, 93, 101.
Werden, Sir John, 173.
Wight, William, fishmonger, half-brother to John Pepys senior, 29 n. 5.
Willshaw, Captain Francis, 57–59, 220, 222, 241.

Willson, 146,
wine, 17, 29, 53.
witnesses: choice of, 125, 127; search for, 89, 90, 93, 105; to be brought from France, 108, 114, 118–19; 120, 126, 127, 132–4, 136, 140–3; expenses of, 94–95, 106, 108, 120; 123, 126, 145; transport of, 100; bribery forbidden, 140, 142; give testimony willingly, 139; Sherwin dies before he can give his testimony, 122; Papist witnesses given permission to land, xxv, 149, 150; French witnesses depart from Dover, 152, 154; *see also under* Scott, Colonel John, *and* Pepys, Samuel.
Wren, Matthew, 69 n. 5, 70.

York, carrier, 12, 29.
York, Duke of, later James II, xi, xiii, 33, 97, 100 n. 1, 172. 200.

PRINTED IN
GREAT BRITAIN
AT THE
UNIVERSITY PRESS
OXFORD
BY
CHARLES BATEY
PRINTER
TO THE
UNIVERSITY

71
72
74
75
76
77
75
85
85